MILTON CANIFF'S
STEVE CANYON

1948

MILTON CANIFF

CHECKER BOOK PUBLISHING GROUP

Library of Congress Cataloging-in-Publication Data

Caniff, Milton Arthur, 1907-
  Milton Caniff's Steve Canyon—1948 / Milton Caniff.
      p. cm.
Reprints comic strips from late 1947 through early 1949.
  ISBN 0-9741664-1-3 (alk. paper)
  I. Title.
  PN6728.S685C35 2003
  741.5'973—dc21
                                        2003012263

*Whether Terry Lee and Jane Allen would ever meet again, their creator did
not know. He had surrendered his godlike right over them and their actions,
which he had guided for eleven years past. Next week, in 220 newspapers
including papers as far away as the Times of Seoul, Korea, Milton Caniff's
byline will appear on a new comic strip, to be known as Steve Canyon.*

*His new hero, Steve Canyon, would be a lean and squinty, older version of
Terry; a fellow with an easy, insolent, Gary Cooperish grace that marked
a breed of plainsmen, and airplanesmen. Canyon knew the world and its
airlines - and its women...*

*Beginning his new strip, Caniff was confident and cool: "It's almost a
mathematical equation," he said. "If I don't know my trade by now,
I'd better quit."*

Time Magazine, January 13, 1947 on the debut of Steve Canyon

Milton Caniff. . . . . Writer, Illustrator

Compilation:

Mark Thompson. . . . . Publisher
Paul Dubuc. . . . . Associate Publisher
Ben Rangel . . . . Art Director

Checker Book Publishing Group
17 N. Main Street, Suite 31
Centerville, OH 45459
Visit us online at www.checkerbpg.com

No solicitations accepted

ISBN# 0-9741664-1-3
Printed in China

No More Pearl Harbors

In the pages of the first volume I touched on the local ties Milton Caniff has with my humble hometown. For this volume I think I would like to touch on the ties Caniff had with the country as a whole.

It may seem peculiar to focus on the writing talents of one of the great artists of the 20th Century, but I thought it's particularly important as we undertake long needed chronicling of the adventures of Major Steve Canyon.

Caniff was a master of crafting and sustaining high adventure within the rigid confines of a short daily strip. He could intertwine this with sex appeal and comic relief, and balance it all out with dashes of intrigue and careful application of the most difficult and final ingredient — social commentary without preachiness. Best selling authors, high-priced screen writers, and other comics writing specialists consistently fail in this balancing act... and they don't have the day job of drawing the thing too.

But let's expand on the stories themselves. The most astonishing thing is the timeliness and prophecy in the tales. Caniff had predicted a Burmese invasion in the panels of Terry and the Pirates before WWII had begun, and Canyon uncovers a communist plot to build secret missile bases in 1959. Later, he finds himself in a thinly disguised version of Viet Nam... in 1964. Most chilling perhaps is Caniff's oft-repeated credo — "No More Pearl Harbors!" This exhortation echoed long after the end of his career — and went sadly unheeded, until the price of our lack of vigilance was paid in human suffering on September 11th.

The reason for Canyon's appeal, however, was Caniff's unapologetic use of overriding themes of patriotism and duty, which were seamlessly incorporated into his perfectly rendered and action-packed cartoons. America is the good guy. America is the hero. We can and will save the world from evil. There are bad people out there with nefarious plans and no regard for human life.

Caniff, by his bomber-jacketed proxy, Steve Canyon, stood his ground during a turbulent period in our history when many people thought being American was a reason for embarrassment or shame. An era brought to an end, ironically, by another Pearl Harbor.

The world is a different place after 9/11/2001. It's a place that can use a man like Steve Canyon again. To stand up and say "No more Pearl Harbors!"

Mark Thompson - Publisher
Checker Book Publishing Group

Steve Canyon: 1948
Table of Contents

Milton Caniff Bibliography

1932 Dumb Dora

1932 Mister Gilfeather

1933 Puffy The Pig

1933 The Gay Thirties
(renamed Gilfeather)

1933 Dickie Dare

1934 Scorchy Smith

1934-1947 Terry and the Pirates

1943-1946 Male Call

1947-1988 Steve Canyon

Stevenson Burton Canyon was born December 1, 1923 in Hillsboro, Ohio. He graduated from Dayton High School and attended Ohio State University in Columbus.

Canyon entered active duty military service in the Army Air Corps as an aviation cadet September 18, 1941, received pilot training in Oklahoma and Texas, and earned his pilot wings on May 28, 1942. He became a bomber pilot in the European Theater of Operations and flew 22 combat missions in a B-25. During a bombing mission, Canyon was wounded by anti-aircraft fire and was awarded the Purple Heart.

He also received a number of other medals for his service in Europe, including the Distinguished Flying Cross, Air Medal, and a Presidential Unit Citation with one oak-leaf cluster.

In May, 1943 he began service in the China-Burma-India Theater of Operations, flying C-46 and C-47 cargo aircraft. He returned Stateside in November, 1944 and was assigned as a C-46 instructor pilot in Nevada. Canyon then was assigned to Hickam Army Air Field in Hawaii in 1945 and then to Scott Field, Illinois as a C-54 instructor.

Steve Canyon was released from active duty in December, 1945. He organized a charter airline involved in air transport services headquartered in New York City. This company, Horizons Unlimited, began operations on January 13, 1947.

(The above is a personnel record developed by the U.S. Air Force in 1989 for use in an official "retirement" ceremony for Steve Canyon a year after Milton Caniff's death and the discontinuation of the Steve Canyon newspaper strip. It was compiled entirely from "facts" about Canyon's background presented in the strip over its 41 years in syndication.)

BARNEY OLDFIELD
Colonel, USAF
Chief of Information

Chapter One

Medical
Sabotage

November 25, 1947 – March 27, 1948

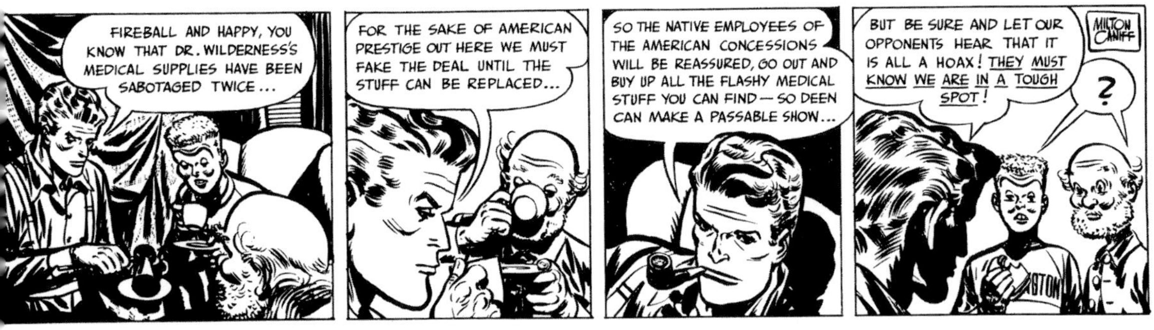
FIREBALL AND HAPPY, YOU KNOW THAT DR. WILDERNESS'S MEDICAL SUPPLIES HAVE BEEN SABOTAGED TWICE...
FOR THE SAKE OF AMERICAN PRESTIGE OUT HERE WE MUST FAKE THE DEAL UNTIL THE STUFF CAN BE REPLACED...
SO THE NATIVE EMPLOYEES OF THE AMERICAN CONCESSIONS WILL BE REASSURED, GO OUT AND BUY UP ALL THE FLASHY MEDICAL STUFF YOU CAN FIND — SO DEEN CAN MAKE A PASSABLE SHOW...
BUT BE SURE AND LET OUR OPPONENTS HEAR THAT IT IS ALL A HOAX! THEY MUST KNOW WE ARE IN A TOUGH SPOT!
?
MILTON CANIFF

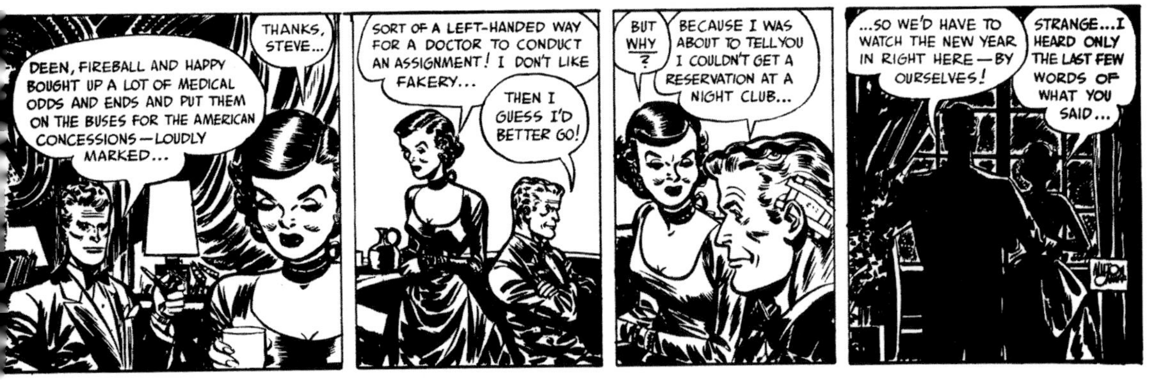
DEEN, FIREBALL AND HAPPY BOUGHT UP A LOT OF MEDICAL ODDS AND ENDS AND PUT THEM ON THE BUSES FOR THE AMERICAN CONCESSIONS — LOUDLY MARKED...
THANKS, STEVE...
SORT OF A LEFT-HANDED WAY FOR A DOCTOR TO CONDUCT AN ASSIGNMENT! I DON'T LIKE FAKERY...
THEN I GUESS I'D BETTER GO!
BUT WHY ?
BECAUSE I WAS ABOUT TO TELL YOU I COULDN'T GET A RESERVATION AT A NIGHT CLUB...
...SO WE'D HAVE TO WATCH THE NEW YEAR IN RIGHT HERE — BY OURSELVES!
STRANGE...I HEARD ONLY THE LAST FEW WORDS OF WHAT YOU SAID...
MILTON CANIFF

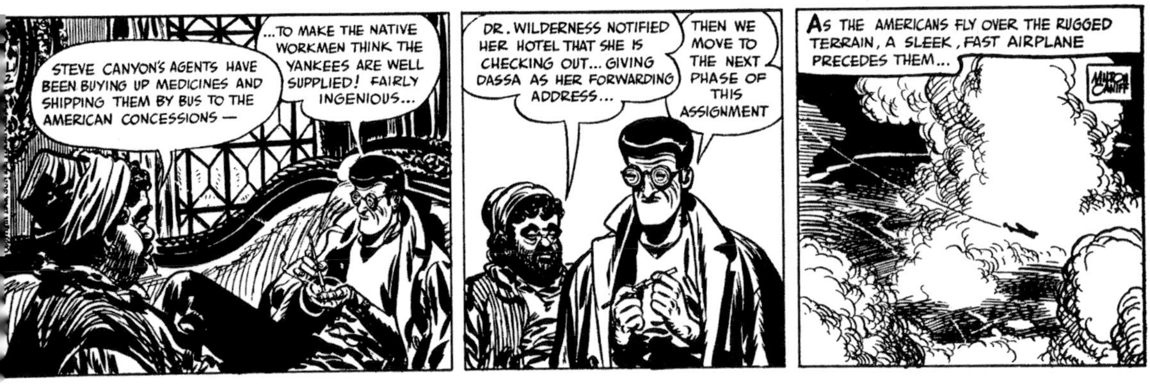
STEVE CANYON'S AGENTS HAVE BEEN BUYING UP MEDICINES AND SHIPPING THEM BY BUS TO THE AMERICAN CONCESSIONS —
...TO MAKE THE NATIVE WORKMEN THINK THE YANKEES ARE WELL SUPPLIED! FAIRLY INGENIOUS...
DR. WILDERNESS NOTIFIED HER HOTEL THAT SHE IS CHECKING OUT... GIVING DASSA AS HER FORWARDING ADDRESS...
THEN WE MOVE TO THE NEXT PHASE OF THIS ASSIGNMENT
AS THE AMERICANS FLY OVER THE RUGGED TERRAIN, A SLEEK, FAST AIRPLANE PRECEDES THEM...
MILTON CANIFF

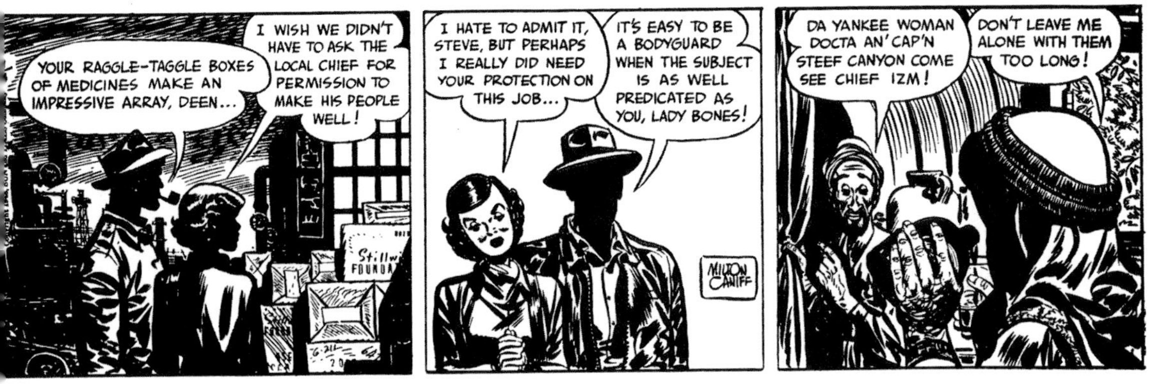
YOUR RAGGLE-TAGGLE BOXES OF MEDICINES MAKE AN IMPRESSIVE ARRAY, DEEN...
I WISH WE DIDN'T HAVE TO ASK THE LOCAL CHIEF FOR PERMISSION TO MAKE HIS PEOPLE WELL!
I HATE TO ADMIT IT, STEVE, BUT PERHAPS I REALLY DID NEED YOUR PROTECTION ON THIS JOB...
IT'S EASY TO BE A BODYGUARD WHEN THE SUBJECT IS AS WELL PREDICATED AS YOU, LADY BONES!
MILTON CANIFF
DA YANKEE WOMAN DOCTA AN' CAP'N STEEF CANYON COME SEE CHIEF IZM!
DON'T LEAVE ME ALONE WITH THEM TOO LONG!

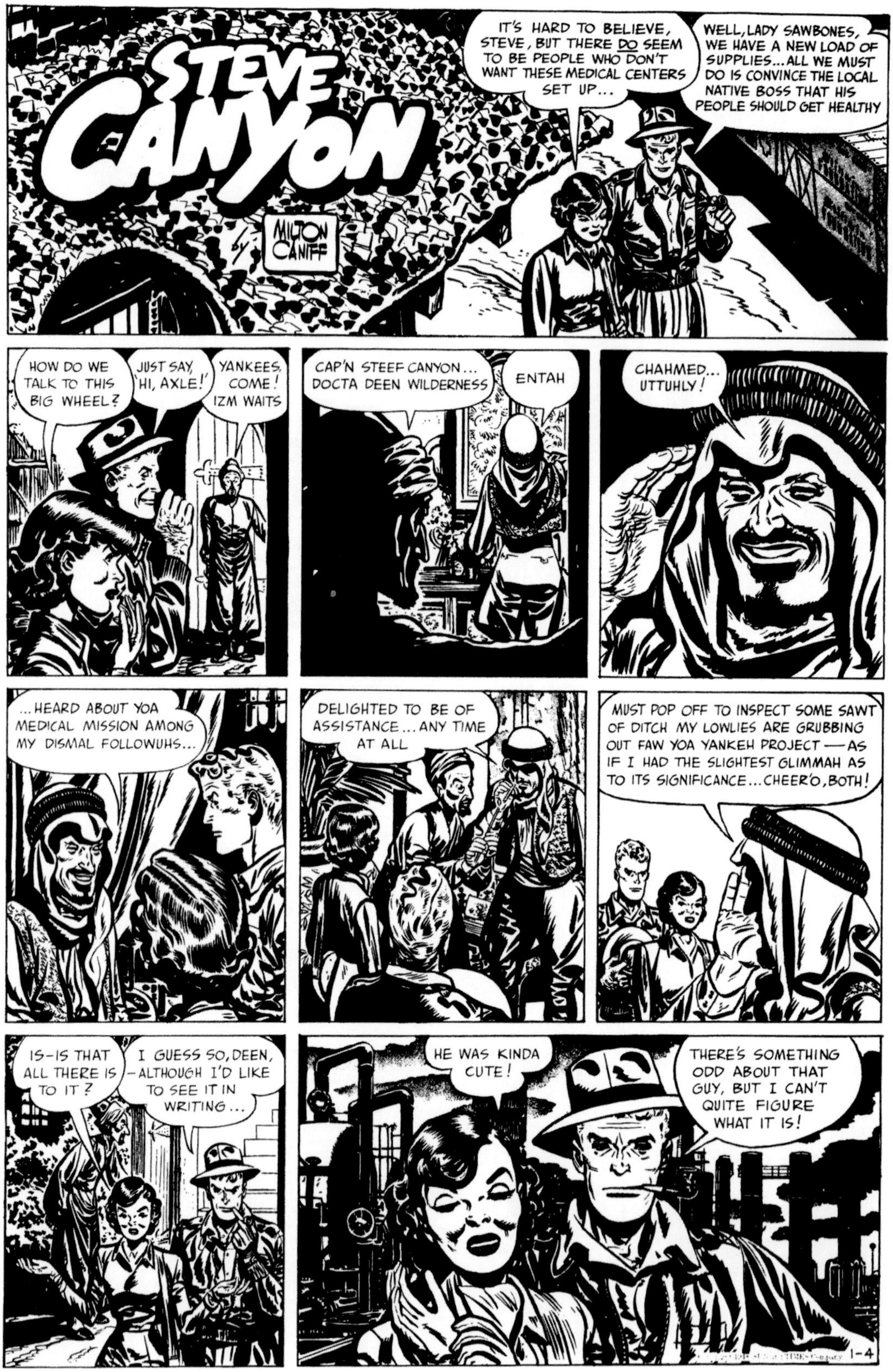
STEVE CANYON
by MILTON CANIFF
IT'S HARD TO BELIEVE, STEVE, BUT THERE DO SEEM TO BE PEOPLE WHO DON'T WANT THESE MEDICAL CENTERS SET UP...
WELL, LADY SAWBONES, WE HAVE A NEW LOAD OF SUPPLIES... ALL WE MUST DO IS CONVINCE THE LOCAL NATIVE BOSS THAT HIS PEOPLE SHOULD GET HEALTHY
HOW DO WE TALK TO THIS BIG WHEEL?
JUST SAY, 'HI, AXLE!'
YANKEES, COME! IZM WAITS
CAP'N STEEF CANYON... DOCTA DEEN WILDERNESS
ENTAH
CHAHMED... UTTUHLY!
...HEARD ABOUT YOA MEDICAL MISSION AMONG MY DISMAL FOLLOWUHS...
DELIGHTED TO BE OF ASSISTANCE... ANY TIME AT ALL
MUST POP OFF TO INSPECT SOME SAWT OF DITCH MY LOWLIES ARE GRUBBING OUT FAW YOA YANKEH PROJECT — AS IF I HAD THE SLIGHTEST GLIMMAH AS TO ITS SIGNIFICANCE... CHEER'O, BOTH!
IS-IS THAT ALL THERE IS TO IT?
I GUESS SO, DEEN, — ALTHOUGH I'D LIKE TO SEE IT IN WRITING...
HE WAS KINDA CUTE!
THERE'S SOMETHING ODD ABOUT THAT GUY, BUT I CAN'T QUITE FIGURE WHAT IT IS!
1-4

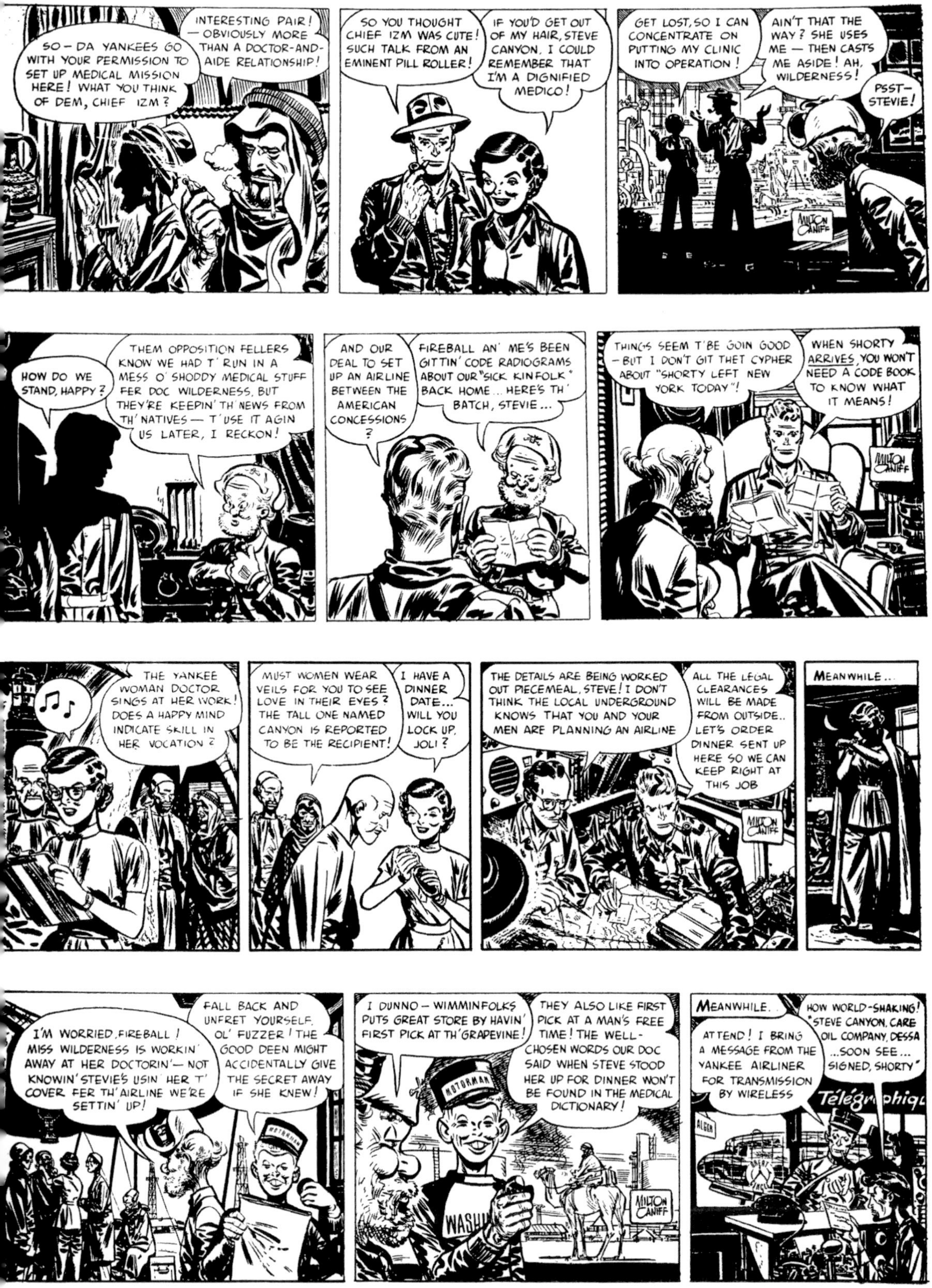

SO—DA YANKEES GO WITH YOUR PERMISSION TO SET UP MEDICAL MISSION HERE! WHAT YOU THINK OF DEM, CHIEF IZM?
INTERESTING PAIR! —OBVIOUSLY MORE THAN A DOCTOR-AND-AIDE RELATIONSHIP!
SO YOU THOUGHT CHIEF IZM WAS CUTE! SUCH TALK FROM AN EMINENT PILL ROLLER!
IF YOU'D GET OUT OF MY HAIR, STEVE CANYON, I COULD REMEMBER THAT I'M A DIGNIFIED MEDICO!
GET LOST, SO I CAN CONCENTRATE ON PUTTING MY CLINIC INTO OPERATION!
AIN'T THAT THE WAY? SHE USES ME — THEN CASTS ME ASIDE! AH, WILDERNESS!
PSST— STEVIE!
MILTON CANIFF
HOW DO WE STAND, HAPPY?
THEM OPPOSITION FELLERS KNOW WE HAD T' RUN IN A MESS O' SHODDY MEDICAL STUFF FER DOC WILDERNESS, BUT THEY'RE KEEPIN' TH' NEWS FROM TH' NATIVES — T'USE IT AGIN US LATER, I RECKON!
AND OUR DEAL TO SET UP AN AIRLINE BETWEEN THE AMERICAN CONCESSIONS?
FIREBALL AN' ME'S BEEN GITTIN' CODE RADIOGRAMS ABOUT OUR "SICK KINFOLK" BACK HOME... HERE'S TH' BATCH, STEVIE...
THINGS SEEM T'BE GOIN GOOD — BUT I DON'T GIT THET CYPHER ABOUT "SHORTY LEFT NEW YORK TODAY"!
WHEN SHORTY ARRIVES, YOU WON'T NEED A CODE BOOK TO KNOW WHAT IT MEANS!
MILTON CANIFF
THE YANKEE WOMAN DOCTOR SINGS AT HER WORK! DOES A HAPPY MIND INDICATE SKILL IN HER VOCATION?
MUST WOMEN WEAR VEILS FOR YOU TO SEE LOVE IN THEIR EYES? THE TALL ONE NAMED CANYON IS REPORTED TO BE THE RECIPIENT!
I HAVE A DINNER DATE... WILL YOU LOCK UP, JOLI?
THE DETAILS ARE BEING WORKED OUT PIECEMEAL, STEVE! I DON'T THINK THE LOCAL UNDERGROUND KNOWS THAT YOU AND YOUR MEN ARE PLANNING AN AIRLINE
ALL THE LEGAL CLEARANCES WILL BE MADE FROM OUTSIDE.. LET'S ORDER DINNER SENT UP HERE SO WE CAN KEEP RIGHT AT THIS JOB
MILTON CANIFF
MEANWHILE...
I'M WORRIED, FIREBALL! MISS WILDERNESS IS WORKIN' AWAY AT HER DOCTORIN' — NOT KNOWIN' STEVIE'S USIN' HER T' COVER FER TH' AIRLINE WE'RE SETTIN' UP!
FALL BACK AND UNFRET YOURSELF, OL' FUZZER! THE GOOD DEEN MIGHT ACCIDENTALLY GIVE THE SECRET AWAY IF SHE KNEW!
MOTORMAN
I DUNNO — WIMMINFOLKS PUTS GREAT STORE BY HAVIN' FIRST PICK AT TH' GRAPEVINE!
THEY ALSO LIKE FIRST PICK AT A MAN'S FREE TIME! THE WELL-CHOSEN WORDS OUR DOC SAID WHEN STEVE STOOD HER UP FOR DINNER WON'T BE FOUND IN THE MEDICAL DICTIONARY!
MOTORMAN
MILTON CANIFF
MEANWHILE...
ATTEND! I BRING A MESSAGE FROM THE YANKEE AIRLINER FOR TRANSMISSION BY WIRELESS
HOW WORLD-SHAKING! "STEVE CANYON, CARE OIL COMPANY, DESSA ...SOON SEE... SIGNED, SHORTY"
ALGER

THAT TAPPING YOU HEAR IS MY FOOT, CANYON! MAKE IT A GOOD STORY!

DEEN, I'M AT YOUR MERCY! I WAS SHOOTING THE BREEZE WITH ONE OF THE ENGINEERS FROM THE OIL COMPANY— AND BEFORE I KNEW IT, THE DINNER HOUR HAD COME AND GONE!

I'D STAY MAD, ONLY THEN I COULDN'T BRAG TO YOU ABOUT HOW WELL MY CLINIC IS GOING!

SWELL — AND YOU'LL SOON HAVE SOMEONE ELSE TO TELL ALL ABOUT IT!

REALLY? ...WHO?

COME TO THE LANDING STRIP WITH ME AND YOU'LL SEE!

WE CAN UNDO THE YANKEE WOMAN DOCTOR'S PUNY EFFORTS AT WILL .. WHAT HAPPENS AT THE MOMENT?

STEVE CANYON RECEIVED A WIRELESS MESSAGE STATING THAT SOMEONE NAMED "SHORTY" WOULD ARRIVE...THE DOCTOR AND EASTER ACCOMPANY HIM TO MEET THE SHUTTLE PLANE

THE SHUTTLE HAD TO WAIT FOR THE CONNECTION AT KALIM...GOT SOMETHING VALUABLE COMING IN ON THAT FLIGHT, STEVE?

YEAH — NICE AND VALUABLE!

THIS MUST BE IMPORTANT—FOR STEVE TO TAKE ME FROM MY WORK TO MEET A PLANE... HAVE YOU ANY IDEA, HAPPY?

I GOT TOO MUCH IMAGINATION F[OR] WHUT I'M IMAGININ', MA'AM!

OPERATION

STEVE CANYON
by MILTON CANIFF

MAYBE STEVE WAS WRONG ABOUT THE OPPOSITION TO OUR HEALTH CENTERS!...THE NATIVE BIGWIG HAS BEEN VERY COOPERATIVE!

TH' AIRYPLANE'S I[N] DOC WILDERNESS, MA'AM

BY THE WAY, HAPPY, WHO IS STEVE MEETING? HE'S BEEN SWEATING OUT THIS FLIGHT FOR HOURS!

I—AH, DON'T RIGHTLY KNOW...

WHY—IT'S A GIRL ...

YUS'M

A PRETTY GIRL ...

UH—I'M AFEERED SO, MA'AM

Steve Canyon

Steve, Happy Easter and Doctor Deen Wilderness are at the airport when Feeta-Feeta, Steve's secretary, steps off the airplane from the United States...

Steve Canyon

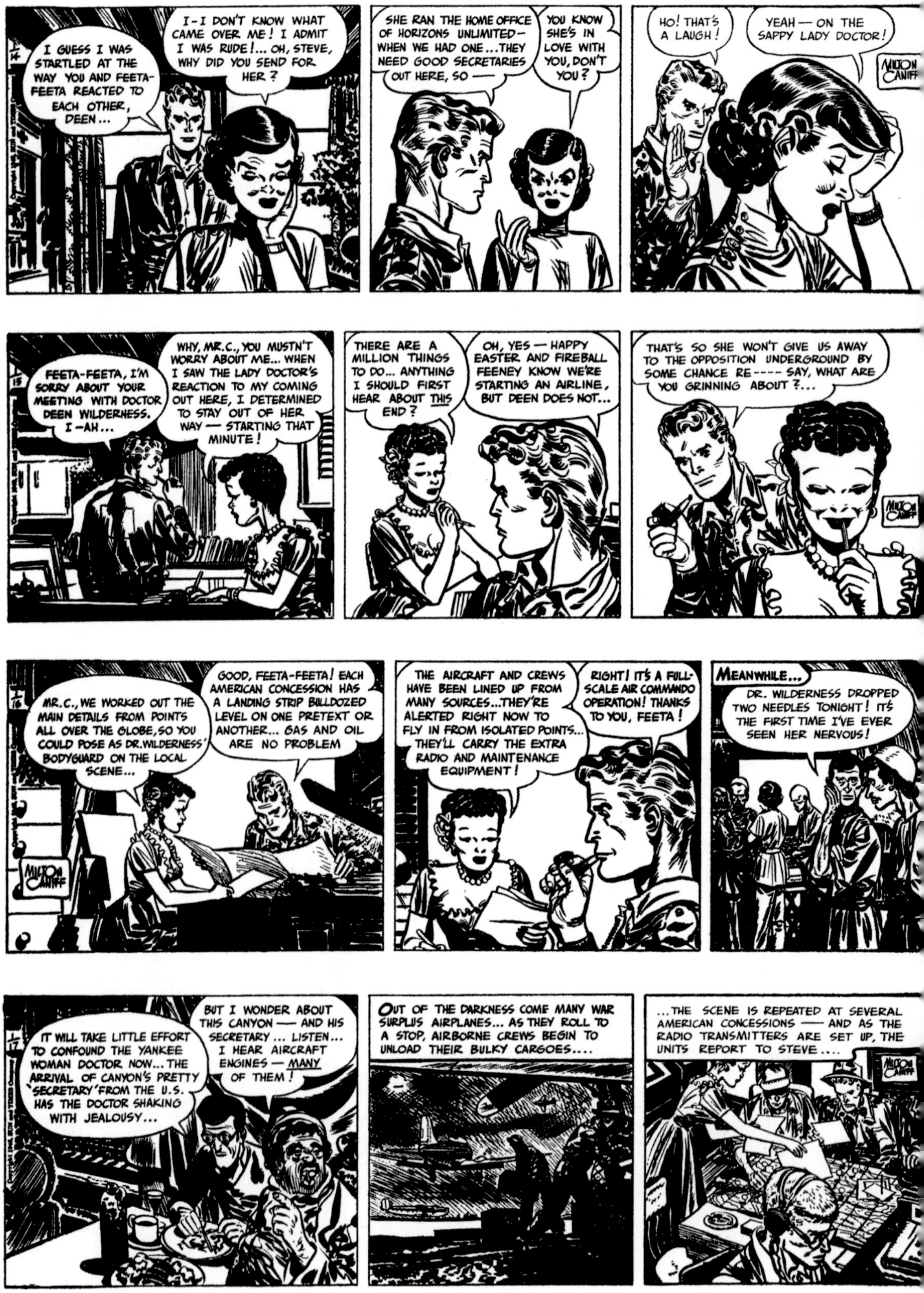
I GUESS I WAS STARTLED AT THE WAY YOU AND FEETA-FEETA REACTED TO EACH OTHER, DEEN...
I-I DON'T KNOW WHAT CAME OVER ME! I ADMIT I WAS RUDE!... OH, STEVE, WHY DID YOU SEND FOR HER?
SHE RAN THE HOME OFFICE OF HORIZONS UNLIMITED—WHEN WE HAD ONE...THEY NEED GOOD SECRETARIES OUT HERE, SO —
YOU KNOW SHE'S IN LOVE WITH YOU, DON'T YOU?
HO! THAT'S A LAUGH!
YEAH — ON THE SAPPY LADY DOCTOR!
MILTON CANIFF
FEETA-FEETA, I'M SORRY ABOUT YOUR MEETING WITH DOCTOR DEEN WILDERNESS. I-AH...
WHY, MR.C., YOU MUSTN'T WORRY ABOUT ME... WHEN I SAW THE LADY DOCTOR'S REACTION TO MY COMING OUT HERE, I DETERMINED TO STAY OUT OF HER WAY — STARTING THAT MINUTE!
THERE ARE A MILLION THINGS TO DO... ANYTHING I SHOULD FIRST HEAR ABOUT THIS END?
OH, YES — HAPPY EASTER AND FIREBALL FEENEY KNOW WE'RE STARTING AN AIRLINE, BUT DEEN DOES NOT...
THAT'S SO SHE WON'T GIVE US AWAY TO THE OPPOSITION UNDERGROUND BY SOME CHANCE RE---- SAY, WHAT ARE YOU GRINNING ABOUT?...
MILTON CANIFF
MR.C., WE WORKED OUT THE MAIN DETAILS FROM POINTS ALL OVER THE GLOBE, SO YOU COULD POSE AS DR.WILDERNESS' BODYGUARD ON THE LOCAL SCENE...
GOOD, FEETA-FEETA! EACH AMERICAN CONCESSION HAS A LANDING STRIP BULLDOZED LEVEL ON ONE PRETEXT OR ANOTHER... GAS AND OIL ARE NO PROBLEM
MILTON CANIFF
THE AIRCRAFT AND CREWS HAVE BEEN LINED UP FROM MANY SOURCES...THEY'RE ALERTED RIGHT NOW TO FLY IN FROM ISOLATED POINTS... THEY'LL CARRY THE EXTRA RADIO AND MAINTENANCE EQUIPMENT!
RIGHT! IT'S A FULL-SCALE AIR COMMANDO OPERATION! THANKS TO YOU, FEETA!
MEANWHILE...
DR. WILDERNESS DROPPED TWO NEEDLES TONIGHT! IT'S THE FIRST TIME I'VE EVER SEEN HER NERVOUS!
IT WILL TAKE LITTLE EFFORT TO CONFOUND THE YANKEE WOMAN DOCTOR NOW... THE ARRIVAL OF CANYON'S PRETTY 'SECRETARY' FROM THE U.S. HAS THE DOCTOR SHAKING WITH JEALOUSY...
BUT I WONDER ABOUT THIS CANYON — AND HIS SECRETARY... LISTEN... I HEAR AIRCRAFT ENGINES — MANY OF THEM!
OUT OF THE DARKNESS COME MANY WAR SURPLUS AIRPLANES... AS THEY ROLL TO A STOP, AIRBORNE CREWS BEGIN TO UNLOAD THEIR BULKY CARGOES....
...THE SCENE IS REPEATED AT SEVERAL AMERICAN CONCESSIONS — AND AS THE RADIO TRANSMITTERS ARE SET UP, THE UNITS REPORT TO STEVE....
MILTON CANIFF

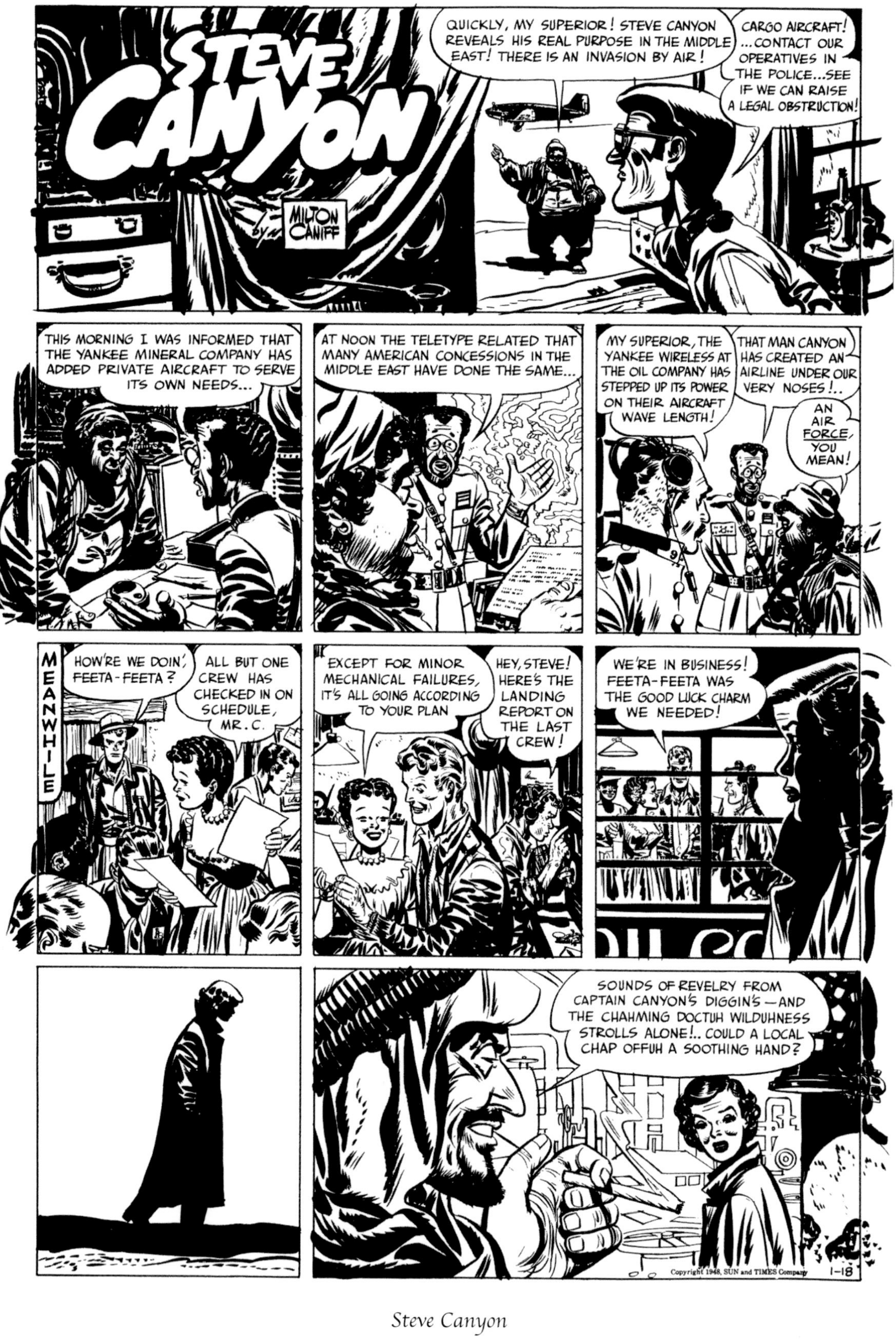
STEVE CANYON
by MILTON CANIFF
QUICKLY, MY SUPERIOR! STEVE CANYON REVEALS HIS REAL PURPOSE IN THE MIDDLE EAST! THERE IS AN INVASION BY AIR!
CARGO AIRCRAFT! ...CONTACT OUR OPERATIVES IN THE POLICE...SEE IF WE CAN RAISE A LEGAL OBSTRUCTION!
THIS MORNING I WAS INFORMED THAT THE YANKEE MINERAL COMPANY HAS ADDED PRIVATE AIRCRAFT TO SERVE ITS OWN NEEDS...
AT NOON THE TELETYPE RELATED THAT MANY AMERICAN CONCESSIONS IN THE MIDDLE EAST HAVE DONE THE SAME...
MY SUPERIOR, THE YANKEE WIRELESS AT THE OIL COMPANY HAS STEPPED UP ITS POWER ON THEIR AIRCRAFT WAVE LENGTH!
THAT MAN CANYON HAS CREATED AN AIRLINE UNDER OUR VERY NOSES!..
AN AIR FORCE, YOU MEAN!
MEANWHILE
HOW'RE WE DOIN', FEETA-FEETA?
ALL BUT ONE CREW HAS CHECKED IN ON SCHEDULE, MR. C.
EXCEPT FOR MINOR MECHANICAL FAILURES, IT'S ALL GOING ACCORDING TO YOUR PLAN
HEY, STEVE! HERE'S THE LANDING REPORT ON THE LAST CREW!
WE'RE IN BUSINESS! FEETA-FEETA WAS THE GOOD LUCK CHARM WE NEEDED!
SOUNDS OF REVELRY FROM CAPTAIN CANYON'S DIGGIN'S—AND THE CHAHMING DOCTUH WILDUHNESS STROLLS ALONE!.. COULD A LOCAL CHAP OFFUH A SOOTHING HAND?
Copyright 1948, SUN and TIMES Company
1-18

ALL THE AIRCRAFT HAVE LANDED AT OUR AMERICAN CONCESSIONS WITHOUT A MAJOR MISHAP! HOW WAS IT HANDLED CAPTAIN CANYON?

THE LOCAL GOVERNMENTS COOPERATED...THEY'RE LESS WORRIED ABOUT THE UNITED STATES THAN ABOUT OTHER COUNTRIES CLOSER AT HAND...

PERSIAN MINERAL Company

TRAFFIC MANAGER

FEETA - FEETA—AND SOME OTHERS WHOSE NAMES I'D BETTER NOT MENTION — DID THE ORGANIZING, HIRING OF PERSONNEL AND SO ON, WHILE I DID THE ADVANCE WORK POSING AS DOCTOR WILDERNESS'S BODYGUARD

WHICH REMINDS ME THAT SHE STILL DOESN'T KNOW ABOUT ALL THIS!.. FEETA, WILL YOU MIND THE STORE WHILE I PUT ON THE BIG EXPLANATION ACT TO DEEN?

♪ A FELLA NEEDS A GIRL ♪

AW, HAVE A HEART!

MILTON CANIFF

OH — CHIEF IZM!

CHEER'O, DOCTUH WILDUHNESS! DOES SOME IMMINENT SUH-JUHRY CALL YOU FROM THE GALA OPENING OF CAPTAIN CANYON'S AIHLINE?

I WASN'T CONSULTED ABOUT THE AIRPLANES —AND I WASN'T INVITED TO THE CELEBRATION!

FRANKLY, NYETHUH WAS I, DOCTUH! WHAT SAY WE POAH OUTCAHSTS SHARE OUAH BITTAH TEA?

MILTON CANIFF

I SAY, THIS IS JOLLY! YOU YANKEES AH SO VEDDY CONSIDERATE... FANCY HAVING THE WIT TO SEND A WOMAN DOCTUH OUT HEAH — A PRETTY WOMAN DOCTUH!

HMM — OH — I'M SORRY!... I'M AFRAID A DOCTOR OFTEN EVEN THINKS SHOP!

HEY, DEEN. I TRIED TO FIND YOU LAST NIGHT TO HELP US CELEBRATE THE START OF THE NEW AIRLINE!

OH YES, I HEARD IT MENTIONED IN A ROUNDABOUT SORT OF WAY, STEVE... CHIEF IZM AND I WERE JUST HAVING DINNER WHEN ---

CHIEF IZM?

YES. HE AND I SEEMED TO BE THE ONLY PEOPLE HERE WHO HAD NO PART IN THE BIG SHOW — SO WE TEAMED UP OUTSIDE THE CELEBRATION CIRCLE!

PERHAPS YOU'D BETTER GO .. I HAVE TO SCRUB UP FOR AN OPERATION! — NOT AS EXCITING AS MAKING AVIATION HISTORY, BUT EACH OF US HAS HIS LITTLE SPECIALTY, EVEN IF IT'S MERELY KNOWING HOW TO REMOVE AN APPENDIX

MILTON CANIFF

WHILE THE YANKEES STILL GLOAT OVER THEIR AIRLINE, WE SHALL FAVOR THEM WITH THE FIRST OF OUR LITTLE ATTENTIONS!

THEIR NUGO PASS WEATHER STATION WAS YOUR CHOICE FOR NUMBER ONE, MY SUPERIOR!

SHORTLY AN UNDERGROUND LISTENING POST IN THE HILLS RECEIVES AN ORDER...

MILTON CANIFF

THEN — AT STEVE'S RADIO ROOM ON THE FLATLAND...

EVERYTHING BUT THE KILKENNY CATS ON THE NUGO PASS WEATHER STATION WAVE LENGTH TODAY...

HEY! THE WEATHER OBSERVER'S LITTLE DAUGHTER IS DOWN WITH WHAT LOOKS LIKE PNEUMONIA.... HE REQUESTS MEDICAL AID...

WHAT'S THE FORECAST FOR THAT AREA?

FOG, SNOW AND ICE!

Steve Canyon

FEETA-FEETA, WE HAVE AN EMERGENCY CALL FROM OUR WEATHER OBSERVER AT NUGO PASS—HIS DAUGHTER HAS PNEUMONIA! DOES STEVE WANT AN AIRPLANE SENT TO DROP MEDICINE?

MR. C. IS OUT AT THE MOMENT—I'LL PHONE YOU BACK!

UNAB, WHERE IS CAPTAIN CANYON?

CAP'N GO HOUSE OF MISSA DOCTA WILDERNESS

SOMEBODY QUICK PULL DRAPES—SO, I GOT NO MORE LOOK TO TELL!

OH...

CAPTAIN CANYON IS STILL OUT, BUT I KNOW HE'D WANT A PLANE SENT— HE IS VERY SENSITIVE TO ANYONE IN DISTRESS!

THE WEATHER MAN AT NUGO PASS IS ON AGAIN! BAD STATIC...THE DAUGHTER IS WORSE! I THINK THE UNDERGROUND IS JAMMING US!

FEETA-FEETA SAYS STEVE IS OUT, BUT THAT HE LEFT A STANDING OPERATING PROCEDURE FOR SUCH EMERGENCIES...SEND THE PLANE

SOON AN AIRPLANE CARRYING EMERGENCY MEDICAL SUPPLIES IN PARACHUTE PACKS IS DISPATCHED TO THE MOUNTAIN AREA...

DID THE YANKEES TAKE THE BAIT?

OF COURSE—YOU HAVE SEEN THEIR MOTION PICTURES!..ALWAYS THEY BECOME SOFT IN THE HEAD AT A CALL FOR HELP! NOW WE WILL PUT THE FALSE BEAM TO WORK! THE SNOW HAS BEGUN!

STEVE, I CAN UNDERSTAND THE NEED FOR SECRECY IN SETTING UP YOUR AIR LINE BETWEEN THE AMERICAN CONCESSIONS IN THE MIDDLE EAST... BUT

BUT WHY DIDN'T I TAKE YOU INTO MY CONFIDENCE... IS THAT THE BEEF?

Steve Canyon by MILTON CANIFF

WELL...

YOU WERE MY FOIL, DEEN! AS THE LADY DOC'S MUSCLE BOY, I WAS ABLE TO LINE UP THE DETAILS BEFORE OUR COMPETITION GOT HEP!

I SUPPOSE MISS FEETA-FEETA HAS BEEN INVALUABLE TO YOU!

OF COURSE! SHE DID THE BIG ORGANIZING JOB ON THE OUTSIDE! ...HEY! I DON'T LIKE THE WAY YOU SAID THAT, LADY SAWBONES!

DON'T LET IT TAKE THE CURL OUT OF YOUR HAIR, STEVIE!.. OH, HERE COMES CHIEF IZM, RIGHT ON TIME FOR OUR DATE!

YES, COMPLETE WITH SNOOD AND ACCENT! GIVE MY REGARDS TO THE HAREM!

Steve Canyon

OUR OPPOSITION DIDN'T WAIT LONG TO POUNCE, MR.C! THEY TRIED TO JAM OUR RADIO!

UH-HUH

WE HAD A DISTRESS CALL FROM THE WEATHER STATION IN NUGO PASS

MHMM

PENICILLIN AND SULFA FOR THE STATION KEEPER'S LITTLE DAUGHTER ... WE SENT CREW NUMBER 5

ROUGH COUNTR... AND SN... SHOWIN... ON TH... WEATHE... CHART...

WAIT A MINUTE! THAT WEATHER MAN AT NUGO PASS ISN'T MARRIED!

FEEL THOSE HORSES PULL!... THIS BEATS DEALIN' OUT HARDWARE IN THE OLD MAN'S STORE BACK HOME, EH, DAN?

FEELS LIKE OLD TIMES—ONLY NOW THE BUTTERFLIES IN MY STOMACH ARE JET-PROPELLED! I'VE GOT QUALMS WITH 29 PALMS!

Copyright 1948, SUN and TIMES Company

STEVE SAYS THE WEATHER-MAN AT NUGO PASS HAS NO DAUGHTER TO BE DOWN WITH PNEUMONIA! IT'S A TRICK! RECALL OUR MERCY AIRPLANE!

SOMEBODY'S JAMMING! I CAN HEAR OUR PILOT, BUT HE'S NOT GETTING ME!

NUGO WEATHER, THIS IS PERSIAN PETROLEUM TC-SRI... I HEAR YOU LOUD AND CLEAR, BUT I CAN'T PICK UP ANY OTHER SIGNAL...OVER

THIS IS NUGO WEATHER! I CAN HEAR YOUR ENGINES! YOU'RE TOO HIGH TO PARACHUTE THE MEDICINE WITH ACCURACY...

DROP DOWN TO 5,000 FEET—IT'S CLEAR RIGHT AT THIS POINT...OVER

NO! NO, TC-SRI! THA... VOICE IS A PHONY! THIS IS NUGO WEATHER STATION! THEY'RE TRYING TO WRECK YOU! OVER! OVER!

I CAN HEAR YOUR ENGINES BUT YOU'RE STILL TOO HIGH TO DROP THE MEDICINE ACCURATELY! YOU'LL BREAK INTO THE CLEAR AT 5,000 FEET... OVER

I CAN'T SEE A THING, BUT YOU SHOULD KNOW!.. COMING DOWN... OVER

STAY UP THERE, TC-SRI! —THIS IS THE REAL NUGO WEATHER STATION... I HEAR THEM TRYING TO WRECK YOU! THEY MUST HAVE ME JAMMED OUT...

HEY, NUGO WEATHER, MY COPILOT JUST CHECKED OUR MAPS...

ARE YOU SURE WE CAN CIRCLE YOUR SHACK AT THAT ALTITUDE?...

NUGO RIDGE IS CHARTE... AS BEING SIX THOU—

DAN! PULL UP!

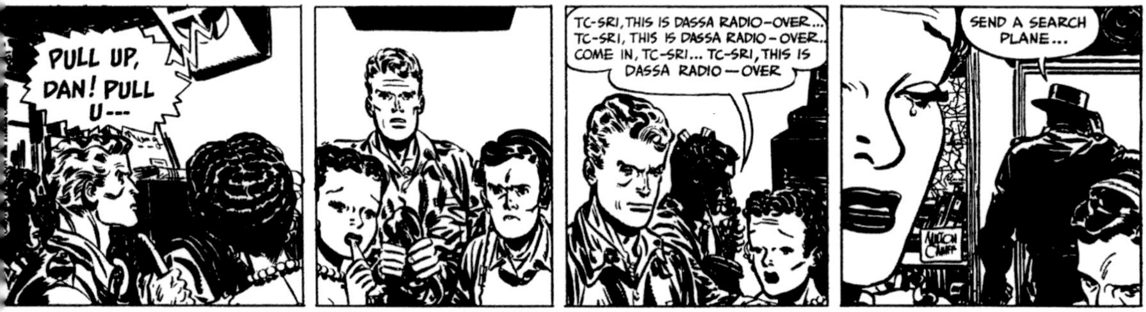
PULL UP, DAN! PULL U---
TC-SRI, THIS IS DASSA RADIO-OVER... TC-SRI, THIS IS DASSA RADIO-OVER.. COME IN, TC-SRI... TC-SRI, THIS IS DASSA RADIO—OVER
SEND A SEARCH PLANE...
MILTON CANIFF

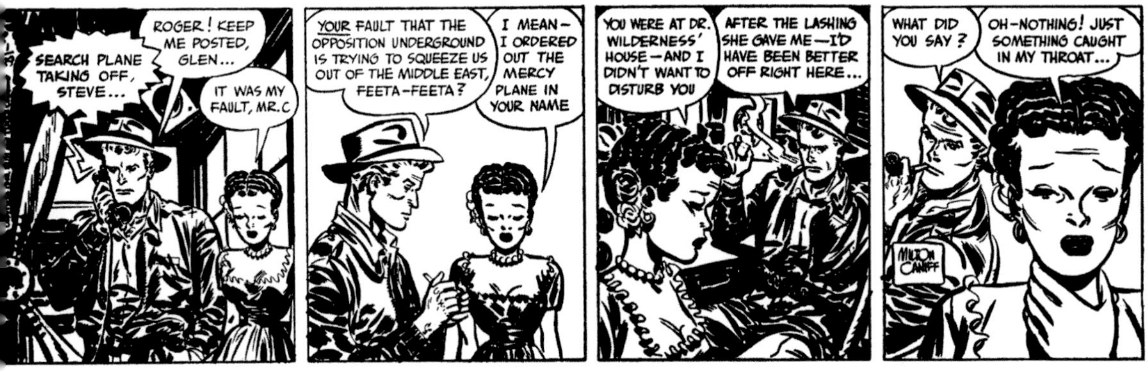
SEARCH PLANE TAKING OFF, STEVE...
ROGER! KEEP ME POSTED, GLEN...
IT WAS MY FAULT, MR. C
YOUR FAULT THAT THE OPPOSITION UNDERGROUND IS TRYING TO SQUEEZE US OUT OF THE MIDDLE EAST, FEETA-FEETA?
I MEAN— I ORDERED OUT THE MERCY PLANE IN YOUR NAME
YOU WERE AT DR. WILDERNESS' HOUSE—AND I DIDN'T WANT TO DISTURB YOU
AFTER THE LASHING SHE GAVE ME—I'D HAVE BEEN BETTER OFF RIGHT HERE...
WHAT DID YOU SAY?
OH—NOTHING! JUST SOMETHING CAUGHT IN MY THROAT...
MILTON CANIFF

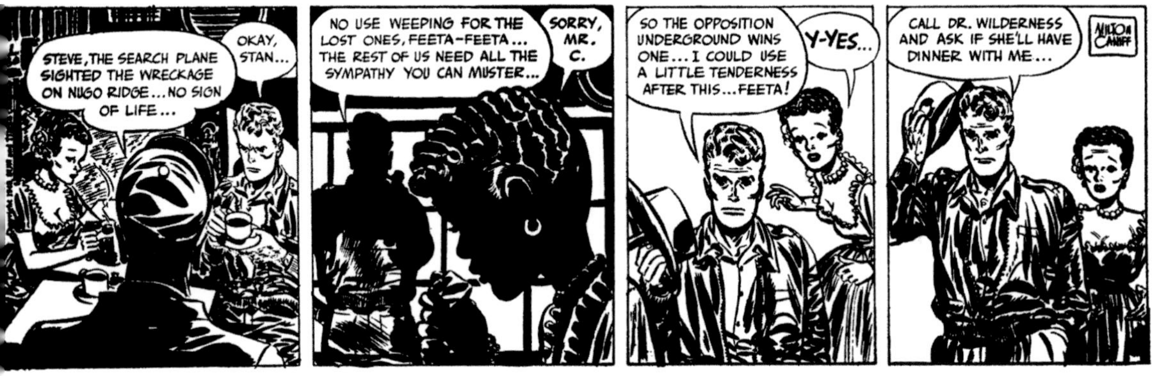
STEVE, THE SEARCH PLANE SIGHTED THE WRECKAGE ON NUGO RIDGE... NO SIGN OF LIFE...
OKAY, STAN...
NO USE WEEPING FOR THE LOST ONES, FEETA-FEETA... THE REST OF US NEED ALL THE SYMPATHY YOU CAN MUSTER...
SORRY, MR. C.
SO THE OPPOSITION UNDERGROUND WINS ONE... I COULD USE A LITTLE TENDERNESS AFTER THIS... FEETA!
Y-YES...
CALL DR. WILDERNESS AND ASK IF SHE'LL HAVE DINNER WITH ME...
MILTON CANIFF

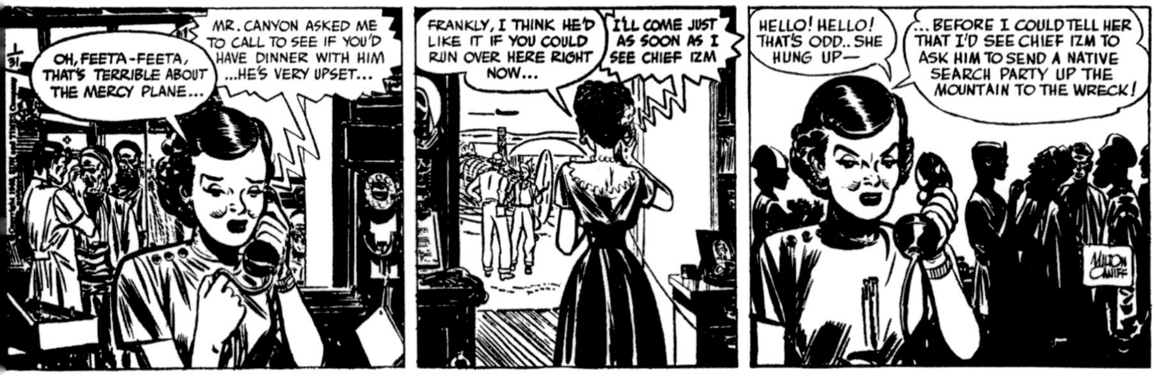
OH, FEETA-FEETA, THAT'S TERRIBLE ABOUT THE MERCY PLANE...
MR. CANYON ASKED ME TO CALL TO SEE IF YOU'D HAVE DINNER WITH HIM ...HE'S VERY UPSET...
FRANKLY, I THINK HE'D LIKE IT IF YOU COULD RUN OVER HERE RIGHT NOW...
I'LL COME JUST AS SOON AS I SEE CHIEF IZM
HELLO! HELLO! THAT'S ODD.. SHE HUNG UP—
...BEFORE I COULD TELL HER THAT I'D SEE CHIEF IZM TO ASK HIM TO SEND A NATIVE SEARCH PARTY UP THE MOUNTAIN TO THE WRECK!
MILTON CANIFF

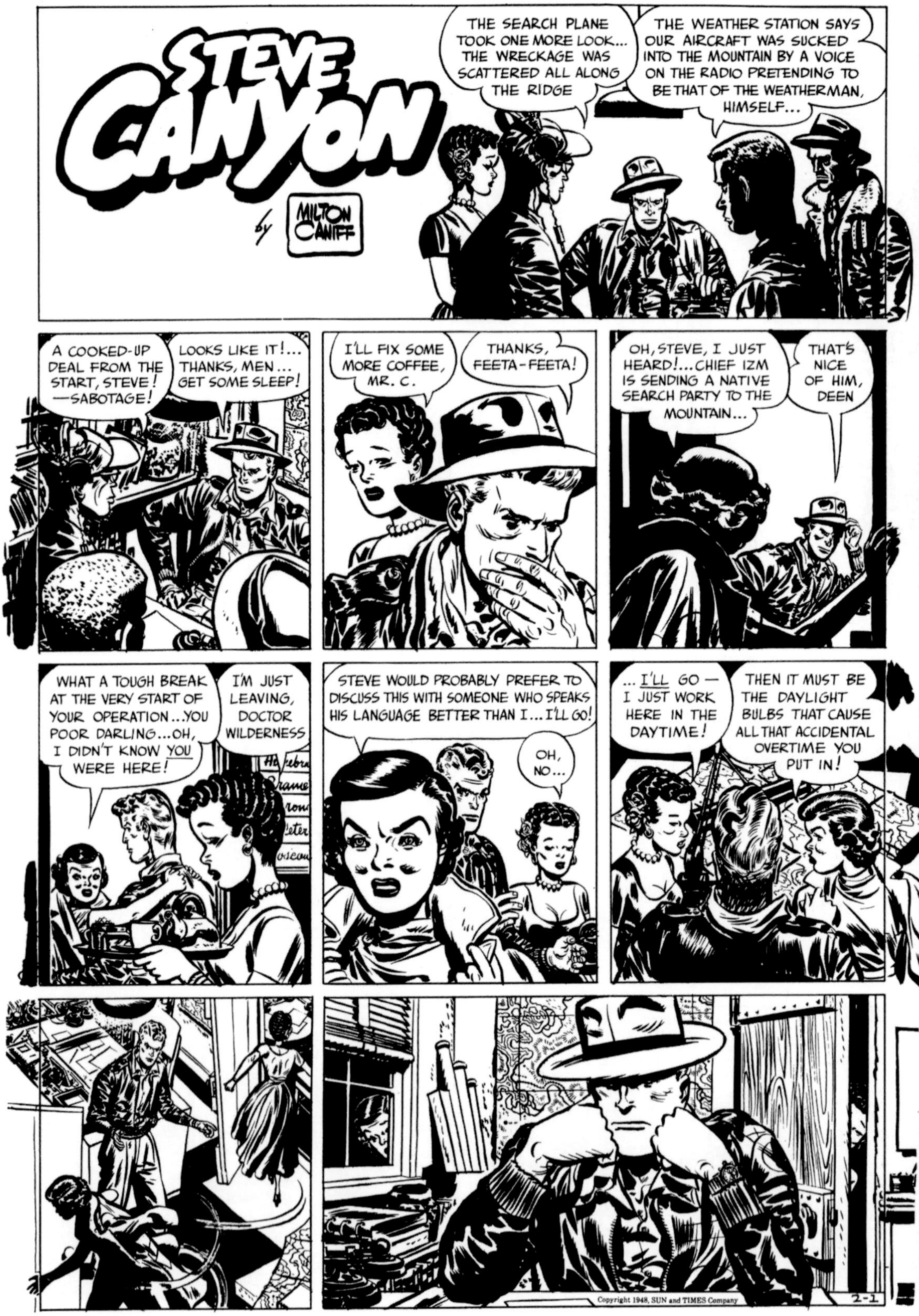
STEVE CANYON
by MILTON CANIFF
THE SEARCH PLANE TOOK ONE MORE LOOK... THE WRECKAGE WAS SCATTERED ALL ALONG THE RIDGE
THE WEATHER STATION SAYS OUR AIRCRAFT WAS SUCKED INTO THE MOUNTAIN BY A VOICE ON THE RADIO PRETENDING TO BE THAT OF THE WEATHERMAN, HIMSELF...
A COOKED-UP DEAL FROM THE START, STEVE! —SABOTAGE!
LOOKS LIKE IT!... THANKS, MEN... GET SOME SLEEP!
I'LL FIX SOME MORE COFFEE, MR. C.
THANKS, FEETA-FEETA!
OH, STEVE, I JUST HEARD!...CHIEF IZM IS SENDING A NATIVE SEARCH PARTY TO THE MOUNTAIN...
THAT'S NICE OF HIM, DEEN
WHAT A TOUGH BREAK AT THE VERY START OF YOUR OPERATION...YOU POOR DARLING...OH, I DIDN'T KNOW YOU WERE HERE!
I'M JUST LEAVING, DOCTOR WILDERNESS
STEVE WOULD PROBABLY PREFER TO DISCUSS THIS WITH SOMEONE WHO SPEAKS HIS LANGUAGE BETTER THAN I...I'LL GO!
OH, NO...
... I'LL GO — I JUST WORK HERE IN THE DAYTIME!
THEN IT MUST BE THE DAYLIGHT BULBS THAT CAUSE ALL THAT ACCIDENTAL OVERTIME YOU PUT IN!
Copyright 1948, SUN and TIMES Company
2-1

NOW IT'S DIPLOMACY! FEETA-FEETA, GOTTA RUN DOWN TO ENJEB! NUMBER FOUR BUSTED THE LOCAL BIG SHEIK'S ELECTRIC WIRE ON AN UNDERSHOT LANDING!

YES, MR. C.

I PHONED DOCTOR WILDERNESS TO SAY THAT MR. CANY--OH, HERE SHE IS NOW...

EXCUSE ME... --I'LL COME BACK WHEN STEVE'S AROUND...

MR. CANYON LEFT ON AN EMERGENCY JOB! I WAS JUST CALLING TO CANCEL YOUR DINNER DATE! MAY I HELP YOU?

WHOM DO I SEE ABOUT ARRANGING SPACE FOR SOME OF MY SUPPLIES TO GO TO THE CONCESSIONS BY AIR?

WITH MR. C. AWAY -- YOU SEE ME!

I WAS AFRAID OF THAT!

SINCE MR. CANYON IS AWAY, I'LL ARRANGE SPACE FOR YOUR MEDICAL STORES TO GO TO THE CONCESSIONS ON COMPANY-OWNED PLANES, DOCTOR WILDERNESS...

THESE AREN'T EXACTLY MEDICAL SUPPLIES

DOCTOR, YOU KNOW THE PRIORITY SYSTEM WE HAVE! THOSE AIRPLANES WERE GOING OUT DANGEROUSLY OVERLOADED!

I COULD HAVE SAID THESE WERE MEDICAL SUPPLIES -- YOU WOULD NEVER HAVE KNOWN!

THE PHONOGRAPHS AND RECORDS YOU ORDERED FOR THE STAFFS OF YOUR CLINICS ARE REALLY THERAPEUTIC! -- I'LL MARK THE BOXES 'MEDICINE'!

SO YOU KNEW MY SECRET! CONGRATULATIONS ON YOUR SPY SYSTEM -- AND THANK YOU FOR YOUR PATRONAGE!

PLEASE WAIT, DR. WILDERNESS... WHY DO YOU RESENT ME SO?

I'M PAST BEING COY ABOUT IT--I'M JEALOUS! I'M SURE YOU RESENT ME -- AND ANY WOMAN WHO TRIES TO TAKE STEVE CANYON FROM YOU... BUT--

YOU HAVE SEVERAL ADVANTAGES OVER YOUR RIVALS... FOR INSTANCE:

IT WOULD BE UNETHICAL FOR A WOMAN DOCTOR TO WEAR A PNEUMONIA BLOUSE TO WORK EVERY DAY -- AS YOU DO!

.. I'M A WITCH TO SAY THAT -- BECAUSE I'D WEAR SUCH CLOTHES IF I ONLY HAD THE NERVE!

IT'S TOO BAD WE DON'T GET ALONG, DR. WILDERNESS! IT WOULD SIMPLIFY MATTERS FOR CAPTAIN CANYON!

OH, I CAN BE VERY CLINICAL ABOUT THIS... A WOMAN DOCTOR HAS LIVED TOO LONG WITH DISCIPLINE TO COMPETE EVENLY WITH A GAL LIKE YOU...

THERE ARE OTHER KINDS OF DISCIPLINE BESIDES MEDICAL STUDY, DOCTOR... DO YOU THINK IT'S EASY FOR ME TO REMEMBER THAT I'M JUST A HIRED HAND IN STEVE CANYON'S LIFE?

OH, WHY DIDN'T YOU USE YOUR OBVIOUS CHARMS TO MARRY STEVE LONG AGO? -- OR DO YOU ENJOY SEEING MUSHY-EYED FEMALES LIKE ME KNOCKING THEMSELVES OUT AGAINST YOUR ODDLY SECURE POSITION?

ACTUALLY -- I THINK MR. C. HATES ME!

Steve Canyon

STEVE CANYON HATES YOU? — YOU'RE KIDDING!

MR. C. IS A REBEL!... I REPRESENT ALL THE ANNOYING REALITIES FROM WHICH HE KEEPS RETREATING, DR. WILDERNESS!

I REMIND HIM OF HIS OVERDUE BILLS, TAXES, APPOINTMENTS HE DOESN'T WISH TO KEEP — ALL THE HALTERS THAT BIND A MAN IN WESTERN CIVILIZATION...

I DON'T BELIEVE STEVE HATES YOU — AND YOU'RE NOT THE SELF-PITYING TYPE...

HE'S JUST STEPPING OUT OF THE AIRPLANE FROM ENJEB... JUDGE FOR YOURSELF BY THE DIFFERENCE IN THE WAY HE GREETS EACH OF US!

HERE COMES MR. CANYON — BACK FROM ENJEB, DR. WILDERNESS! NOW WE'LL SEE WHICH OF US HIS GREETINGS FAVOR!

HI, DEEN! HI, FEETA-FEETA!... OH, BEFORE I FORGET IT...

I SAW BRECK NAZAIRE AT ENJEB! HE SAID TO BE SURE AND GIVE YOU A BIG KISS FOR HIM! --- HEY! WHAT'S WRONG WITH DEEN?

SEND IN THE NEXT PATIENT, PLEASE

STEVE CANYON
by MILTON CANIFF

STEVE CANYON'S FAITHFUL FEETA-FEETA! IS THIS YOUR IDEA OF A JOKE?

NO, DR. WILDERNESS, IT'S THE ONLY WAY I COULD BE SURE OF SEEING YOU!

MY PLANE IS WAITING... IF YOU AREN'T ILL, DON'T TAKE UP THE TIME OF PEOPLE WHO NEED A DOCTOR'S ATTENTION...

THAT'S WHY I CAME HERE — BECAUSE YOU ARE MOVING YOUR MEDICAL HEADQUARTERS TO ANOTHER TOWN...

THAT SHOULD MAKE YOU HAPPY... YOU AND STEVE CAN LAUGH ABOUT THE MOONSTRUCK LADY DOCTOR WHO SHOULD HAVE STUCK TO HER PILL ROLLING!

BUT I CAME TO ASK YOU TO STAY HERE HE NEEDS YOU!

Steve Canyon

THE DISPENSARY WILL GIVE HIM ASPIRIN FOR HIS AIRLINE HEADACHES!

NOT THAT! HE'S AT EASE AROUND YOU—HE LAUGHS AND MAKES JOKES! YOU DO HIM GOOD!

HE RELAXES WITH YOU, TOO... MORE THAN MEETS THE EYE, I AM SURE!

I SUPPOSE I SHOULD BE ANGRY ABOUT WHAT YOU JUST SAID, BUT YOU'RE NOT A MEANIE AT HEART!

WHY ALL THIS SWEETNESS AND LIGHT?.. WHY ARE YOU DELIBERATELY PUNISHING YOURSELF BY TRYING TO THROW ME INTO STEVE'S ARMS?

MAYBE I'M NUTS!... ANYHOW, I'VE MADE MY SPEECH. I'LL GO NOW...

... HEY, FIREBALL! DOC WILDERNESS JUST PHONED... SHE'S CHANGED HER MIND ABOUT MOVING HER HEADQUARTERS!

?

2-8   Copyright 1948, SUN and TIMES Company

MISSA DOCTA WILDERNESS, IS CHIEF IZM WAITS...

OH, I ALMOST FORGOT OUR DATE!

YOU KNOW, CHIEF IZM, IT'S GOOD OF YOU TO SQUIRE ME AROUND THIS PLACE

AND WELL I MIGHT, DOCTUH! YOU AH A COOL BREATH OF SPRING IN THIS WINTAH OF SAND AND SUN!

WELL—YOU'VE MADE MY JOB SO MUCH EASIER

BY GIVING YOU SOMETHING TO MAKE THE CANYON CHAP JEALOUS—WITHOUT BOTHUHRING YOU BY MAKING LOVE TO YOU, MYSELF ... RIGHT?

Steve Canyon

YOU SENT FOR ME, DEEN?

YES, STEVE! I'M JEALOUS OF FEETA-FEETA, AND I REALIZE I'VE BEEN USING CHIEF IZM TO MAKE YOU JEALOUS... I'M GOING BACK TO PILL ROLLING — FULL TIME!

I'VE ALWAYS KNOWN EDUCATION FOR WOMEN WAS A DANGEROUS THING... I'M TAKING YOU INTO PROTECTIVE CUSTODY FOR BEING LICENSED WITHOUT PRACTICING

HEY, FEETA-FEETA! THOUGHT YOU'D BE WORKING TONIGHT! HOW ABOUT GOING TO THE MOVIES?

YEAH — IT'S LOVE STORY. IT'LL TAKE YOUR MIND OFF THE EVERY-DAY GRIND!

I MUST BE OUT OF MY HEAD, STEVE! YOU PROBABLY HAVE A STRING OF GIRLS LIKE ME ALL OVER THE WORLD...

...ALTHOUGH FOR THEIR OWN SAKES I HOPE THEY'RE NOT LIKE ME!

DO YOU THINK IT'S FAIR FOR BIG, YELLOW-HAIRED PILOTS TO GO AROUND BREAKING THE HEARTS OF LADY MEDICS?...

DON'T ANSWER THAT QUESTION!

HEY, FEETA-FEETA'S LEAVING!

WHADYA KNOW... FEETA WALKED OUT JUST BEFORE THE FELLA GOT THE GIRL!

... I WILL REPEAT THE HEADLINES UP TO THIS HOUR... THERE IS NO CHANGE IN THE CRITICAL SITUATION IN PALESTINE...

...THE PREVAILING EPIDEMIC IN THE MIDDLE EAST HAS AGAIN BROKEN OUT IN A REMOTE SPOT—THIS TIME IN A MOUNTAIN VILLAGE EAST OF DASSA IN THE---

THAT'S IN MY TERRITORY —AND I HEAR ABOUT IT FROM A RADIO STATION IN THE BALKANS!

THIS IS DASSA RADIO, DR. WILDERNESS —WE JUST GOT A CALL ABOUT AN EPIDEMIC IN THE MOUNTA---

I JUST HEARD ABOUT IT ON A NEWSCAST FROM THE BALKANS! NO TIME TO GO INTO THAT NOW.... I'LL ROUND UP MY CREW...

MISTA PILOT FIREBALL FEENEY! MISSY DOCTA WILDERNESS SAY YOU FLYBOY HER IMMEDIATE!

SHORE, MA'AM, HE'S RIGHT HERE! DON'T YE GO SOARIN' INTA TH' NIGHT TILL MY STEVIE KNOWS MORE ABOUT IT...

WHY, TO BE SHUAH, DOCTUH WILDUHNESS! THAT IS INDEED BANDIT COUNTRY — AND I INSIST UPON ACCOMPANYING YOU!...AS A CHIEF I SHALL HAVE INFLUENCE WITH THE HILL PEOPLE...

BY GOOD FAWTUNE I AM ALREADY DRESSED AND READY TO DEPAHT!

Steve Canyon

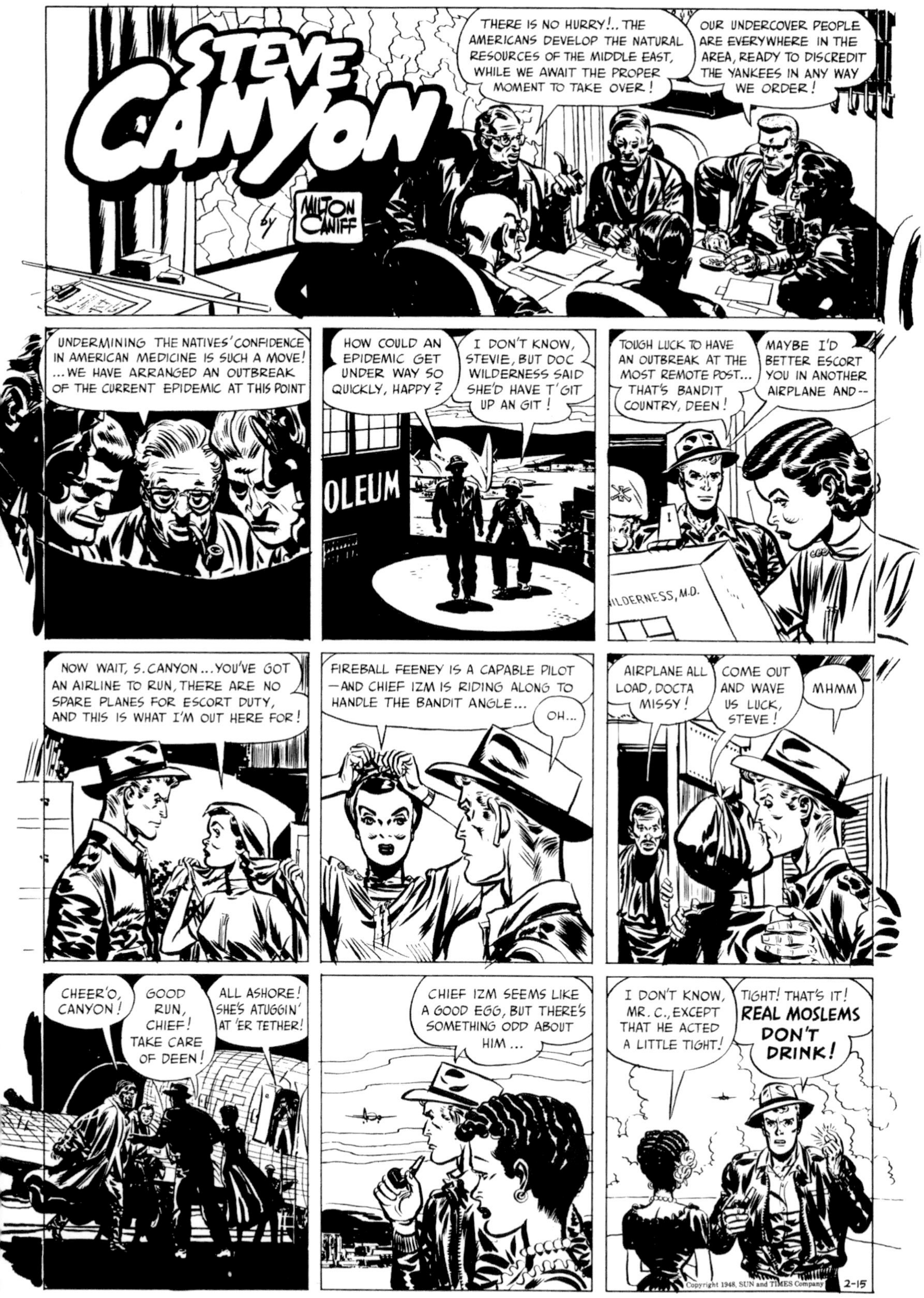
STEVE CANYON
by MILTON CANIFF
THERE IS NO HURRY!.. THE AMERICANS DEVELOP THE NATURAL RESOURCES OF THE MIDDLE EAST, WHILE WE AWAIT THE PROPER MOMENT TO TAKE OVER!
OUR UNDERCOVER PEOPLE ARE EVERYWHERE IN THE AREA, READY TO DISCREDIT THE YANKEES IN ANY WAY WE ORDER!
UNDERMINING THE NATIVES' CONFIDENCE IN AMERICAN MEDICINE IS SUCH A MOVE! ...WE HAVE ARRANGED AN OUTBREAK OF THE CURRENT EPIDEMIC AT THIS POINT
HOW COULD AN EPIDEMIC GET UNDER WAY SO QUICKLY, HAPPY?
I DON'T KNOW, STEVIE, BUT DOC WILDERNESS SAID SHE'D HAVE T'GIT UP AN GIT!
OLEUM
TOUGH LUCK TO HAVE AN OUTBREAK AT THE MOST REMOTE POST... THAT'S BANDIT COUNTRY, DEEN!
MAYBE I'D BETTER ESCORT YOU IN ANOTHER AIRPLANE AND--
ILDERNESS, M.D.
NOW WAIT, S. CANYON... YOU'VE GOT AN AIRLINE TO RUN, THERE ARE NO SPARE PLANES FOR ESCORT DUTY, AND THIS IS WHAT I'M OUT HERE FOR!
FIREBALL FEENEY IS A CAPABLE PILOT —AND CHIEF IZM IS RIDING ALONG TO HANDLE THE BANDIT ANGLE...
OH...
AIRPLANE ALL LOAD, DOCTA MISSY!
COME OUT AND WAVE US LUCK, STEVE!
MHMM
CHEER'O, CANYON!
GOOD RUN, CHIEF! TAKE CARE OF DEEN!
ALL ASHORE! SHE'S ATUGGIN' AT 'ER TETHER!
CHIEF IZM SEEMS LIKE A GOOD EGG, BUT THERE'S SOMETHING ODD ABOUT HIM...
I DON'T KNOW, MR. C., EXCEPT THAT HE ACTED A LITTLE TIGHT!
TIGHT! THAT'S IT! REAL MOSLEMS DON'T DRINK!
Copyright 1948, SUN and TIMES Company
2-15

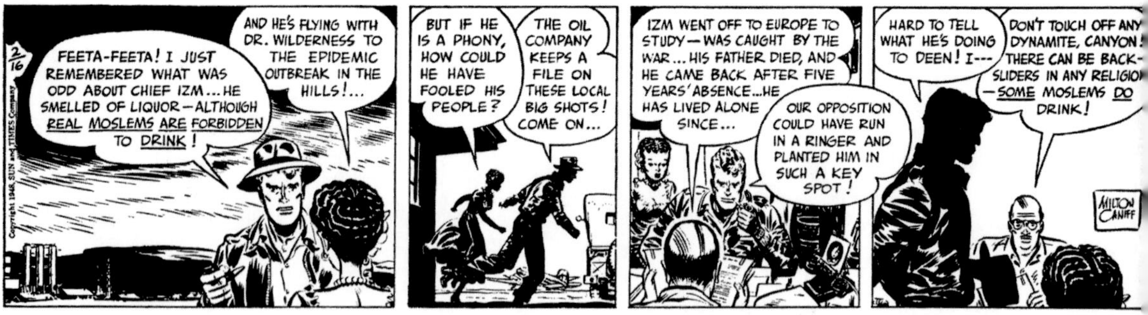
2/16
Copyright 1948, SUN and TIMES Company
FEETA-FEETA! I JUST REMEMBERED WHAT WAS ODD ABOUT CHIEF IZM... HE SMELLED OF LIQUOR—ALTHOUGH REAL MOSLEMS ARE FORBIDDEN TO DRINK!
AND HE'S FLYING WITH DR. WILDERNESS TO THE EPIDEMIC OUTBREAK IN THE HILLS!...
BUT IF HE IS A PHONY, HOW COULD HE HAVE FOOLED HIS PEOPLE?
THE OIL COMPANY KEEPS A FILE ON THESE LOCAL BIG SHOTS! COME ON...
IZM WENT OFF TO EUROPE TO STUDY—WAS CAUGHT BY THE WAR... HIS FATHER DIED, AND HE CAME BACK AFTER FIVE YEARS' ABSENCE...HE HAS LIVED ALONE SINCE...
OUR OPPOSITION COULD HAVE RUN IN A RINGER AND PLANTED HIM IN SUCH A KEY SPOT!
HARD TO TELL WHAT HE'S DOING TO DEEN! I---
DON'T TOUCH OFF ANY DYNAMITE, CANYON! THERE CAN BE BACK-SLIDERS IN ANY RELIGION—SOME MOSLEMS DO DRINK!
MILTON CANIFF

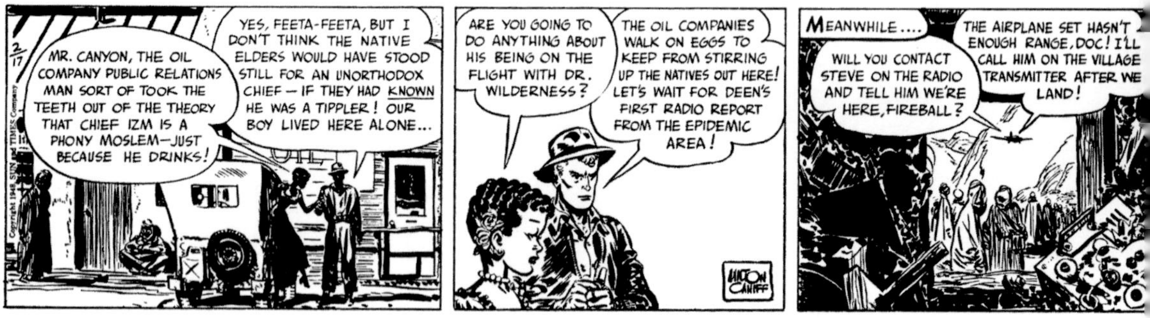
2/17
Copyright 1948, SUN and TIMES Company
MR. CANYON, THE OIL COMPANY PUBLIC RELATIONS MAN SORT OF TOOK THE TEETH OUT OF THE THEORY THAT CHIEF IZM IS A PHONY MOSLEM—JUST BECAUSE HE DRINKS!
YES, FEETA-FEETA, BUT I DON'T THINK THE NATIVE ELDERS WOULD HAVE STOOD STILL FOR AN UNORTHODOX CHIEF—IF THEY HAD KNOWN HE WAS A TIPPLER! OUR BOY LIVED HERE ALONE...
ARE YOU GOING TO DO ANYTHING ABOUT HIS BEING ON THE FLIGHT WITH DR. WILDERNESS?
THE OIL COMPANIES WALK ON EGGS TO KEEP FROM STIRRING UP THE NATIVES OUT HERE! LET'S WAIT FOR DEEN'S FIRST RADIO REPORT FROM THE EPIDEMIC AREA!
MILTON CANIFF
MEANWHILE....
WILL YOU CONTACT STEVE ON THE RADIO AND TELL HIM WE'RE HERE, FIREBALL?
THE AIRPLANE SET HASN'T ENOUGH RANGE, DOC! I'LL CALL HIM ON THE VILLAGE TRANSMITTER AFTER WE LAND!

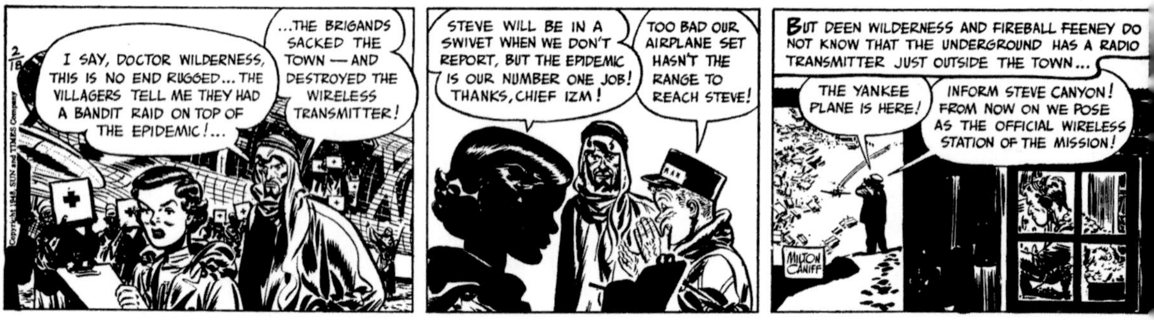
2/18
Copyright 1948, SUN and TIMES Company
I SAY, DOCTOR WILDERNESS, THIS IS NO END RUGGED... THE VILLAGERS TELL ME THEY HAD A BANDIT RAID ON TOP OF THE EPIDEMIC!...
...THE BRIGANDS SACKED THE TOWN — AND DESTROYED THE WIRELESS TRANSMITTER!
STEVE WILL BE IN A SWIVET WHEN WE DON'T REPORT, BUT THE EPIDEMIC IS OUR NUMBER ONE JOB! THANKS, CHIEF IZM!
TOO BAD OUR AIRPLANE SET HASN'T THE RANGE TO REACH STEVE!
BUT DEEN WILDERNESS AND FIREBALL FEENEY DO NOT KNOW THAT THE UNDERGROUND HAS A RADIO TRANSMITTER JUST OUTSIDE THE TOWN...
THE YANKEE PLANE IS HERE!
INFORM STEVE CANYON! FROM NOW ON WE POSE AS THE OFFICIAL WIRELESS STATION OF THE MISSION!
MILTON CANIFF

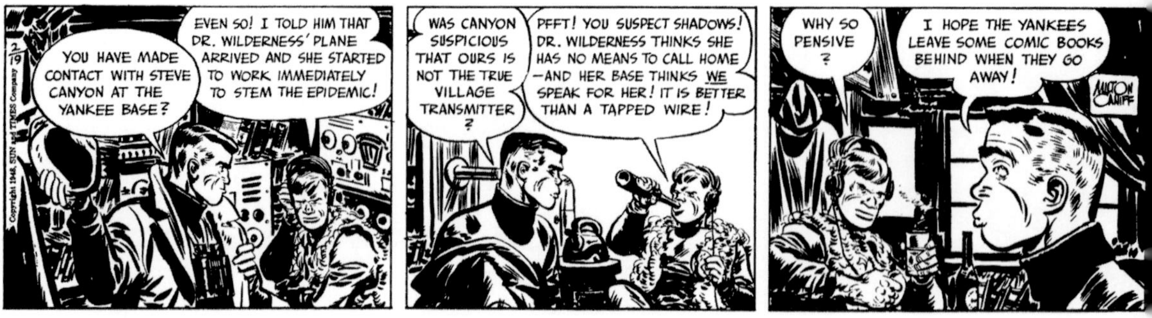
2/19
Copyright 1948, SUN and TIMES Company
YOU HAVE MADE CONTACT WITH STEVE CANYON AT THE YANKEE BASE?
EVEN SO! I TOLD HIM THAT DR. WILDERNESS' PLANE ARRIVED AND SHE STARTED TO WORK IMMEDIATELY TO STEM THE EPIDEMIC!
WAS CANYON SUSPICIOUS THAT OURS IS NOT THE TRUE VILLAGE TRANSMITTER?
PFFT! YOU SUSPECT SHADOWS! DR. WILDERNESS THINKS SHE HAS NO MEANS TO CALL HOME—AND HER BASE THINKS WE SPEAK FOR HER! IT IS BETTER THAN A TAPPED WIRE!
WHY SO PENSIVE?
I HOPE THE YANKEES LEAVE SOME COMIC BOOKS BEHIND WHEN THEY GO AWAY!
MILTON CANIFF

I SAY, DOCTOR WILDERNESS —I'M NOT MUCH OF AN AIDE IN YOUR EFFORTS TO STEM THE EPIDEMIC!

MY CREW OF TRAINED NATIVES IS DOING THE WORK, CHIEF IZM —YOUR PRESENCE HAS DOUBTLESS KEPT THE VILLAGERS FROM PANICKING!

DOES IT GO BADLY?

I CAN'T SEEM TO GET THE SPREAD OF INFECTION UNDER CONTROL! IF IT EVER HIT THE CROWDED CITIES IN THE HOT LOWLANDS IT WOULD SWEEP LIKE A PRAIRIE FIRE!

FIREBALL, ME LAD, STEVE CANYON WILL GIVE YOU FITS FOR NOT GETTING SOME KIND OF RADIO REPORT BACK TO HIM— EVEN THOUGH BANDITS DID WRECK THE VILLAGE SET...

I'LL TRY AGAIN TO RAISE HIM ON THE AIRPLANE TRANSMITTER!

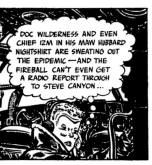

DOC WILDERNESS AND EVEN CHIEF IZM IN HIS MAW HUBBARD NIGHTSHIRT ARE SWEATING OUT THE EPIDEMIC —AND THE FIREBALL CAN'T EVEN GET A RADIO REPORT THROUGH TO STEVE CANYON...

NO USE... NOT ENOUGH POWER TO REACH STEVE AT DASSA... HEY! THERE'S SOME MORSE!... STRONG SIGNAL!... TALKING TO STEVE CANYON ABOUT ME!

SOMEBODY'S TRANSMITTING FROM NEAR-BY—PRETENDING TO SPEAK FOR OUR MEDICAL MISSION!... MY DIRECTION FINDER SHOULD LOCATE THEIR POSITION...

IT'S FUNNY—BACK HOME I OFTEN THOUGHT OF LOOKING FOR A RADIO STATION WITH A GUN IN MY HAND...

YOU ARE TIRED, DOCTUH WILDUHNESS!

CHIEF IZM, THE PATTERN OF THIS EPIDEMIC IS ALL WRONG...

JUST AS I GET CONTROL IN ONE AREA THE DISEASE BREAKS OUT IN ANOTHER PART OF THE SETTLEMENT

MOST DISTRESSIN'

I CAN'T BELIEVE THE UNDERGROUND WOULD DELIBERATELY START A THING LIKE THIS...

THAT WOULD BE BAHBARIC!

... THEY TOLD US WHEN WE ARRIVED THAT THE RADIO WAS SMASHED BY BANDITS... SO WE CAN'T CALL FOR HELP...

TRUE...

Steve Canyon

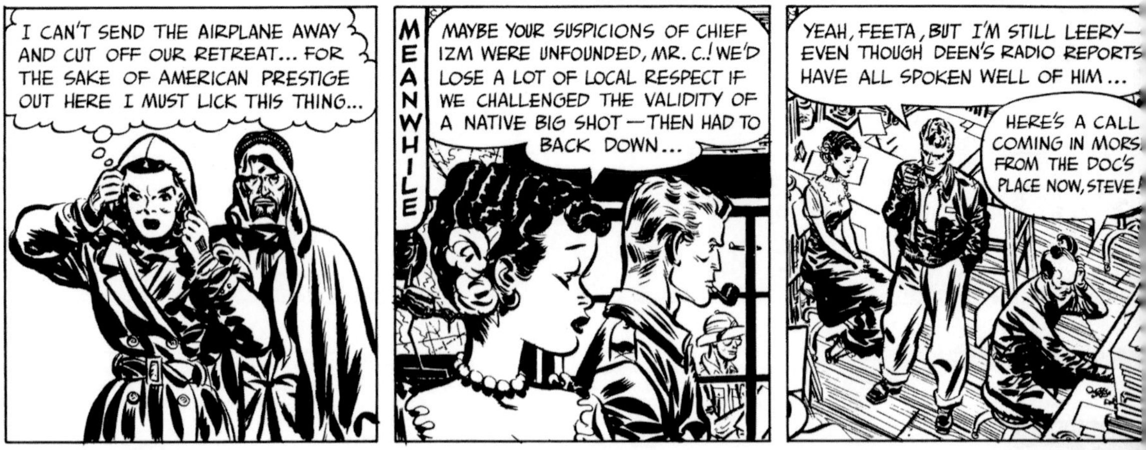
I CAN'T SEND THE AIRPLANE AWAY AND CUT OFF OUR RETREAT... FOR THE SAKE OF AMERICAN PRESTIGE OUT HERE I MUST LICK THIS THING...
MEANWHILE
MAYBE YOUR SUSPICIONS OF CHIEF IZM WERE UNFOUNDED, MR. C.! WE'D LOSE A LOT OF LOCAL RESPECT IF WE CHALLENGED THE VALIDITY OF A NATIVE BIG SHOT—THEN HAD TO BACK DOWN...
YEAH, FEETA, BUT I'M STILL LEERY— EVEN THOUGH DEEN'S RADIO REPORTS HAVE ALL SPOKEN WELL OF HIM...
HERE'S A CALL COMING IN MORS FROM THE DOC'S PLACE NOW, STEVE!

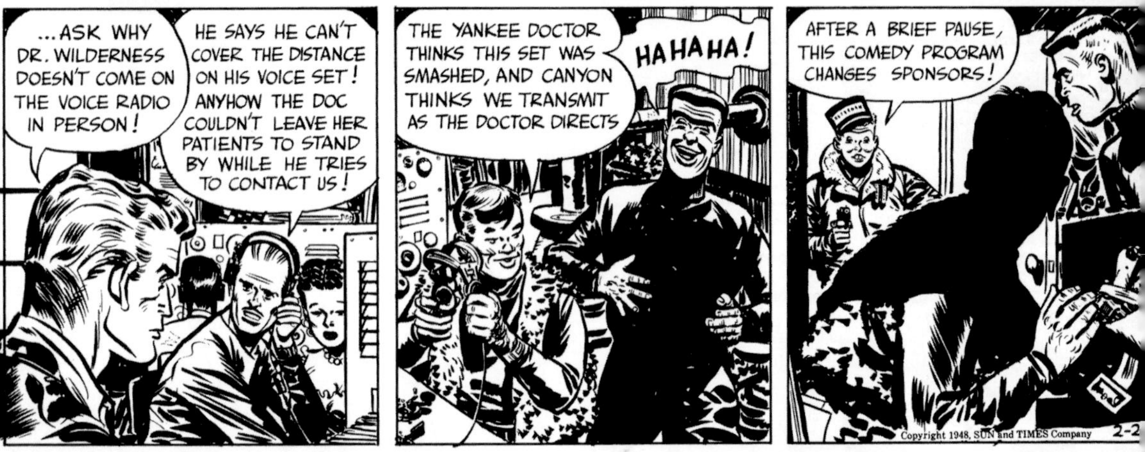
...ASK WHY DR. WILDERNESS DOESN'T COME ON THE VOICE RADIO IN PERSON!
HE SAYS HE CAN'T COVER THE DISTANCE ON HIS VOICE SET! ANYHOW THE DOC COULDN'T LEAVE HER PATIENTS TO STAND BY WHILE HE TRIES TO CONTACT US!
THE YANKEE DOCTOR THINKS THIS SET WAS SMASHED, AND CANYON THINKS WE TRANSMIT AS THE DOCTOR DIRECTS
HAHAHA!
AFTER A BRIEF PAUSE, THIS COMEDY PROGRAM CHANGES SPONSORS!
Copyright 1948, SUN and TIMES Company
2-2

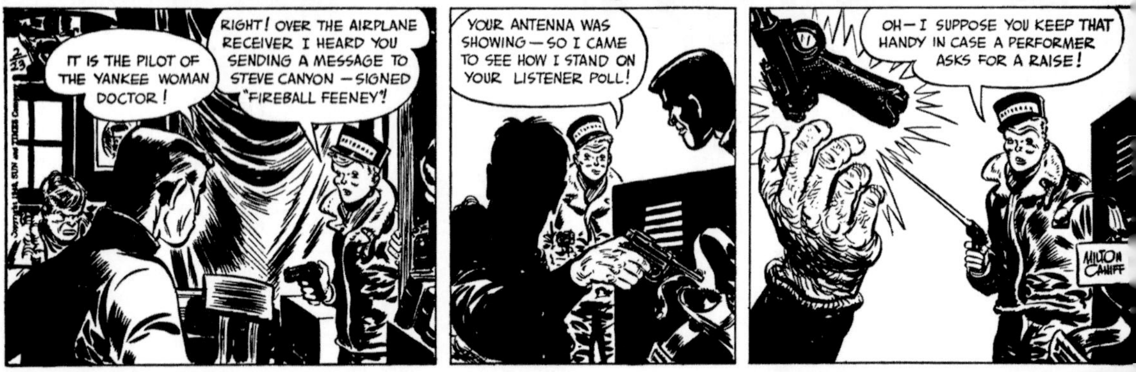
IT IS THE PILOT OF THE YANKEE WOMAN DOCTOR!
RIGHT! OVER THE AIRPLANE RECEIVER I HEARD YOU SENDING A MESSAGE TO STEVE CANYON —SIGNED "FIREBALL FEENEY"!
YOUR ANTENNA WAS SHOWING—SO I CAME TO SEE HOW I STAND ON YOUR LISTENER POLL!
OH—I SUPPOSE YOU KEEP THAT HANDY IN CASE A PERFORMER ASKS FOR A RAISE!
MILTON CANIFF

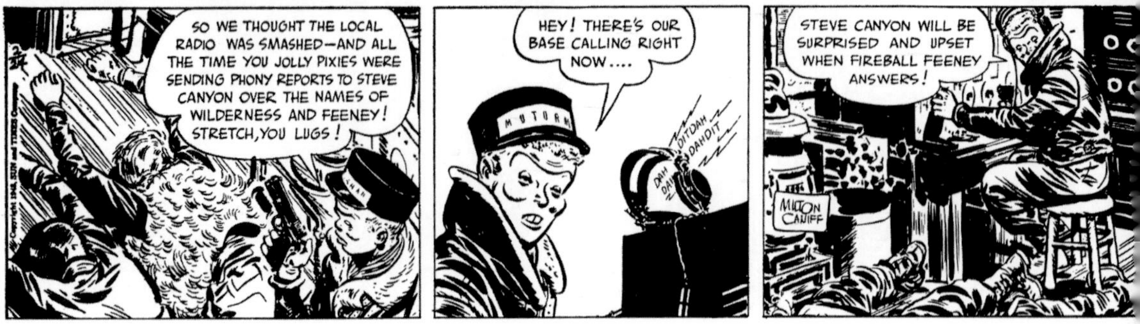
SO WE THOUGHT THE LOCAL RADIO WAS SMASHED—AND ALL THE TIME YOU JOLLY PIXIES WERE SENDING PHONY REPORTS TO STEVE CANYON OVER THE NAMES OF WILDERNESS AND FEENEY! STRETCH, YOU LUGS!
HEY! THERE'S OUR BASE CALLING RIGHT NOW....
STEVE CANYON WILL BE SURPRISED AND UPSET WHEN FIREBALL FEENEY ANSWERS!
MILTON CANIFF

ANSWER THE CALL FROM CANYON! I WILL DISPOSE OF FEENEY!

MORE SICK IN NORTH OF VILLAGE, MISSA DOCTA WILDERNESS!

AND I AM RUNNING OUT OF HELP! I CAN'T SEEM TO ISOLATE THE INFECTION! THIS MUST BE A SABOTAGE JOB!

CHIEF IZM, I THINK THE UNDERGROUND IS CLOSING IN ON US! SINCE THE TOWN RADIO WAS SMASHED, FIREBALL WILL HAVE TO FLY OUT FOR ARMED HELP!

MY WORD, HOW GRIM!

WILL YOU FIND FIREBALL AND ALERT HIM FOR THE RUN?

BUT OF COURSE, MY DEAR!

THE TIME FOR INJURING YANKEE MEDICAL PRESTIGE IS AT HAND! YOU KNOW THE PLAN!

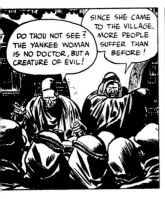
DO THOU NOT SEE? THE YANKEE WOMAN IS NO DOCTOR, BUT A CREATURE OF EVIL!

SINCE SHE CAME TO THE VILLAGE, MORE PEOPLE SUFFER THAN BEFORE!

MISSA DOCTA WILDERNESS, IS MOB RISING!

I KNOW... LISTEN! CHIEF IZM IS OUT THERE! HE'S SPEAKING TO THEM...

I SAY...

THE YANKEE WOMAN IS NEXT!

TH-THE MOB SHOT CHIEF IZM!

THEY COME, MISSA DOCTA! YOU GO TRAP DOOR! THEY NO KILL US LOWLY NATIVES — MERELY HELPERS!

WHAT WOULD YOU GIVE TO BE EATIN' A HOT FUDGE IN THAT LITTLE PLACE ACROSS FROM JOHNS HOPKINS RIGHT THIS MINUTE?

Steve Canyon

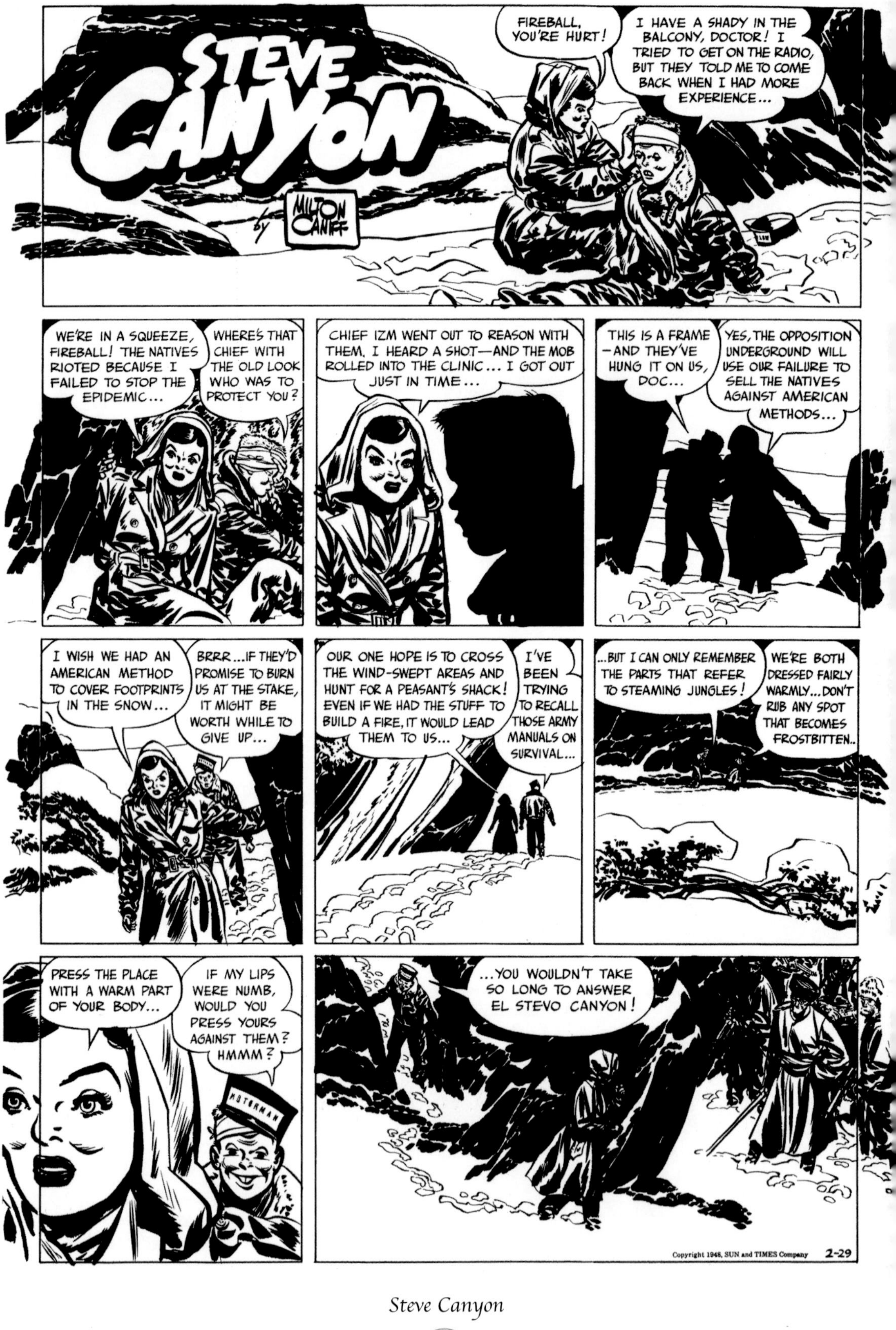
STEVE CANYON
by MILTON CANIFF
FIREBALL, YOU'RE HURT!
I HAVE A SHADY IN THE BALCONY, DOCTOR! I TRIED TO GET ON THE RADIO, BUT THEY TOLD ME TO COME BACK WHEN I HAD MORE EXPERIENCE...
WE'RE IN A SQUEEZE, FIREBALL! THE NATIVES RIOTED BECAUSE I FAILED TO STOP THE EPIDEMIC...
WHERE'S THAT CHIEF WITH THE OLD LOOK WHO WAS TO PROTECT YOU?
CHIEF IZM WENT OUT TO REASON WITH THEM. I HEARD A SHOT—AND THE MOB ROLLED INTO THE CLINIC... I GOT OUT JUST IN TIME...
THIS IS A FRAME—AND THEY'VE HUNG IT ON US, DOC...
YES, THE OPPOSITION UNDERGROUND WILL USE OUR FAILURE TO SELL THE NATIVES AGAINST AMERICAN METHODS...
I WISH WE HAD AN AMERICAN METHOD TO COVER FOOTPRINTS IN THE SNOW...
BRRR...IF THEY'D PROMISE TO BURN US AT THE STAKE, IT MIGHT BE WORTH WHILE TO GIVE UP...
OUR ONE HOPE IS TO CROSS THE WIND-SWEPT AREAS AND HUNT FOR A PEASANT'S SHACK! EVEN IF WE HAD THE STUFF TO BUILD A FIRE, IT WOULD LEAD THEM TO US...
I'VE BEEN TRYING TO RECALL THOSE ARMY MANUALS ON SURVIVAL...
...BUT I CAN ONLY REMEMBER THE PARTS THAT REFER TO STEAMING JUNGLES!
WE'RE BOTH DRESSED FAIRLY WARMLY...DON'T RUB ANY SPOT THAT BECOMES FROSTBITTEN..
PRESS THE PLACE WITH A WARM PART OF YOUR BODY...
IF MY LIPS WERE NUMB, WOULD YOU PRESS YOURS AGAINST THEM? HMMM?
MOTORMAN
...YOU WOULDN'T TAKE SO LONG TO ANSWER EL STEVO CANYON!
Copyright 1948, SUN and TIMES Company
2-29

WHY SO QUIET, DOC WILDERNESS? ARE YOU SORE BECAUSE YOU HAD TO BANDAGE MY HEAD ON A HOLIDAY?

F—FIREBALL!

YOUR TEETH ARE CHATTERING, DOC!

WHY, Y---

YOU WILL FORCE THE INTOXICANT DRUG UPON THESE YANKEES — THEN PARADE THEM THROUGH THE STREETS FOR ALL THE NATIVES TO OBSERVE!

WHY DO YOU DO THIS? WHAT HAVE WE DONE TO YOU? WHO ARE YOU?

MY GOVERNMENT WISHES THE YANKEE MEDICAL MISSION TO FAIL AND YOU TO BE HUMILIATED IN THE EYES OF THE PEOPLE OF THE MIDDLE EAST!

WHY DOESN'T YOUR GOVERNMENT HELP THESE PEOPLE OF THE OIL COUNTRY—INSTEAD OF TRYING TO HARM US?

WE DON'T NEED THEM—AND WE DON'T NEED OIL—BUT WE CAN'T AFFORD TO ALLOW YOU YANKEES TO HAVE THEM!

THEY'RE BECOMING GLASSY-EYED, MY LEADER!

THE DRUG MAKES THE YANKEE WOMAN DOCTOR AND HER PILOT APPEAR VERY DRUNK!

OUR AGENTS AMONG THE NATIVES ARE TALKING UP THE 'DISGRACEFUL' PERFORMANCE!

GOTTA GET OFFA STREET

THROW THEM BACK INTO THE SQUARE — WHERE ALL MAY OBSERVE THEIR SHAME!

YES! ONLY YANKEES WOULD SEND A STUPID WOMAN TO DOCTOR OUR PEOPLE!

SHALL WE ALLOW THE PEOPLE TO STONE THEM TO DEATH?

NOT YET! I SHOULD HAVE A LITTLE FUN FROM THIS AFTER ALL MY WORK! BRING THE WOMAN TO ME!

MR. CANYON, YOUR NEW SERIAL NUMBER AND AIR RESERVE ASSIGNMENT TO THE 55th TROOP CARRIER SQUADRON CAME IN THE MAIL FROM THE STATES...

MMHMM

AND YOUR FRIEND ROOSIE SENT YOU A NEW BOOK THAT'S BEING SOLD FOR THE BENEFIT OF THE AIR FORCES AID SOCIETY!

... IT'S NICE OF YOU TO TRY AND DIVERT MY MIND, FEETA-FEETA, BUT IF THAT RADIO STATION AT DEEN WILDERNESS' PLACE DOESN'T SOON ANSWER OUR CALL, I'M TAKING OFF!

STEVE! GOTTA CONTACT!

Steve Canyon

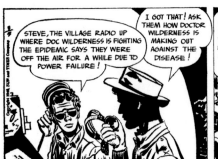

STEVE, THE VILLAGE RADIO UP WHERE DOC WILDERNESS IS FIGHTING THE EPIDEMIC SAYS THEY WERE OFF THE AIR FOR A WHILE DUE TO POWER FAILURE!

I GOT THAT! ASK THEM HOW DOCTOR WILDERNESS IS MAKING OUT AGAINST THE DISEASE!

THE OPERATOR SAYS ALL OUR PEOPLE ARE WORKING HARD IN THE HOSPITAL! ANY MESSAGES HE CAN CARRY TO THEM?

I DON'T LIKE THIS REMOTE-CONTROL STUFF... FIREBALL COULD GO TO THAT STATION AND TAP OUT MORSE CODE ON HIS OWN! I'M GOING TO TEST THAT SETUP... SEND THIS ---

...ASK FIREBALL FEENEY TO SETTLE A BET FOR US... WHO IS THE NEW FOOTBALL COACH AT THE UNIVERSITY OF WASHINGTON?

CAPTAIN CANYON ASKS FIREBALL FEENEY TO SETTLE A BET BY TELLING HIM WHO IS THE NEW FOOTBALL COACH AT THE UNIVERSITY OF WASHINGTON, U.S.A.

FEENEY IS NOW OUR PRISONER! IT WILL BE EASY TO BEAT THAT INFORMATION FROM HIM!

HOW MUCH FLOGGING CAN THE MAN ENDURE?

THE HOT IRON WILL DO IT!

I'LL TELL! I'LL TELL!

STEVE, DO YOU THINK FIREBALL KNOWS WHO IS THE NEW COACH AT U.W.?

SURE! WE HAD A BET ON THE APPOINTMENT!— HIS MAN WON! HEY! THEY'RE ANSWERING...

FEENEY SAYS IT WAS LEWIS N. CLARK WHO WENT TO WASHINGTON!

BREAK OUT THE GUN LOCKE AND WARM U NUMBER FOU WE'RE TAKIN OFF!

RAJAH

STEVE CANYON
by MILTON CANIFF

ARE YOU SURE SOMETHING'S WRONG AT DOC WILDERNESS' MEDICAL OUTPOST, STEVE? THEIR RADIO CONTACT IS GOOD, EVEN IF WE CAN ONLY GET THEM IN MORSE CODE!

I TRIED SOME VERY LOCAL AMERICAN QUESTIONS ON THEIR OPERATOR AND HE DIDN'T GIVE WITH THE RIGHT ANSWERS.

MEANWHILE...

BRING IN THE YANKEE WOMAN DOCTOR...

THE GOOD PEOPLE OF THE VILLAGE HAVE SEEN YOU AND YOUR PILOT LURCHING THROUGH THE STREETS — DRUNK, WHILE THE EPIDEMIC GOES ON — OUT OF CONTROL...

YOU DRUGGED US!

AND YOU WILL BE DRUGGED AGAIN WHEN YOU OPERATE ON THE TRIBAL LEADER'S SON!

...HE HAS APPENDICITIS. IT WILL BE RUPTURED BY THE TIME YOU ARE READY!

Steve Canyon

NO! UNDER THAT ARTIFICIAL INTOXICATION COULD KILL HIM! I WON'T DO IT!

WE SHALL HAVE YOUR PILOT ON AN ADJOINING TABLE... IF YOU HESITATE...

...WE SHALL PERFORM AN AMATEUR APPENDECTOMY ON HIM — WITHOUT ANESTHESIA

OH, NO!

THE NATIVES OF THE MIDDLE EAST SHALL SOON HEAR OF THE DRUNKEN, INCOMPETENT YANKEE DOCTOR...

YOU WON'T GET AWAY WITH IT!

YOU HAVEN'T SHOWN ME CHIEF IZM'S BODY! I THINK HE ESCAPED!.. HE'LL BRING HELP...

HAHA HOHO!

WHAT'S FUNNY!

I AM CHIEF IZM!

3-7

IT CAN'T BE!

YES, DOCTOR WILDERNESS...

BY PLACING CAPS ON MY TEETH..

ADDING THE THEATRICAL BEARD...

DONNING THE NATIVE HEADDRESS AND REMOVING THE THICK GLASSES...

I BECOME THE LATE CHIEF IZM —COMPLETE WITH ACCENT **AND** EUROPEAN EDUCATION... I SAY, MY DEAH, THE JEST'S ON YOU — BUT I'M JOLLY AFRAID IT WILL BE NO LOFFING MATTUH!

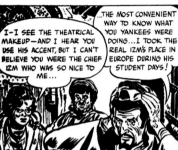

I-I SEE THE THEATRICAL MAKEUP—AND I HEAR YOU USE HIS ACCENT, BUT I CAN'T BELIEVE YOU WERE THE CHIEF IZM WHO WAS SO NICE TO ME...

...THE MOST CONVENIENT WAY TO KNOW WHAT YOU YANKEES WERE DOING... I TOOK THE REAL IZM'S PLACE IN EUROPE DURING HIS STUDENT DAYS!

BUT THE MOB SHOT THE CHIEF—JUST A WHILE AGO ..!

THAT WAS STAGED TO CONFUSE YOU! THEY WILL BE TOLD **YOU** KILLED CHIEF IZM BECAUSE HE THREATENED TO EXPOSE YOU AS AN INCOMPETENT DRUNKARD!

I SUPPOSE THAT'S TO INCITE THEM TO KILL FIREBALL AND ME...

...ESPECIALLY AFTER I GIVE YOU MORE OF THE INTOXICATION DRUG **AND** HAVE YOU TAKE OUT THE TRIBAL LEADER'S SON'S APPENDIX...

Steve Canyon

YOU MIGHT AS WELL RELAX, DR. WILDERNESS... WE ARE QUITE EXPERT AT THESE THINGS!

HAVEN'T YOU DONE ENOUGH? MUST YOU KILL A CHILD TO ALIENATE THE NATIVES?

THOU SAW THE YANKEE WOMAN INTOXICATED IN THE SQUARE! DOST THOU STILL TRUST THY SON TO HER DUBIOUS SKILL?

THERE IS NO CHOICE! MY SON WEEPS FROM THE PAIN IN HIS SIDE!

WE HAVE PREPARED THE OPERATING THEATRE FROM YOUR OWN CHARTS... WHEN THE INTOXICATION DRUG TAKES FULL EFFECT, YOU WILL BEGIN...

MEANWHILE— A NATIVE SLIPS FROM THE CROWD WAITING FOR DEEN'S ORDEAL...

DOWN THE VALLEY FROM THE VILLAGE WHERE DR. DEEN WILDERNESS AND FIREBALL FEENEY ARE BEING TORTURED...

DID YOU GET IN AND OUT OF THE TOWN WITHOUT BEING SUSPECTED?

YES, CAP'N CANYON! BUT YOU WERE WISE TO LAND FAR FROM THE PLACE AND APPROACH ON FOOT! THE UNDERGROUND HAS TAKEN OVER!

TO HUMILIATE DR. WILDERNESS THEY EVEN NOW FORCE HER TO OPERATE — YET SHE APPEARS TO BE UNDER THE INFLUENCE OF SOME DRUG!

WHERE IS CHIEF IZM WHILE ALL THIS IS GOING ON?

THE NATIVES HAD NOT SEEN HIM SINCE THE HOSPITAL WAS MOBBED... IT WAS THEN THE UNDERGROUND TOOK OVER, COMMANDED BY A TALL STRANGER WEARING THICK GLASSES...

AND I'LL BET HE SMELLS OF THE SAME LIQUOR THAT MADE ME SUSPICIOUS OF CHIEF IZM!

CAP'N CANYON, THE UNDERGROUNDERS WHO TORTURE DR. WILDERNESS AND PILOT FEENEY IN YONDER TOWN ARE FEW IN NUMBER! WE COULD RUSH THE PLACE!

BUT WE NEED TO DISCREDIT THEM THE WAY THEY ARE TRYING TO TURN THE NATIVES AGAINST U.S. MEDICAL METHODS!

HAPPY, REMEMBER HOW THE OLD ROAD AGENTS WOULD DRIFT INTO A FRONTIER SETTLEMENT IN DISGUISE, THEN GUN THEIR WAY OUT AFTER THE STICKUP?

YOP! MUSTA SEEN IT IN A DOZEN WESTERN MOVIN' PITCHERS!

I THINK WE CAN PULL A TWIST ON THAT TRICK!... HOW MUCH WOULD YOU CHARGE FOR A SWATCH OF YOUR BEARD?

TENSION IS HIGH AS THE VILLAGERS WAIT FOR DR. DEEN WILDERNESS TO REMOVE THE APPENDIX OF THE TRIBAL LEADER'S SON...

'MDRUGGED... CAN'T SEE.... CAN'T SAVE HIM...

HE'S DEAD!

YOU ARE WITNESS TO THIS ACT OF MURDER UPON THE INNOCENT PERSON OF YOUR TRIBAL LEADER'S SON!

THE YANKEE WOMAN IS INTOXICATED! SHE MUST PAY FOR THIS CRIME!

IT IS SIMPLE JUSTICE! I SHALL INFORM THE ASSEMBLY— SO THAT ACTION MAY FOLLOW!

WHILE AT THE EDGE OF THE TOWN...

THE CROWD SOUND REACHES AN ANGRY PITCH! NOW IS THE TIME, CAP'N CANYON!

ROGER! LET'S GO, HAP!

Steve Canyon

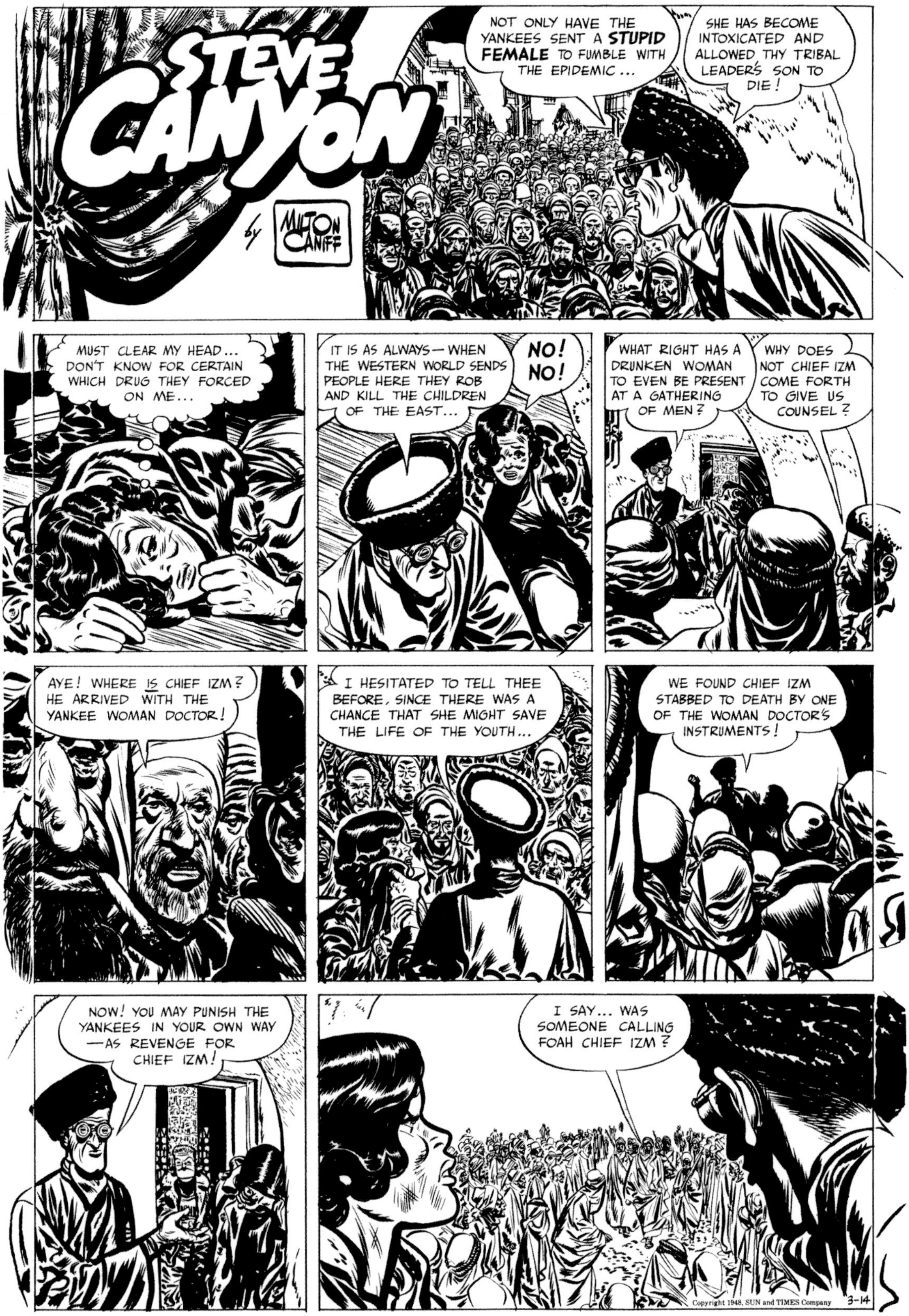
STEVE CANYON
by MILTON CANIFF
NOT ONLY HAVE THE YANKEES SENT A **STUPID FEMALE** TO FUMBLE WITH THE EPIDEMIC ...
SHE HAS BECOME INTOXICATED AND ALLOWED THY TRIBAL LEADER'S SON TO DIE!
MUST CLEAR MY HEAD... DON'T KNOW FOR CERTAIN WHICH DRUG THEY FORCED ON ME...
IT IS AS ALWAYS— WHEN THE WESTERN WORLD SENDS PEOPLE HERE THEY ROB AND KILL THE CHILDREN OF THE EAST...
NO! NO!
WHAT RIGHT HAS A DRUNKEN WOMAN TO EVEN BE PRESENT AT A GATHERING OF MEN?
WHY DOES NOT CHIEF IZM COME FORTH TO GIVE US COUNSEL?
AYE! WHERE IS CHIEF IZM? HE ARRIVED WITH THE YANKEE WOMAN DOCTOR!
I HESITATED TO TELL THEE BEFORE, SINCE THERE WAS A CHANCE THAT SHE MIGHT SAVE THE LIFE OF THE YOUTH...
WE FOUND CHIEF IZM STABBED TO DEATH BY ONE OF THE WOMAN DOCTOR'S INSTRUMENTS!
NOW! YOU MAY PUNISH THE YANKEES IN YOUR OWN WAY —AS REVENGE FOR CHIEF IZM!
I SAY... WAS SOMEONE CALLING FOAH CHIEF IZM?
Copyright 1948, SUN and TIMES Company
3-14

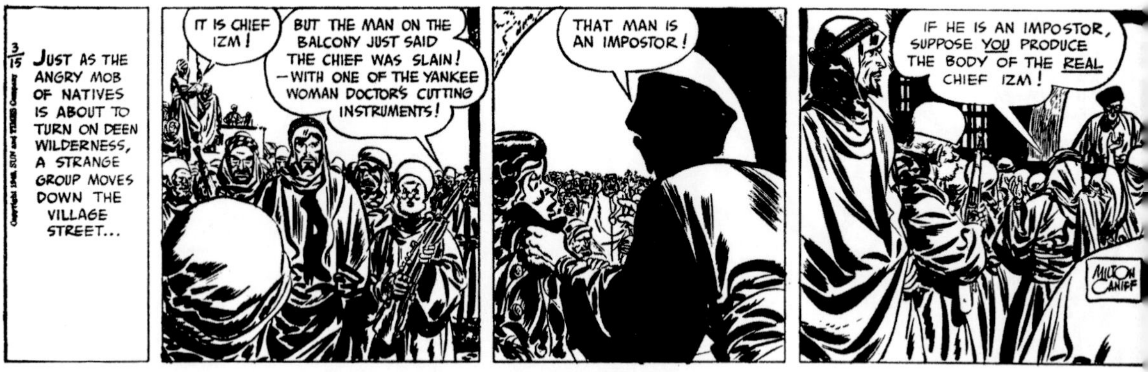
3/15
JUST AS THE ANGRY MOB OF NATIVES IS ABOUT TO TURN ON DEEN WILDERNESS, A STRANGE GROUP MOVES DOWN THE VILLAGE STREET...
IT IS CHIEF IZM!
BUT THE MAN ON THE BALCONY JUST SAID THE CHIEF WAS SLAIN! —WITH ONE OF THE YANKEE WOMAN DOCTOR'S CUTTING INSTRUMENTS!
THAT MAN IS AN IMPOSTOR!
IF HE IS AN IMPOSTOR, SUPPOSE YOU PRODUCE THE BODY OF THE REAL CHIEF IZM!
MILTON CANIFF

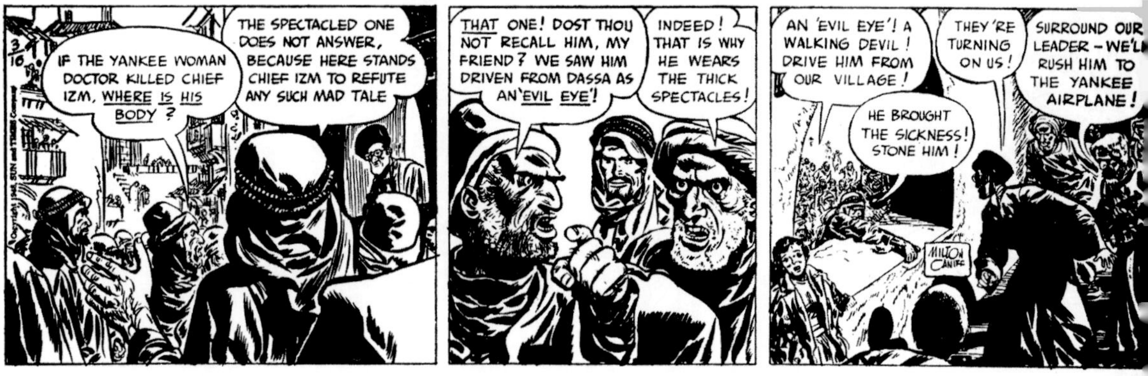
3/16
IF THE YANKEE WOMAN DOCTOR KILLED CHIEF IZM, WHERE IS HIS BODY?
THE SPECTACLED ONE DOES NOT ANSWER, BECAUSE HERE STANDS CHIEF IZM TO REFUTE ANY SUCH MAD TALE
THAT ONE! DOST THOU NOT RECALL HIM, MY FRIEND? WE SAW HIM DRIVEN FROM DASSA AS AN 'EVIL EYE'!
INDEED! THAT IS WHY HE WEARS THE THICK SPECTACLES!
AN 'EVIL EYE'! A WALKING DEVIL! DRIVE HIM FROM OUR VILLAGE!
HE BROUGHT THE SICKNESS! STONE HIM!
THEY'RE TURNING ON US!
SURROUND OUR LEADER – WE'L RUSH HIM TO THE YANKEE AIRPLANE!
MILTON CANIFF

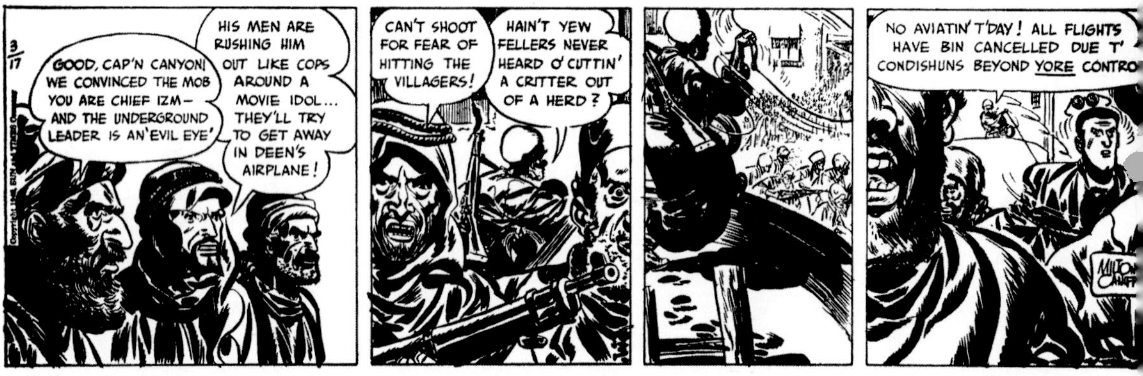
3/17
GOOD, CAP'N CANYON! WE CONVINCED THE MOB YOU ARE CHIEF IZM— AND THE UNDERGROUND LEADER IS AN 'EVIL EYE'
HIS MEN ARE RUSHING HIM OUT LIKE COPS AROUND A MOVIE IDOL... THEY'LL TRY TO GET AWAY IN DEEN'S AIRPLANE!
CAN'T SHOOT FOR FEAR OF HITTING THE VILLAGERS!
HAIN'T YEW FELLERS NEVER HEARD O' CUTTIN' A CRITTER OUT OF A HERD?
NO AVIATIN' T'DAY! ALL FLIGHTS HAVE BIN CANCELLED DUE T' CONDISHUNS BEYOND YORE CONTRO
MILTON CANIFF

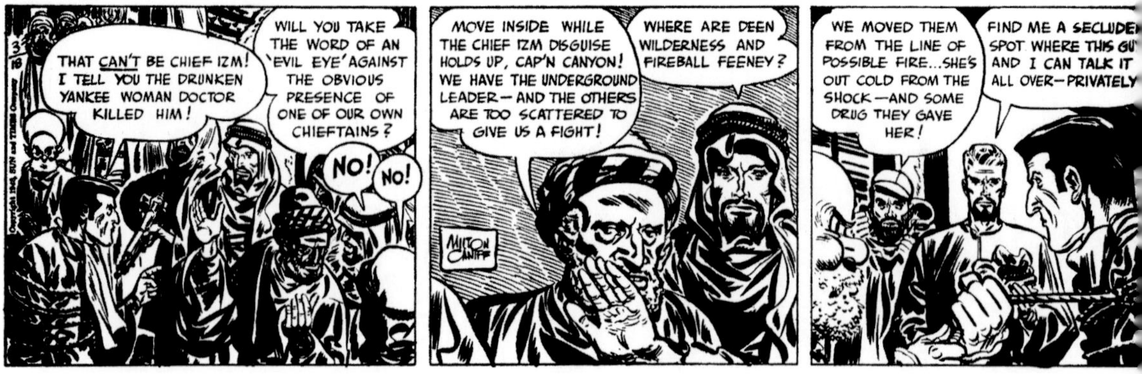
3/18
THAT CAN'T BE CHIEF IZM! I TELL YOU THE DRUNKEN YANKEE WOMAN DOCTOR KILLED HIM!
WILL YOU TAKE THE WORD OF AN 'EVIL EYE' AGAINST THE OBVIOUS PRESENCE OF ONE OF OUR OWN CHIEFTAINS?
NO!
NO!
MOVE INSIDE WHILE THE CHIEF IZM DISGUISE HOLDS UP, CAP'N CANYON! WE HAVE THE UNDERGROUND LEADER—AND THE OTHERS ARE TOO SCATTERED TO GIVE US A FIGHT!
WHERE ARE DEEN WILDERNESS AND FIREBALL FEENEY?
MILTON CANIFF
WE MOVED THEM FROM THE LINE OF POSSIBLE FIRE...SHE'S OUT COLD FROM THE SHOCK—AND SOME DRUG THEY GAVE HER!
FIND ME A SECLUDE SPOT WHERE THIS GU AND I CAN TALK IT ALL OVER—PRIVATELY

THE UNDERGROUNDERS LOADED DR. WILDERNESS WITH SOME SORT OF DRUG... SHE'S OUT!

WE SCATTERED THEM — BUT STEVE CANYON TOOK THEIR LEADER DOWN THE VALLEY FOR A 'CHAT'!...

I THOUGHT IF YOU COULD MAKE UP AS A NATIVE CHIEFTAIN, WHY SHOULDN'T I? GET UP AND KEEP MOVING!

I WAS HOPING YOU'D DO SOMETHING LIKE THAT... NOW I WON'T HAVE TO MAKE A SPEECH ABOUT WHAT YOU DID TO DEEN WILDERNESS!

I THINK THAT WILL BE FOR THE TROUBLE YOU CAUSED DOCTOR WILDERNESS — AS A DOCTOR!

AND THAT'S FOR THE TROUBLE YOU CAUSED ME WHILE I WAS TRYING TO MAKE HER FORGET SHE'S A DOCTOR!

MEANWHILE — ON THE CLIFF ABOVE THE VILLAGE...

A MAN-BIRD RESTS IN THE VALLEY — AND THE TOWNSPEOPLE APPEAR DISTURBED OVER SOMETHING!

AH! PERHAPS WE SHALL GAIN MORE FOR OUR PAINS THAN FRESH FOOD! MOVE IN AS I DIRECTED!

... RELAX, DR. WILDERNESS

OH, HAPPY, THAT WAS STEVE CANYON POSING AS CHIEF IZM, WASN'T IT?

YES'M! STEVIE CALMED DOWN TH' TOWN FOLKS — NOW HIM AN' TH' BIG UNDERGROUND FELLER ARE DOWN TH' HOLLER CLEARIN' UP A FEW POINTS!

STEVE CANYON

by MILTON CANIFF

YOU SHOULDN'T HAVE RUN UP SUCH A LARGE BILL WITH DR. WILDERNESS! IT WILL HURT TO PAY THROUGH THAT NOSE OF YOURS!

AH! A GAY BLADE!

HADN'T YOU HEARD? A POINT IS NOT POLITE!

Steve Canyon

DROP, STEVIE!

WON'T YEW EASTERNERS NEVER LEARN THET RATTLYSNAKES GENER'LY RUNS IN PAIRS?

Copyright 1948, SUN and TIMES Company

HAPPY EASTER! WHAT HAPPENED?

YEW GIT A RUSH O' INNOCENCE TO TH' HEAD SOMETIMES, STEVIE CANYON...

ONE O' THEM UNDERGROUNDERS POTTED A SHOT AT YE FROM YONDER LEDGE WHILST YE WUZ CUFFIN' WITH THEIR LEADER!—I VENTILATED HIM A LEETLE!

THANKS, HAP!...HEY! LISTEN! SHOTS! —FROM THE VILLAGE...

MILTON CANIFF

WHILE IN THE TOWN ...

NOMADS! MOUNTAIN BANDITS!

THEY'LL GO FOR THE FOOD STORES FIRST GET DR. WILDERNES TO THE AIRPLANE BEFOR THEY FIND HER — OR S WON'T WANT TO GET WELL!

FIREBALL! IT'S A NOMAD BANDIT RAID! ARE YOU WELL ENOUGH TO FLY DEEN OUT OF HERE IN THE AIRPLANE?

SURE! I DIDN'T HAVE THE SLUG THEY GAVE HER!

THE BANDITS ARE LOOTING THE FOOD STORES — WE CAN CARRY THE DOCTOR DOWN THE BACK STREET TO THE LANDING STRIP!

STOP GORGING LONG ENOUGH TO LISTEN! THE GREAT NINE SAID TO SEIZE THE MAN—BIRD!

OOPF, F'GOT! C'MON! GREAT NINE'LL BE ANGRY!

WHILE ABOVE THE TOWN ....

STEVIE! HERE'S WHERE THEM UNDERGROUNDERS SMASHED THEIR RADIO WHEN WE CLOSED IN!

SEE IF THEY LEFT ANYTHIN THAT WILL BUI BRIGHTLY, HAF HURRY!

Steve Canyon

STEVIE, HERE'S SOME OIL THEM UNDERGROUND RADIO FELLERS MUSTA HAD IN THEIR SHACK!

THAT'LL DO IT, HAP! I'LL CURL THE EDGE OF THIS PIECE OF ROOFING, LIGHT THE OIL—AND WE'RE OFF!

YEEIE YEEIPEE!

MILTON CANIFF

AND INTO THE MIDST OF THE NOMADS LOOTING THE EPIDEMIC VILLAGE

...I AIN'T SLID S'MUCH SINCE TH' BUNG BLOWED ON TH' MOLASSES KEG!

RACING THROUGH THE TOWN ON A MAKESHIFT SLED, STEVE AND HAPPY THROW THE NOMAD RAID INTO MOMENTARY CONFUSION

ONE OF THE STUPID TOWNSMEN HAS STOLEN MY HORSE! HE WILL WARN THE NEARBY VILLAGES TO RISE AGAINST US!

DEEN WILDERNESS HAS BEEN CARRIED ABOARD THE AIRPLANE AND FIREBALL FEENEY WARMS THE ENGINES...

STAND BY! HERE COME STEVE AND HAP NOW!

WITH THE NOMAD BOYS RIGHT BEHIND —LOOKIN' AS IF THEY'RE YES-MADS!

MILTON CANIFF

THROW US SOME SHEETS, SUPPLY PACKS, A RIFLE AND AMMO— THEN TAKE OFF HOT— FULL FLAPS! WE'LL TRIP THESE HILL-WILLIES AND JOIN YOU LATER IN THE AIRPLANE WE PARKED DOWN THE VALLEY!

BUT, STEVE, THOSE NOMADS WILL TEAR YOU TO PIECES

THAT'S AN ORDER!

THEY'RE RIDIN' RIGHT FOR US! MAYBE THEY'LL GO INTO THEM PROPS AN' WRECK TH' WORKS!

SNUB THE LINE AROUND THE TAIL WHEEL GEAR...

AND WE'LL HAVE SOME ROBERT-SLEDDING THEY NEVER SAW IN THE WINTER OLYMPICS!

MILTON CANIFF

STOP THE MAN-BIRD OR THE GREAT NINE WILL HANG US ALL!

THE MAN-BIRD SPITS BULLETS!

HE'S LIFTING, HAP! LET GO THE LINE!

IN THE FLYING SNOW AND CONFUSION, STEVE AND HAPPY EASTER FLASH PAST THE ASTONISHED NOMADS ON THE IMPROVISED SLED...

WHERE NOW, STEVIE?

INTO THE PASS THEY CAME THROUGH! WE MAY BE ABLE TO CORK THEM UP UNTIL THE NEIGHBORING VILLAGES ARE AROUSED...

...AS IF I'M FOOLING HAP!

MILTON CANIFF

Steve Canyon

Chapter Two
The Nine Maid
March 28 – May 23, 1948

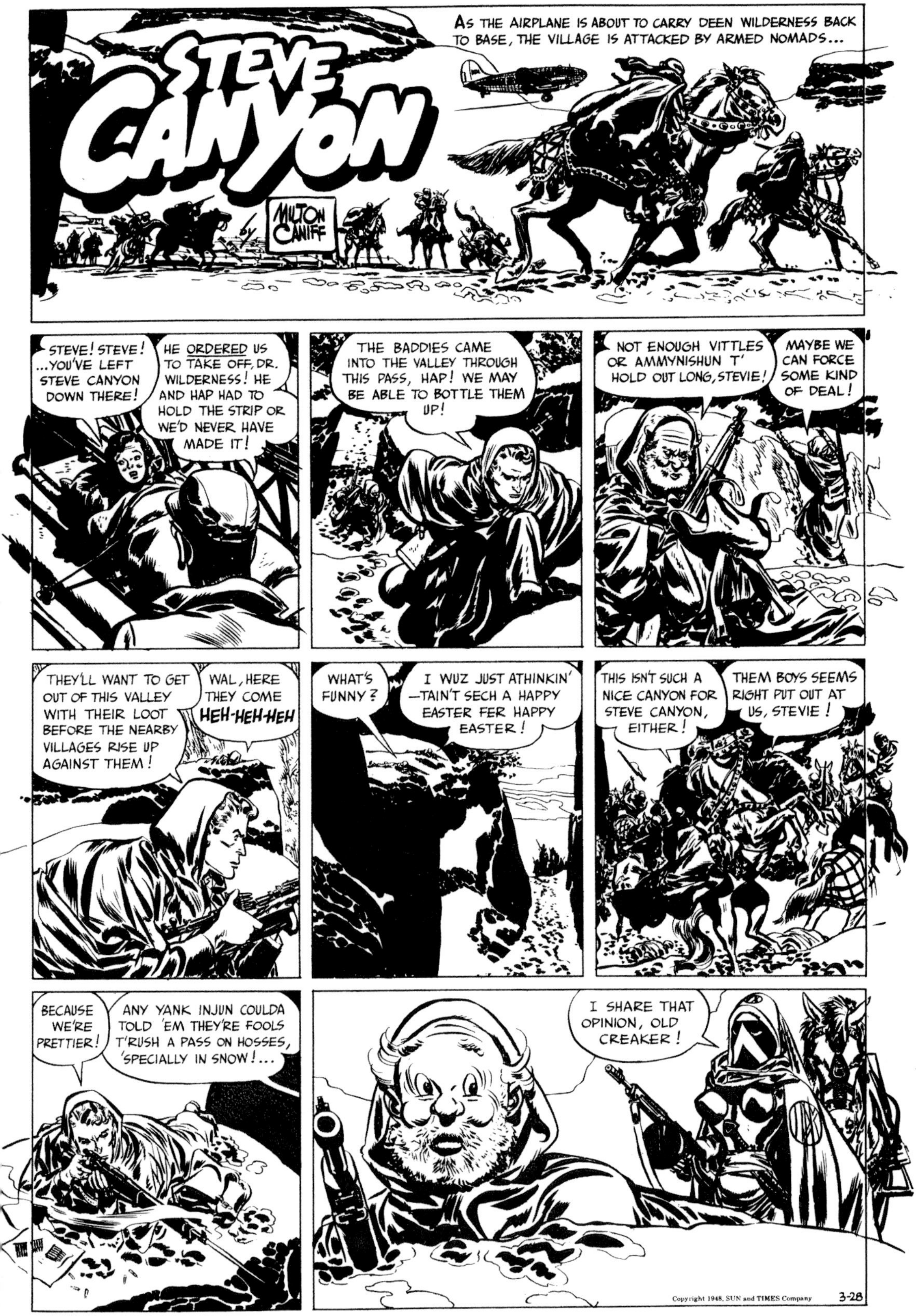
STEVE CANYON
by MILTON CANIFF
AS THE AIRPLANE IS ABOUT TO CARRY DEEN WILDERNESS BACK TO BASE, THE VILLAGE IS ATTACKED BY ARMED NOMADS...
STEVE! STEVE! ...YOU'VE LEFT STEVE CANYON DOWN THERE!
HE ORDERED US TO TAKE OFF, DR. WILDERNESS! HE AND HAP HAD TO HOLD THE STRIP OR WE'D NEVER HAVE MADE IT!
THE BADDIES CAME INTO THE VALLEY THROUGH THIS PASS, HAP! WE MAY BE ABLE TO BOTTLE THEM UP!
NOT ENOUGH VITTLES OR AMMYNISHUN T' HOLD OUT LONG, STEVIE!
MAYBE WE CAN FORCE SOME KIND OF DEAL!
THEY'LL WANT TO GET OUT OF THIS VALLEY WITH THEIR LOOT BEFORE THE NEARBY VILLAGES RISE UP AGAINST THEM!
WAL, HERE THEY COME HEH-HEH-HEH
WHAT'S FUNNY?
I WUZ JUST ATHINKIN' —TAIN'T SECH A HAPPY EASTER FER HAPPY EASTER!
THIS ISN'T SUCH A NICE CANYON FOR STEVE CANYON, EITHER!
THEM BOYS SEEMS RIGHT PUT OUT AT US, STEVIE!
BECAUSE WE'RE PRETTIER!
ANY YANK INJUN COULDA TOLD 'EM THEY'RE FOOLS T'RUSH A PASS ON HOSSES, 'SPECIALLY IN SNOW!...
I SHARE THAT OPINION, OLD CREAKER!
Copyright 1948, SUN and TIMES Company
3-28

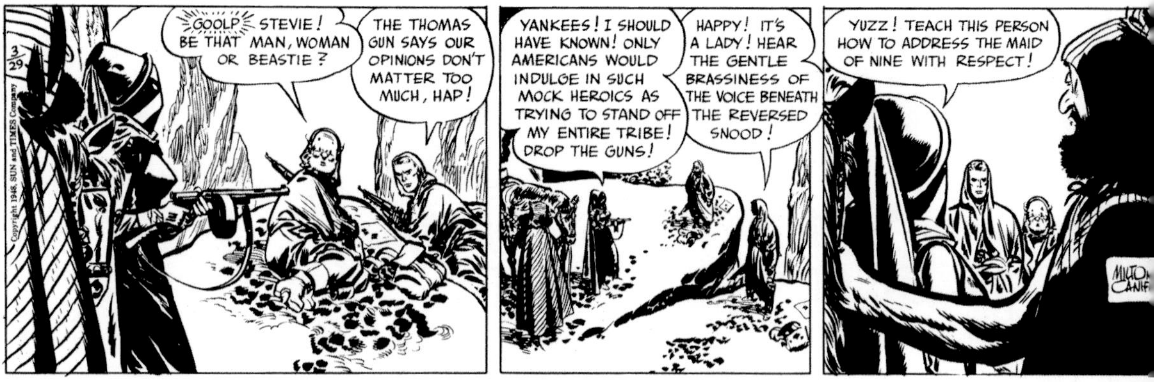
3/29
Copyright 1948, SUN and TIMES Company
GOOLP! STEVIE! BE THAT MAN, WOMAN OR BEASTIE?
THE THOMAS GUN SAYS OUR OPINIONS DON'T MATTER TOO MUCH, HAP!
YANKEES! I SHOULD HAVE KNOWN! ONLY AMERICANS WOULD INDULGE IN SUCH MOCK HEROICS AS TRYING TO STAND OFF MY ENTIRE TRIBE! DROP THE GUNS!
HAPPY! IT'S A LADY! HEAR THE GENTLE BRASSINESS OF THE VOICE BENEATH THE REVERSED SNOOD!
YUZZ! TEACH THIS PERSON HOW TO ADDRESS THE MAID OF NINE WITH RESPECT!
MILTON CANIFF

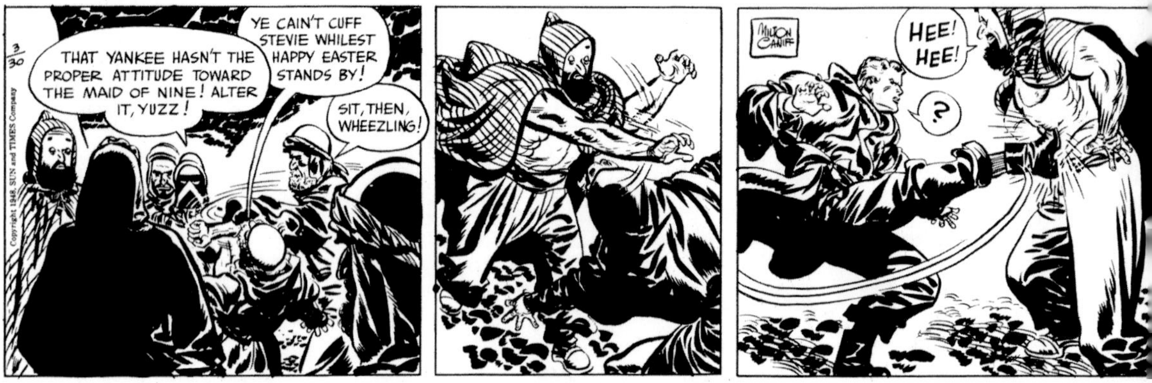
3/30
Copyright 1948, SUN and TIMES Company
THAT YANKEE HASN'T THE PROPER ATTITUDE TOWARD THE MAID OF NINE! ALTER IT, YUZZ!
YE CAIN'T CUFF STEVIE WHILEST HAPPY EASTER STANDS BY!
SIT, THEN, WHEEZLING!
MILTON CANIFF
HEE! HEE!
?

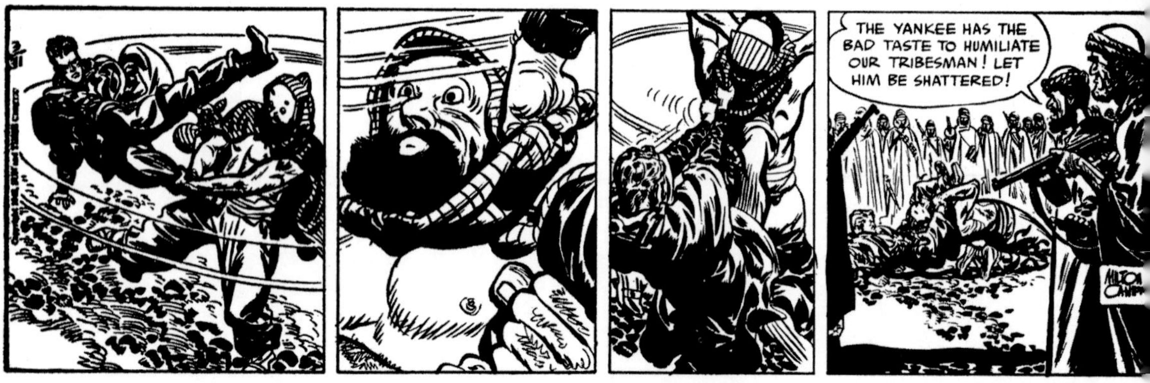
3/31
THE YANKEE HAS THE BAD TASTE TO HUMILIATE OUR TRIBESMAN! LET HIM BE SHATTERED!
MILTON CANIFF

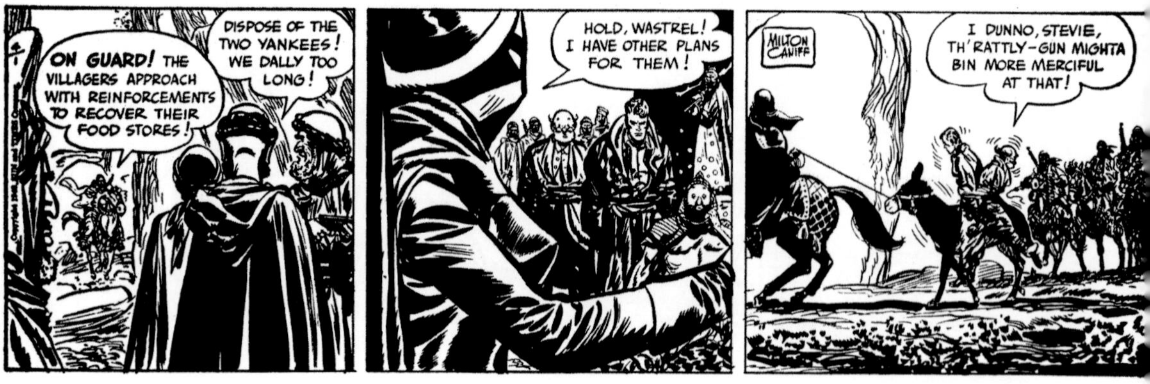
4/1
ON GUARD! THE VILLAGERS APPROACH WITH REINFORCEMENTS TO RECOVER THEIR FOOD STORES!
DISPOSE OF THE TWO YANKEES! WE DALLY TOO LONG!
HOLD, WASTREL! I HAVE OTHER PLANS FOR THEM!
MILTON CANIFF
I DUNNO, STEVIE, TH' RATTLY-GUN MIGHTA BIN MORE MERCIFUL AT THAT!

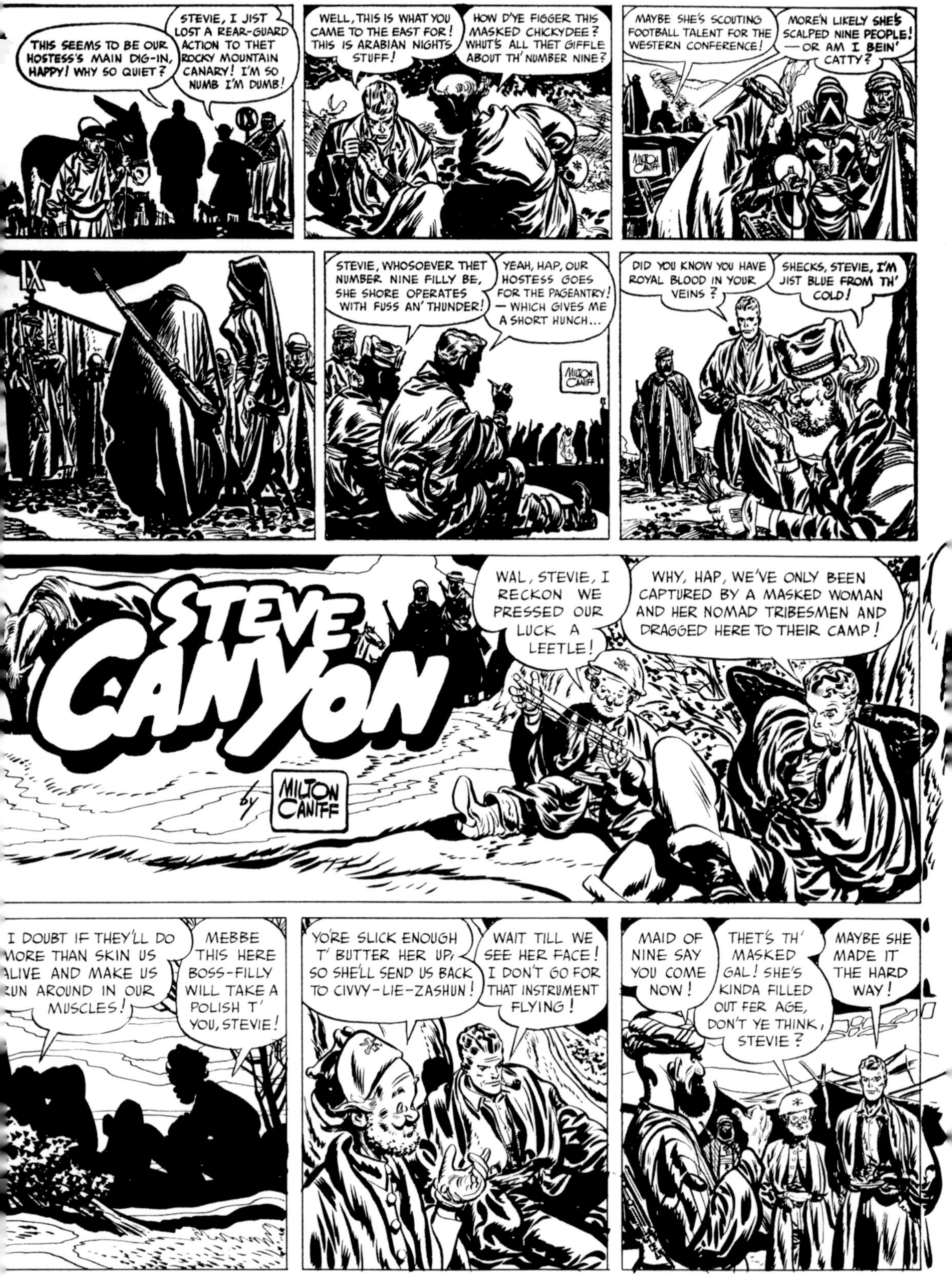
THIS SEEMS TO BE OUR HOSTESS'S MAIN DIG-IN, HAPPY! WHY SO QUIET?
STEVIE, I JIST LOST A REAR-GUARD ACTION TO THET ROCKY MOUNTAIN CANARY! I'M SO NUMB I'M DUMB!
IX
WELL, THIS IS WHAT YOU CAME TO THE EAST FOR! THIS IS ARABIAN NIGHTS STUFF!
HOW D'YE FIGGER THIS MASKED CHICKYDEE? WHUT'S ALL THET GIFFLE ABOUT TH' NUMBER NINE?
MAYBE SHE'S SCOUTING FOOTBALL TALENT FOR THE WESTERN CONFERENCE!
MORE'N LIKELY SHE'S SCALPED NINE PEOPLE! —OR AM I BEIN' CATTY?
MILTON CANIFF
IX
STEVIE, WHOSOEVER THET NUMBER NINE FILLY BE, SHE SHORE OPERATES WITH FUSS AN' THUNDER!
YEAH, HAP, OUR HOSTESS GOES FOR THE PAGEANTRY! —WHICH GIVES ME A SHORT HUNCH...
MILTON CANIFF
DID YOU KNOW YOU HAVE ROYAL BLOOD IN YOUR VEINS?
SHECKS, STEVIE, I'M JIST BLUE FROM TH' COLD!
STEVE CANYON
by MILTON CANIFF
WAL, STEVIE, I RECKON WE PRESSED OUR LUCK A LEETLE!
WHY, HAP, WE'VE ONLY BEEN CAPTURED BY A MASKED WOMAN AND HER NOMAD TRIBESMEN AND DRAGGED HERE TO THEIR CAMP!
I DOUBT IF THEY'LL DO MORE THAN SKIN US ALIVE AND MAKE US RUN AROUND IN OUR MUSCLES!
MEBBE THIS HERE BOSS-FILLY WILL TAKE A POLISH T' YOU, STEVIE!
YO'RE SLICK ENOUGH T' BUTTER HER UP, SO SHE'LL SEND US BACK TO CIVVY-LIE-ZASHUN!
WAIT TILL WE SEE HER FACE! I DON'T GO FOR THAT INSTRUMENT FLYING!
MAID OF NINE SAY YOU COME NOW!
THET'S TH' MASKED GAL! SHE'S KINDA FILLED OUT FER AGE, DON'T YE THINK, STEVIE?
MAYBE SHE MADE IT THE HARD WAY!

MAID OF NINE, COMES PRIS---
HIT THE GRIT, VARLET! MAKE WAY FOR HAPPY THE EASTER, COUNT DE COLORADO, DUKE DE RIMROCK...
?
...THE MINISTER INTERDENOMINARY OF THE ROCKY MOUNTAIN EMPIRE WAITS UPON THE MAID OF NINE!
WHAT IS ALL THIS — AND WHY DID YOU NOT MENTION IT BEFORE?
DOES THE MAID OF NINE REVEAL HER TRUE IDENTITY WHEN SHE GOES AMONG ALIENS IN THE LOW COUNTRY?
CERTAINLY NOT...THERE IS A PRICE UPON MY HEAD!
THEN YOU WILL, OF COURSE, DO HAPPY THE EASTER THE HONOR OF SETTING A HIGH RANSOM UPON HIS HEAD!
HMMM! THIS I SHALL TAKE UNDER ADVISEMENT!
WHUT KIND O' SATAN BAITIN' BE YE UP TO, STEVIE CANYON?
THIS BABE WOULD KILL TWO NOBODIES JUST TO SAVE RATIONS, BUT THE ROYALTY GABBLE MAY BOARD US TILL WE CAN MAKE A BREAK! GET THE WRINKLES OUT OF YOUR COAT OF ARMS, COUNT!
Copyright 1948, SUN and TIMES Company
WHEN SUMMONED TO THE TENT OF THE STRANGE MASKED GIRL, STEVE INTRODUCES HAPPY EASTER AS A MEMBER OF THE NOBILITY!
THIS MAN IS WHAT?
THE MARQUIS OF MILWAUKEE, THE SHAH OF CHEYENNE, EARL OF AZUSA AND BEY OF CHESAPEAKE — HAPPY THE EASTER!
AND WHAT IS ONE OF ROYAL BIRTH DOING HERE?
EXCHANGE EXILE, MILADY! YOUR BOYS GO TO THE U.S. TO STUDY OUR NIGHT LIFE—HIS EASTERICAL HIGHNESS IS HERE TO STUDY YOUR INSECT LIFE!
PSST, HAPPY, DON'T OVERPLAY THE JOKE!
WHO'S JOKING?
MILTON CANIFF
4/6
SO THE SMALL YANKEE IS A NOBLEMAN! I DID NOT KNOW THERE WAS A TITLED GROUP IN AMERICA...
YOU'VE NEVER HEARD OF THE HOUSE OF FULL? IF WE HAD A COPY OF "JERK'S PEERAGE" OR "ALMANACH DE GOTHAM" I COULD POINT OUT HAPPY!
SO YOU THINK HAPPY THE EASTER SHOULD COMMAND A HIGH RANSOM, EH — AH, WHAT IS YOUR TITLE?
I MERELY SERVE HIS GRACE — FOR WHICH HE HAS MOST GRACIOUSLY DUBBED ME "KEEPER OF THE GRAND CANYON" I SHARE HIS EXILE!
AND IF THE MAID OF NINE ELECTS TO HANG YOU BOTH?
MILTON CANIFF
THEN OUR SEARCH FOR A REAL-LIFE BEAUTY TO PLAY IN HAPPY THE EASTER'S MOVIE ON EMANCIPATED ASIATIC WOMEN WILL BE OVER FOREVER!

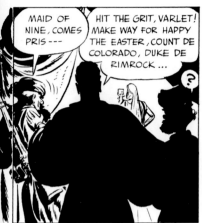

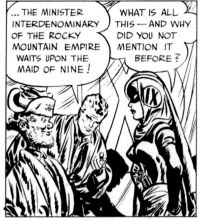

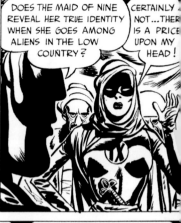

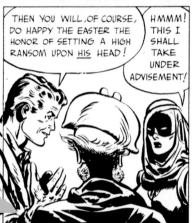

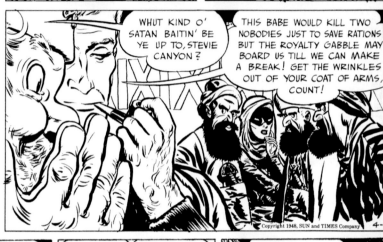

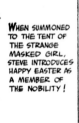

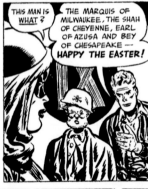

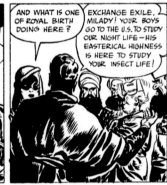

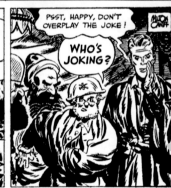

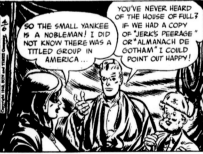

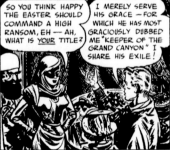

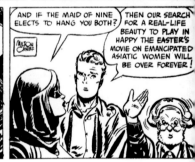

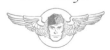

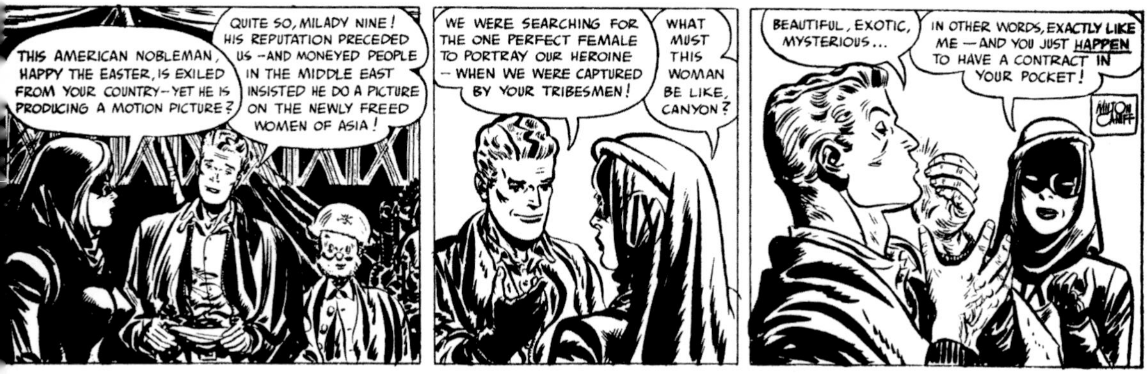
THIS AMERICAN NOBLEMAN, HAPPY THE EASTER, IS EXILED FROM YOUR COUNTRY--YET HE IS PRODUCING A MOTION PICTURE?
QUITE SO, MILADY NINE! HIS REPUTATION PRECEDED US --AND MONEYED PEOPLE IN THE MIDDLE EAST INSISTED HE DO A PICTURE ON THE NEWLY FREED WOMEN OF ASIA!
WE WERE SEARCHING FOR THE ONE PERFECT FEMALE TO PORTRAY OUR HEROINE -- WHEN WE WERE CAPTURED BY YOUR TRIBESMEN!
WHAT MUST THIS WOMAN BE LIKE, CANYON?
BEAUTIFUL, EXOTIC, MYSTERIOUS...
IN OTHER WORDS, EXACTLY LIKE ME -- AND YOU JUST HAPPEN TO HAVE A CONTRACT IN YOUR POCKET!
MILTON CANIFF

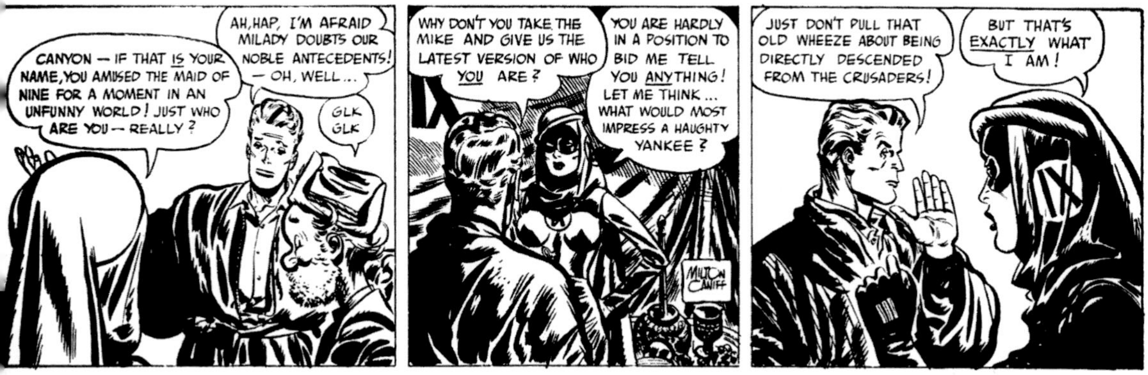
CANYON -- IF THAT IS YOUR NAME, YOU AMUSED THE MAID OF NINE FOR A MOMENT IN AN UNFUNNY WORLD! JUST WHO ARE YOU -- REALLY?
AH, HAP, I'M AFRAID MILADY DOUBTS OUR NOBLE ANTECEDENTS! -- OH, WELL...
GLK GLK
WHY DON'T YOU TAKE THE MIKE AND GIVE US THE LATEST VERSION OF WHO YOU ARE?
YOU ARE HARDLY IN A POSITION TO BID ME TELL YOU ANYTHING! LET ME THINK... WHAT WOULD MOST IMPRESS A HAUGHTY YANKEE?
MILTON CANIFF
JUST DON'T PULL THAT OLD WHEEZE ABOUT BEING DIRECTLY DESCENDED FROM THE CRUSADERS!
BUT THAT'S EXACTLY WHAT I AM!

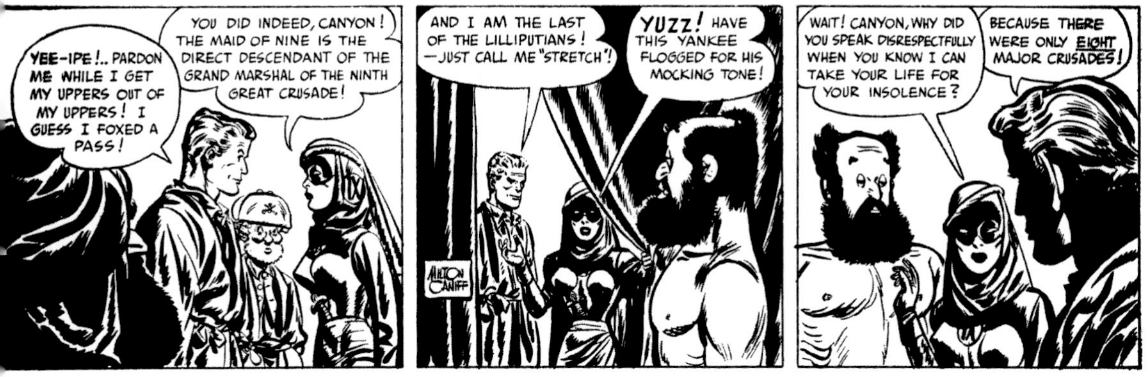
YEE-IPE!.. PARDON ME WHILE I GET MY UPPERS OUT OF MY UPPERS! I GUESS I FOXED A PASS!
YOU DID INDEED, CANYON! THE MAID OF NINE IS THE DIRECT DESCENDANT OF THE GRAND MARSHAL OF THE NINTH GREAT CRUSADE!
AND I AM THE LAST OF THE LILLIPUTIANS! --JUST CALL ME "STRETCH"!
YUZZ! HAVE THIS YANKEE FLOGGED FOR HIS MOCKING TONE!
MILTON CANIFF
WAIT! CANYON, WHY DID YOU SPEAK DISRESPECTFULLY WHEN YOU KNOW I CAN TAKE YOUR LIFE FOR YOUR INSOLENCE?
BECAUSE THERE WERE ONLY EIGHT MAJOR CRUSADES!

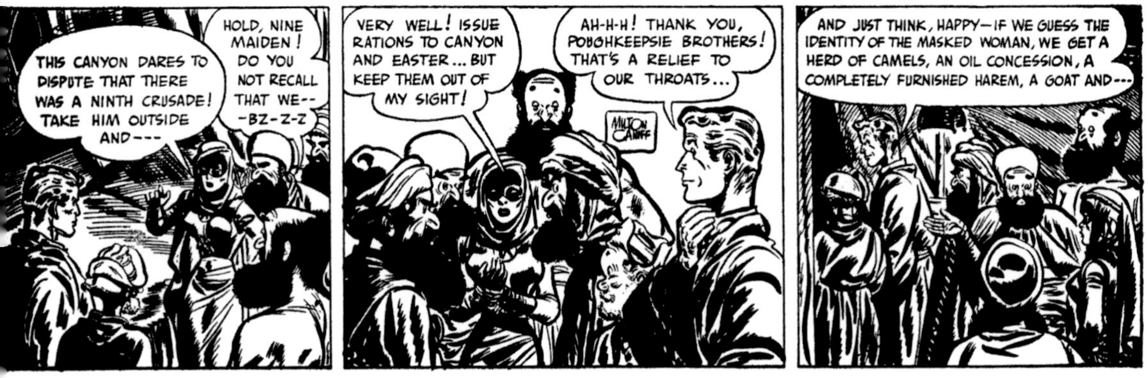
THIS CANYON DARES TO DISPUTE THAT THERE WAS A NINTH CRUSADE! TAKE HIM OUTSIDE AND---
HOLD, NINE MAIDEN! DO YOU NOT RECALL THAT WE-- -BZ-Z-Z
VERY WELL! ISSUE RATIONS TO CANYON AND EASTER... BUT KEEP THEM OUT OF MY SIGHT!
AH-H-H! THANK YOU, POUGHKEEPSIE BROTHERS! THAT'S A RELIEF TO OUR THROATS...
MILTON CANIFF
AND JUST THINK, HAPPY-- IF WE GUESS THE IDENTITY OF THE MASKED WOMAN, WE GET A HERD OF CAMELS, AN OIL CONCESSION, A COMPLETELY FURNISHED HAREM, A GOAT AND---

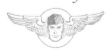

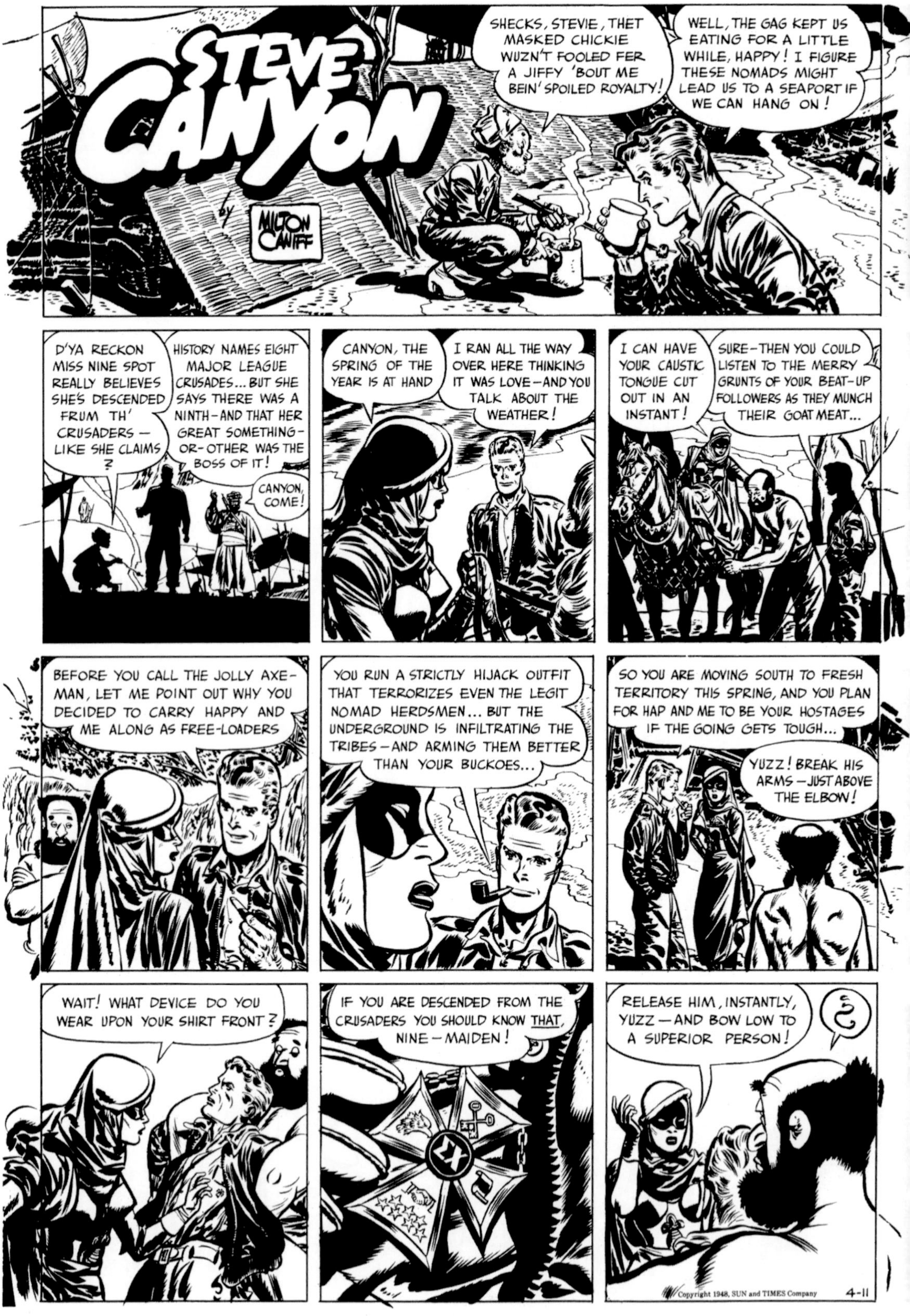
STEVE CANYON
by MILTON CANIFF
SHECKS, STEVIE, THET MASKED CHICKIE WUZN'T FOOLED FER A JIFFY 'BOUT ME BEIN' SPOILED ROYALTY!
WELL, THE GAG KEPT US EATING FOR A LITTLE WHILE, HAPPY! I FIGURE THESE NOMADS MIGHT LEAD US TO A SEAPORT IF WE CAN HANG ON!
D'YA RECKON MISS NINE SPOT REALLY BELIEVES SHE'S DESCENDED FRUM TH' CRUSADERS — LIKE SHE CLAIMS?
HISTORY NAMES EIGHT MAJOR LEAGUE CRUSADES... BUT SHE SAYS THERE WAS A NINTH — AND THAT HER GREAT SOMETHING-OR-OTHER WAS THE BOSS OF IT!
CANYON, COME!
CANYON, THE SPRING OF THE YEAR IS AT HAND
I RAN ALL THE WAY OVER HERE THINKING IT WAS LOVE — AND YOU TALK ABOUT THE WEATHER!
I CAN HAVE YOUR CAUSTIC TONGUE CUT OUT IN AN INSTANT!
SURE — THEN YOU COULD LISTEN TO THE MERRY GRUNTS OF YOUR BEAT-UP FOLLOWERS AS THEY MUNCH THEIR GOAT MEAT...
BEFORE YOU CALL THE JOLLY AXE-MAN, LET ME POINT OUT WHY YOU DECIDED TO CARRY HAPPY AND ME ALONG AS FREE-LOADERS
YOU RUN A STRICTLY HIJACK OUTFIT THAT TERRORIZES EVEN THE LEGIT NOMAD HERDSMEN... BUT THE UNDERGROUND IS INFILTRATING THE TRIBES — AND ARMING THEM BETTER THAN YOUR BUCKOES...
SO YOU ARE MOVING SOUTH TO FRESH TERRITORY THIS SPRING, AND YOU PLAN FOR HAP AND ME TO BE YOUR HOSTAGES IF THE GOING GETS TOUGH...
YUZZ! BREAK HIS ARMS — JUST ABOVE THE ELBOW!
WAIT! WHAT DEVICE DO YOU WEAR UPON YOUR SHIRT FRONT?
IF YOU ARE DESCENDED FROM THE CRUSADERS YOU SHOULD KNOW THAT, NINE-MAIDEN!
RELEASE HIM, INSTANTLY, YUZZ — AND BOW LOW TO A SUPERIOR PERSON!
Copyright 1948, SUN and TIMES Company
4-11

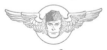

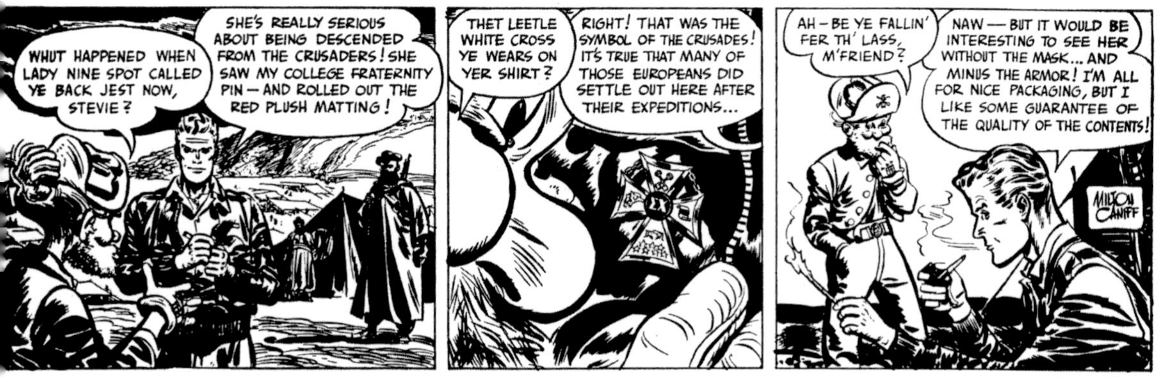
WHUT HAPPENED WHEN LADY NINE SPOT CALLED YE BACK JEST NOW, STEVIE?
SHE'S REALLY SERIOUS ABOUT BEING DESCENDED FROM THE CRUSADERS! SHE SAW MY COLLEGE FRATERNITY PIN — AND ROLLED OUT THE RED PLUSH MATTING!
THET LEETLE WHITE CROSS YE WEARS ON YER SHIRT?
RIGHT! THAT WAS THE SYMBOL OF THE CRUSADES! IT'S TRUE THAT MANY OF THOSE EUROPEANS DID SETTLE OUT HERE AFTER THEIR EXPEDITIONS...
AH - BE YE FALLIN' FER TH' LASS, M'FRIEND?
NAW — BUT IT WOULD BE INTERESTING TO SEE HER WITHOUT THE MASK... AND MINUS THE ARMOR! I'M ALL FOR NICE PACKAGING, BUT I LIKE SOME GUARANTEE OF THE QUALITY OF THE CONTENTS!
MILTON CANIFF

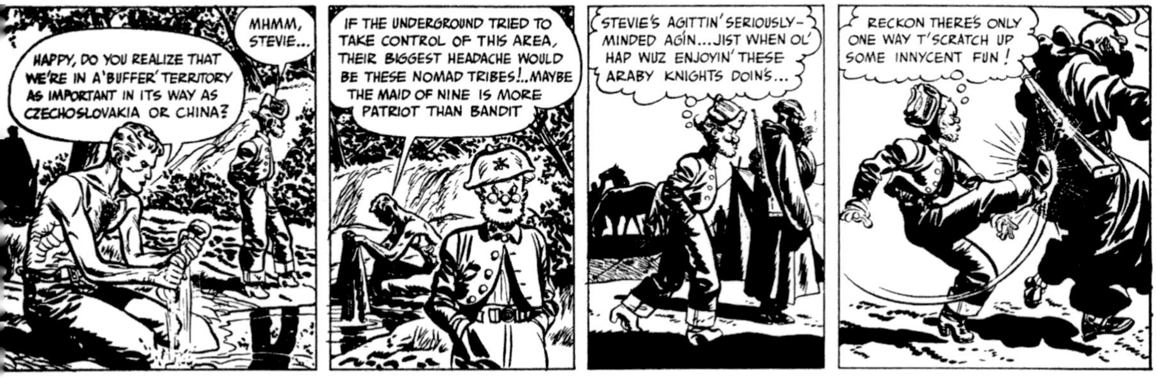
HAPPY, DO YOU REALIZE THAT WE'RE IN A 'BUFFER' TERRITORY AS IMPORTANT IN ITS WAY AS CZECHOSLOVAKIA OR CHINA?
MHMM, STEVIE...
IF THE UNDERGROUND TRIED TO TAKE CONTROL OF THIS AREA, THEIR BIGGEST HEADACHE WOULD BE THESE NOMAD TRIBES!..MAYBE THE MAID OF NINE IS MORE PATRIOT THAN BANDIT
STEVIE'S AGITTIN' SERIOUSLY-MINDED AGIN...JIST WHEN OL' HAP WUZ ENJOYIN' THESE ARABY KNIGHTS DOIN'S...
RECKON THERE'S ONLY ONE WAY T'SCRATCH UP SOME INNYCENT FUN!

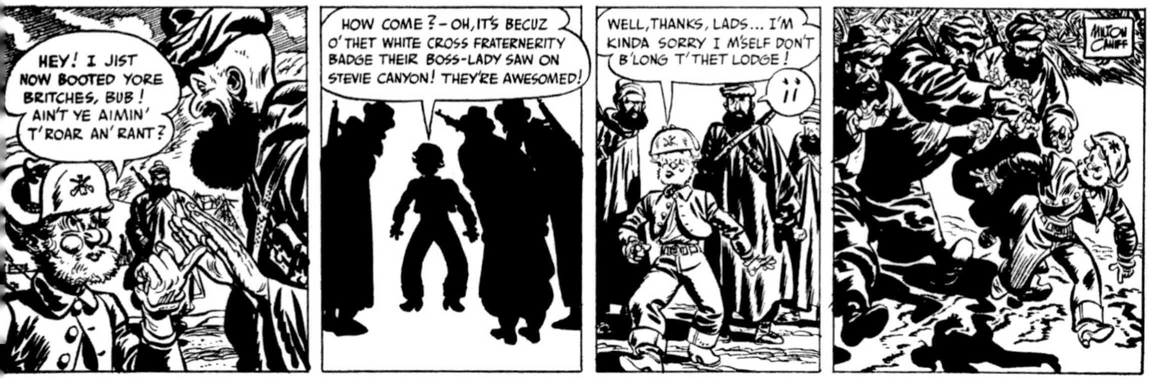
HEY! I JIST NOW BOOTED YORE BRITCHES, BUB! AIN'T YE AIMIN' T'ROAR AN' RANT?
HOW COME? - OH, IT'S BECUZ O'THET WHITE CROSS FRATERNERITY BADGE THEIR BOSS-LADY SAW ON STEVIE CANYON! THEY'RE AWESOMED!
WELL, THANKS, LADS... I'M KINDA SORRY I M'SELF DON'T B'LONG T'THET LODGE!
!!
MILTON CANIFF

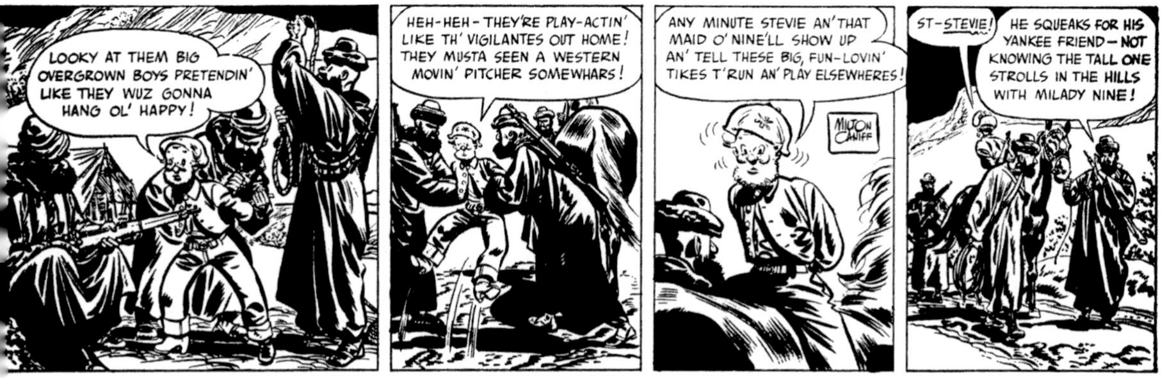
LOOKY AT THEM BIG OVERGROWN BOYS PRETENDIN' LIKE THEY WUZ GONNA HANG OL' HAPPY!
HEH-HEH- THEY'RE PLAY-ACTIN' LIKE TH' VIGILANTES OUT HOME! THEY MUSTA SEEN A WESTERN MOVIN' PITCHER SOMEWHARS!
ANY MINUTE STEVIE AN' THAT MAID O' NINE'LL SHOW UP AN' TELL THESE BIG, FUN-LOVIN' TIKES T'RUN AN' PLAY ELSEWHERES!
MILTON CANIFF
ST-STEVIE!
HE SQUEAKS FOR HIS YANKEE FRIEND — NOT KNOWING THE TALL ONE STROLLS IN THE HILLS WITH MILADY NINE!

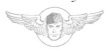

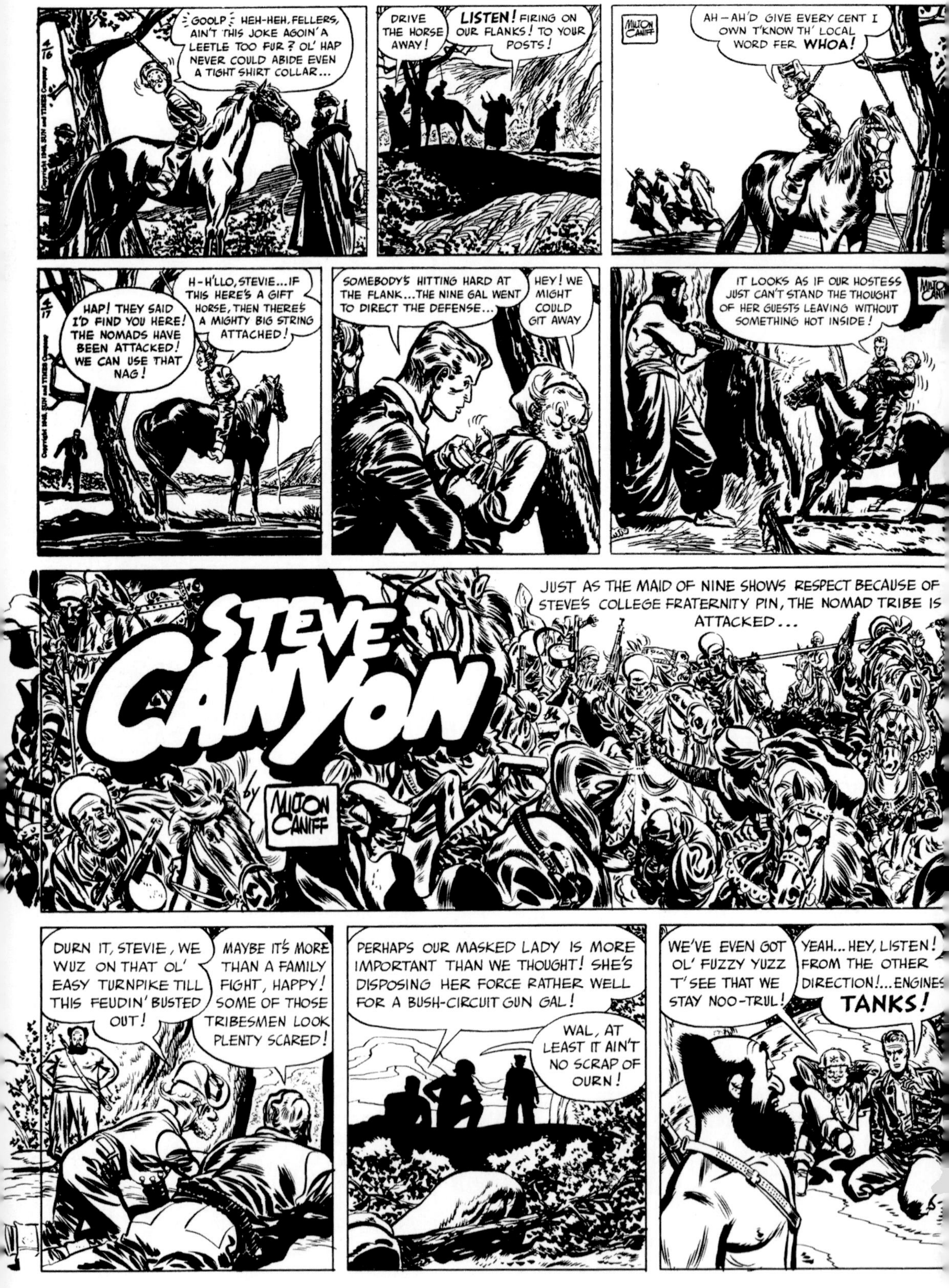

GOOLP! HEH-HEH, FELLERS, AIN'T THIS JOKE AGOIN' A LEETLE TOO FUR? OL' HAP NEVER COULD ABIDE EVEN A TIGHT SHIRT COLLAR...
4/16
DRIVE THE HORSE AWAY!
LISTEN! FIRING ON OUR FLANKS! TO YOUR POSTS!
MILTON CANIFF
AH–AH'D GIVE EVERY CENT I OWN T'KNOW TH' LOCAL WORD FER WHOA!
4/17
HAP! THEY SAID I'D FIND YOU HERE! THE NOMADS HAVE BEEN ATTACKED! WE CAN USE THAT NAG!
H-H'LLO, STEVIE... IF THIS HERE'S A GIFT HORSE, THEN THERE'S A MIGHTY BIG STRING ATTACHED!
SOMEBODY'S HITTING HARD AT THE FLANK... THE NINE GAL WENT TO DIRECT THE DEFENSE...
HEY! WE MIGHT COULD GIT AWAY
IT LOOKS AS IF OUR HOSTESS JUST CAN'T STAND THE THOUGHT OF HER GUESTS LEAVING WITHOUT SOMETHING HOT INSIDE!
STEVE CANYON
by MILTON CANIFF
JUST AS THE MAID OF NINE SHOWS RESPECT BECAUSE OF STEVE'S COLLEGE FRATERNITY PIN, THE NOMAD TRIBE IS ATTACKED...
DURN IT, STEVIE, WE WUZ ON THAT OL' EASY TURNPIKE TILL THIS FEUDIN' BUSTED OUT!
MAYBE IT'S MORE THAN A FAMILY FIGHT, HAPPY! SOME OF THOSE TRIBESMEN LOOK PLENTY SCARED!
PERHAPS OUR MASKED LADY IS MORE IMPORTANT THAN WE THOUGHT! SHE'S DISPOSING HER FORCE RATHER WELL FOR A BUSH-CIRCUIT GUN GAL!
WAL, AT LEAST IT AIN'T NO SCRAP OF OURN!
WE'VE EVEN GOT OL' FUZZY YUZZ T'SEE THAT WE STAY NOO-TRUL!
YEAH... HEY, LISTEN! FROM THE OTHER DIRECTION!... ENGINES TANKS!

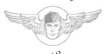

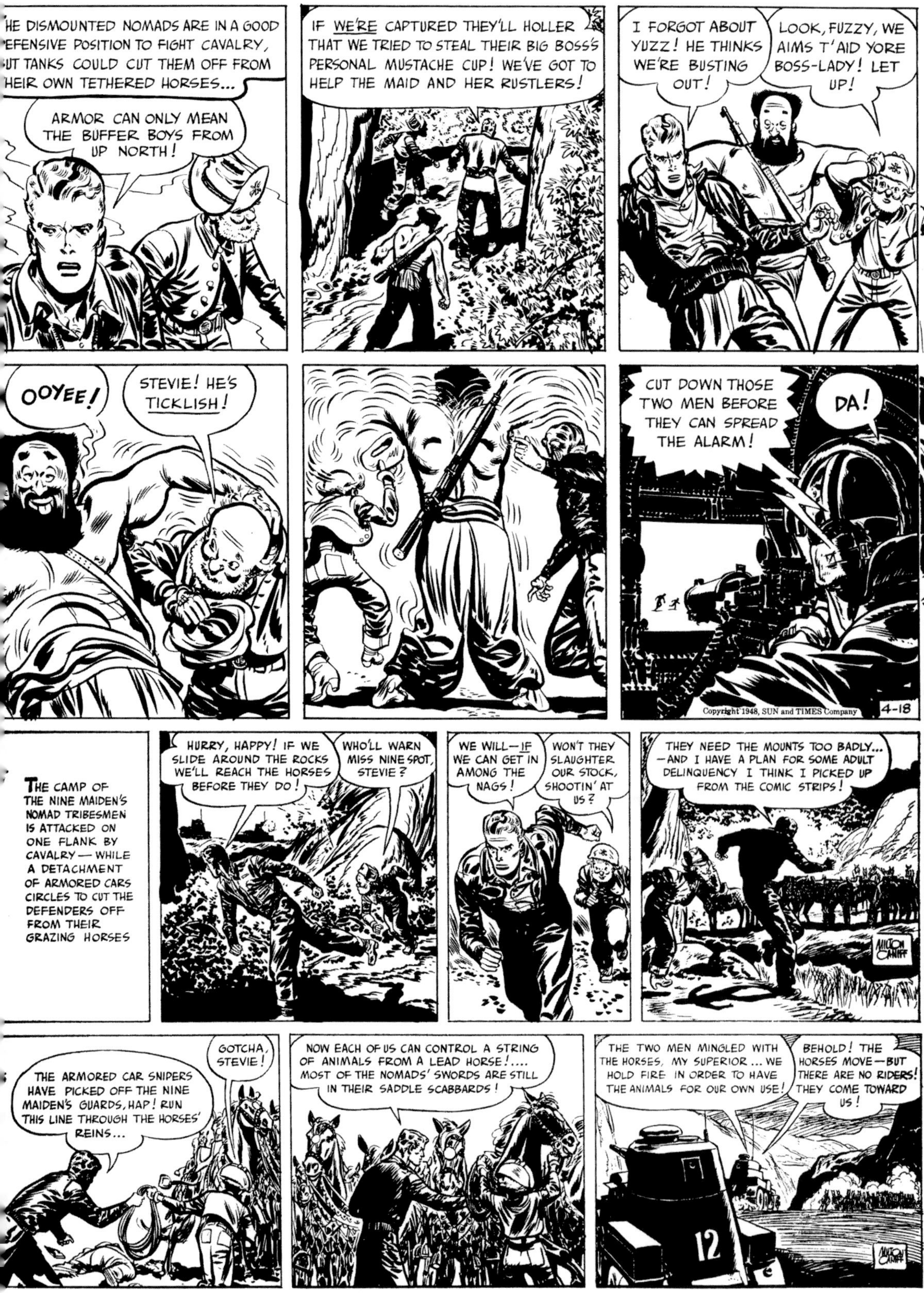
HE DISMOUNTED NOMADS ARE IN A GOOD EFENSIVE POSITION TO FIGHT CAVALRY, UT TANKS COULD CUT THEM OFF FROM HEIR OWN TETHERED HORSES...
ARMOR CAN ONLY MEAN THE BUFFER BOYS FROM UP NORTH!
IF WE'RE CAPTURED THEY'LL HOLLER THAT WE TRIED TO STEAL THEIR BIG BOSS'S PERSONAL MUSTACHE CUP! WE'VE GOT TO HELP THE MAID AND HER RUSTLERS!
I FORGOT ABOUT YUZZ! HE THINKS WE'RE BUSTING OUT!
LOOK, FUZZY, WE AIMS T' AID YORE BOSS-LADY! LET UP!
OOYEE!
STEVIE! HE'S TICKLISH!
CUT DOWN THOSE TWO MEN BEFORE THEY CAN SPREAD THE ALARM!
DA!
Copyright 1948, SUN and TIMES Company
4-18
THE CAMP OF THE NINE MAIDEN'S NOMAD TRIBESMEN IS ATTACKED ON ONE FLANK BY CAVALRY — WHILE A DETACHMENT OF ARMORED CARS CIRCLES TO CUT THE DEFENDERS OFF FROM THEIR GRAZING HORSES
HURRY, HAPPY! IF WE SLIDE AROUND THE ROCKS WE'LL REACH THE HORSES BEFORE THEY DO!
WHO'LL WARN MISS NINE SPOT, STEVIE?
WE WILL — IF WE CAN GET IN AMONG THE NAGS!
WON'T THEY SLAUGHTER OUR STOCK, SHOOTIN' AT US?
THEY NEED THE MOUNTS TOO BADLY... — AND I HAVE A PLAN FOR SOME ADULT DELINQUENCY I THINK I PICKED UP FROM THE COMIC STRIPS!
MILTON CANIFF
THE ARMORED CAR SNIPERS HAVE PICKED OFF THE NINE MAIDEN'S GUARDS, HAP! RUN THIS LINE THROUGH THE HORSES' REINS...
GOTCHA, STEVIE!
NOW EACH OF US CAN CONTROL A STRING OF ANIMALS FROM A LEAD HORSE!.... MOST OF THE NOMADS' SWORDS ARE STILL IN THEIR SADDLE SCABBARDS!
THE TWO MEN MINGLED WITH THE HORSES, MY SUPERIOR ... WE HOLD FIRE IN ORDER TO HAVE THE ANIMALS FOR OUR OWN USE!
BEHOLD! THE HORSES MOVE — BUT THERE ARE NO RIDERS! THEY COME TOWARD US!
12
MILTON CANIFF

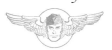

THE NOMADS' HORSES COME TOWARD US — CONTROLLED BY SOME UNSEEN HAND!

WE WERE TO GUARD THEM UNTIL OUR OWN HORSEMEN BROKE THROUGH TO TAKE THEM IN CHARGE — BUT NOW THEY ENGULF US!

BUT FROM UNDER THE BELLIES OF TWO OF THE HORSES, RAZOR-SHARP NATIVE SWORDS SLASH AT THE TIRES OF THE ARMORED CARS...

BAM BAM BAM

I THINK THE THIRD 'BAM' WAS THE COMMANDER OF THOSE CARS BLOWING HIS WIG!

WE DONE IT TO 'EM, STEVIE! THEM CLANK-WAGON TIRES BLOWED LIKE BUBBLY GUM!

THEY CAN HARDLY MOVE NOW, HAP! — GET THAT AXLE GREASE, GOAT HAIR AND LAMP OIL FROM THE SUPPLY TENT!

THEM CREWS MUST BE WAITIN' FER THEIR FLANK ATTACK T'BREAK THROUGH!

JUST THE TIME WE NEED! I HAVE THE OIL-SOAKED GOAT HAIR WADDED WITH A HUNK OF GREASE! HOLD THE CATAPULT WHILE I LIGHT UP!

BUMS AWAY-Y-Y!!

WHAT OCCURS HERE?

WE ARRIVED AS CANYON AND EASTER SET THE VEHICLES AFIRE WITH IMPROVISED MORTARS, MILADY NINE!

THE HEAT DROVE THE CREWS INTO THE OPEN...

I DID NOT ANTICIPATE HAVING TO CITE PRISONERS FOR VALOR!

DON'T RATTLE YOUR CHAIN OF COMMAND, DUCHESS

WE DIDN'T DO THIS FOR YOUR SAKE!... IF THOSE LADDIES FROM UP NORTH CAPTURED US, THEIR NEWSPAPERS WOULD SCREAM THAT UNCLE SUGAR HAD TWO DIVISIONS OF TROOPS THREATENING THEIR SOUTHERN BOUNDARY!

HORSES? FOR HAPPY AND ME?

THE NINE MAIDEN SO ORDERS, FOR YOUR PARTISAN EFFORTS ON BEHALF OF THIS TRIBE!

DID MY MEN SELECT ADEQUATE MOUNTS FOR YOU, CANYON?

BEATS THE HEE-HAW EXPRESS, DUCHESS!

I SEE YOU ARE BREAKING UP YOUR FORCE, LADY NINE

OUR VISITORS FROM THE NORTH WILL RETURN WITH AIRPLANES TO FIND THEIR ARMORED PATROL AND HORSEMEN... WE WILL DISPERSE AND RENDEZVOUS AFTER THEIR AIRCRAFT HAVE MOVED ON!

THAT'S MODERN STUFF! WHO ARE YOU, WOMAN?

YOU MIGHT BE QUITE SURPRISE —AND, AGA MAYBE NO

Steve Canyon

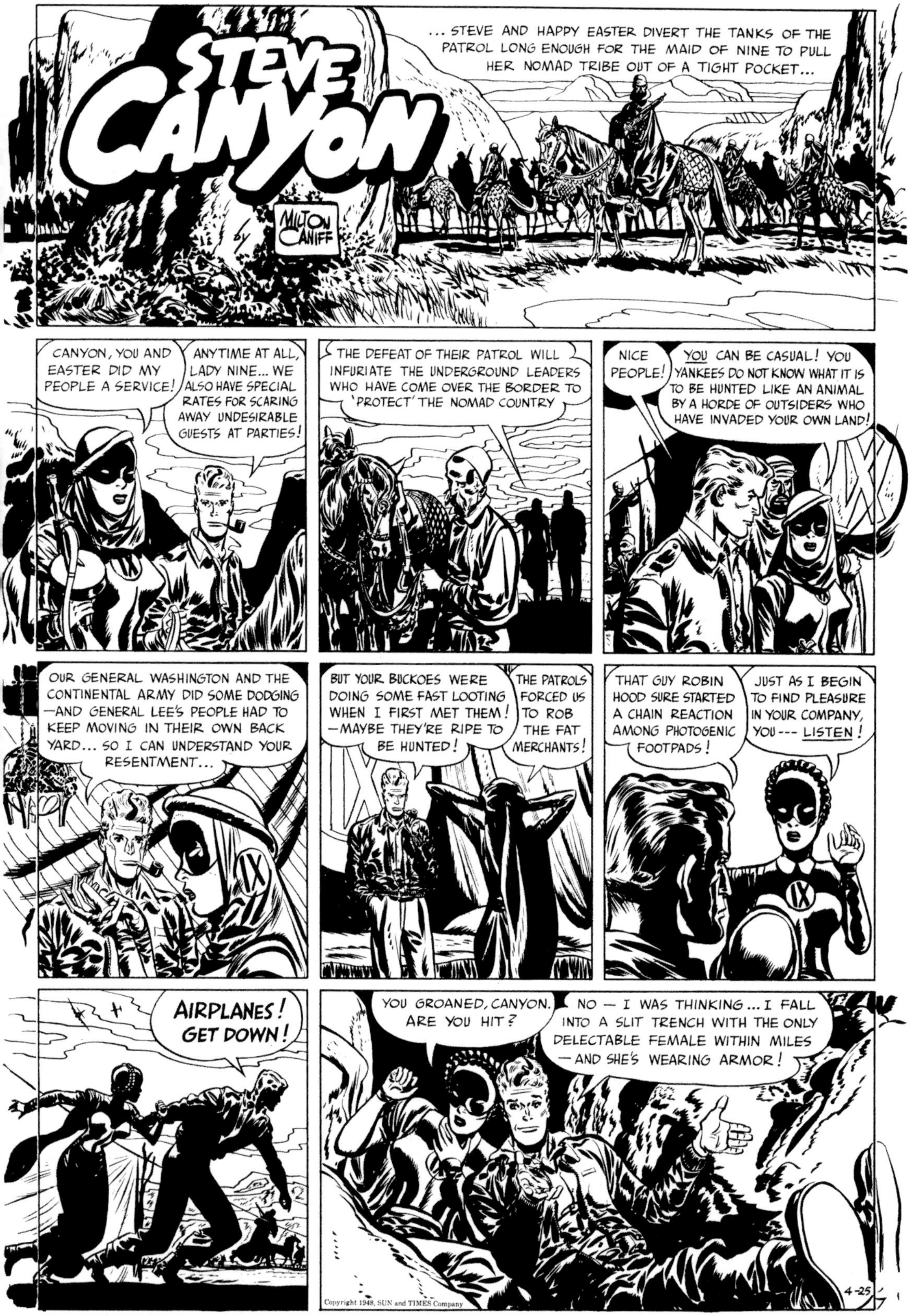
STEVE CANYON
by MILTON CANIFF
... STEVE AND HAPPY EASTER DIVERT THE TANKS OF THE PATROL LONG ENOUGH FOR THE MAID OF NINE TO PULL HER NOMAD TRIBE OUT OF A TIGHT POCKET...
CANYON, YOU AND EASTER DID MY PEOPLE A SERVICE!
ANYTIME AT ALL, LADY NINE... WE ALSO HAVE SPECIAL RATES FOR SCARING AWAY UNDESIRABLE GUESTS AT PARTIES!
THE DEFEAT OF THEIR PATROL WILL INFURIATE THE UNDERGROUND LEADERS WHO HAVE COME OVER THE BORDER TO 'PROTECT' THE NOMAD COUNTRY
NICE PEOPLE!
YOU CAN BE CASUAL! YOU YANKEES DO NOT KNOW WHAT IT IS TO BE HUNTED LIKE AN ANIMAL BY A HORDE OF OUTSIDERS WHO HAVE INVADED YOUR OWN LAND!
OUR GENERAL WASHINGTON AND THE CONTINENTAL ARMY DID SOME DODGING —AND GENERAL LEE'S PEOPLE HAD TO KEEP MOVING IN THEIR OWN BACK YARD... SO I CAN UNDERSTAND YOUR RESENTMENT...
BUT YOUR BUCKOES WERE DOING SOME FAST LOOTING WHEN I FIRST MET THEM! —MAYBE THEY'RE RIPE TO BE HUNTED!
THE PATROLS FORCED US TO ROB THE FAT MERCHANTS!
THAT GUY ROBIN HOOD SURE STARTED A CHAIN REACTION AMONG PHOTOGENIC FOOTPADS!
JUST AS I BEGIN TO FIND PLEASURE IN YOUR COMPANY, YOU --- LISTEN!
AIRPLANES! GET DOWN!
YOU GROANED, CANYON. ARE YOU HIT?
NO — I WAS THINKING... I FALL INTO A SLIT TRENCH WITH THE ONLY DELECTABLE FEMALE WITHIN MILES —AND SHE'S WEARING ARMOR!
Copyright 1948, SUN and TIMES Company
4-25

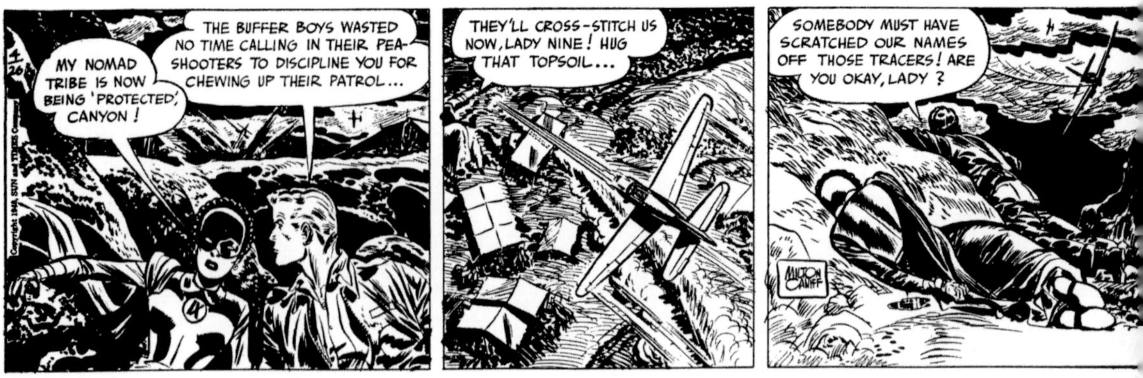
MY NOMAD TRIBE IS NOW BEING 'PROTECTED,' CANYON !
THE BUFFER BOYS WASTED NO TIME CALLING IN THEIR PEA-SHOOTERS TO DISCIPLINE YOU FOR CHEWING UP THEIR PATROL...
THEY'LL CROSS-STITCH US NOW, LADY NINE! HUG THAT TOPSOIL...
SOMEBODY MUST HAVE SCRATCHED OUR NAMES OFF THOSE TRACERS! ARE YOU OKAY, LADY ?
MILTON CANIFF

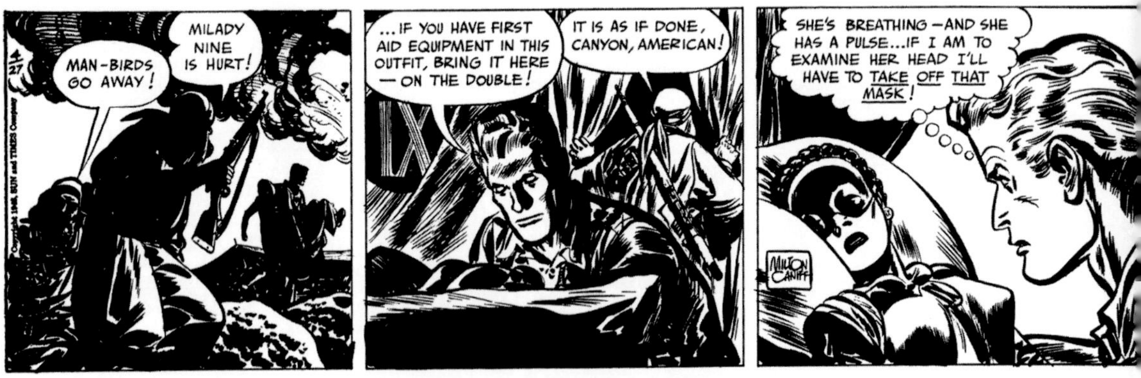
MAN-BIRDS GO AWAY !
MILADY NINE IS HURT!
...IF YOU HAVE FIRST AID EQUIPMENT IN THIS OUTFIT, BRING IT HERE —ON THE DOUBLE!
IT IS AS IF DONE, CANYON, AMERICAN!
SHE'S BREATHING —AND SHE HAS A PULSE...IF I AM TO EXAMINE HER HEAD I'LL HAVE TO TAKE OFF THAT MASK !
MILTON CANIFF

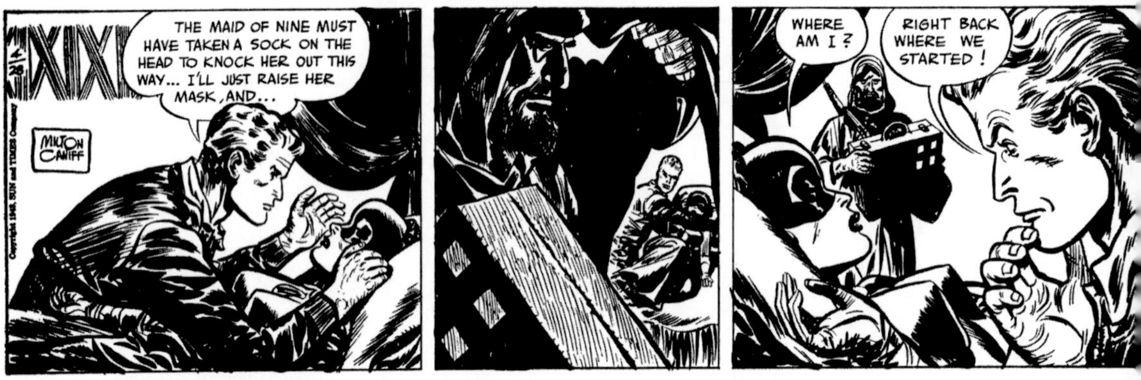
THE MAID OF NINE MUST HAVE TAKEN A SOCK ON THE HEAD TO KNOCK HER OUT THIS WAY... I'LL JUST RAISE HER MASK, AND...
MILTON CANIFF
WHERE AM I ?
RIGHT BACK WHERE WE STARTED !

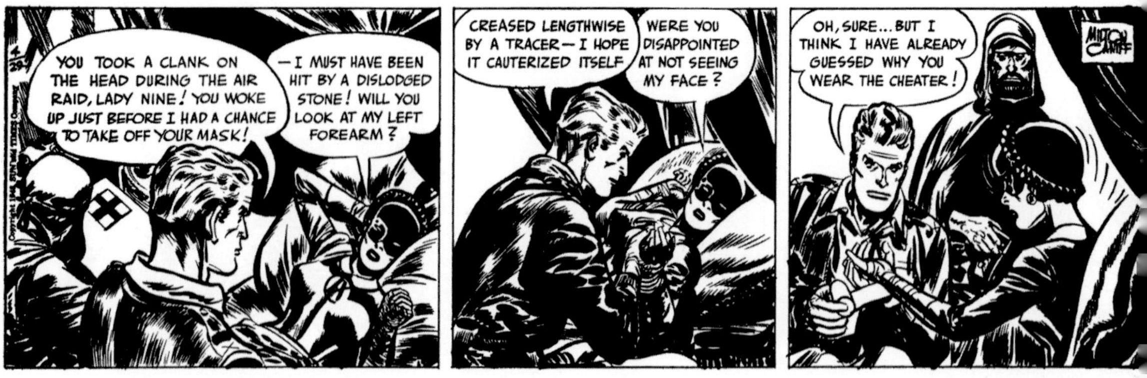
YOU TOOK A CLANK ON THE HEAD DURING THE AIR RAID, LADY NINE! YOU WOKE UP JUST BEFORE I HAD A CHANCE TO TAKE OFF YOUR MASK!
—I MUST HAVE BEEN HIT BY A DISLODGED STONE! WILL YOU LOOK AT MY LEFT FOREARM ?
CREASED LENGTHWISE BY A TRACER—I HOPE IT CAUTERIZED ITSELF
WERE YOU DISAPPOINTED AT NOT SEEING MY FACE ?
OH, SURE...BUT I THINK I HAVE ALREADY GUESSED WHY YOU WEAR THE CHEATER!
MILTON CANIFF

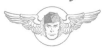

CANYON, WHAT DO YOU MEAN YOU'VE GUESSED WHY I WEAR THIS MASK?

IF THE UNDERGROUND HAS INFILTRATED AGENTS INTO YOUR NOMAD TRIBE, YOU CAN MOVE IN AND OUT FROM UNDER THEIR NOSES IF THEY DON'T KNOW YOUR FACE!

OH—YES, OF COURSE...

THERE WOULDN'T NEED TO BE ANY OTHER REASON, WOULD THERE?

...SUCH AS THE FACT THAT I MIGHT KNOW YOUR FACE FROM SOMEWHERE...

...AND SHE JUST SAT THERE WONDERING WHETHER TO SLUG THE LUG—OR TAKE HIM COMPLETELY INTO HER CONFIDENCE!

SO YOU WON'T TALK, EH? SORE BECAUSE I YAPPED ABOUT YOUR MASK, LADY NINE?

NO, CANYON—SURPRISED AT MYSELF FOR RISKING MY SECURITY! I THINK PERHAPS YOU ARE MORE DANGEROUS THAN THE BULLETS OF MY ENEMIES! —YOU WRAP A BANDAGE TOO TENDERLY!

MEANWHILE

WHAT CAN THIS BE?

A STAINED, BULLET-TORN JACKET! MARKED WITH THE SIGN OF NINE!

AND HERE IS A TAG ADDRESSED TO OUR MAID OF NINE!

IT MUST HAVE BEEN DROPPED FROM ONE OF THE ATTACKING MAN-BIRDS. IF MY GUESS IS CORRECT THIS WILL BE A SAD DAY IN OUR CAMP!

STEVE CANYON

LADY NINE, YOU MAY OR MAY NOT BE DESCENDED FROM THE CRUSADERS, BUT THE BIG BOYS TO THE NORTH ARE CLOBBERING YOUR PEOPLE — AND THAT'S ENOUGH FOR HAPPY EASTER AND ME...

YOU WILL PROBABLY REGRET THAT DECISION, CANYON! YOUR PIONEERS TREATED THE AMERICAN INDIANS AS WE ARE BEING TORMENTED NOW!

ONE WAR AT A TIME, DUCHESS... BESIDES, HAP'S HIDE AND MINE ARE IN THE VAT ON THIS DEAL...BRIEF US!

EVERY SPRING WE NOMADS LEAVE THE LOW COUNTRY AND GO TO THE GRAZING LANDS... WE KNEW THE UNDERGROUND HAD TAKEN OVER SUCH POLICE AS EXIST IN THESE HILLS...

Steve Canyon

WE KNEW THEY WOULD MERELY HAVE TO WAIT AT THE WATER STOPS TO ARREST THE NOMAD LEADERS AND TAKE OVER THE TRIBES WITH A MINIMUM OF FIGHTING...

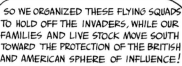

SO WE ORGANIZED THESE FLYING SQUADS TO HOLD OFF THE INVADERS, WHILE OUR FAMILIES AND LIVE STOCK MOVE SOUTH TOWARD THE PROTECTION OF THE BRITISH AND AMERICAN SPHERE OF INFLUENCE!

YES, ALOI!

THIS WAS FOUND AFTER THE AIR ATTACK, NINE MAIDEN... IT MUST HAVE BEEN DROPPED FROM ONE OF THE MAN-BIRDS! IT BEARS A TAG — ADDRESSED TO YOU!

IT IS A MAN'S BLOUSE!

IT BEARS THE SIGN OF NINE! IT BELONGS TO MY FATHER!

BUT IT IS DARKLY STAINED — AND THERE ARE HOLES

GENTLEMEN, THERE WILL BE SOME CHANGES IN MY PLANS...

Copyright 1948, SUN and TIMES Company 5-2

STEVIE! I WUZ WORRIED MEBBE THEM IRON JAYBIRDS HAD DRILLED YE!

NEAR MISS, HAPPY! — DID YOU HEAR THEY DROPPED A BULLET-TORN BLOUSE THAT BELONGED TO THE NINE MAIDEN'S DAD?

DID SHE BOIL?

WORSE — SHE ICED! I'M AFRAID SHE'LL TRY FOR REVENGE — AND PLAY INTO THEIR HANDS!

I GAVE HER FIRST AID — AND ALMOST SAW HER FACE!

MEBBE YE SHOULDN'T NEVER SEE HER UNMASKED, STEVIE!

WHY NOT?

MOST WIMMIN WOULD LIKE T'PLAY MASKYRADE ALL TH' TIME — IT'S US FELLERS WHICH TELLS 'EM T' COME DOWN T'EAT AN' GIT TO TH' KITCHEN!... THEN WE EAT HEARTY AN' GO OUT LOOKIN' FER ANOTHER FILLY WHO'S GOT SOME MYSTERY ABOUT HER!

CAN MILADY NINE BE BLAMED FOR SEEKING REVENGE? THE HATED UNDERGROUND HAS DESTROYED HER FATHER!

WE HAVE BUT SLENDER PROOF OF SUCH!

PERHAPS THE AMERICAN COULD REASON WITH MILADY!

SUMMON HIM, THEN!

I DID NOT SEND FOR YOU, CANYON!

MEDICAL CORPSMAN CANYON TO YOU, DUCHESS! TIME TO CHECK THAT BULLET CREASE ON YOUR ARM...

LATER

WELL — WHEN DO YOU START TO BEGUILE ME FROM MY TASK OF PLANNING FULL REPRISALS ON MY FOES?

HMMM — SOME PROUD FLESH AROUND THE WOUND, AS LONG AS IT'S THERE THE INFECTION MAY SPREAD AND ENDANGER THE ENTIRE BODY...

Steve Canyon

LADY NINE, YOU EXPLAINED TO ME THAT YOUR NOMAD TRIBE IS MOVING SOUTH TOWARD THE BRITISH AND AMERICAN SPHERE OF INFLUENCE INSTEAD OF TO THE USUAL INTERIOR GRAZING COUNTRY...

YES, CANYON! THE UNDERGROUND HIRELINGS LIE IN WAIT INLAND... NEAR OUR USUAL CAMP

BUT OUR FAMILIES AND LIVE-STOCK MOVE DOWN THE SAFE COASTAL ROAD, WHILE WE FORM A SCREEN BETWEEN THEM AND OUR ENEMIES...

THEN YOU DO REALIZE THAT THE BUFFER BOYS WANT TO BAIT YOU INTO LEAVING YOUR SUPPLY COLUMN VULNERABLE!

I WOULD NOT TAKE MY TROOPS — I SHALL GO ALONE!

WHY SO SURPRISED THAT I SHOULD LEAVE MY TROOPS TO GO ALONE TO AVENGE MY FATHER'S DEATH? WOULDN'T YOU, CANYON?

I SUPPOSE I WOULD — BUT A BLOODY SHIRT DOESN'T PROVE ITS OWNER IS DEAD, LADY NINE...

IF YOUR FATHER IS DEAD YOU CAN'T HELP HIM! BUT YOU CAN LEAD YOUR TRIBESMEN!... AND — BESIDES...

BESIDES — WHAT, CANYON?

YOUR NOMAD RIDERS AND THEIR FAMILIES PROBABLY LOOK TO YOU FOR SPIRITUAL STRENGTH AS WELL AS GENERALSHIP IN WARFARE... ARE YOU LISTENING TO ME?

— OH, YES... OF COURSE

CANYON, THE UNDERGROUND AGENTS MUST KNOW BY NOW THAT MY TRIBESMEN'S FAMILIES MOVE DOWN THE RELATIVELY SAFE COAST ROAD — WHILE WE RIDE PARALLEL A FEW MILES INLAND!

RIGHT, LADY NINE! AND THEY'LL HAVE TO ATTACK AGAIN — JUST TO SAVE FACE WITH THE OTHER NOMADS

THEN THEY MUST HURRY, FOR WE ARE ABOUT TO RENDEZVOUS AT A CERTAIN COASTAL VILLAGE, WITH HIRED BARGES — AND A TUG TO HAUL THE TRIBE OVERWATER TO SAFETY

WHO KNOWS THIS MEETING PLACE?

THE LEADER OF MY OTHER COLUMN, MY SCOUTS, THE TUG CAPTAIN AND I...

AND THIS IS THE RENDEZVOUS TOWN — IN WHICH NOTHING SEEMS WRONG ...UNLESS YOU LOOK VERY CLOSELY...

CANYON, THE POINT OF CONTACT WITH OUR FAMILIES AND THE TUG AND BARGES WHICH WILL EVACUATE US — IS JUST BEYOND THAT RANGE ...

YOU HAVE YOUR SCOUTS COMBING THE PLACE FOR A TRAP — I HOPE, MILADY NINE!

WHICH, INDEED, SHE HAS...

THE TUG AND BARGES LIE OFFSHORE AS ORDERED, MY FRIEND

AND THE COLUMN OF WOMEN AND CHILDREN AND ANIMALS CAMPS JUST BEYOND THE TOWN!

THEN YOU MAY RIDE TO SO INFORM THE MAID OF NINE!... I SHALL BE WAITING AMONG THESE FRIENDLY VILLAGERS...

IT WOULD APPEAR, GENTLE COUSIN, THAT THE TEMPERATURE MIGHT SOON BE SUBJECT TO A CHANGE... ART THOU PREPARED FOR SUCH?

AYE, GRACIOUS TOWNSMAN

Steve Canyon

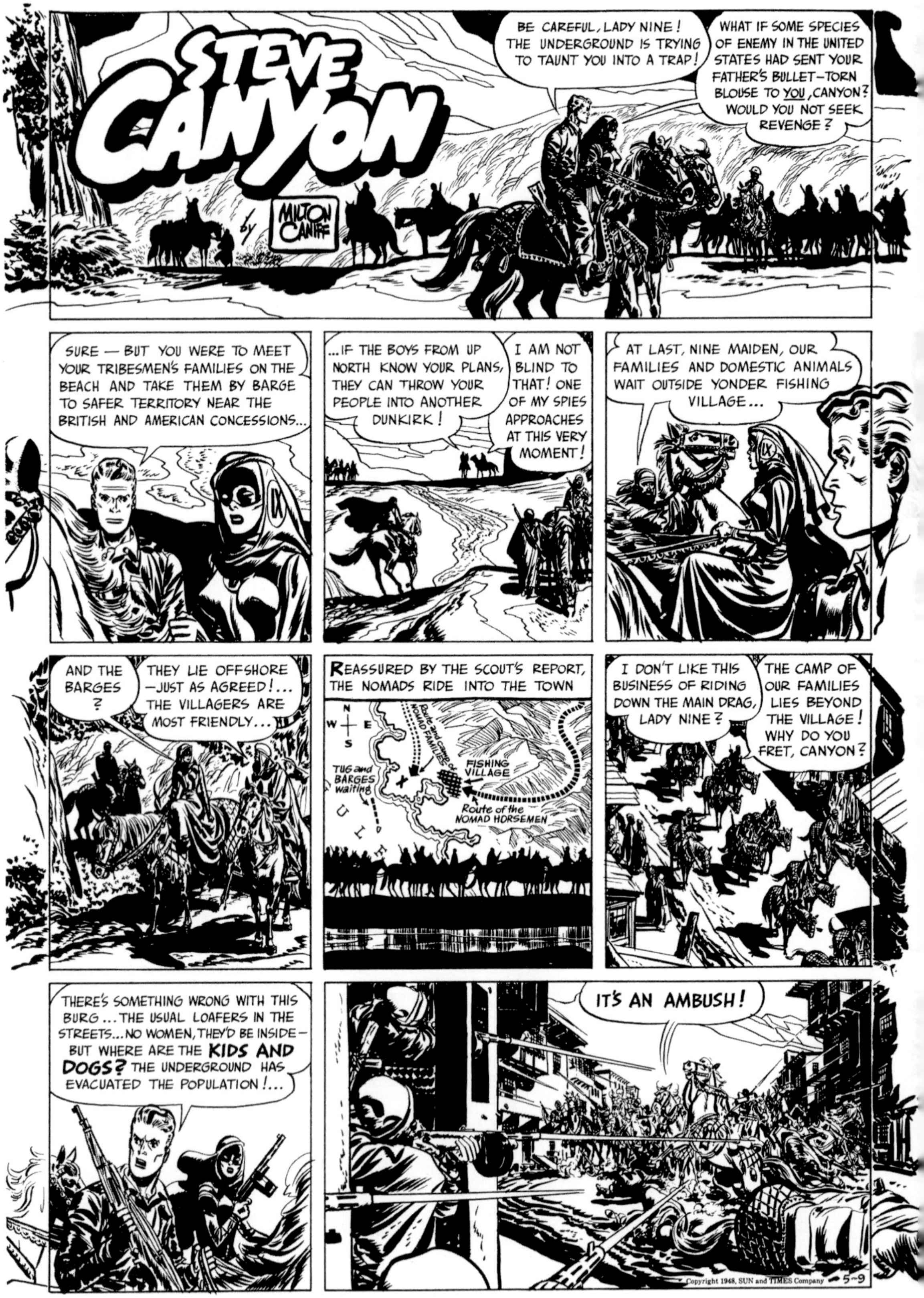
STEVE CANYON
by MILTON CANIFF
BE CAREFUL, LADY NINE! THE UNDERGROUND IS TRYING TO TAUNT YOU INTO A TRAP!
WHAT IF SOME SPECIES OF ENEMY IN THE UNITED STATES HAD SENT YOUR FATHER'S BULLET-TORN BLOUSE TO YOU, CANYON? WOULD YOU NOT SEEK REVENGE?
SURE — BUT YOU WERE TO MEET YOUR TRIBESMEN'S FAMILIES ON THE BEACH AND TAKE THEM BY BARGE TO SAFER TERRITORY NEAR THE BRITISH AND AMERICAN CONCESSIONS...
...IF THE BOYS FROM UP NORTH KNOW YOUR PLANS, THEY CAN THROW YOUR PEOPLE INTO ANOTHER DUNKIRK!
I AM NOT BLIND TO THAT! ONE OF MY SPIES APPROACHES AT THIS VERY MOMENT!
AT LAST, NINE MAIDEN, OUR FAMILIES AND DOMESTIC ANIMALS WAIT OUTSIDE YONDER FISHING VILLAGE...
AND THE BARGES?
THEY LIE OFFSHORE —JUST AS AGREED!... THE VILLAGERS ARE MOST FRIENDLY...
REASSURED BY THE SCOUT'S REPORT, THE NOMADS RIDE INTO THE TOWN
N
W E
S
Route and camp of NOMAD FAMILIES
TUG and BARGES waiting
X
FISHING VILLAGE
Route of the NOMAD HORSEMEN
I DON'T LIKE THIS BUSINESS OF RIDING DOWN THE MAIN DRAG, LADY NINE?
THE CAMP OF OUR FAMILIES LIES BEYOND THE VILLAGE! WHY DO YOU FRET, CANYON?
THERE'S SOMETHING WRONG WITH THIS BURG... THE USUAL LOAFERS IN THE STREETS... NO WOMEN, THEY'D BE INSIDE— BUT WHERE ARE THE KIDS AND DOGS? THE UNDERGROUND HAS EVACUATED THE POPULATION!...
IT'S AN AMBUSH!
Copyright 1948, SUN and TIMES Company
5-9

AGAINST STEVE'S ADVICE, THE NINE MAIDEN'S NOMADS RIDE THROUGH THE CENTER OF THE RENDEZVOUS TOWN — THEN GUNS BLAZE FROM EVERY BUILDING...

AMBUSH!

AS THE NINE MAIDEN'S HORSE FALTERS, STEVE FORCES THE WOUNDED ANIMAL OFF INTO AN ALLEYWAY TO BREAK THE LINE OF FIRE FROM THE BUILDINGS

'TAIN'T LIKE MY OL' SEVENTH CAVALRY CARBEEN, BUT A FELLER CAIN'T HAVE EVERYTHING!

RALLY OUR MEN AT THE BRIDGE NORTH OF TOWN! WE SHALL HOLD OFF THE UNDERGROUND UNTIL OUR FAMILIES BOARD THE BARGES LYING OFFSHORE...

AYE, MILADY NINE!

I SHOULD HAVE HEEDED YOUR WARNING, CANYON!

WELL, NINE LADY, I HEAR THAT SOME OF THE EUROPEAN NEWSPAPERS ARE SAYING WE AMERICAN SAVAGES DO THIS SORT OF THING EVERY DAY — SO WE SHOULD KNOW THE TECHNIQUE!

THE NINE MAIDEN'S HORN RALLIES HER MEN AT THE BRIDGE ABOVE THE TOWN —
...WHERE THEY CAN COMMAND MOVEMENT OF TRAFFIC IN EITHER DIRECTION..

THROW SOME RIFLEMEN ON THE FLANKS TO NICK ANY UNDERGROUNDER WHO TRIES TO SWIM THE STREAM!...

OUR FAMILIES HEARD THE SHOTS AND STARTED TO BOARD THE WAITING BARGES, MILADY NINE...

GOOD...

THAT'S GOOD, BUT THIS ISN'T! A BUS MUST HAVE BUNGLED INTO THE TOWN ON ITS REGULAR RUN — THE BUFFER BOYS HAVE LINED UP BEHIND IT TO CROSS THE BRIDGE — WITH THE PASSENGERS TRAPPED INSIDE — AS A SHIELD...

NINE MAIDEN, THOSE UNDERGROUND JOKERS ARE LINING UP BEHIND THAT ONCOMING BUS SO WE CAN'T FIRE WITHOUT HITTING THE PASSENGERS! — WE CAN REVERSE THAT DODGE!

YES, CANYON?

HAVE YOUR RIFLEMEN KEEP THEM BACK THERE — AND GIVE ME A FLYING SQUAD TO CARRY THESE SECTIONS OF FENCING...

WITH THE BUS TO CUT THEIR ENEMIES' LINE OF FIRE, STEVE LEADS THE NOMADS STRAIGHT AT THE VEHICLE...

Steve Canyon

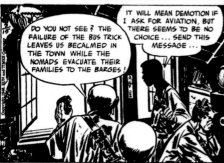

DO YOU NOT SEE? THE FAILURE OF THE BUS TRICK LEAVES US BECALMED IN THE TOWN WHILE THE NOMADS EVACUATE THEIR FAMILIES TO THE BARGES!

IT WILL MEAN DEMOTION IF I ASK FOR AVIATION, BUT THERE SEEMS TO BE NO CHOICE ... SEND THIS MESSAGE ...

THE EMBARKING CONTINUES WITH ALL HASTE, NINE MAIDEN!

BETTER START MOVING BACK TO THE BEACH, LADY NINE...THAT TUG CAPTAIN'S PROBABLY GETTING ITCHY TOWLINES!

YOU AND THE OTHERS MAY FALL BACK ... I TOLD YOU I SHALL REMAIN AND LEARN WHO KILLED MY FATHER!

IN SPITE OF THE AMBUSH BY THE UNDERGROUND, THE MAID OF NINE GETS MANY OF HER PEOPLE ABOARD THE WAITING BARGES—AS STEVE CANYON AND HAPPY EASTER HELP COVER THE EVACUATION...

STEVE CANYON

Registered U. S. Patent Office.

by MILTON CANIFF

HURRY, LADY NINE — YOU'LL MISS THE LAST BOAT!

LISTEN! AIRPLANES! FIGHTERS! THERE WON'T BE A LAST BOAT NOW!

HOW ABOUT THE BUS THAT WAS STALLED BY THE STREET FIGHTING?

THE UNDERGROUNDERS ARE GAWKING AT THEIR OWN AIRCRAFT...

THIS HERE'S TH' FUST TIME A BUS EVER DID WAIT FER ME!

IF THE PLANES SPOT US — JUST ASK FOR A TRANSFER!

THERE IS A CITY ON THE SHORE TO THE SOUTH...IF WE CAN ELUDE THE AIRCRAFT!

Steve Canyon

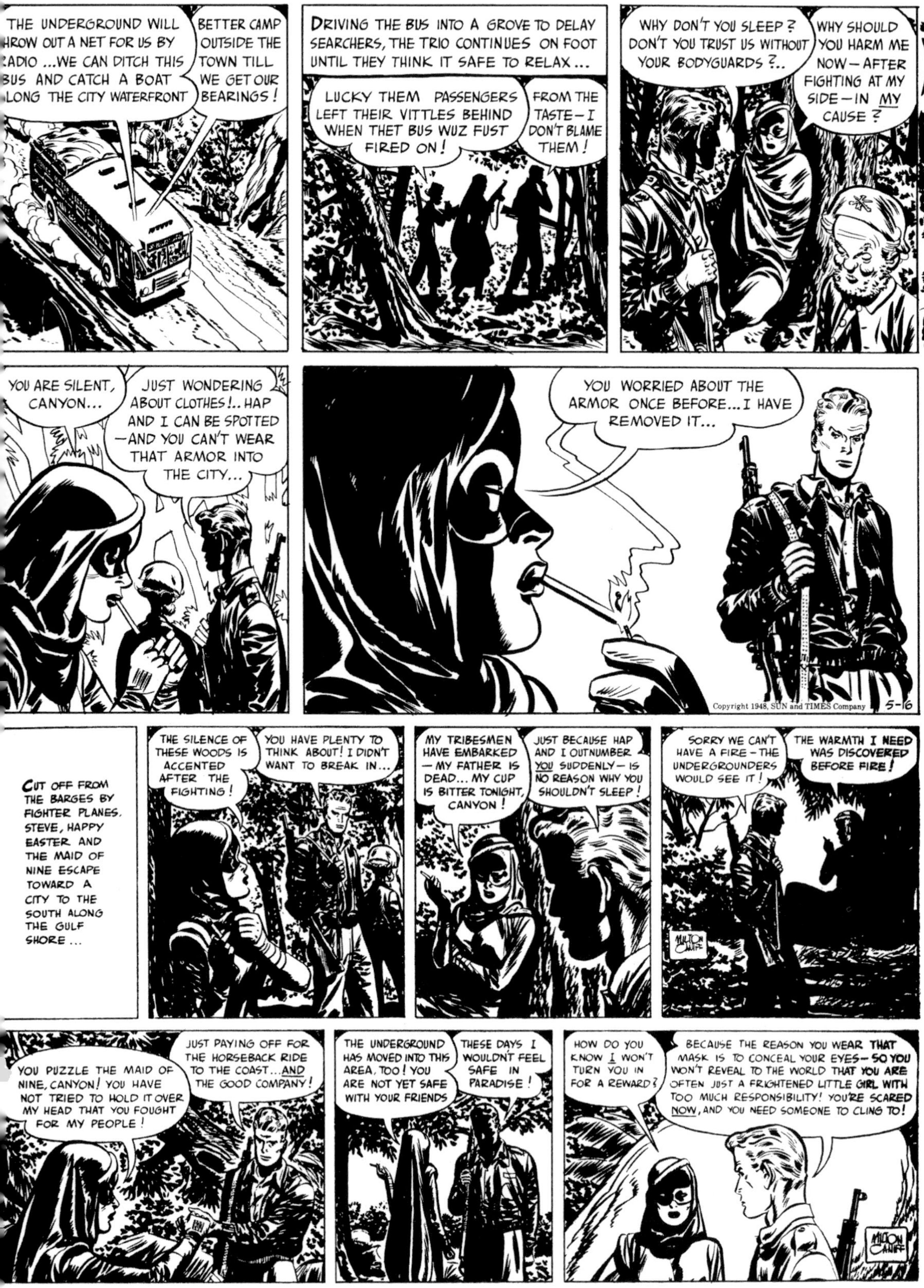
THE UNDERGROUND WILL HROW OUT A NET FOR US BY ADIO ...WE CAN DITCH THIS US AND CATCH A BOAT LONG THE CITY WATERFRONT
BETTER CAMP OUTSIDE THE TOWN TILL WE GET OUR BEARINGS!
DRIVING THE BUS INTO A GROVE TO DELAY SEARCHERS, THE TRIO CONTINUES ON FOOT UNTIL THEY THINK IT SAFE TO RELAX...
LUCKY THEM PASSENGERS LEFT THEIR VITTLES BEHIND WHEN THET BUS WUZ FUST FIRED ON!
FROM THE TASTE—I DON'T BLAME THEM!
WHY DON'T YOU SLEEP? DON'T YOU TRUST US WITHOUT YOUR BODYGUARDS?..
WHY SHOULD YOU HARM ME NOW—AFTER FIGHTING AT MY SIDE—IN MY CAUSE?
YOU ARE SILENT, CANYON...
JUST WONDERING ABOUT CLOTHES!.. HAP AND I CAN BE SPOTTED —AND YOU CAN'T WEAR THAT ARMOR INTO THE CITY...
YOU WORRIED ABOUT THE ARMOR ONCE BEFORE...I HAVE REMOVED IT...
Copyright 1948, SUN and TIMES Company
5-16
CUT OFF FROM THE BARGES BY FIGHTER PLANES, STEVE, HAPPY EASTER AND THE MAID OF NINE ESCAPE TOWARD A CITY TO THE SOUTH ALONG THE GULF SHORE...
THE SILENCE OF THESE WOODS IS ACCENTED AFTER THE FIGHTING!
YOU HAVE PLENTY TO THINK ABOUT! I DIDN'T WANT TO BREAK IN...
MY TRIBESMEN HAVE EMBARKED —MY FATHER IS DEAD... MY CUP IS BITTER TONIGHT, CANYON!
JUST BECAUSE HAP AND I OUTNUMBER YOU SUDDENLY—IS NO REASON WHY YOU SHOULDN'T SLEEP!
SORRY WE CAN'T HAVE A FIRE—THE UNDERGROUNDERS WOULD SEE IT!
THE WARMTH I NEED WAS DISCOVERED BEFORE FIRE!
MILTON CANIFF
YOU PUZZLE THE MAID OF NINE, CANYON! YOU HAVE NOT TRIED TO HOLD IT OVER MY HEAD THAT YOU FOUGHT FOR MY PEOPLE!
JUST PAYING OFF FOR THE HORSEBACK RIDE TO THE COAST...AND THE GOOD COMPANY!
THE UNDERGROUND HAS MOVED INTO THIS AREA, TOO! YOU ARE NOT YET SAFE WITH YOUR FRIENDS
THESE DAYS I WOULDN'T FEEL SAFE IN PARADISE!
HOW DO YOU KNOW I WON'T TURN YOU IN FOR A REWARD?
BECAUSE THE REASON YOU WEAR THAT MASK IS TO CONCEAL YOUR EYES—SO YOU WON'T REVEAL TO THE WORLD THAT YOU ARE OFTEN JUST A FRIGHTENED LITTLE GIRL WITH TOO MUCH RESPONSIBILITY! YOU'RE SCARED NOW, AND YOU NEED SOMEONE TO CLING TO!
MILTON CANIFF

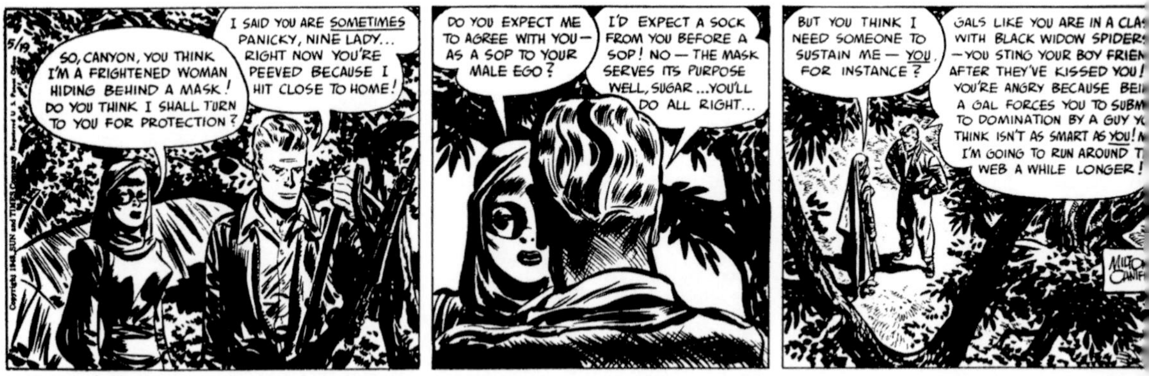
5/19
SO, CANYON, YOU THINK I'M A FRIGHTENED WOMAN HIDING BEHIND A MASK! DO YOU THINK I SHALL TURN TO YOU FOR PROTECTION?
I SAID YOU ARE SOMETIMES PANICKY, NINE LADY... RIGHT NOW YOU'RE PEEVED BECAUSE I HIT CLOSE TO HOME!
DO YOU EXPECT ME TO AGREE WITH YOU— AS A SOP TO YOUR MALE EGO?
I'D EXPECT A SOCK FROM YOU BEFORE A SOP! NO — THE MASK SERVES ITS PURPOSE WELL, SUGAR ...YOU'LL DO ALL RIGHT...
BUT YOU THINK I NEED SOMEONE TO SUSTAIN ME — YOU, FOR INSTANCE?
GALS LIKE YOU ARE IN A CLA WITH BLACK WIDOW SPIDER —YOU STING YOUR BOY FRIEN AFTER THEY'VE KISSED YOU! YOU'RE ANGRY BECAUSE BEI A GAL FORCES YOU TO SUBM TO DOMINATION BY A GUY Y THINK ISN'T AS SMART AS YOU! I'M GOING TO RUN AROUND T WEB A WHILE LONGER!
MILTON CANIFF

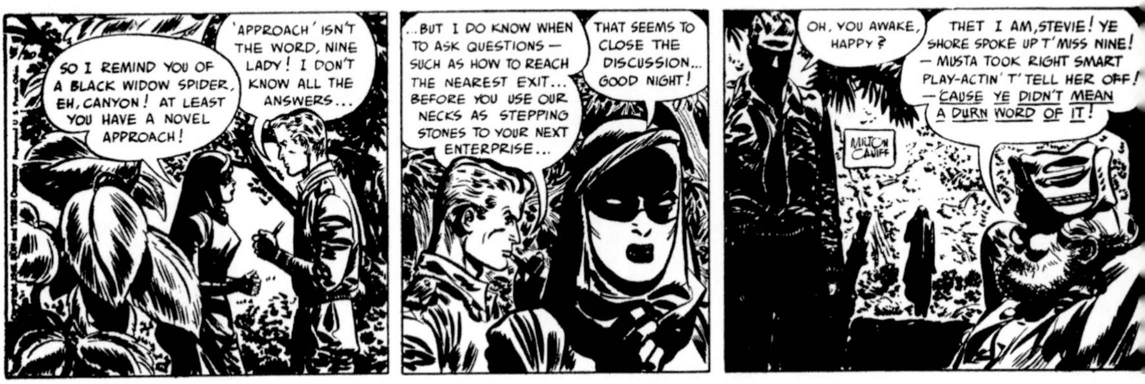
5/20
SO I REMIND YOU OF A BLACK WIDOW SPIDER, EH, CANYON! AT LEAST YOU HAVE A NOVEL APPROACH!
'APPROACH' ISN'T THE WORD, NINE LADY! I DON'T KNOW ALL THE ANSWERS...
...BUT I DO KNOW WHEN TO ASK QUESTIONS — SUCH AS HOW TO REACH THE NEAREST EXIT... BEFORE YOU USE OUR NECKS AS STEPPING STONES TO YOUR NEXT ENTERPRISE...
THAT SEEMS TO CLOSE THE DISCUSSION... GOOD NIGHT!
OH, YOU AWAKE, HAPPY?
THET I AM, STEVIE! YE SHORE SPOKE UP T'MISS NINE! — MUSTA TOOK RIGHT SMART PLAY-ACTIN' T'TELL HER OFF! —'CAUSE YE DIDN'T MEAN A DURN WORD OF IT!
MILTON CANIFF

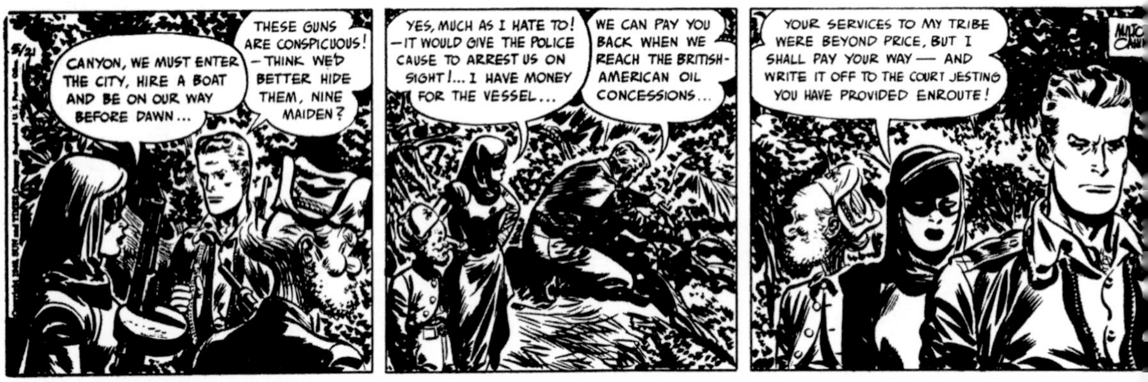
5/21
CANYON, WE MUST ENTER THE CITY, HIRE A BOAT AND BE ON OUR WAY BEFORE DAWN...
THESE GUNS ARE CONSPICUOUS! — THINK WE'D BETTER HIDE THEM, NINE MAIDEN?
YES, MUCH AS I HATE TO! —IT WOULD GIVE THE POLICE CAUSE TO ARREST US ON SIGHT!... I HAVE MONEY FOR THE VESSEL...
WE CAN PAY YOU BACK WHEN WE REACH THE BRITISH-AMERICAN OIL CONCESSIONS...
YOUR SERVICES TO MY TRIBE WERE BEYOND PRICE, BUT I SHALL PAY YOUR WAY — AND WRITE IT OFF TO THE COURT JESTING YOU HAVE PROVIDED ENROUTE!

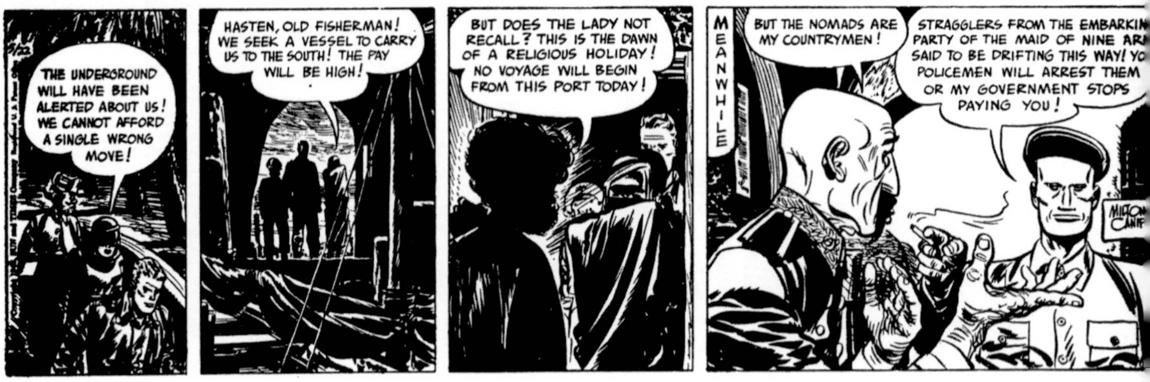
5/22
THE UNDERGROUND WILL HAVE BEEN ALERTED ABOUT US! WE CANNOT AFFORD A SINGLE WRONG MOVE!
HASTEN, OLD FISHERMAN! WE SEEK A VESSEL TO CARRY US TO THE SOUTH! THE PAY WILL BE HIGH!
BUT DOES THE LADY NOT RECALL? THIS IS THE DAWN OF A RELIGIOUS HOLIDAY! NO VOYAGE WILL BEGIN FROM THIS PORT TODAY!
MEANWHILE
BUT THE NOMADS ARE MY COUNTRYMEN!
STRAGGLERS FROM THE EMBARKI PARTY OF THE MAID OF NINE AR SAID TO BE DRIFTING THIS WAY! YO POLICEMEN WILL ARREST THEM OR MY GOVERNMENT STOPS PAYING YOU!

Chapter Three

Operation Convoy

May 24 - September 3, 1948

STEVE CANYON

by MILTON CANIFF

Registered U. S. Patent Office

Unable to find a boatman willing to transport them, Steve, Happy Easter and the Maid of Nine are caught in a coastal town by the coming of daylight....

THOSE UNDERPAID POLICEMEN USUALLY EARN EXTRA MONEY FROM THE UNDERGROUND— BY PICKING UP FUGITIVES SUCH AS WE!

I SHALL 'PURCHASE' THE CLOAK OF THIS WAYFARER BY LEAVING HIM A COIN! THE BAZAARS WILL BE OPENING AND I CAN BUY HOODED ROBES FOR YOU TWO! WAIT HERE!

WHAT IF LADY NINE-SPOT DON'T COME BACK, STEVIE?

JUST TO BE COLDLY PRACTICAL—SHE NEEDS US TO HELP HER GET AWAY FROM THE BUFFER BOYS FROM UP NORTH!

BAKSHEESH, YONKEE! BAKSHEESH!

WOT IN THONDER...?

THEY WANT A HANDOUT... AND WE'RE BUSTED!

HUSH, KIDS! NIX BAKSHEESH!

BAKSHEESH, YONKEE!

WE GOT LAW, STEVIE! DO WE TALK, TANGLE, OR TAKE OFF?

CAN'T DRAW FIRE TO THESE CHILDREN...

THE KIDS CALLED US YANKEES— WHICH MEANS AMERICAN TROOPS WERE NEAR HERE DURING THE WAR!... MAYBE WE CAN CONNECT WITH SOMEONE WHO RECALLS THOSE FAST U.S. BUCKS!

WHAT ABOUT MISS EYE-EX?

....ALL SHE HAD TO DO TO DISGUISE HERSELF WAS TO REMOVE THE MASK! MAYBE WE'RE LOOKING AT HER RIGHT NOW!

Copyright 1948, SUN and TIMES Company   5-23

Steve Canyon

ACCIDENTALLY BETRAYED TO THE POLICE BY NATIVE CHILDREN SEEKING ALMS, STEVE AND HAPPY EASTER SUBMIT RATHER THAN DRAW FIRE TO THE YOUNGSTERS, BUT THE MAID OF NINE IS ABLE TO DON A ROBE AND MINGLE WITH THE CROWD AT A STREET BAZAAR

... SEEING STEVE AND HAPPY EASTER BEING HURRIED OFF BY THE POLICE, THE MAID OF NINE MOVES BEHIND THE BAZAAR BOOTHS ALONG THEIR LINE OF MARCH

Steve Canyon

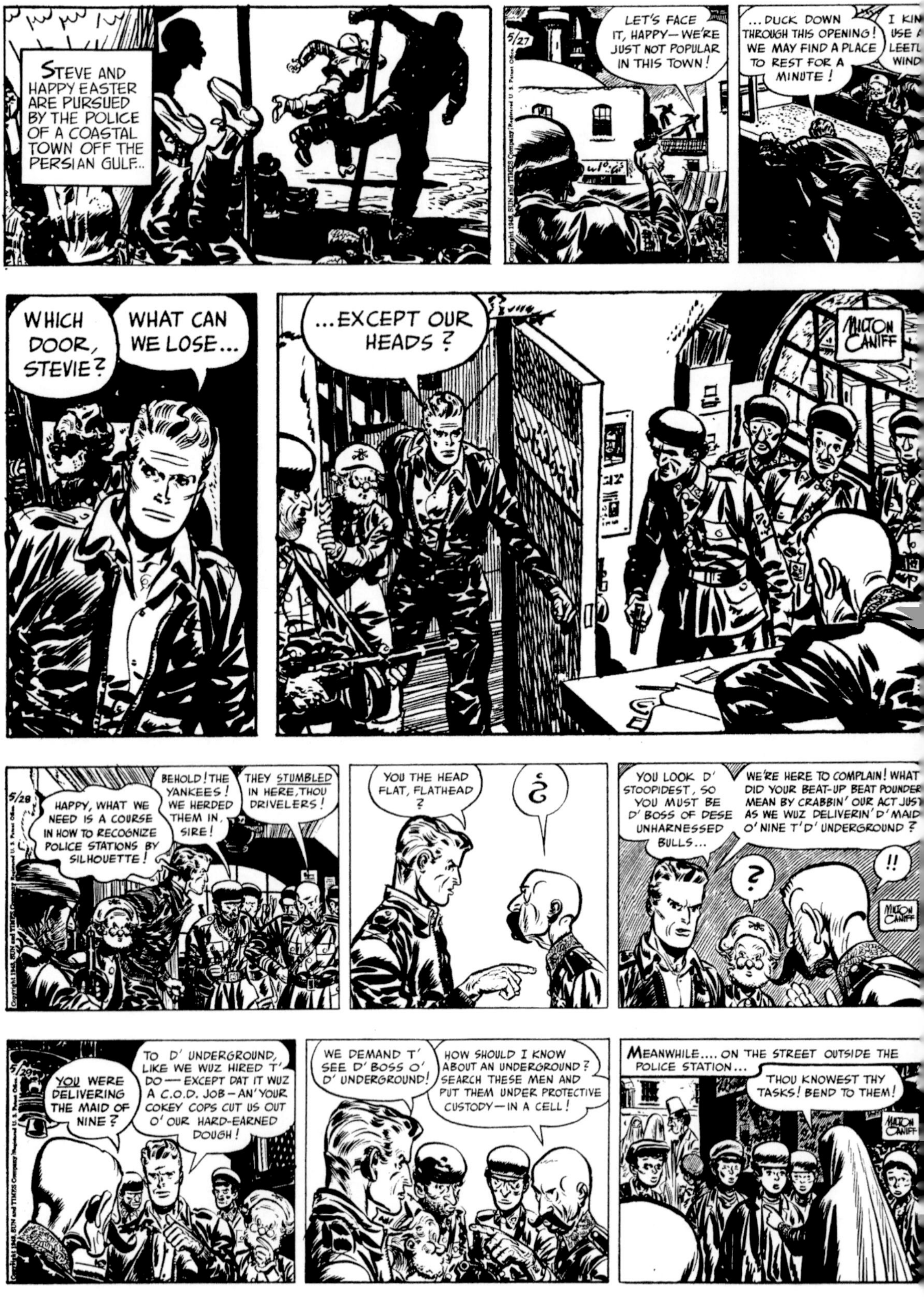
STEVE AND HAPPY EASTER ARE PURSUED BY THE POLICE OF A COASTAL TOWN OFF THE PERSIAN GULF...
LET'S FACE IT, HAPPY— WE'RE JUST NOT POPULAR IN THIS TOWN!
... DUCK DOWN THROUGH THIS OPENING! WE MAY FIND A PLACE TO REST FOR A MINUTE!
WHICH DOOR, STEVIE?
WHAT CAN WE LOSE...
...EXCEPT OUR HEADS?
MILTON CANIFF
HAPPY, WHAT WE NEED IS A COURSE IN HOW TO RECOGNIZE POLICE STATIONS BY SILHOUETTE!
BEHOLD! THE YANKEES! WE HERDED THEM IN, SIRE!
THEY STUMBLED IN HERE, THOU DRIVELERS!
YOU THE HEAD FLAT, FLATHEAD?
YOU LOOK D' STOOPIDEST, SO YOU MUST BE D' BOSS OF DESE UNHARNESSED BULLS...
WE'RE HERE TO COMPLAIN! WHAT DID YOUR BEAT-UP BEAT POUNDER MEAN BY CRABBIN' OUR ACT JUST AS WE WUZ DELIVERIN' D' MAID O' NINE T' D' UNDERGROUND?
?
!!
MILTON CANIFF
YOU WERE DELIVERING THE MAID OF NINE?
TO D' UNDERGROUND, LIKE WE WUZ HIRED T' DO — EXCEPT DAT IT WUZ A C.O.D. JOB — AN' YOUR COKEY COPS CUT US OUT O' OUR HARD-EARNED DOUGH!
WE DEMAND T' SEE D' BOSS O' D' UNDERGROUND!
HOW SHOULD I KNOW ABOUT AN UNDERGROUND? SEARCH THESE MEN AND PUT THEM UNDER PROTECTIVE CUSTODY — IN A CELL!
MEANWHILE.... ON THE STREET OUTSIDE THE POLICE STATION...
THOU KNOWEST THY TASKS! BEND TO THEM!
MILTON CANIFF

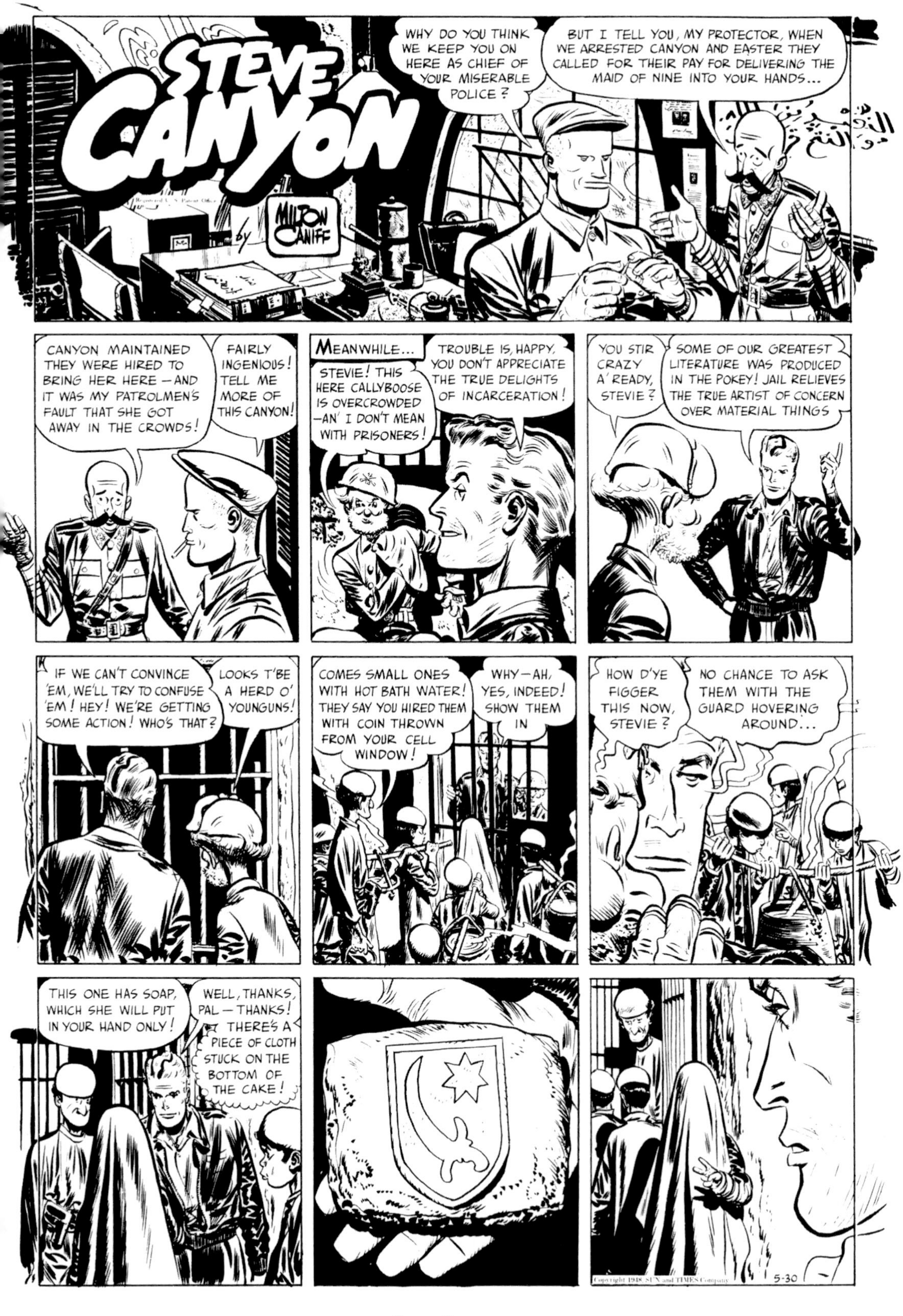
STEVE CANYON
Registered U.S. Patent Office
by MILTON CANIFF
WHY DO YOU THINK WE KEEP YOU ON HERE AS CHIEF OF YOUR MISERABLE POLICE?
BUT I TELL YOU, MY PROTECTOR, WHEN WE ARRESTED CANYON AND EASTER THEY CALLED FOR THEIR PAY FOR DELIVERING THE MAID OF NINE INTO YOUR HANDS...
CANYON MAINTAINED THEY WERE HIRED TO BRING HER HERE—AND IT WAS MY PATROLMEN'S FAULT THAT SHE GOT AWAY IN THE CROWDS!
FAIRLY INGENIOUS! TELL ME MORE OF THIS CANYON!
MEANWHILE...
STEVIE! THIS HERE CALLYBOOSE IS OVERCROWDED—AN' I DON'T MEAN WITH PRISONERS!
TROUBLE IS, HAPPY, YOU DON'T APPRECIATE THE TRUE DELIGHTS OF INCARCERATION!
YOU STIR CRAZY A'READY, STEVIE?
SOME OF OUR GREATEST LITERATURE WAS PRODUCED IN THE POKEY! JAIL RELIEVES THE TRUE ARTIST OF CONCERN OVER MATERIAL THINGS
IF WE CAN'T CONVINCE 'EM, WE'LL TRY TO CONFUSE 'EM! HEY! WE'RE GETTING SOME ACTION! WHO'S THAT?
LOOKS T'BE A HERD O' YOUNGUNS!
COMES SMALL ONES WITH HOT BATH WATER! THEY SAY YOU HIRED THEM WITH COIN THROWN FROM YOUR CELL WINDOW!
WHY—AH, YES, INDEED! SHOW THEM IN
HOW D'YE FIGGER THIS NOW, STEVIE?
NO CHANCE TO ASK THEM WITH THE GUARD HOVERING AROUND...
THIS ONE HAS SOAP, WHICH SHE WILL PUT IN YOUR HAND ONLY!
WELL, THANKS, PAL—THANKS!
THERE'S A PIECE OF CLOTH STUCK ON THE BOTTOM OF THE CAKE!
Copyright 1948 SUN and TIMES Company
5-30

5/31

STEVE AND HAPPY EASTER HAVE HARDLY HAD TIME TO START SPARRING WITH THE SMALLER INMATES OF THE JAIL BEFORE A CONTINGENT OF CHILDREN APPEAR, LADEN WITH HOT WATER AND SOAP... THEY ARE LED BY A GIRL—WHO SLIPS STEVE A....

...PERSIAN GULF COMMAND SHOULDER PATCH FROM THE WAR!

AN' SHE GAVE YE THET 'V' SIGN WITH HER FINGERS, STEVIE!

WHO BE SHE? IS THIS HERE BOILY WATER A TRICK?

MAYBE THE KID WAS TREATED WELL BY AMERICAN TROOPS AND SHE'S PAYING OFF...

MEANWHILE...

THEY CARRIED NO PAPERS, BUT THE TALL ONE HAD THE NAME 'CANYON' STENCILED IN HIS JACKET, MY PROTECTOR!

HIS SPEECH WAS THAT OF THE BAD ONES IN THE YANKEE CINEMA!

PLACE A MAN WITH A MACHINE GUN BEHIND THAT SCREEN —THEN BRING CANYON IN!

6/1

STEVIE, DID YE PUT ON TH' ROUGHNECK TOMFOOLERY SO'S T' MAKE TH' LOCAL LAW THINK WE WUZ SHIFTLESS FELLERS?

RIGHT, HAP! MANY OF THESE PEOPLE HAVE BEEN TOLD ALL AMERICAN CIVILIANS ACT LIKE MOVIE-TYPE MUGS! OUR REAL IDENTITIES WOULD SET OFF A LOUD SPY SCARE!

D'YE RECKON MISS NINE GOT AWAY GOOD? SHE WUZ A HIGH-STEPPIN' FILLY!

CANYON! YOU COME WITH ME

HIYA, HEAD FLAT! IF Y' STOOGE BEHIND D' SCREEN LIKED DETECATIV STORIES, TELL HIM T' RELAX! HE CAN GET MY AUTOGRAPH WIDOUT DAT CHOP-GUN!

6/2

YANKEE NAMED CANYON, WHY ARE YOU IN THIS AREA?

I TOLD Y' ONCE'T, OL' HANDLEBARS, WE WUZ HIRED T' DELIVER D' MAID O' NINE TO D' UNDERGROUND — ONLY YOUR FLATS BULLED IN!... SHE RAN INTO D' CROWD!

...WHO'S DIS HERE CHARACTER?

NEVER MIND!... WHO HIRED YOU TO CAPTURE THE MAID OF NINE?

I AIN'T TALKIN' NO MORE TILL I GET A LAWYER!

WHAT'S Y' FRIEND LAUGHIN' SO HARD FOR?

AT YOUR QUAINT YANKEE CUSTOMS!

6/3

HOW MANY OF YOU YANKEE SPIES ARE IN THIS VICINITY?

CERTAIN PARTIES IN D' U.S. WOULD HOWL T' HEAR ME CALLED A SPY!

THAT'S AN AMERICAN AVIATOR'S JACKET YOU'RE WEARING... THE NAME STENCILED INSIDE IS 'CANYON'

I DIDN'T ASK D' GUY'S NAME I GOT IT FROM...

WE WILL HAVE THAT NAME CHECKED AGAINST YOUR DESCRIPTION... I THINK IT MIGHT BRING FORTH SOME INTERESTING MILITARY DATA!

YOU DO DAT!... AN' GIVE ME REGARDS TO D' F.B.I. WHILE Y' SCHMOOZIN' WIT' WASHINGTON!

OH—WE WON'T CHECK YOUR RECORD IN THAT CAPITAL!

Steve Canyon

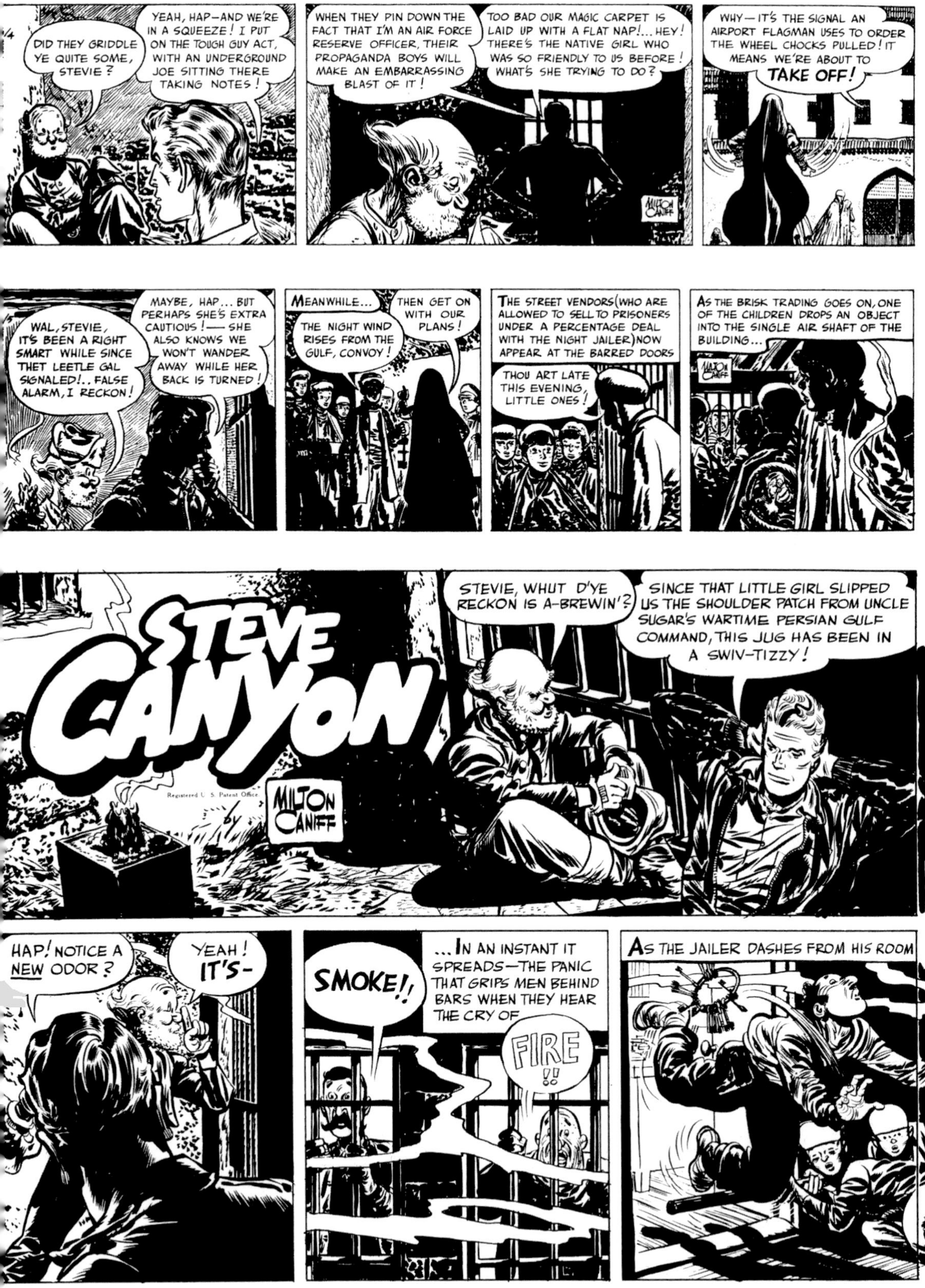
DID THEY GRIDDLE YE QUITE SOME, STEVIE?
YEAH, HAP—AND WE'RE IN A SQUEEZE! I PUT ON THE TOUGH GUY ACT, WITH AN UNDERGROUND JOE SITTING THERE TAKING NOTES!
WHEN THEY PIN DOWN THE FACT THAT I'M AN AIR FORCE RESERVE OFFICER, THEIR PROPAGANDA BOYS WILL MAKE AN EMBARRASSING BLAST OF IT!
TOO BAD OUR MAGIC CARPET IS LAID UP WITH A FLAT NAP!... HEY! THERE'S THE NATIVE GIRL WHO WAS SO FRIENDLY TO US BEFORE! WHAT'S SHE TRYING TO DO?
MILTON CANIFF
WHY—IT'S THE SIGNAL AN AIRPORT FLAGMAN USES TO ORDER THE WHEEL CHOCKS PULLED! IT MEANS WE'RE ABOUT TO TAKE OFF!
WAL, STEVIE, IT'S BEEN A RIGHT SMART WHILE SINCE THET LEETLE GAL SIGNALED!.. FALSE ALARM, I RECKON!
MAYBE, HAP... BUT PERHAPS SHE'S EXTRA CAUTIOUS!— SHE ALSO KNOWS WE WON'T WANDER AWAY WHILE HER BACK IS TURNED!
MEANWHILE...
THE NIGHT WIND RISES FROM THE GULF, CONVOY!
THEN GET ON WITH OUR PLANS!
THE STREET VENDORS (WHO ARE ALLOWED TO SELL TO PRISONERS UNDER A PERCENTAGE DEAL WITH THE NIGHT JAILER) NOW APPEAR AT THE BARRED DOORS
THOU ART LATE THIS EVENING, LITTLE ONES!
AS THE BRISK TRADING GOES ON, ONE OF THE CHILDREN DROPS AN OBJECT INTO THE SINGLE AIR SHAFT OF THE BUILDING...
MILTON CANIFF
STEVE CANYON
Registered U. S. Patent Office
by MILTON CANIFF
STEVIE, WHUT D'YE RECKON IS A-BREWIN'?
SINCE THAT LITTLE GIRL SLIPPED US THE SHOULDER PATCH FROM UNCLE SUGAR'S WARTIME PERSIAN GULF COMMAND, THIS JUG HAS BEEN IN A SWIV-TIZZY!
HAP! NOTICE A NEW ODOR?
YEAH! IT'S-
SMOKE!!
...IN AN INSTANT IT SPREADS—THE PANIC THAT GRIPS MEN BEHIND BARS WHEN THEY HEAR THE CRY OF
FIRE!!
AS THE JAILER DASHES FROM HIS ROOM

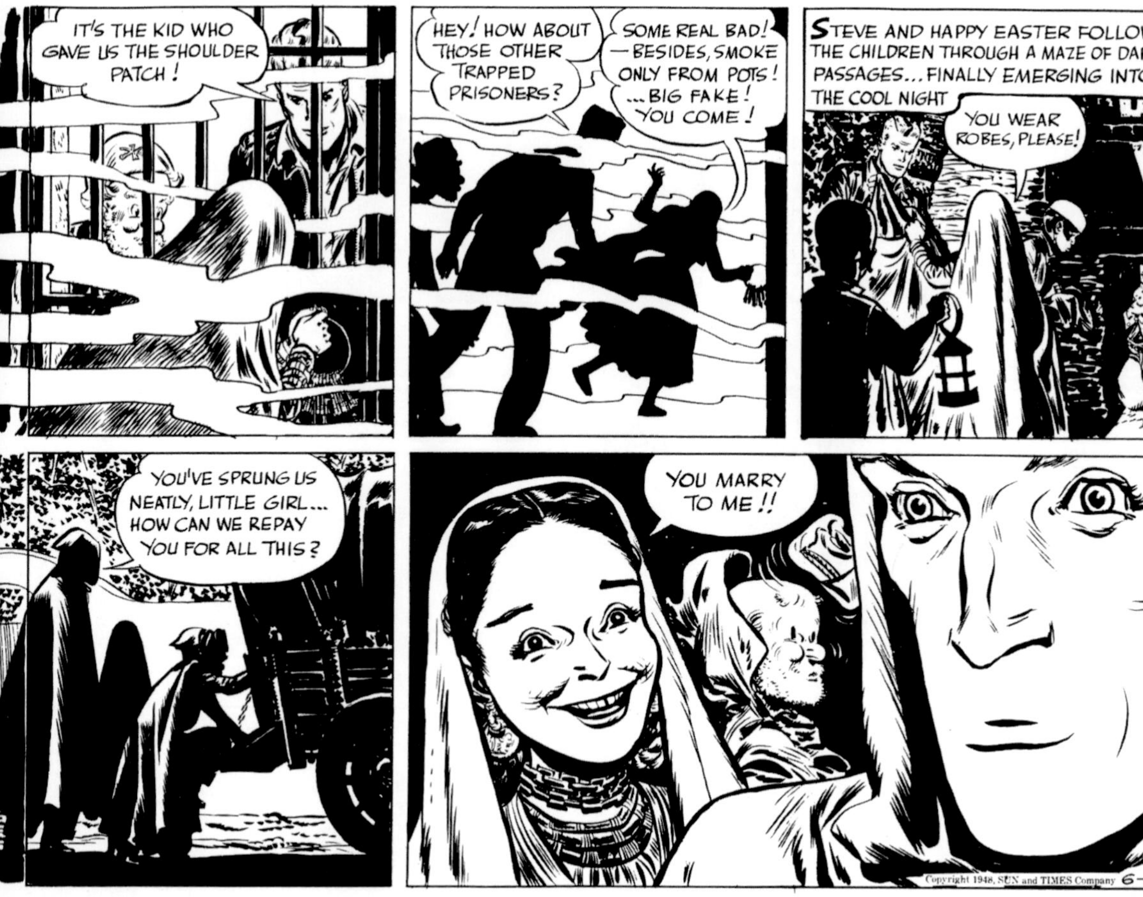
IT'S THE KID WHO GAVE US THE SHOULDER PATCH!
HEY! HOW ABOUT THOSE OTHER TRAPPED PRISONERS?
SOME REAL BAD! —BESIDES, SMOKE ONLY FROM POTS! ...BIG FAKE! YOU COME!
STEVE AND HAPPY EASTER FOLLOW THE CHILDREN THROUGH A MAZE OF DARK PASSAGES... FINALLY EMERGING INTO THE COOL NIGHT
YOU WEAR ROBES, PLEASE!
YOU'VE SPRUNG US NEATLY, LITTLE GIRL... HOW CAN WE REPAY YOU FOR ALL THIS?
YOU MARRY TO ME!!
Copyright 1948, SUN and TIMES Company 6-6

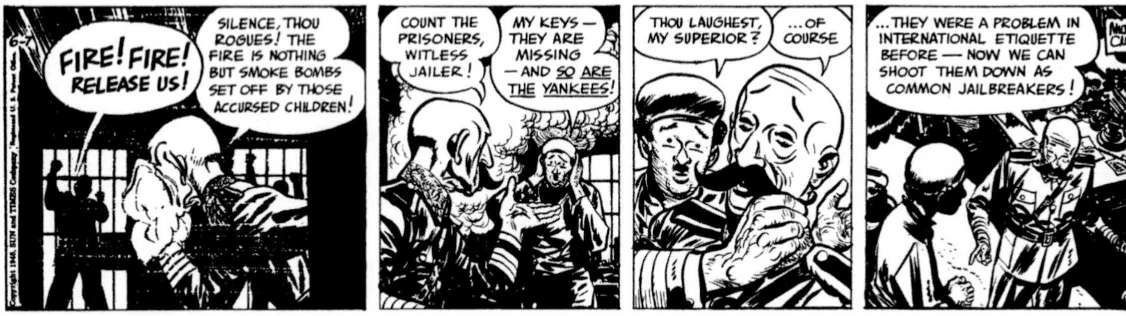
6-7
FIRE! FIRE! RELEASE US!
SILENCE, THOU ROGUES! THE FIRE IS NOTHING BUT SMOKE BOMBS SET OFF BY THOSE ACCURSED CHILDREN!
COUNT THE PRISONERS, WITLESS JAILER!
MY KEYS— THEY ARE MISSING —AND SO ARE THE YANKEES!
THOU LAUGHEST, MY SUPERIOR?
...OF COURSE
...THEY WERE A PROBLEM IN INTERNATIONAL ETIQUETTE BEFORE — NOW WE CAN SHOOT THEM DOWN AS COMMON JAILBREAKERS!

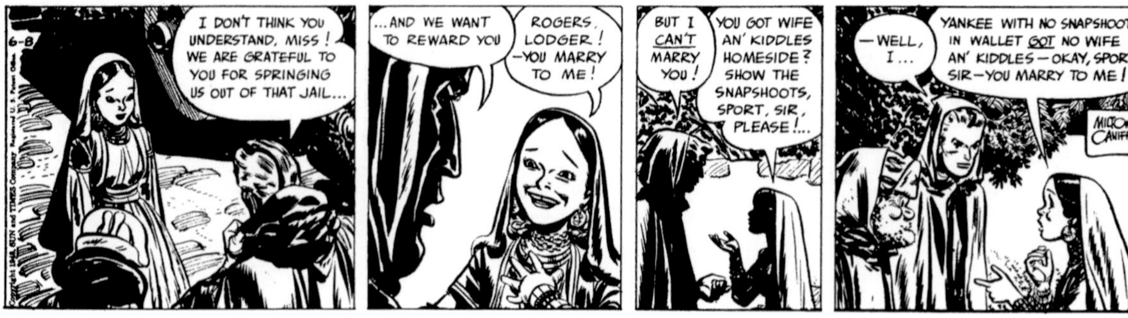
6-8
I DON'T THINK YOU UNDERSTAND, MISS! WE ARE GRATEFUL TO YOU FOR SPRINGING US OUT OF THAT JAIL...
...AND WE WANT TO REWARD YOU
ROGERS. LODGER! —YOU MARRY TO ME!
BUT I CAN'T MARRY YOU!
YOU GOT WIFE AN' KIDDLES HOMESIDE? SHOW THE SNAPSHOOTS, SPORT, SIR, PLEASE!...
—WELL, I...
YANKEE WITH NO SNAPSHOOTS IN WALLET GOT NO WIFE AN' KIDDLES—OKAY, SPORT, SIR—YOU MARRY TO ME!
MILTON CANIFF

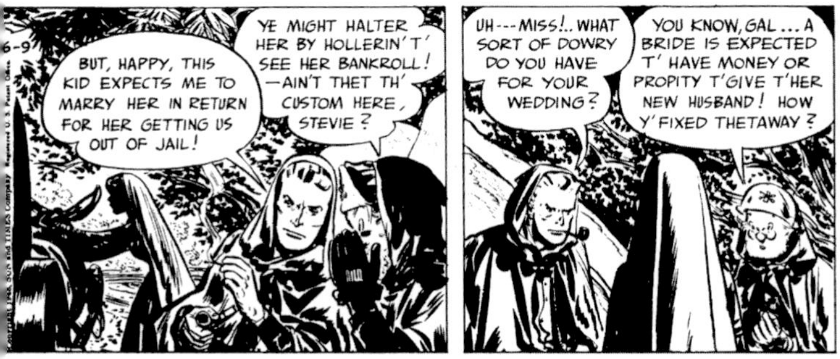
6-9
BUT, HAPPY, THIS KID EXPECTS ME TO MARRY HER IN RETURN FOR HER GETTING US OUT OF JAIL!
YE MIGHT HALTER HER BY HOLLERIN' T' SEE HER BANKROLL! —AIN'T THET TH' CUSTOM HERE, STEVIE?
UH---MISS!.. WHAT SORT OF DOWRY DO YOU HAVE FOR YOUR WEDDING?
YOU KNOW, GAL... A BRIDE IS EXPECTED T' HAVE MONEY OR PROPITY T'GIVE T'HER NEW HUSBAND! HOW Y'FIXED THETAWAY?
U.S. OF A. ARMY LEAVE BEHIND HERE BIG STOREHOUSE FULL UP OF SURPLUS STUFF...
...LOVER, SIR, I GIVE YOU KEY TO WHOLE SHEBANGS!
MILTON CANIFF

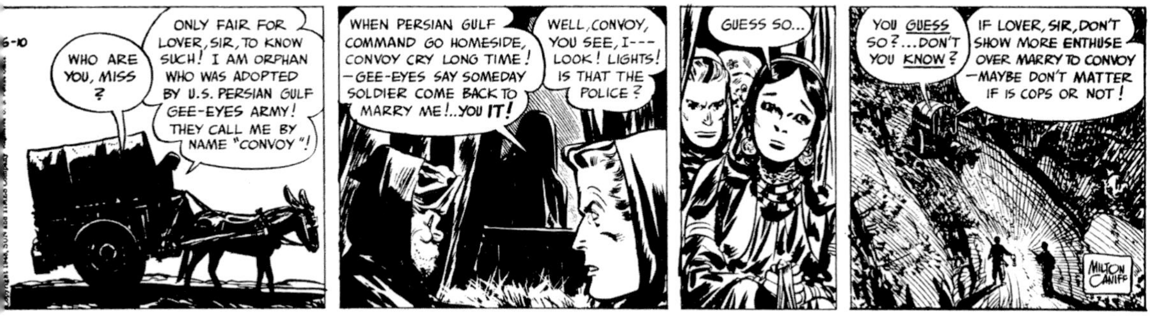
6-10
WHO ARE YOU, MISS?
ONLY FAIR FOR LOVER, SIR, TO KNOW SUCH! I AM ORPHAN WHO WAS ADOPTED BY U.S. PERSIAN GULF GEE-EYES ARMY! THEY CALL ME BY NAME "CONVOY"!
WHEN PERSIAN GULF COMMAND GO HOMESIDE, CONVOY CRY LONG TIME! —GEE-EYES SAY SOMEDAY SOLDIER COME BACK TO MARRY ME!..YOU IT!
WELL, CONVOY, YOU SEE, I--- LOOK! LIGHTS! IS THAT THE POLICE?
GUESS SO...
YOU GUESS SO?...DON'T YOU KNOW?
IF LOVER, SIR, DON'T SHOW MORE ENTHUSE OVER MARRY TO CONVOY —MAYBE DON'T MATTER IF IS COPS OR NOT!
MILTON CANIFF

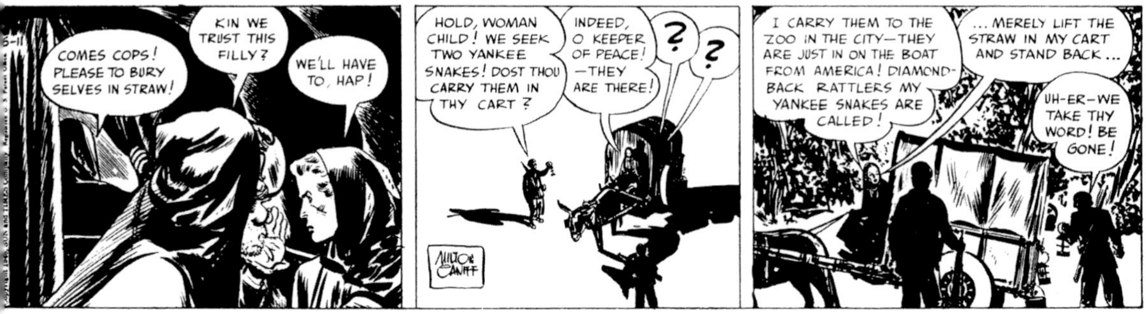
6-11
COMES COPS! PLEASE TO BURY SELVES IN STRAW!
KIN WE TRUST THIS FILLY?
WE'LL HAVE TO, HAP!
HOLD, WOMAN CHILD! WE SEEK TWO YANKEE SNAKES! DOST THOU CARRY THEM IN THY CART?
INDEED, O KEEPER OF PEACE! —THEY ARE THERE!
?
?
MILTON CANIFF
I CARRY THEM TO THE ZOO IN THE CITY—THEY ARE JUST IN ON THE BOAT FROM AMERICA! DIAMOND-BACK RATTLERS MY YANKEE SNAKES ARE CALLED!
...MERELY LIFT THE STRAW IN MY CART AND STAND BACK...
UH-ER-WE TAKE THY WORD! BE GONE!

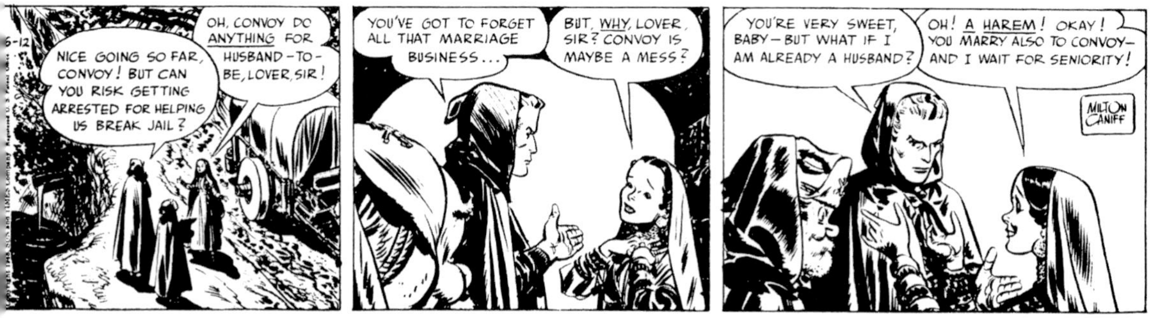
6-12
NICE GOING SO FAR, CONVOY! BUT CAN YOU RISK GETTING ARRESTED FOR HELPING US BREAK JAIL?
OH, CONVOY DO ANYTHING FOR HUSBAND-TO-BE, LOVER, SIR!
YOU'VE GOT TO FORGET ALL THAT MARRIAGE BUSINESS...
BUT, WHY, LOVER, SIR? CONVOY IS MAYBE A MESS?
YOU'RE VERY SWEET, BABY—BUT WHAT IF I AM ALREADY A HUSBAND?
OH! A HAREM! OKAY! YOU MARRY ALSO TO CONVOY— AND I WAIT FOR SENIORITY!
MILTON CANIFF

STEVIE, THEM UNDERGROUNDERS IS REALLY BAYIN', AT OUR HEELS!

I DON'T KNOW WHICH I'M MORE CONCERNED ABOUT, HAPPY...THE BADDIES — OR THE LITTLE GAL THINKING I CAME HERE TO MARRY HER!

YOU CAN SEE WHAT HAPPENED...PERSIAN GULF COMMAND GEE-EYES FOUND A CUTE ORPHAN KID, NAMED HER "CONVOY" AND TOLD HER AN AMERICAN WOULD SOMEDAY TURN UP FOR THE BIG ROMANCE...

I'M THE FIRST WORLD WAR II YANK TO SHOW MY FACE — SO I'M ELECTED...

SSST! THET SOUNDS LIKE LAW OUTSIDE!

HOLD, GIRL-CHILD! WE WILL SEARCH THY CART FOR TWO FUGITIVES!

I AM FORTUNATE TO MEET THEE, NOBLE KEEPERS OF THE PEACE...

I NEED THY HELP! MY RESPECTED PARENT LIES ILL IN THE CART...

ILL?

AYE! SHE IS GRIPPED BY A FEVER... RED SPOTS APPEAR ON HER SICKLY COUNTENANCE! PLEASE HASTEN TO ASSIST HER!

WHY — AH — THAT IS A MATTER FOR THE HEALTH AUTHORITIES! MOVE ON !..BUT AT ONCE!

NICE GOING, CONVOY! THAT LOCAL CHIN-CHIN YOU PUT OUT SENT THE BADGE BOYS AWAY PRONTO!

SUCH IS DUTY OF WIFE-ENGAGED, LOVER, SIR! I --- — QUICKLY, DUCK! REAL DANGER ON DECK!

THE WAY SHE'S DRIVING THIS LATE MODEL ICE-AGE CONVERTIBLE WE MUST BE SIDE-STEPPING THE TOPSOIL OF THE UNDERGROUND!

WITH SUCH RECKLESS CART DRIVERS ON THE LOOSE, IT IS NO LONGER SAFE FOR THE YOUNG LADIES OF MY SCHOOL TO GO WALKING!

6-13

Steve Canyon

CONVOY, HOW FAR DO WE RIDE IN THIS TORTURE RACK?

OH, LOVER CANYON, SIR, CONVOY DEEPLY REGRETS BEAT-UP TRANSPORT DEAL! END OF LINE COMING UP!

OOOH — AT THE SOUND OF THE CREAK IT WILL BE MY CART-IAC CONDITION!... WHERE ARE WE? WHAT'S THIS PLACE?

ABANDONED FORT, LOVER, SIR! ONE TIME DEFENDED RIVER MOUTH!

LOOKS LIKE A GOOD PLACE TO HIDE OUT FROM THE UNDERGROUND AND THEIR POLICE STOOGES!

EVEN BETTER PLACE FOR HONEYMOONSHINES, LOVER, SIR!

LOVER CANYON, SIR, PLEASE TO ENJOY VIEW FROM HONEYMOONER FORT — WHILE CONVOY WHIPS UP CHOW

...UH—YEAH, CONVOY— OKAY!

STEVIE, TH' LEETLE PULLET'S GOT YE TOEIN' DIRT LIKE A SCHOOLBOY

THIS IS A NEW KIND OF SNAFFLE HAPPY! — IT'S JUST THAT I'M THE FIRST AMERICAN EX-SOLDIER TO COME BACK HERE...

I'M A EX-SOLJER, TOO, STEVIE — AN' NO SQUABBIES IS AFUSSIN' OVER OL' HAPPY!

MEBBE I OUGHTA TAKE M'SELF A LEETLE STROLL RIGHT AFTER MESS! MIGHTY FINE SCENERY!

YOU WALK OUT ON ME, HAPPY EASTER, AND I'LL TELL THE SEVENTH CAVALRY ASSOCIATION YOU SECRETLY LIKE JEEPS BETTER THAN HORSES!

I THOUGHT THIS HAD A FAMILIAR TASTE! WHERE DID YOU GET THE U.S. ISSUE RATIONS?

DO YOU NOT RECALL, LOVER CANYON, SIR, I OFFERED TO YOU A KEY TO WAREHOUSE OF SURPLUS WAR STUFF?

BUT THAT STUFF DOESN'T BELONG TO YOU, CONVOY!

OH, YES, LOVER, SIR! MESS SERGEANT GAVE TO CONVOY HIS KEY BEFORE GOING HOMESIDE!

HE SAID PLEASE TO HAND OUT GRUB TO NATIVES!.. SAND-HAPPY SOULS WHO MUST LIVE ON PERSIAN GULF DESERVE PRIVATE LEND — WITH NO LEASE!

I'M MIGHTY SOOTHED! TOO BAD WE AIN'T YET SHOOK TH' LOCAL LAW FROM OUR HEELS, STEVIE!

WE CAN PLAN SOMETHING IN THE MORNING, HAPPY!

...LOVER, SIR, WHERE WILL YOU TAKE CONVOY AFTER WE MARRY TOGETHER? NEW YORK — OR MAYBE HOLLYWOODS?

LOOK, CONVOY, I DON'T WANT TO HURT YOUR FEELINGS, BUT WE CAN'T BE MARRIED!

OF COURSE, NOT WITHOUT PREACHMAN, LOVER, SIR...

WELL, THAT'S SETTLED...

CHECK, CHUM, SIR!... CONVOY'S FRIENDS IN CITY ALL ARRANGED TO KIDNAP PREACHMAN FROM U.S. MISSION! ARRIVE SOON!

Steve Canyon

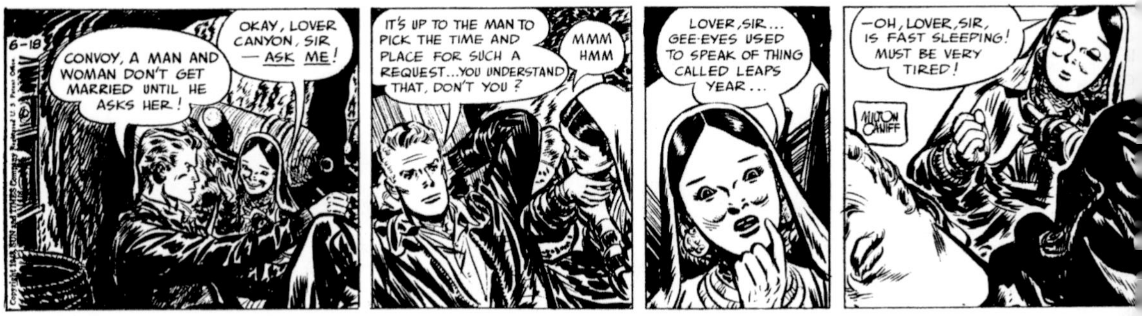
6-18
CONVOY, A MAN AND WOMAN DON'T GET MARRIED UNTIL HE ASKS HER!
OKAY, LOVER CANYON, SIR — ASK ME!
IT'S UP TO THE MAN TO PICK THE TIME AND PLACE FOR SUCH A REQUEST...YOU UNDERSTAND THAT, DON'T YOU?
MMM HMM
LOVER, SIR... GEE-EYES USED TO SPEAK OF THING CALLED LEAPS YEAR...
—OH, LOVER, SIR, IS FAST SLEEPING! MUST BE VERY TIRED!
MILTON CANIFF

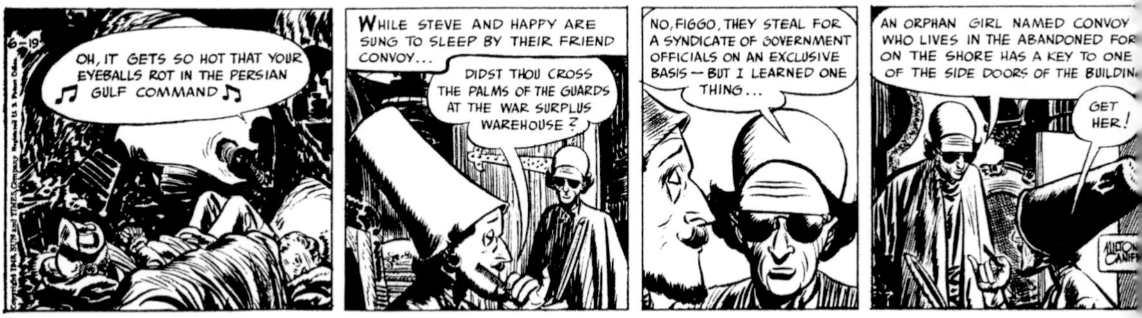
6-19
OH, IT GETS SO HOT THAT YOUR EYEBALLS ROT IN THE PERSIAN GULF COMMAND ♫
WHILE STEVE AND HAPPY ARE SUNG TO SLEEP BY THEIR FRIEND CONVOY...
DIDST THOU CROSS THE PALMS OF THE GUARDS AT THE WAR SURPLUS WAREHOUSE?
NO, FIGGO, THEY STEAL FOR A SYNDICATE OF GOVERNMENT OFFICIALS ON AN EXCLUSIVE BASIS — BUT I LEARNED ONE THING...
AN ORPHAN GIRL NAMED CONVOY WHO LIVES IN THE ABANDONED FOR ON THE SHORE HAS A KEY TO ONE OF THE SIDE DOORS OF THE BUILDIN
GET HER!
MILTON CANIFF

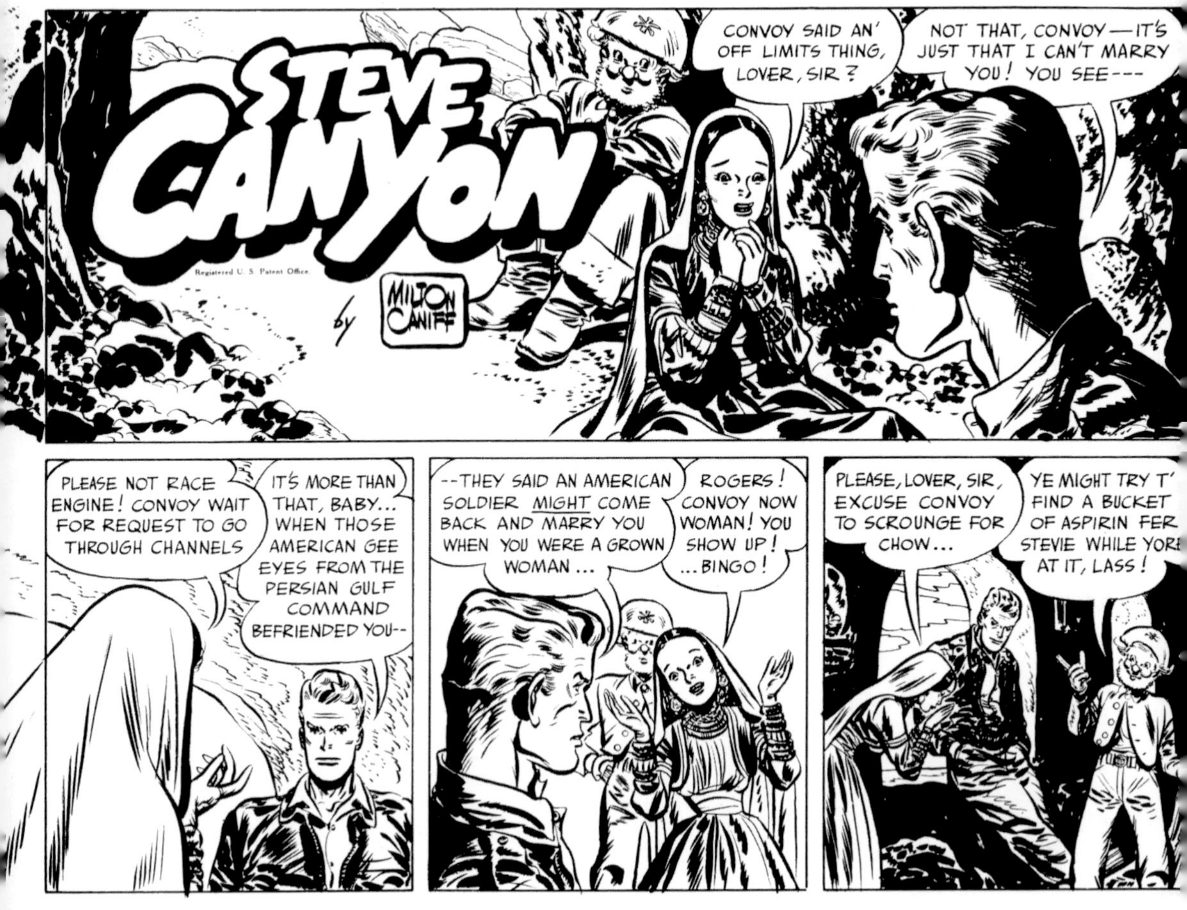
STEVE CANYON
Registered U. S. Patent Office.
by MILTON CANIFF
CONVOY SAID AN' OFF LIMITS THING, LOVER, SIR?
NOT THAT, CONVOY — IT'S JUST THAT I CAN'T MARRY YOU! YOU SEE---
PLEASE NOT RACE ENGINE! CONVOY WAIT FOR REQUEST TO GO THROUGH CHANNELS
IT'S MORE THAN THAT, BABY... WHEN THOSE AMERICAN GEE EYES FROM THE PERSIAN GULF COMMAND BEFRIENDED YOU--
--THEY SAID AN AMERICAN SOLDIER MIGHT COME BACK AND MARRY YOU WHEN YOU WERE A GROWN WOMAN...
ROGERS! CONVOY NOW WOMAN! YOU SHOW UP! ...BINGO!
PLEASE, LOVER, SIR, EXCUSE CONVOY TO SCROUNGE FOR CHOW...
YE MIGHT TRY T' FIND A BUCKET OF ASPIRIN FER STEVIE WHILE YOR AT IT, LASS!

HAPPY, IT LOOKS AS IF I'M BREACHED ON SOMEONE ELSE'S PROMISE!

WAL, YE KIN HIRE A BABY SITTER FOR YORE BRIDE IF'N YE WANTS A NIGHT OUT WITH TH' BOYS!

THE KID'S SERIOUS, HAP... AND SHE COULD TURN US OVER TO THE UNDERGROUND AS EASILY AS SHE RESCUED US FROM IT!

I KNOW, STEVIE! RECKON WE'D BEST HITCH AN' GIT AFORE ALL TINKUM BUSTS LOOSE!

IT'S PROBABLY THE HUMANE THING TO DO...

SHORE! WE KIN SEND TH' LEETLE GAL A REE-WARD WHEN WE GITS BACK T' CIVVY-LIE-ZA-SHUN!

WHY SO MIGHTY QUIET, STEVIE?

I THINK WE'D BETTER STAY RIGHT HERE FOR A WHILE, HAP!

WHUT'RE YOU ALOOKIN' AT THET'S SO MIND-CHANGIN'?

I DON'T SEE A DURN THING!

NOT NOW!.. IT WAS A SUBMARINE — AND IT WASN'T BRITISH OR AMERICAN!

Copyright 1948, SUN and TIMES Company   6-20

IF THIS ORPHAN HAS A KEY TO THE WAREHOUSE FILLED WITH SURPLUS YANKEE WAR MATERIAL, THEN BRING HER TO ME!

AH, FIGGO, I SAVED THE BEST NEWS! THIS CHILD CALLED 'CONVOY' ALSO SHELTERS THE TWO YANKEES WHO FLED FROM THE JAIL!

SHE HARBORS THESE MEN IN THE ABANDONED FORT? THEN THIS WILL BE EASY!

SHE HAS ARMS FROM THE WAR SUPPLIES... WE MUST USE CARE!

THE YANKEES WILL SOONER OR LATER HAVE THE GIRL CONTACT THEIR CONSULAR REPRESENTATIVE! — IF WE KEEP WATCH AND SEIZE HER AS SHE APPROACHES THE BUILDING...

OF COURSE!.. THOU ART ALMOST AS CLEVER AS FIGGO!

YOU SAW WHUT, STEVIE?

A SUBMARINE, HAP! MY EAGLE EYE HAS EASED OFF SINCE THE WAR, BUT I'M CERTAIN IT WASN'T BRITISH OR AMERICAN!

WHUT DOES THET MAKE US?

IT MAKES US STAY HERE UNTIL WE FIND OUT WHOSE SUB IT REALLY IS!

WAL, I'VE HEERD O' FELLERS RUNNIN' OFF T' WAR TO ESCAPE FROM MARRIED LIFE...

BUT I NEVER KNEW A LAD T' RISK GITTIN' A SLUG IN TH' HEAD AND A WIFE IN ONE PACKAGE!

DON'T LOOK NOW, BUT YOU SEEM TO BE MORE RIGHT THAN YOU EXPECTED!

Steve Canyon

73

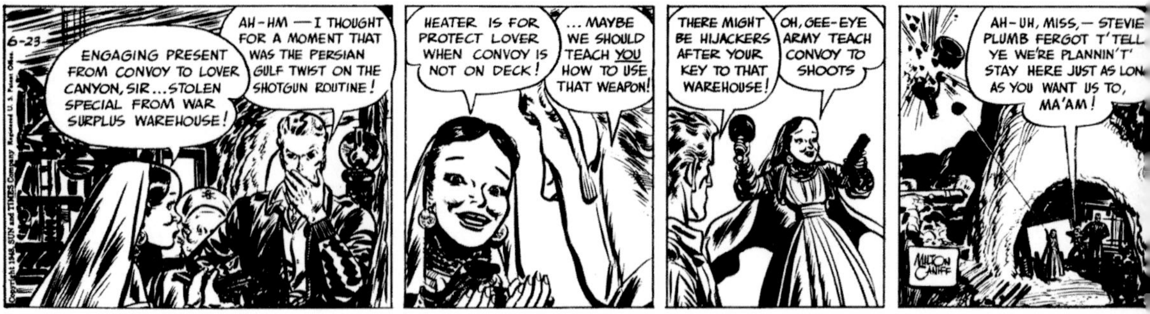
6-23
ENGAGING PRESENT FROM CONVOY TO LOVER CANYON, SIR... STOLEN SPECIAL FROM WAR SURPLUS WAREHOUSE!
AH-HM — I THOUGHT FOR A MOMENT THAT WAS THE PERSIAN GULF TWIST ON THE SHOTGUN ROUTINE!
HEATER IS FOR PROTECT LOVER WHEN CONVOY IS NOT ON DECK!
... MAYBE WE SHOULD TEACH YOU HOW TO USE THAT WEAPON!
THERE MIGHT BE HIJACKERS AFTER YOUR KEY TO THAT WAREHOUSE!
OH, GEE-EYE ARMY TEACH CONVOY TO SHOOTS
AH-UH, MISS, — STEVIE PLUMB FERGOT T' TELL YE WE'RE PLANNIN' T' STAY HERE JUST AS LON AS YOU WANT US TO, MA'AM!
MILTON CANIFF

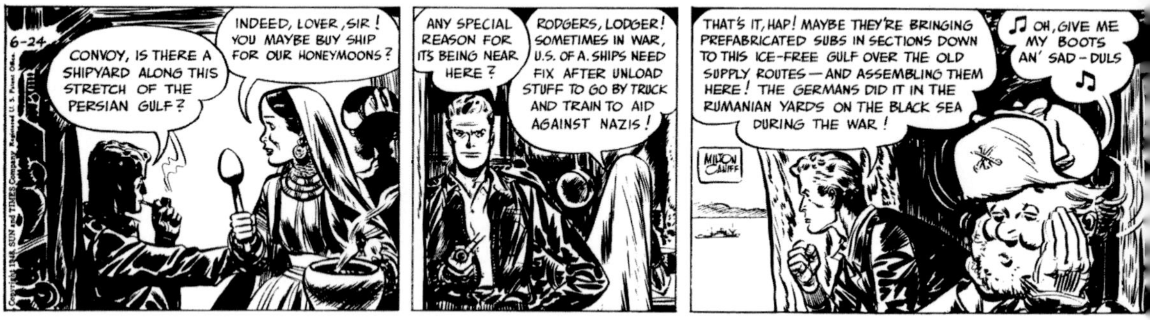
6-24
CONVOY, IS THERE A SHIPYARD ALONG THIS STRETCH OF THE PERSIAN GULF?
INDEED, LOVER, SIR! YOU MAYBE BUY SHIP FOR OUR HONEYMOONS?
ANY SPECIAL REASON FOR ITS BEING NEAR HERE?
RODGERS, LODGER! SOMETIMES IN WAR, U.S. OF A. SHIPS NEED FIX AFTER UNLOAD STUFF TO GO BY TRUCK AND TRAIN TO AID AGAINST NAZIS!
THAT'S IT, HAP! MAYBE THEY'RE BRINGING PREFABRICATED SUBS IN SECTIONS DOWN TO THIS ICE-FREE GULF OVER THE OLD SUPPLY ROUTES — AND ASSEMBLING THEM HERE! THE GERMANS DID IT IN THE RUMANIAN YARDS ON THE BLACK SEA DURING THE WAR!
MILTON CANIFF
♫ OH, GIVE ME MY BOOTS AN' SAD-DULS ♫

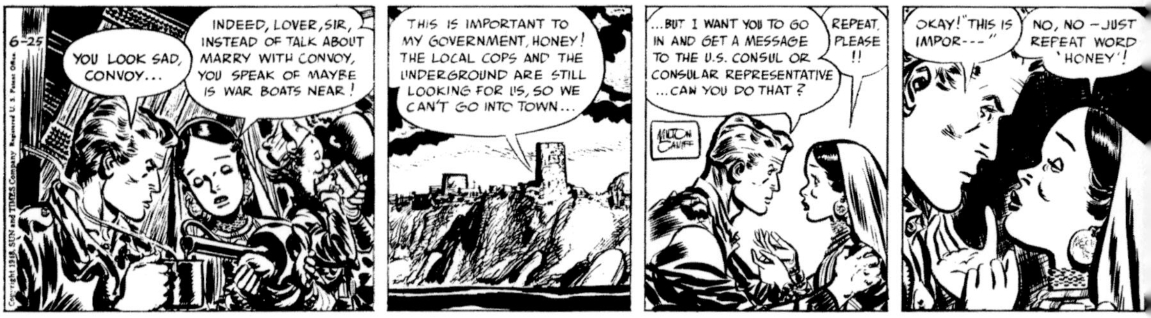
6-25
YOU LOOK SAD, CONVOY...
INDEED, LOVER, SIR, INSTEAD OF TALK ABOUT MARRY WITH CONVOY, YOU SPEAK OF MAYBE IS WAR BOATS NEAR!
THIS IS IMPORTANT TO MY GOVERNMENT, HONEY! THE LOCAL COPS AND THE UNDERGROUND ARE STILL LOOKING FOR US, SO WE CAN'T GO INTO TOWN...
... BUT I WANT YOU TO GO IN AND GET A MESSAGE TO THE U.S. CONSUL OR CONSULAR REPRESENTATIVE ... CAN YOU DO THAT?
REPEAT, PLEASE !!
MILTON CANIFF
OKAY! "THIS IS IMPOR---"
NO, NO — JUST REPEAT WORD 'HONEY'!

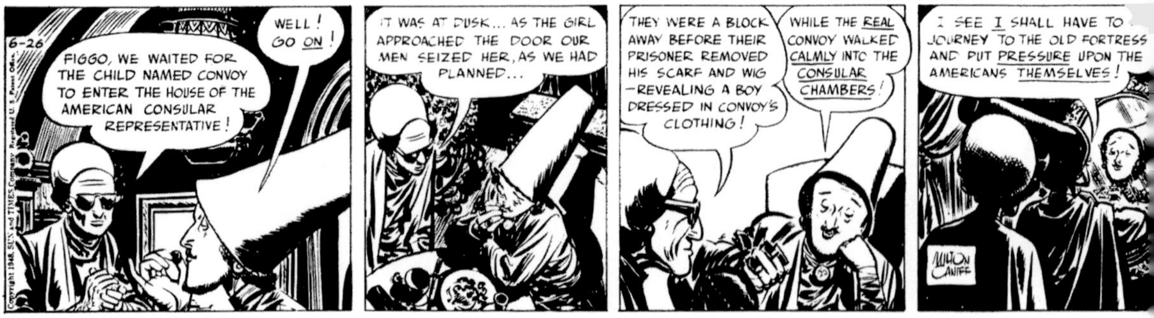
6-26
FIGGO, WE WAITED FOR THE CHILD NAMED CONVOY TO ENTER THE HOUSE OF THE AMERICAN CONSULAR REPRESENTATIVE!
WELL! GO ON!
IT WAS AT DUSK... AS THE GIRL APPROACHED THE DOOR OUR MEN SEIZED HER, AS WE HAD PLANNED...
THEY WERE A BLOCK AWAY BEFORE THEIR PRISONER REMOVED HIS SCARF AND WIG — REVEALING A BOY DRESSED IN CONVOY'S CLOTHING!
WHILE THE REAL CONVOY WALKED CALMLY INTO THE CONSULAR CHAMBERS!
I SEE I SHALL HAVE TO JOURNEY TO THE OLD FORTRESS AND PUT PRESSURE UPON THE AMERICANS THEMSELVES!
MILTON CANIFF

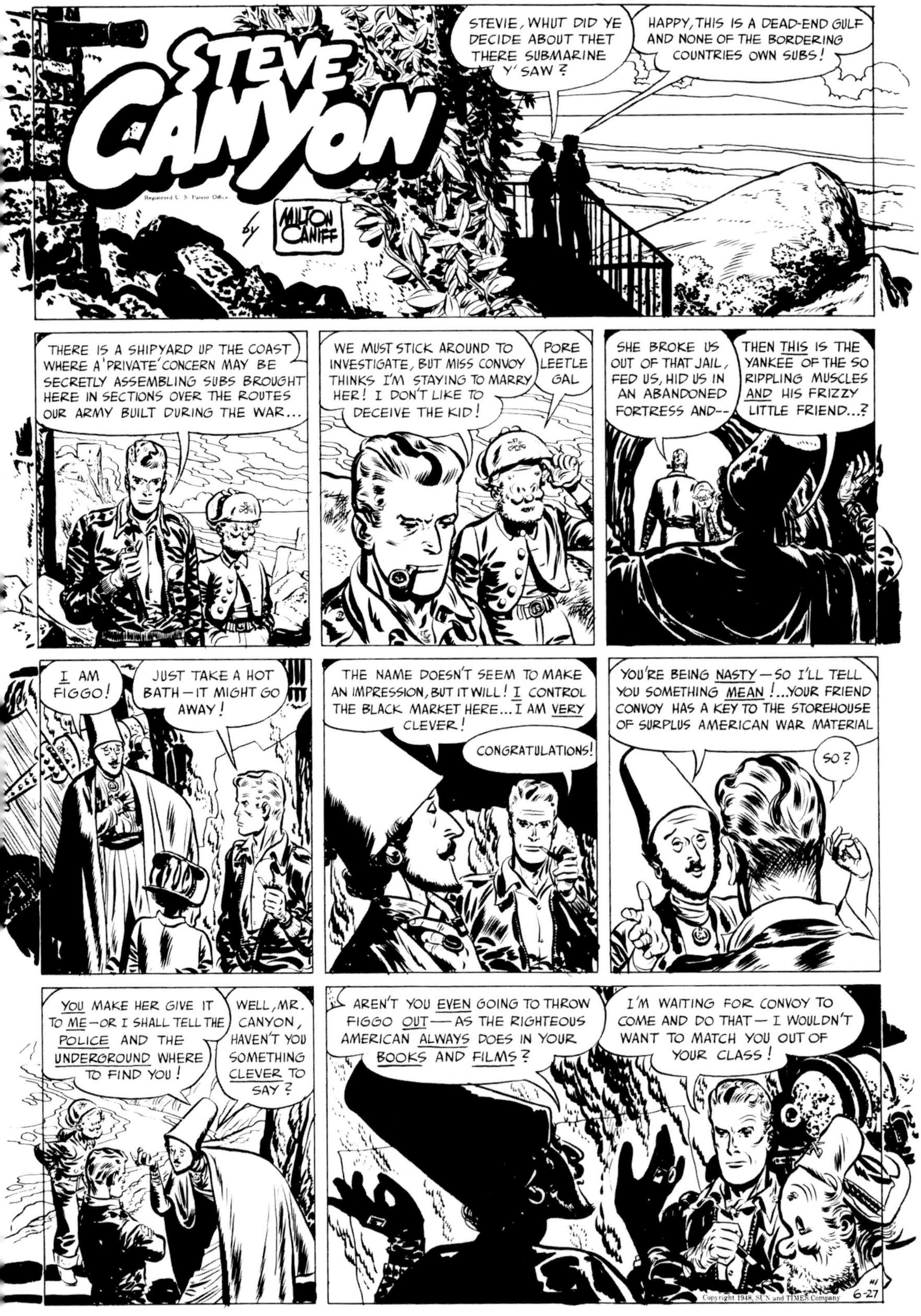
STEVE CANYON
Registered U. S. Patent Office
by MILTON CANIFF
STEVIE, WHUT DID YE DECIDE ABOUT THET THERE SUBMARINE Y' SAW ?
HAPPY, THIS IS A DEAD-END GULF AND NONE OF THE BORDERING COUNTRIES OWN SUBS !
THERE IS A SHIPYARD UP THE COAST WHERE A 'PRIVATE' CONCERN MAY BE SECRETLY ASSEMBLING SUBS BROUGHT HERE IN SECTIONS OVER THE ROUTES OUR ARMY BUILT DURING THE WAR...
WE MUST STICK AROUND TO INVESTIGATE, BUT MISS CONVOY THINKS I'M STAYING TO MARRY HER ! I DON'T LIKE TO DECEIVE THE KID !
PORE LEETLE GAL
SHE BROKE US OUT OF THAT JAIL, FED US, HID US IN AN ABANDONED FORTRESS AND--
THEN THIS IS THE YANKEE OF THE SO RIPPLING MUSCLES AND HIS FRIZZY LITTLE FRIEND...?
I AM FIGGO !
JUST TAKE A HOT BATH — IT MIGHT GO AWAY !
THE NAME DOESN'T SEEM TO MAKE AN IMPRESSION, BUT IT WILL ! I CONTROL THE BLACK MARKET HERE... I AM VERY CLEVER !
CONGRATULATIONS !
YOU'RE BEING NASTY — SO I'LL TELL YOU SOMETHING MEAN !...YOUR FRIEND CONVOY HAS A KEY TO THE STOREHOUSE OF SURPLUS AMERICAN WAR MATERIAL
SO ?
YOU MAKE HER GIVE IT TO ME — OR I SHALL TELL THE POLICE AND THE UNDERGROUND WHERE TO FIND YOU !
WELL, MR. CANYON, HAVEN'T YOU SOMETHING CLEVER TO SAY ?
AREN'T YOU EVEN GOING TO THROW FIGGO OUT — AS THE RIGHTEOUS AMERICAN ALWAYS DOES IN YOUR BOOKS AND FILMS ?
I'M WAITING FOR CONVOY TO COME AND DO THAT — I WOULDN'T WANT TO MATCH YOU OUT OF YOUR CLASS !
Copyright 1948, SUN and TIMES Company
6-27

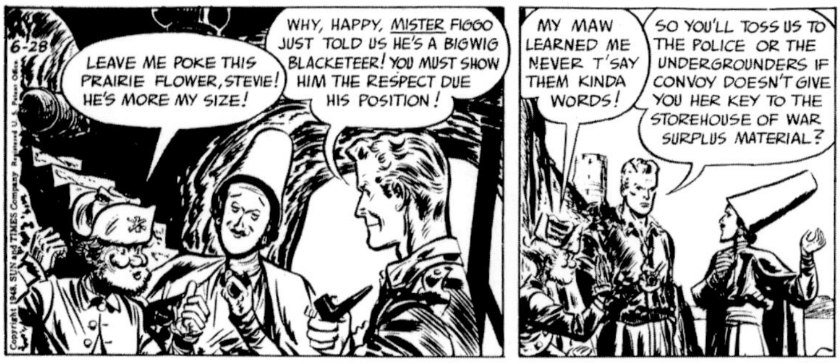
6-28
LEAVE ME POKE THIS PRAIRIE FLOWER, STEVIE! HE'S MORE MY SIZE!
WHY, HAPPY, MISTER FIGGO JUST TOLD US HE'S A BIGWIG BLACKETEER! YOU MUST SHOW HIM THE RESPECT DUE HIS POSITION!
MY MAW LEARNED ME NEVER T'SAY THEM KINDA WORDS!
SO YOU'LL TOSS US TO THE POLICE OR THE UNDERGROUNDERS IF CONVOY DOESN'T GIVE YOU HER KEY TO THE STOREHOUSE OF WAR SURPLUS MATERIAL?
...I'VE THOUGHT IT OVER AND DECIDED YOU'VE GOT US HOG-TIED, FIGGO! I GUESS YOU TALKED YOURSELF INTO A KEY!
?
MILTON CANIFF

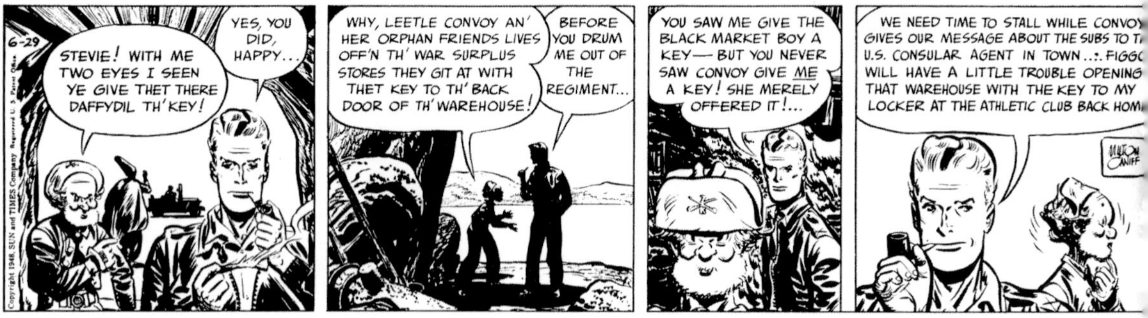
6-29
STEVIE! WITH ME TWO EYES I SEEN YE GIVE THET THERE DAFFYDIL TH' KEY!
YES, YOU DID, HAPPY...
WHY, LEETLE CONVOY AN' HER ORPHAN FRIENDS LIVES OFF'N TH' WAR SURPLUS STORES THEY GIT AT WITH THET KEY TO TH' BACK DOOR OF TH' WAREHOUSE!
BEFORE YOU DRUM ME OUT OF THE REGIMENT...
YOU SAW ME GIVE THE BLACK MARKET BOY A KEY— BUT YOU NEVER SAW CONVOY GIVE ME A KEY! SHE MERELY OFFERED IT!...
WE NEED TIME TO STALL WHILE CONVOY GIVES OUR MESSAGE ABOUT THE SUBS TO T U.S. CONSULAR AGENT IN TOWN...FIGGO WILL HAVE A LITTLE TROUBLE OPENING THAT WAREHOUSE WITH THE KEY TO MY LOCKER AT THE ATHLETIC CLUB BACK HOM
MILTON CANIFF

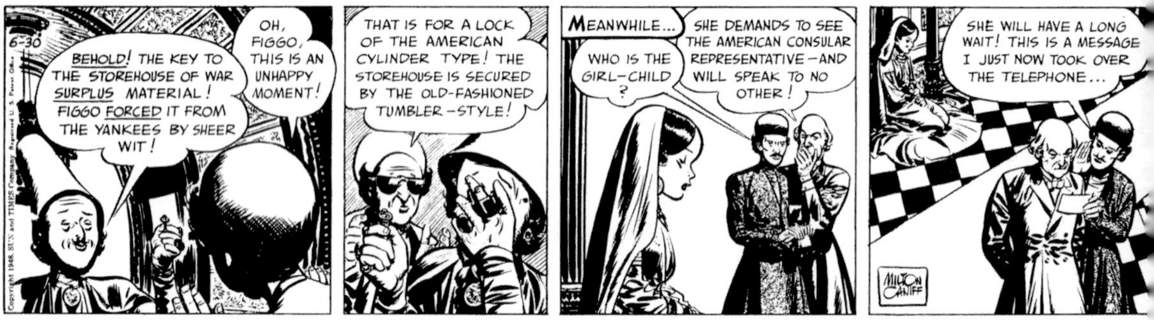
6-30
BEHOLD! THE KEY TO THE STOREHOUSE OF WAR SURPLUS MATERIAL! FIGGO FORCED IT FROM THE YANKEES BY SHEER WIT!
OH, FIGGO, THIS IS AN UNHAPPY MOMENT!
THAT IS FOR A LOCK OF THE AMERICAN CYLINDER TYPE! THE STOREHOUSE IS SECURED BY THE OLD-FASHIONED TUMBLER-STYLE!
MEANWHILE...
WHO IS THE GIRL-CHILD?
SHE DEMANDS TO SEE THE AMERICAN CONSULAR REPRESENTATIVE—AND WILL SPEAK TO NO OTHER!
SHE WILL HAVE A LONG WAIT! THIS IS A MESSAGE I JUST NOW TOOK OVER THE TELEPHONE...
MILTON CANIFF

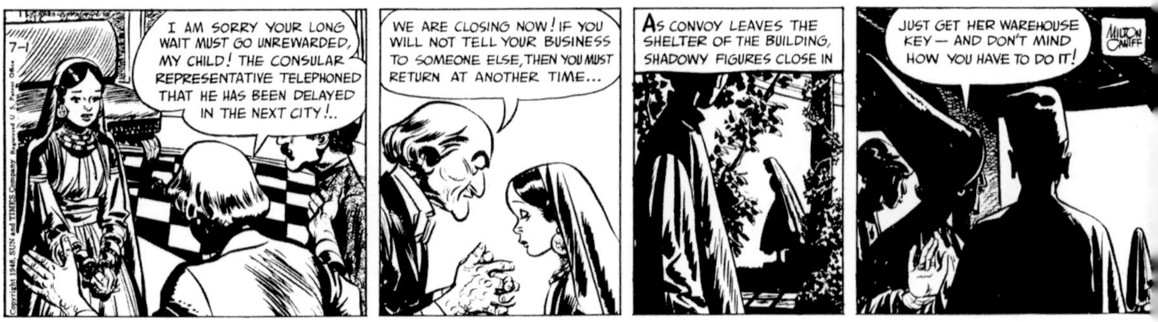
7-1
I AM SORRY YOUR LONG WAIT MUST GO UNREWARDED, MY CHILD! THE CONSULAR REPRESENTATIVE TELEPHONED THAT HE HAS BEEN DELAYED IN THE NEXT CITY!..
WE ARE CLOSING NOW! IF YOU WILL NOT TELL YOUR BUSINESS TO SOMEONE ELSE, THEN YOU MUST RETURN AT ANOTHER TIME...
AS CONVOY LEAVES THE SHELTER OF THE BUILDING, SHADOWY FIGURES CLOSE IN
JUST GET HER WAREHOUSE KEY— AND DON'T MIND HOW YOU HAVE TO DO IT!
MILTON CANIFF

BEHOLD! WE GAIN ON THE GIRL NAMED CONVOY— BUT WE ARE BEING FOLLOWED!

SHE HAS LED US TO A LONELY SECTION...

PERHAPS WE SHOULD TURN BACK...

THEY ARE MERE CHILDREN—

...BUT TINY ANTS CAN STRIP THE FLESH FROM YOUR BONES IN A FEW SECONDS...IF THERE ARE ENOUGH OF THEM...

FIGGO— OUR MEN WERE BEATEN BY YOUNG HOODLUMS AS THEY TRIED TO CATCH THE CHILD NAMED CONVOY!

OH, TO BE FOILED BY A FEMALE IS JUST— OH, DEAR, IT IS SIMPLY INFURIATING!

NOW IT IS MORE THAN POSSESSION OF THE STOREHOUSE KEY— FIGGO SHALL HAVE PAYMENT IN FULL FROM BOTH THAT URCHIN AND THE TWO YANKEES!

MEANWHILE...
I SEE IT, TOO, STEVIE! YOU KIN BET IT'S A U-BOAT!

IT'S HEADING FOR THE NEAR-BY SHIPYARD! WHEN CONVOY COMES, WE'RE GOING UP THERE AND BE SUBVERSIVE AMONG THE SUBMARINES!

STEVIE, D'YE RECKON THET DAFFYDIL TURNED US IN TO TH' LAW— OR TO TH' UNDERGROUND —LIKE HE ALLOWED T'DO?

...CAN'T BE SURE, HAPPY —BUT WE WON'T LEAVE LITTLE CONVOY TO BUCK MR. FIGGO AND THE LOCAL BLACKETEERS ALL BY HERSELF!

ALSO, WE'RE GOING TO FIND OUT WHY THOSE SUBMARINES KEEP COMING OUT OF A NARROW, DEAD-END GULF!

OUR CONVOY FILLY AIN'T AROUND... RECKON THET RUSTLY RUSTLER DID HER ANY HURT?

LISTEN! SHOTS! FIGGO MUST HAVE SICKED THE COPS ON US!

HE SAID HE WOULD IF CONVOY DIDN'T GIVE HIM THE KEY TO THE WAREHOUSE FULL OF SURPLUS AMERICAN WAR MATERIAL!

TH' FIRIN'S COMIN FROM TH' MAIN PATH!

Steve Canyon

KIN WE GIT AWAY BY TH' CLIFF?

THE TIDE COVERS... THE PATH!

WE'RE TRAPPED, HAPPY!

'PEARS SO!

NOTHING TO DO BUT SLUG IT OUT WHEN THEY COME AROUND THE BEND!

I'M BRACED FER [...] LISTEN! THEY'R[...] A-SCREECHIN' SOMETHIN'—LIKE AMERICKY INJUN[...] ON TH' WARPATH

♪ YONKEE DUDDLE KIB IT OP YONKEE DUDDLE DENDY ♪

MINE D' MOOSIC AN[...] D' STEB AN' WIT' D[...] GELS BE HENDY[...]

Copyright 1948, SUN and TIMES Company   7-[...]

CONVOY, HAPPY AND I FEEL CERTAIN THE SUBMARINES WE'VE SEEN ARE CONNECTED WITH THAT SHIPYARD UP THE COAST...

WE'RE GOING UP THERE TO LOOK FOR OURSELVES

OH, LOVER CANYON, SIR, CONVOY WILL GO ALONG---

NO, BABY, YOU WILL TAKE A LETTER TO THE U.S. AUTHORITIES IN THE MAIN PORT—TO TELL THEM WHAT'S UP, IN CASE WE DON'T COME BACK!

MILTON CANIFF

MEANWHILE....

FIGGO, THE BLACK MARKETEER, WANTS NO PAY FOR TELLING WHERE WE MAY FIND CANYON AND EASTER?

IT SHALL BE PAY ENOUGH TO SE[...] WHAT YOU OF TH[...] UNDERGROUND[...] WILL DO TO TH[...] MAN WHO MAD[...] FIGGO APPEA[...] THE FOOL!

THE AMERICAN CONSUL WOULD PROBABLY STOP US IF HE KNEW HAP AND I WERE GOING TO TRACK THOSE SUBS DOWN TO THAT 'NEUTRAL' SHIPYARD...

OH, LOVER CANYON, SIR...

...BUT THIS LETTER WILL TELL HIM THE STORY— IN CASE WE HIT A SNAG...

CONVOY MUST BE THERE TO PROTECT YOU!

YOU MUST CARRY THE LETTER! IT WILL BE OF GREAT IMPORTANCE TO OUR ARMS PROGRAM!

MILTON CANIFF

THAT IS DIFFERENCE! CONVOY DELIVER ON DOUBLE— START BIG ARMS PROGRAM WITH LOVER, SIR, JUST AS SOON AS COME BACK

Steve Canyon

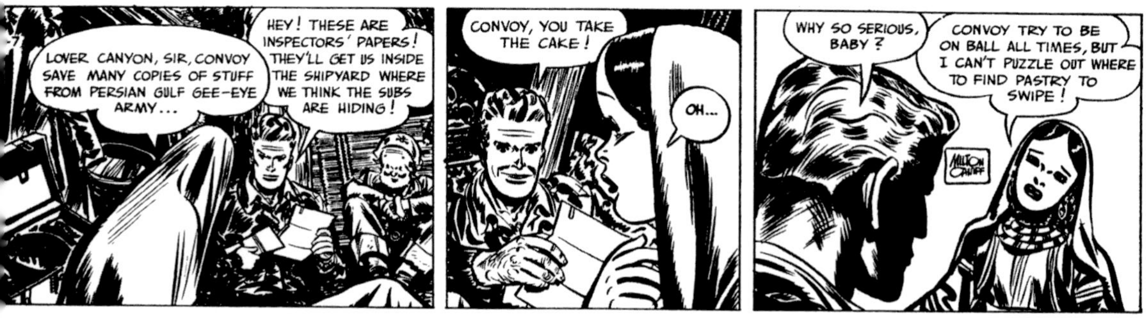
LOVER CANYON, SIR, CONVOY SAVE MANY COPIES OF STUFF FROM PERSIAN GULF GEE-EYE ARMY...
HEY! THESE ARE INSPECTORS' PAPERS! THEY'LL GET US INSIDE THE SHIPYARD WHERE WE THINK THE SUBS ARE HIDING!
CONVOY, YOU TAKE THE CAKE!
OH...
WHY SO SERIOUS, BABY?
CONVOY TRY TO BE ON BALL ALL TIMES, BUT I CAN'T PUZZLE OUT WHERE TO FIND PASTRY TO SWIPE!
MILTON CANIFF

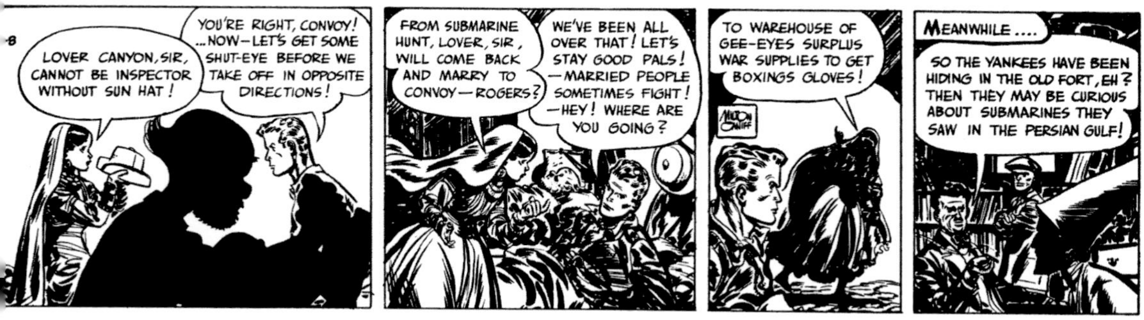
LOVER CANYON, SIR, CANNOT BE INSPECTOR WITHOUT SUN HAT!
YOU'RE RIGHT, CONVOY! ..NOW—LET'S GET SOME SHUT-EYE BEFORE WE TAKE OFF IN OPPOSITE DIRECTIONS!
FROM SUBMARINE HUNT, LOVER, SIR, WILL COME BACK AND MARRY TO CONVOY—ROGERS?
WE'VE BEEN ALL OVER THAT! LET'S STAY GOOD PALS! —MARRIED PEOPLE SOMETIMES FIGHT! —HEY! WHERE ARE YOU GOING?
TO WAREHOUSE OF GEE-EYES SURPLUS WAR SUPPLIES TO GET BOXINGS GLOVES!
MILTON CANIFF
MEANWHILE....
SO THE YANKEES HAVE BEEN HIDING IN THE OLD FORT, EH? THEN THEY MAY BE CURIOUS ABOUT SUBMARINES THEY SAW IN THE PERSIAN GULF!

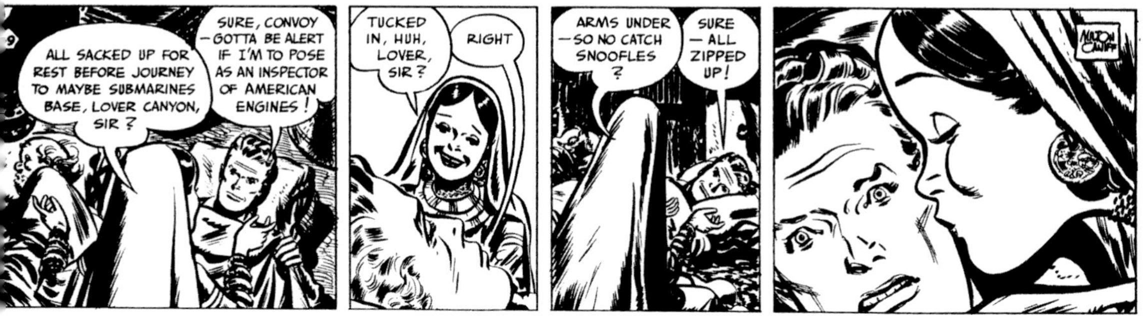
ALL SACKED UP FOR REST BEFORE JOURNEY TO MAYBE SUBMARINES BASE, LOVER CANYON, SIR?
SURE, CONVOY —GOTTA BE ALERT IF I'M TO POSE AS AN INSPECTOR OF AMERICAN ENGINES!
TUCKED IN, HUH, LOVER, SIR?
RIGHT
ARMS UNDER —SO NO CATCH SNOOFLES?
SURE —ALL ZIPPED UP!
MILTON CANIFF

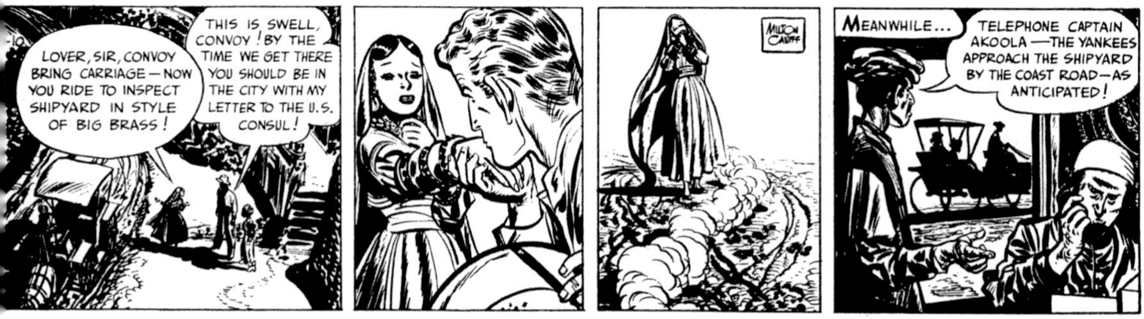
LOVER, SIR, CONVOY BRING CARRIAGE—NOW YOU RIDE TO INSPECT SHIPYARD IN STYLE OF BIG BRASS!
THIS IS SWELL, CONVOY! BY THE TIME WE GET THERE YOU SHOULD BE IN THE CITY WITH MY LETTER TO THE U.S. CONSUL!
MILTON CANIFF
MEANWHILE...
TELEPHONE CAPTAIN AKOOLA —THE YANKEES APPROACH THE SHIPYARD BY THE COAST ROAD—AS ANTICIPATED!

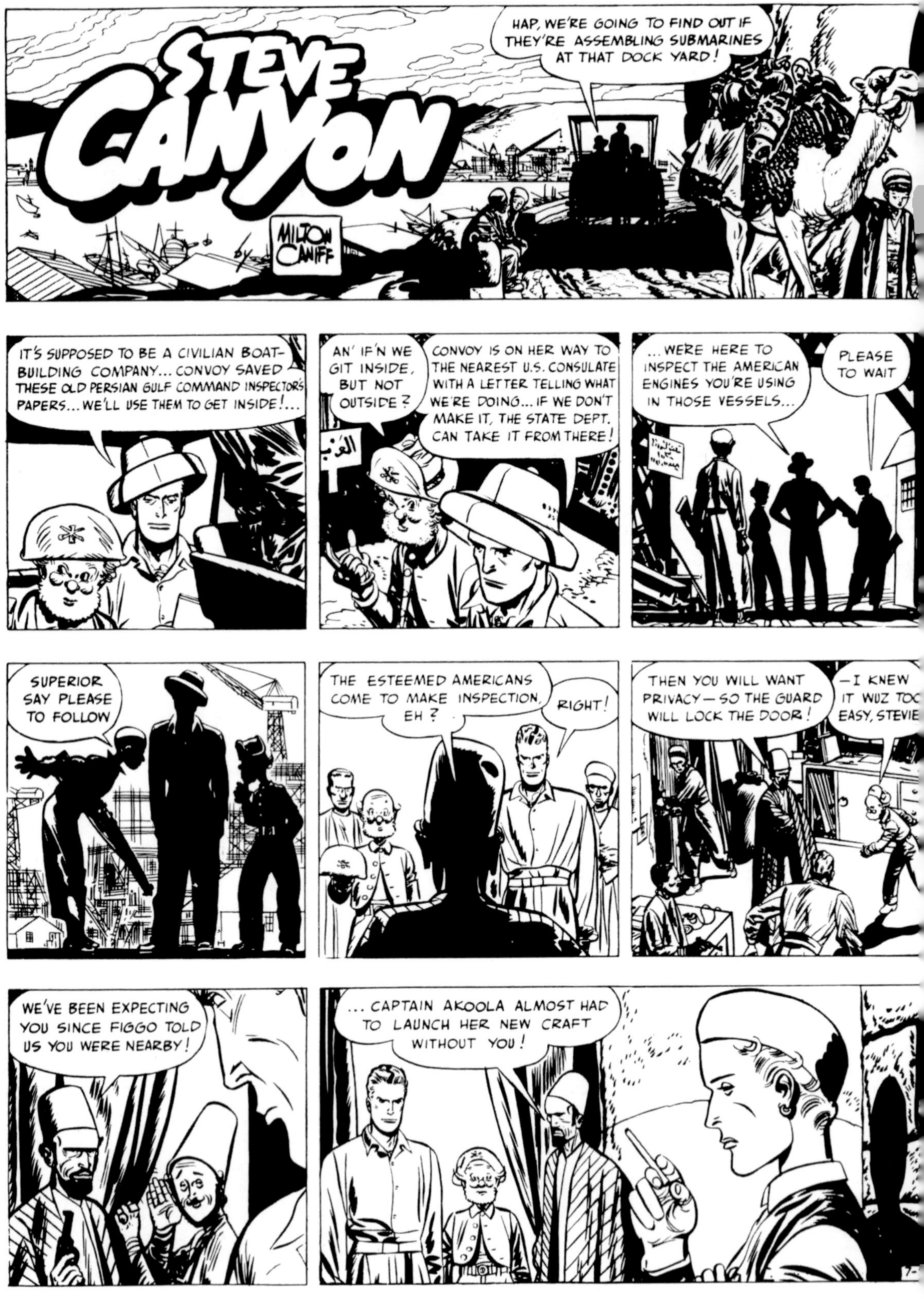

STEVE CANYON
by MILTON CANIFF
HAP, WE'RE GOING TO FIND OUT IF THEY'RE ASSEMBLING SUBMARINES AT THAT DOCK YARD!
IT'S SUPPOSED TO BE A CIVILIAN BOAT-BUILDING COMPANY... CONVOY SAVED THESE OLD PERSIAN GULF COMMAND INSPECTOR'S PAPERS... WE'LL USE THEM TO GET INSIDE!...
AN' IF'N WE GIT INSIDE, BUT NOT OUTSIDE?
CONVOY IS ON HER WAY TO THE NEAREST U.S. CONSULATE WITH A LETTER TELLING WHAT WE'RE DOING... IF WE DON'T MAKE IT, THE STATE DEPT. CAN TAKE IT FROM THERE!
...WE'RE HERE TO INSPECT THE AMERICAN ENGINES YOU'RE USING IN THOSE VESSELS...
PLEASE TO WAIT
SUPERIOR SAY PLEASE TO FOLLOW
THE ESTEEMED AMERICANS COME TO MAKE INSPECTION, EH?
RIGHT!
THEN YOU WILL WANT PRIVACY—SO THE GUARD WILL LOCK THE DOOR!
—I KNEW IT WUZ TOO EASY, STEVIE
WE'VE BEEN EXPECTING YOU SINCE FIGGO TOLD US YOU WERE NEARBY!
...CAPTAIN AKOOLA ALMOST HAD TO LAUNCH HER NEW CRAFT WITHOUT YOU!

As STEVE AND HAPPY EASTER ENTER THE OFFICE OF THE SHIPYARD WHERE THEY SUSPECT SUBMARINES ARE BEING ASSEMBLED — THEY ARE MET BY GUNS — AND A FAMILIAR FIGURE...

THET DAFFYDIL IN TH' DUNCE HAT HAS GOT US AMBUSHED, STEVIE!

YOU'RE SO RIGHT, FUZZY-FACE! THE BIG, BLONDE CANYON GAVE FIGGO THE WRONG KEY — SO THIS IS HIS REWARD!

...ENOUGH OF THIS PITTERPATTER! TAKE THE BLACK MARKET INFORMER OUT OF HERE!

CAPTAIN AKOOLA HAS SPOKEN! GO, FIGGO!

ALWAYS LIKE T' HELP TH' NEIGHBORS WITH THEIR HOUSE CLEANIN'!

CANYON, I AM CAPTAIN AKOOLA — I WILL COMMAND THE VESSEL NOW IN THE DRYDOCK!

CAPTAIN OF A SHIP — WEARING LIEUTENANT COMMANDER'S STRIPES! — ABOUT THE RIGHT RANK FOR A SUBMARINE ASSIGNMENT

MY RANK COULD COMMAND ANY TYPE CRAFT!

BUT FEW WOMEN COMMAND SHIPS OF WHATEVER SORT, MADAME...

CONGRATULATIONS!

?

WH---

CATCH CANYON AND EASTER ALIVE!

GRAB THE BEAM, HAP!

WELL, CANYON

Steve Canyon

7-16

MOST VIRILE EXHIBITION, CANYON — NOW YOU PLEASE DESCEND AND SURRENDER — OR WE RIDDLE YOUR SMALL FRIEND!

DON'T YE DO IT, STEVIE!

MADAME BLIGH HAS US IN A SQUEEZE, HAPPY — WE STILL HAVE CONVOY AND THE NOTES SHE'S CARRYING AS OUR ACE TO PLAY LATER

GIT — WHILE YE GOT A WHOLE SKIN, PODNUH!

7-17

THAT BLOW WILL REMIND YOU NOT TO ASK FOR YOUR YANKEE CONCEPTION OF JUSTICE!

I'M HALF ASLEEP, BUT I'D NEVER DREAM OF HOPING FOR THAT!

NOW, CANYON, CAPTAIN AKOOLA WILL POINT OUT THINGS OF INTEREST!

WHAT HAVE YOU TO TOP THE SOLAR SYSTEM JUST PASSED THROUGH?

I THINK YOU WILL FIND THIS A DIFFERENT KIND OF NAVIGATIONAL PROBLEM!

IT'S DIFFERENT ALREADY — AND I'VE JUST COME TO THE SEE PART — NOT THE S-E-A!

STEVE CANYON

I THINK WE'LL CONCEDE THAT YOU'RE IN COMMAND HERE, CAPTAIN AKOOLA!

YOU HESITATE MAKING PRONOUNCEMENT OF MY NAM CANYON! IT MEANS IN ENGLI "SHARK"!

VERY DASHING! AND WHERE DO YOU DASH TO, CAPTAIN SHARK?

CANYON, COME... EASTER, WAIT!

YOU SEE WHAT?

LOOKS LIKE A SMALL FREIGHTER OR TANKER FROM HERE

AND FROM HERE IT LOOKS HOW?

WHY — IT'S A FALSE HULL — BELOW THE WATER LINE IT'S A SUBMARINE!

Steve Canyon

HULL AND FITTINGS RE VERY LIGHT METAL IT ALL SUBMERGES S BUT ONE PIECE!

—YOU COULD SURFACE IT AT NIGHT ON ANY NAVIGABLE WATER AND STILL NO ONE WOULD KNOW IT'S A SUB!

QUITE CORRECT!

YOU COULD SAIL UNDER ANY FLAG — AND COLLECT INFORMATION OR FIRE A TORPEDO AT CLOSE RANGE — THEN SINK OUT OF SIGHT!

BUT WHY DO YOU SHOW ME ALL THIS?

IS IT NOT WHAT YOU CAME TO LEARN?... OF COURSE MY PLANS FOR YOU DO NOT ALLOW THAT YOU SHALL EVER REPEAT THE INFORMATION!

...DO I DETECT A SLY LOOK? DOES CANYON THINK THE U.S. MARINES WILL ARRIVE BY THE NICK OF THE CLOCK?

IF SO, YOU MAY REGROUP YOUR THOUGHTS! I HAVE IN MY HAND THE LETTER YOU SENT TO THE U.S. CONSUL — SO HE COULD INVESTIGATE IF YOU FAILED TO ESCAPE FROM HERE! YOU CAN SEE BY THE BLOODSTAINS THAT YOUR YOUNG GIRL MESSENGER PUT UP A GOOD FIGHT!

Copyright 1948, SUN and TIMES Company 7-18

19

WAS THE YANKEE CANYON SURPRISED WHEN YOU SHOWED HIM THE UNIQUE VESSEL YOU WILL COMMAND, MY CAPTAIN?

DOUBLY SO WHEN I SHOWED HIM THE TORN AND BLOOD-STAINED LETTER HE THOUGHT HIS GIRL MESSENGER WAS CARRYING TO THE UNITED STATES CONSUL!

NOW CANYON KNOWS HE IS CUT OFF FROM HIS OWN GOVERNMENT

IS IT NOT A RISK TO USE THESE AMERICANS IN THE MANNER YOU HAVE PLANNED, MY CAPTAIN?

I DID NOT BECOME THE FIRST WOMAN COMMANDER OF A SUBMARINE BY AVOIDING RISKS!... OR BY HESITATING TO BREAK SUBORDINATES WHO QUESTION MY METHODS!

20

WHOA UP, STEVIE! THET THERE SKIPPER FILLY SHOWED YOU TH' BLOODY LETTER LEETLE CONVOY WUZ A CARRYIN' T' TH' U.S. CONSUL...

...BUT TH' KID JUST MIGHTA GOT CLEAN AWAY AN' WENT ON T' SPEAK T' TH' MAN, PUSSONAL!

MAYBE...

THET SHE-SAILOR SAID HER NAME MEANS 'SHARK' IN ENGLISH TALK!...BET SHE JIST MADE THET UP T' SCARE FOLKS!

PUT THE YANKEES ON BOARD UNDER GUARD—WE'LL FLOAT THE SHIP AND CAST OFF...

Steve Canyon

83

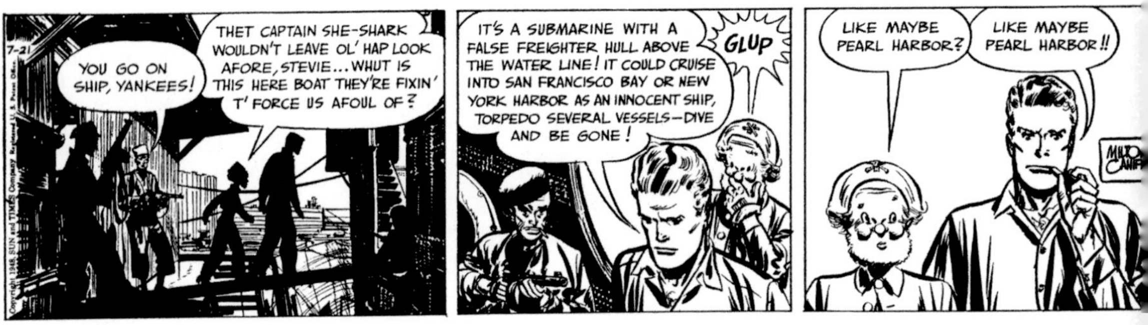
7-21
Copyright 1948, SUN and TIMES Company. Registered U.S. Patent Office.
YOU GO ON SHIP, YANKEES!
THET CAPTAIN SHE-SHARK WOULDN'T LEAVE OL' HAP LOOK AFORE, STEVIE... WHUT IS THIS HERE BOAT THEY'RE FIXIN' T' FORCE US AFOUL OF?
IT'S A SUBMARINE WITH A FALSE FREIGHTER HULL ABOVE THE WATER LINE! IT COULD CRUISE INTO SAN FRANCISCO BAY OR NEW YORK HARBOR AS AN INNOCENT SHIP, TORPEDO SEVERAL VESSELS—DIVE AND BE GONE!
GLUP
LIKE MAYBE PEARL HARBOR?
LIKE MAYBE PEARL HARBOR!!

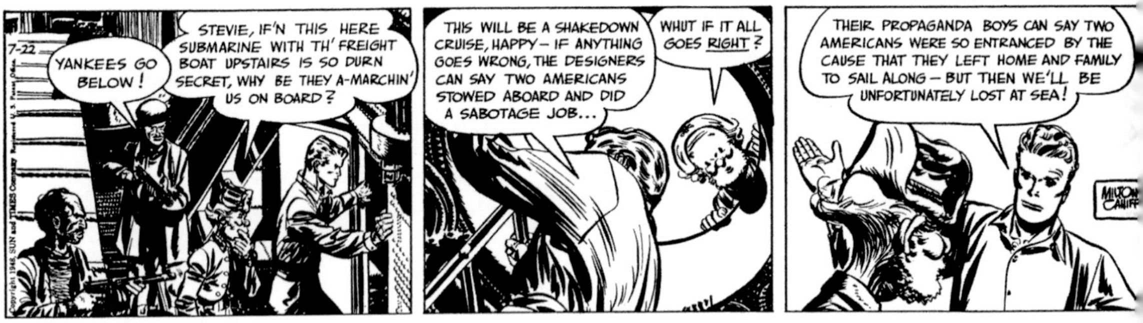
7-22
Copyright 1948, SUN and TIMES Company. Registered U.S. Patent Office.
YANKEES GO BELOW!
STEVIE, IF'N THIS HERE SUBMARINE WITH TH' FREIGHT BOAT UPSTAIRS IS SO DURN SECRET, WHY BE THEY A-MARCHIN' US ON BOARD?
THIS WILL BE A SHAKEDOWN CRUISE, HAPPY—IF ANYTHING GOES WRONG, THE DESIGNERS CAN SAY TWO AMERICANS STOWED ABOARD AND DID A SABOTAGE JOB...
WHUT IF IT ALL GOES RIGHT?
THEIR PROPAGANDA BOYS CAN SAY TWO AMERICANS WERE SO ENTRANCED BY THE CAUSE THAT THEY LEFT HOME AND FAMILY TO SAIL ALONG—BUT THEN WE'LL BE UNFORTUNATELY LOST AT SEA!

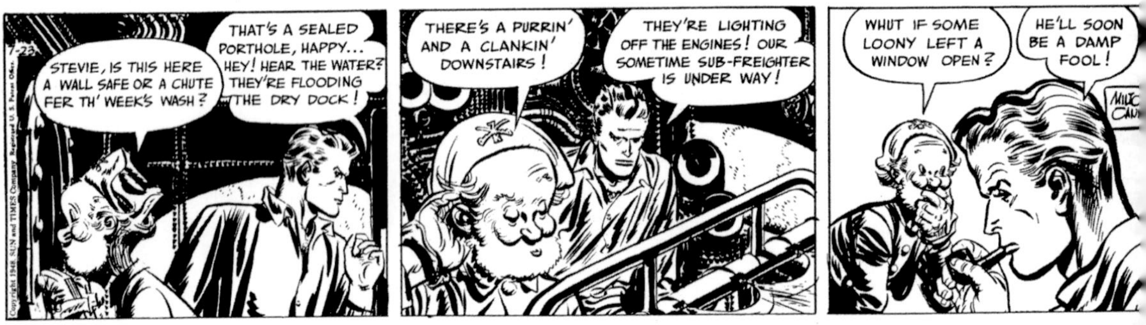
7-23
Copyright 1948, SUN and TIMES Company. Registered U.S. Patent Office.
STEVIE, IS THIS HERE A WALL SAFE OR A CHUTE FER TH' WEEK'S WASH?
THAT'S A SEALED PORTHOLE, HAPPY... HEY! HEAR THE WATER? THEY'RE FLOODING THE DRY DOCK!
THERE'S A PURRIN' AND A CLANKIN' DOWNSTAIRS!
THEY'RE LIGHTING OFF THE ENGINES! OUR SOMETIME SUB-FREIGHTER IS UNDER WAY!
WHUT IF SOME LOONY LEFT A WINDOW OPEN?
HE'LL SOON BE A DAMP FOOL!

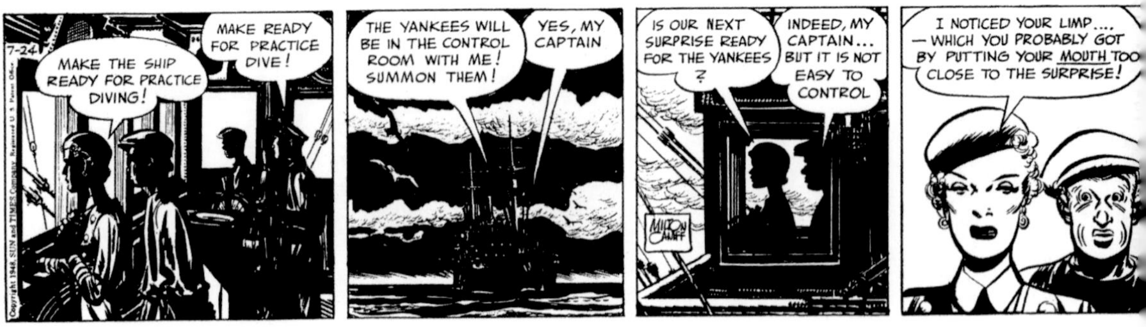
7-24
Copyright 1948, SUN and TIMES Company. Registered U.S. Patent Office.
MAKE THE SHIP READY FOR PRACTICE DIVING!
MAKE READY FOR PRACTICE DIVE!
THE YANKEES WILL BE IN THE CONTROL ROOM WITH ME! SUMMON THEM!
YES, MY CAPTAIN
IS OUR NEXT SURPRISE READY FOR THE YANKEES?
INDEED, MY CAPTAIN... BUT IT IS NOT EASY TO CONTROL
MILTON CANIFF
I NOTICED YOUR LIMP.... —WHICH YOU PROBABLY GOT BY PUTTING YOUR MOUTH TOO CLOSE TO THE SURPRISE!

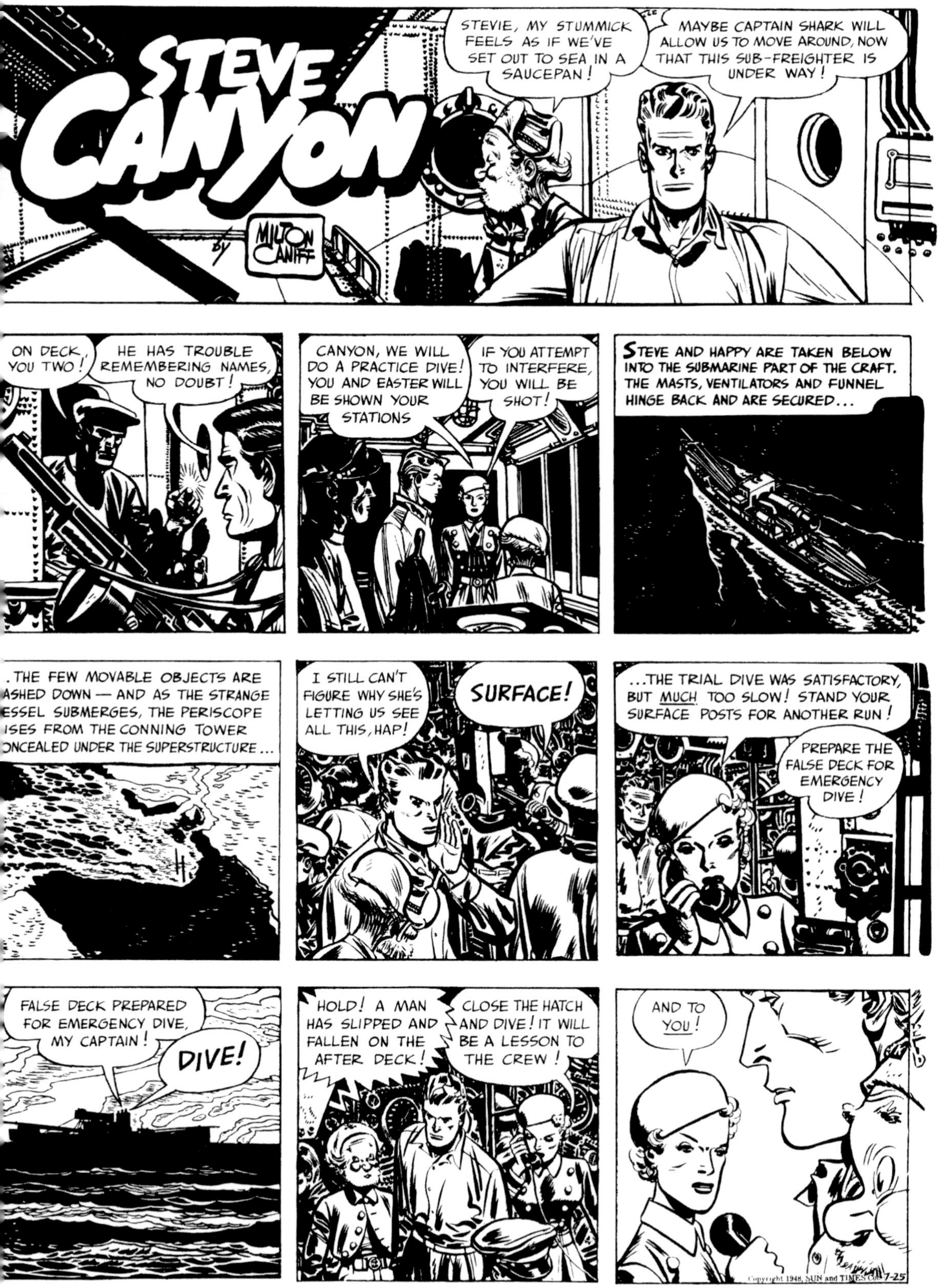
STEVE CANYON
by MILTON CANIFF
STEVIE, MY STUMMICK FEELS AS IF WE'VE SET OUT TO SEA IN A SAUCEPAN!
MAYBE CAPTAIN SHARK WILL ALLOW US TO MOVE AROUND, NOW THAT THIS SUB-FREIGHTER IS UNDER WAY!
ON DECK, YOU TWO!
HE HAS TROUBLE REMEMBERING NAMES, NO DOUBT!
CANYON, WE WILL DO A PRACTICE DIVE! YOU AND EASTER WILL BE SHOWN YOUR STATIONS
IF YOU ATTEMPT TO INTERFERE, YOU WILL BE SHOT!
STEVE AND HAPPY ARE TAKEN BELOW INTO THE SUBMARINE PART OF THE CRAFT. THE MASTS, VENTILATORS AND FUNNEL HINGE BACK AND ARE SECURED...
.THE FEW MOVABLE OBJECTS ARE ASHED DOWN — AND AS THE STRANGE ESSEL SUBMERGES, THE PERISCOPE ISES FROM THE CONNING TOWER ONCEALED UNDER THE SUPERSTRUCTURE...
I STILL CAN'T FIGURE WHY SHE'S LETTING US SEE ALL THIS, HAP!
SURFACE!
...THE TRIAL DIVE WAS SATISFACTORY, BUT MUCH TOO SLOW! STAND YOUR SURFACE POSTS FOR ANOTHER RUN!
PREPARE THE FALSE DECK FOR EMERGENCY DIVE!
FALSE DECK PREPARED FOR EMERGENCY DIVE, MY CAPTAIN!
DIVE!
HOLD! A MAN HAS SLIPPED AND FALLEN ON THE AFTER DECK!
CLOSE THE HATCH AND DIVE! IT WILL BE A LESSON TO THE CREW!
AND TO YOU!
Copyright 1948, SUN and TIMES Co. 7-25

7-26

YOU HAVE WITNESSED A PRACTICE DIVE OF THIS SUBMARINE DISGUISED AS A FREIGHTER! WHAT DO YOU THINK, CANYON?

WRAP UP SIX TO GO OUT, SHARKY — I'LL PEDDLE THEM AROUND THE UNITED NATIONS ON CONSIGNMENT!

BUT HOW CAN I TELL MY GRANDCHILDREN WHAT I DID IN THE COLD WAR IF YOU DON'T TIP HAPPY AND ME TO WHY WE'RE HERE?

YOU ARE AN INTELLIGENT AMERICAN — WE WANT YOUR REACTION TO THIS CRAFT!

GLADLY! IT'S A CUTE STUNT THAT COULD RAISE CAIN IN A HARBOR FULL OF SHIPPING AT THE START OF AN UNDECLARED WAR... WHICH IS WHAT I WILL TELL THE U.S. NAVY WHEN I GET TO A RADIO!

BUT, OF COURSE YOU KNOW YOU ARE NOT GOIN' TO GET TO A RADIO, DON'T YOU?

7-27

WE GUESSED THAT YOU'D TOSS US TO THE DEEP SIX AFTER WE HAD SERVED YOUR PURPOSE — DO WE GET THE SLUG NOW, CAPTAIN SHARK?

YOU ARE CASUAL ABOUT THE PROSPECT OF DEATH, CANYON!

NO, I'M JUST STUPID — NO IMAGINATION! .. FOR INSTANCE, I DON'T SEE HOW YOU COULD GET THIS SUB DISGUISED AS A FREIGHTER INTO A MAJOR AMERICAN HARBOR ...

YOU WOULD HAVE TO CALL FOR A PILOT, PRESENT YOUR PAPERS AND IDENTIFY YOURSELF AND YOUR MISSION ...

OH, WE THOUGHT OF THAT FIRST!

THEN YOU WON'T NEED ANY FURTHER OPINIONS FROM HAP AND ME ....

YES, I WILL — A IF YOU DON'T GI THEM FREELY, HAVE A WAY O PERSUADING YO TO TALK

7-28

OKAY, CAPTAIN SHARK, SINCE HAPPY EASTER AND I ARE SCHEDULED TO BE KNOCKED OFF, ASK US ANYTHING! — WE'LL GIVE YOU SOME NEW ARABIAN NIGHTS TALES!

YOU CAN TELL ME LITTLE I DON'T KNOW, CANYON — BUT IF WE ARE CHALLENGED BY UNFRIENDLY CRAFT, ONE OF YOU WILL ANSWER!

HAPPY AND I AGREED THAT IF YOU MADE A 'FRONT' OF EITHER OF US BY HOLDING A GUN TO THE HEAD OF THE OTHER, BACKSTAGE — THAT THE SPEAKER WOULD TELL THAT THIS 'FREIGHTER' IS REALLY A SUBMARINE!

VERY FARSIGHTED, BUT RATHER A WASTE OF YOUR YANKEE HEROICS! MATE, BRING THE SUPERCARGO TO ME!

7-29

CONVOY!

TO BE SURE, CANYON! DID YOU THINK WE WOULD DESTROY SUCH A USEFUL TOOL?

SHE FOUGHT TO RETAIN THE LETTER SHE CARRIED FROM YOU TO THE U.S. CONSUL ... THE BLOOD ON THE TORN PAPER RESULTED WHEN SHE BIT THE HAND OF ONE OF MY MEN!

REMOVE THE GAG!

I LOVE YOU, SIR!

DO I SEE A CHANGE OF HEART MIRRORED IN THE EYES OF THE SO NOBLE YANKEE ..?

Steve Canyon

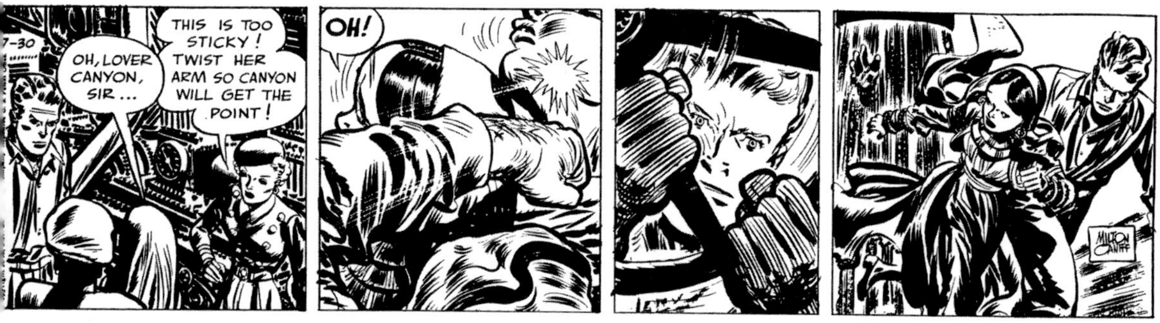
7-30
OH, LOVER CANYON, SIR ...
THIS IS TOO STICKY! TWIST HER ARM SO CANYON WILL GET THE POINT!
OH!
MILTON CANIFF

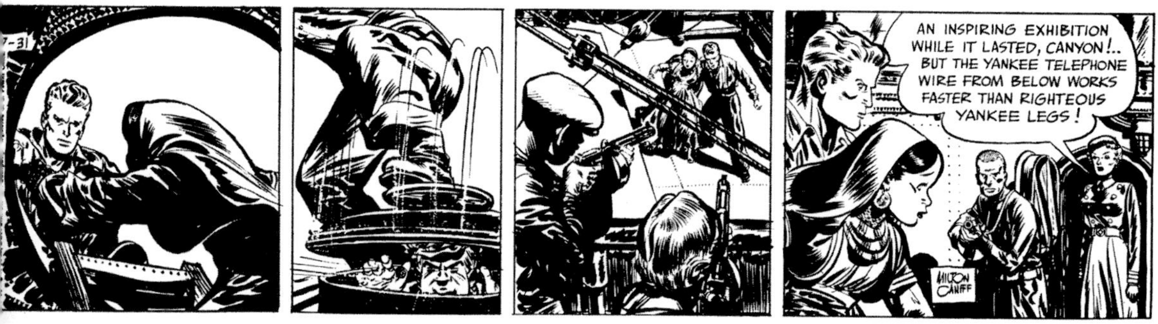
7-31
AN INSPIRING EXHIBITION WHILE IT LASTED, CANYON!.. BUT THE YANKEE TELEPHONE WIRE FROM BELOW WORKS FASTER THAN RIGHTEOUS YANKEE LEGS!
MILTON CANIFF

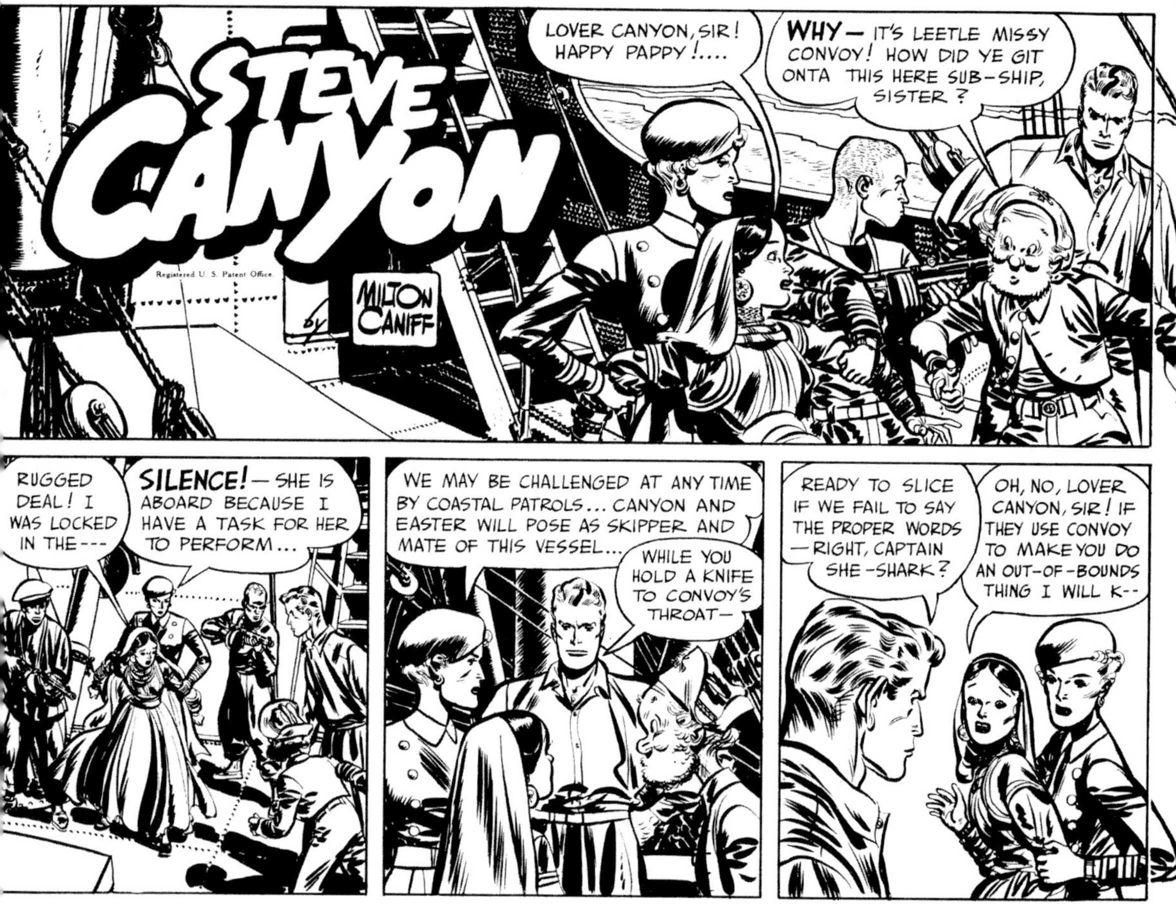
STEVE CANYON
Registered U. S. Patent Office.
BY MILTON CANIFF
LOVER CANYON, SIR! HAPPY PAPPY!....
WHY— IT'S LEETLE MISSY CONVOY! HOW DID YE GIT ONTA THIS HERE SUB-SHIP, SISTER?
RUGGED DEAL! I WAS LOCKED IN THE---
SILENCE!— SHE IS ABOARD BECAUSE I HAVE A TASK FOR HER TO PERFORM...
WE MAY BE CHALLENGED AT ANY TIME BY COASTAL PATROLS... CANYON AND EASTER WILL POSE AS SKIPPER AND MATE OF THIS VESSEL...
WHILE YOU HOLD A KNIFE TO CONVOY'S THROAT—
READY TO SLICE IF WE FAIL TO SAY THE PROPER WORDS —RIGHT, CAPTAIN SHE-SHARK?
OH, NO, LOVER CANYON, SIR! IF THEY USE CONVOY TO MAKE YOU DO AN OUT-OF-BOUNDS THING I WILL K--

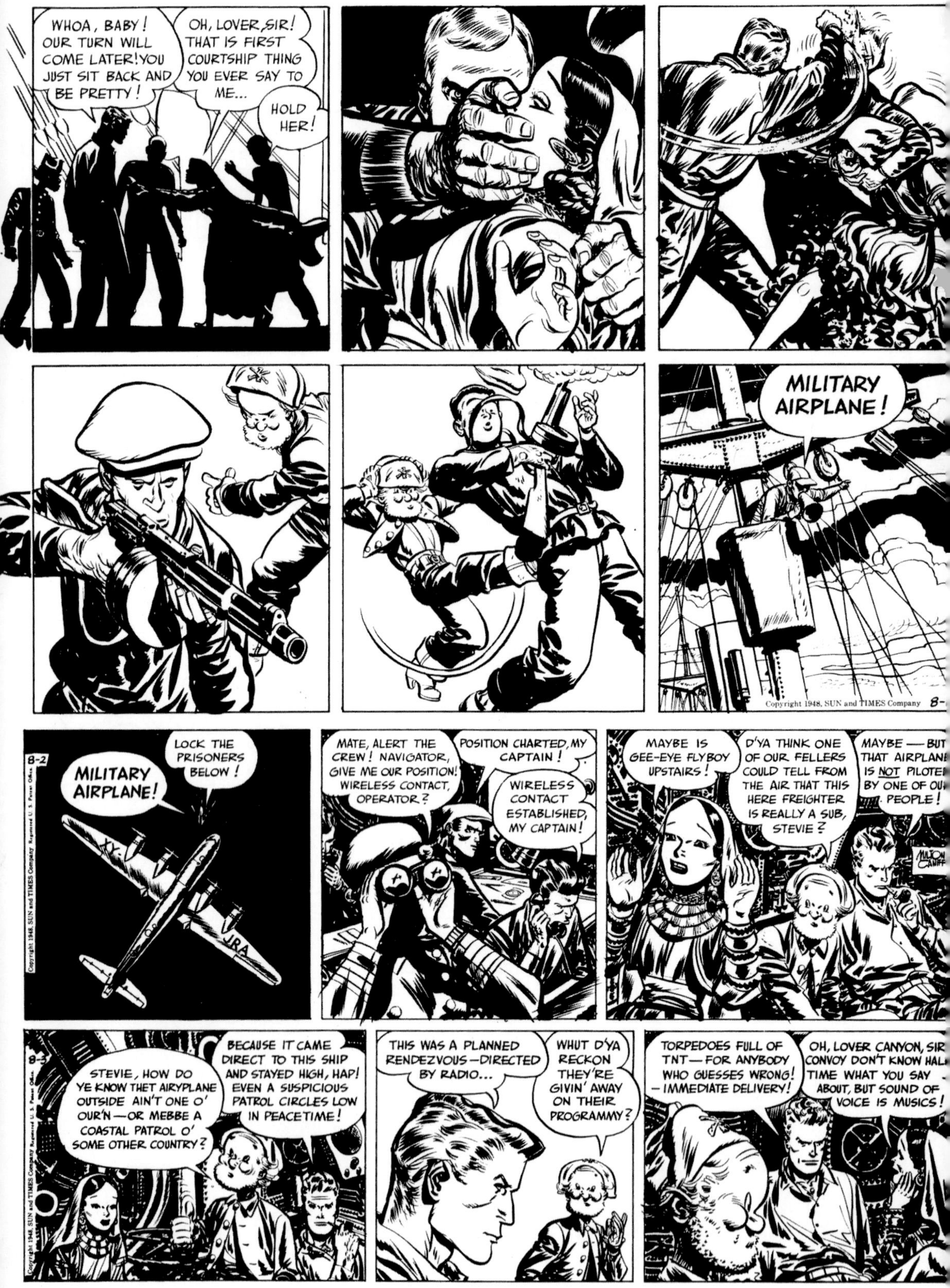
WHOA, BABY! OUR TURN WILL COME LATER! YOU JUST SIT BACK AND BE PRETTY!
OH, LOVER, SIR! THAT IS FIRST COURTSHIP THING YOU EVER SAY TO ME...
HOLD HER!
MILITARY AIRPLANE!
Copyright 1948, SUN and TIMES Company
MILITARY AIRPLANE!
LOCK THE PRISONERS BELOW!
MATE, ALERT THE CREW! NAVIGATOR, GIVE ME OUR POSITION! WIRELESS CONTACT, OPERATOR?
POSITION CHARTED, MY CAPTAIN!
WIRELESS CONTACT ESTABLISHED, MY CAPTAIN!
MAYBE IS GEE-EYE FLYBOY UPSTAIRS!
D'YA THINK ONE OF OUR FELLERS COULD TELL FROM THE AIR THAT THIS HERE FREIGHTER IS REALLY A SUB, STEVIE?
MAYBE —BUT THAT AIRPLANE IS NOT PILOTE BY ONE OF OU PEOPLE!
MILTON CANIFF
STEVIE, HOW DO YE KNOW THET AIRYPLANE OUTSIDE AIN'T ONE O' OUR'N —OR MEBBE A COASTAL PATROL O' SOME OTHER COUNTRY?
BECAUSE IT CAME DIRECT TO THIS SHIP AND STAYED HIGH, HAP! EVEN A SUSPICIOUS PATROL CIRCLES LOW IN PEACETIME!
THIS WAS A PLANNED RENDEZVOUS—DIRECTED BY RADIO...
WHUT D'YA RECKON THEY'RE GIVIN' AWAY ON THEIR PROGRAMMY?
TORPEDOES FULL OF TNT—FOR ANYBODY WHO GUESSES WRONG! —IMMEDIATE DELIVERY!
OH, LOVER CANYON, SIR CONVOY DON'T KNOW HAL TIME WHAT YOU SAY ABOUT, BUT SOUND OF VOICE IS MUSICS!

THE AIRCRAFT IS TRANSMITTING IN CODE M, AS AGREED, MY CAPTAIN!

INFORM THE AIRMEN THAT WE RECEIVE THEIR SOUND VERY WELL! THEY MAY PROCEED WITH THE OTHER SIGNAL...

FOR SOME TIME THE AIRCRAFT AND THE SUBMARINE DISGUISED AS A FREIGHTER EXCHANGE RADIO COMMUNICATIONS...

QUITE SATISFACTORY—ESPECIALLY THE IMAGE OF THE ISLAND AND HARBOR!...IS THERE DANGER OF OUTSIDERS KNOWING THIS EXPERIMENT IS BEING CONDUCTED?

NONE!.. WE FLY FROM AN ABANDONED YANKEE RUNWAY ON AN ISLAND THE AMERICANS THINK HAS GONE BACK TO JUNGLE!

STEVE, HAPPY EASTER AND CONVOY ARE IMPRISONED BELOW DECKS AS AN AIRPLANE SLOWLY CIRCLES THE SUBMARINE DISGUISED AS A FREIGHTER...

FOOTSTEPS, STEVIE! CAPTAIN SHARK'S BULLY-BOYS ARE ARUNNIN' HITHER AN' YITHER UPSTAIRS!

DRILLS AND FORMATIONS TO MEET VARIOUS SIMULATED CONDITIONS, HAP!

OUR FUTURE AIN'T A VERY PRETTY PICTURE, PODNUH!

PICTURE! THAT'S IT!

PICTURE, STEVIE?

RIGHT, HAP!

AS AN EX-CAVALRYMAN YOU KNOW WHY YOU TROOPERS WERE CALLED "THE EYES OF THE ARMY"...

WHY, SHORE...

WE WUZ TH' SCOUTS! WE'D RIDE OUT AN' SEE WHUT WUZ UP —THEN REPORT BACK SO TH' COMMANDIN' OFFICER COULD PLAN HIS TACTICS!

OUR INVASION OF JAPAN WAS TO HAVE BEEN COVERED BY A NEW KIND OF EYE, BUT, OF COURSE, WE NEVER HAD TO USE IT...

...CAPTAIN SHARK'S PEOPLE MAY BE TESTING A VERSION OF IT...IN WHICH THE COMMANDER STAYS AT SEA, DIRECTING SHORE OPERATIONS FROM TELEVISION IMAGES RELAYED FROM AIRCRAFT...

STEVIE, YE'VE GOT T' H'IST OFF'N THIS HERE BOAT AN' TELL THE AMERICKY NAVY FOLKS WHUT CAPTAIN SHARK AN' HER PEOPLE ARE UP TO...

HOW STRONG A SWIMMER ARE YOU, HAPPY?

DON'T YOU WORRY NONE ABOUT ME, PODNUH!...JIST GIT AWAY AN' LIGHT OUT!

WE MIGHT FOOL THE CREW OF THIS VESSEL, BUT CAPTAIN SHARK WON'T BE SO EASY!

LOVER CANYON, SIR...

...YES, CONVOY

...MAYBE CONVOY KNOWS A WAY TO SNAFFLE UP THE LADY BRASS!

Steve Canyon

I'M BEGINNING TO SEE DAYLIGHT ON THE SHAKEDOWN CRUISE OF THIS SUBMARINE DISGUISED AS A FREIGHTER!... THE MILITARY AIRPLANE THAT CIRCLED US WAS NOT A COASTAL PATROL JOB—IT WAS FRIENDLY TO THIS CROWD!

THAT AIRPLANE DIDN'T JUST EXCHANGE IDENTIFICATION CHITCHAT BY RADIO WITH THIS SHIP... OUR CAPTAIN SHARK RAN UP A TELEVISION AERIAL!

WHUT FER, STEVIE—WRASSLIN' MATCHES?

TESTING, HAPPY!...IF THAT AIRCRAFT HAD JUST MAPPED OR PHOTOGRAPHED A PLACE LIKE PEARL HARBOR, THEY WOULDN'T HAVE TO FLY THE PLATES BACK TO BASE...

...THEY COULD TRANSMIT THE EXACT PLAN OF ANCHORAGE BY TELEVISION OR FACSIMILE TO SUBS LYING JUST OFFSHORE—WHICH COULD MOVE IN AND FIRE THEIR TORPEDOES WITHOUT RAISING A PERISCOPE!

WHUT D'WE AIM T'DO ABOUT IT, PODNUH?

WE MUST BE NEAR SHORE...THIS SHIP IS TRAILING A GROUND WIRE DISGUISED AS A LINE FOR THE DINGHY!

IF WE CAN GET INTO THE SMALL BOAT TONIGHT WE CAN ROW ASHORE AND PASS ON THIS INFO TO OUR OWN NAVY PEOPLE!

LATER... MY CAPTAIN, THE GUARD OVER THE PRISONERS HAS BEEN FOUND DAZED! THEY HAVE ESCAPED!

THE SMALL BOAT HAS ALSO TAKEN LEAVE!

PUT THE SHIP ABOUT, STEERSMAN! NO SEARCHLIGHT... IT MIGHT EXCITE SUSPICION ASHORE!

HOW DOES MY CAPTAIN HOPE TO FIND THEM IN THIS BLACK OCEAN?

CANYON DOES NOT KNOW IT, BUT THE STERN OF THAT DINGHY IS COATED WITH LUMINOUS PAINT!

Copyright 1948, SUN and TIMES Company   8-8

Steve Canyon

GIRL GO TO CAPTAIN!

GLUP! STEVIE, THET SHE-SHARK COULD DO ANYTHIN' TO OUR LEETLE CONVOY...

I KNOW, HAP! —AND CONVOY DIDN'T HAVE TIME TO TELL US WHAT SHE KNEW ABOUT THE CAPTAIN!

LEAVE THE CHILD WITH ME...

I THOUGHT I KNEW THIS SUBMARINE FROM BOW TO STERN, BUT YOU WILL NOW TELL ME SOMETHING ABOUT IT I HAVE NOT BEEN ABLE TO PUZZLE OUT...

BUT, MADAME CAPTAIN SHARK, WHAT COULD CONVOY TELL YOU OF YOUR OWN SUBMARINE?

BEFORE I SHOWED YOU TO CANYON AND EASTER, YOU WERE IMPRISONED IN THE CAPTAIN'S LOCKER

YOU CAREFULLY EXAMINED EVERYTHING THEREIN, EVEN PICKING LOCKS LIKE AN EXPERT, BUT ONLY ONE THING IS ACTUALLY MISSING...

WHAT DID YOU DO WITH IT?

ANSWER ME!

I ATE IT!

YOU ATE WHAT YOU STOLE FROM MY LOCKER?

YES, MADAME CAPTAIN SHARK! —EVERY BIT...

WHY?

IF CONVOY COULD FIND IT SO EASILY, CREW COULD LIKEWISE... I ATE IT TO PROTECT THE CAPTAIN...

TO PROTECT ME?

ROGERS!... IF CREW KNEW WHAT CONVOY KNOWS, MADAME CAPTAIN WOULD QUICK TIME BE BACK AT DESK! —IF NOT ON SHORT END OF FIRING SQUAD! CONVOY ALSO WOMAN IN LOVE!

WHAT DO YOU MEAN, "LOVE"?

IF CONVOY NOT NUTS WITH LOVE OVER MR. CANYON, MAYBE WOULD NOT HAVE CATCH ON THAT MADAME CAPTAIN IN SAME HAPPY PICKLE!

IN YOUR COUNTRY WOMAN CAPTAIN OF SUBMARINE MUST BE ALL TIME BOOK SAILOR— STRICTLY BRASS BY THE NUMBERS! IF THEY KNEW YOU IN LOVE — SKXXX! HELLO, ENSIGN!

CONVOY FOUND EVIDENCE OF LOVE— ATE IT —NOW NO CHANCE FOR CREW TO SNITCH!

WHAT IF I WERE TO TELL YOU THAT YOU DID NOT EAT ALL OF THE EVIDENCE?!

Steve Canyon

THERE IS *MORE* PROOF THAT MADAME CAPTAIN IS IN LOVE THAN THAT WHICH I STOLE FROM HER LOCKER?

YES... BUT THIS I KEEP IN THE SAFE! —TO WHICH ONLY I HOLD THE COMBINATION...

YOU SEE—IT WAS COMPLETED BEFORE YOU ATE THE TISSUE-PAPER PATTERN!

NOT A WORD FROM LEETLE CONVOY...D'YE RECKON THET SHE-SHARK WOULD TAKE OUT ALL HER SPITE ON TH' GAL, STEVIE?

I'VE JUST GONE OVER IN MY MIND THE 106TH PLAN OF WHAT I'LL TRY TO DO TO ANYONE WHO HARMS THE KID, HAP...

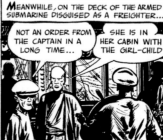

MEANWHILE, ON THE DECK OF THE ARMED SUBMARINE DISGUISED AS A FREIGHTER...

NOT AN ORDER FROM THE CAPTAIN IN A LONG TIME...

SHE IS IN HER CABIN WITH THE GIRL-CHILD

SOME HARM MAY HAVE BEFALLEN OUR COMMANDER —I SHALL GO BELOW AND INQUIRE...

HAPPY, IF THE SPACE ON THIS SUBMARINE DISGUISED AS A FREIGHTER WEREN'T SO JAMMED, WE'D EACH BE IN SOLITARY CONFINEMENT—AFTER THE WAY I SNAFFLED THAT ESCAPE TRY!

DON'T STEW, STEVIE...IF'N WE'D GOT ON LAND WE MIGH HAVE T' GO T' WORK!

MY REAL CONCERN IS WHAT CAPTAIN SHARK DID TO CONVOY WHEN SHE SEPARATED THE CHILD FROM US...

YOP — THET FROWNIN' FILLY MIGHT DO HURT TO OUR LEETLE ORPHAN!

WHILE IN THE CAPTAIN'S CABIN...

IS THERE NO HOPE?

NONE!

OH, PLEASE, MADAME CAPTAIN SHARK...

YOUR PLAINTS WILL NOT CAUSE ME TO RELENT, URCHIN!

Steve Canyon

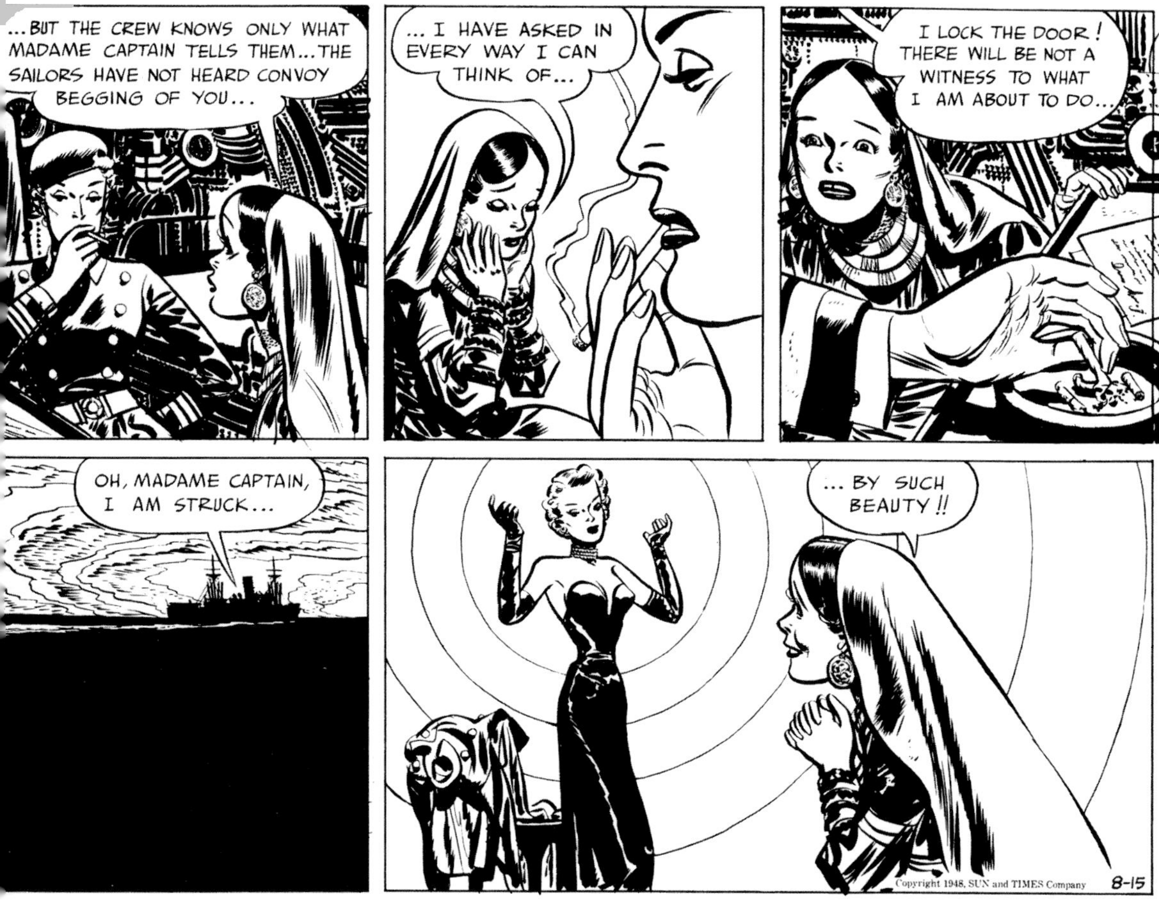
...BUT THE CREW KNOWS ONLY WHAT MADAME CAPTAIN TELLS THEM...THE SAILORS HAVE NOT HEARD CONVOY BEGGING OF YOU...
... I HAVE ASKED IN EVERY WAY I CAN THINK OF...
I LOCK THE DOOR! THERE WILL BE NOT A WITNESS TO WHAT I AM ABOUT TO DO...
OH, MADAME CAPTAIN, I AM STRUCK...
... BY SUCH BEAUTY!!
Copyright 1948, SUN and TIMES Company
8-15

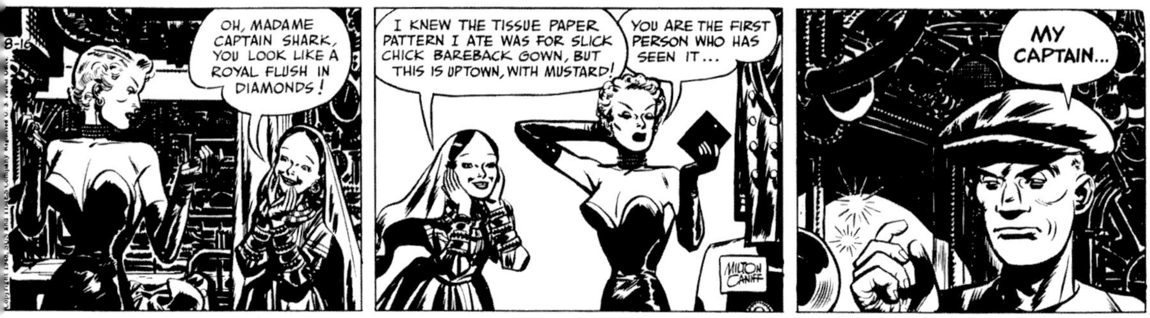
8-16
OH, MADAME CAPTAIN SHARK, YOU LOOK LIKE A ROYAL FLUSH IN DIAMONDS!
I KNEW THE TISSUE PAPER PATTERN I ATE WAS FOR SLICK CHICK BAREBACK GOWN, BUT THIS IS UPTOWN, WITH MUSTARD!
YOU ARE THE FIRST PERSON WHO HAS SEEN IT...
MILTON CANIFF
MY CAPTAIN...

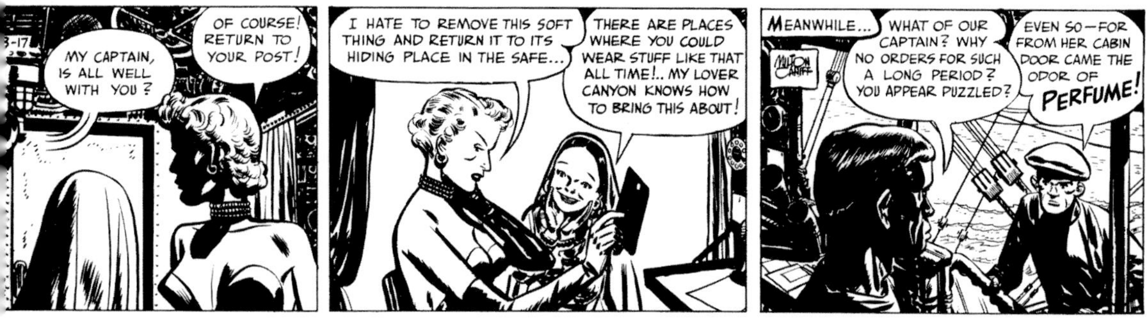
8-17
MY CAPTAIN, IS ALL WELL WITH YOU?
OF COURSE! RETURN TO YOUR POST!
I HATE TO REMOVE THIS SOFT THING AND RETURN IT TO ITS HIDING PLACE IN THE SAFE...
THERE ARE PLACES WHERE YOU COULD WEAR STUFF LIKE THAT ALL TIME!.. MY LOVER CANYON KNOWS HOW TO BRING THIS ABOUT!
MEANWHILE...
MILTON CANIFF
WHAT OF OUR CAPTAIN? WHY NO ORDERS FOR SUCH A LONG PERIOD? YOU APPEAR PUZZLED?
EVEN SO—FOR FROM HER CABIN DOOR CAME THE ODOR OF PERFUME!

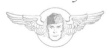

8-18

I AM A FAITHFUL FOLLOWER OF THE AMERICAN FILMS!..YOU WOULD BE SOCKEROOPS IN HOLLYWOODS...

OH, COME NOW, CHILD

IS TRUE, MADAME CAPTAIN—YOU COME FROM SKIPPERING SUBMARINE TO CINEMA—IS SENSASHE!

ABSURD!

BUT MY LOVER CANYON CAN ARRANGE THIS—HE IS CONNECTED! LET ME GO AND TELL ONLY HIS PERSONAL EAR OF THIS AMAZEMENT THING!

MEANWHILE—ON THE BRIDGE ABOVE..

PERFUME SCENT FROM OUR CAPTAIN'S CABIN, EH?—AND I HAVE NOTICED DEEPER COLOR IN HER CHEEKS AND LIPS...

...SINCE THE BIG YANKEE APPEARED—I PUT IT DOWN TO WIND AND SUN—BUT COULD IT BE ROUGE?

8-19

THE GOWN GOES BACK TO THE SAFE—AND I RETURN TO THE BRIDGE!

—BUT, MADAME CAPTAIN—IF YOU ALLOW ME TO TALK TO MY LOVER CANYON, HE CAN ARRANGE A TRIUMPH FOR YOU IN HOLLYWOODS!

ENOUGH OF THIS FOOLISH CHATTER! YOUR YANKEE WILL GET EXERCISE ON THE AFTER-DECK AT 2100 AND THAT IS AS CLOSE AS HE WILL BE TO CALIFORNIA!

OH, LOVER CANYON, SHE ALMOST FELL FOR SONG WITH DANCE

BUT ALL ENDS WITH CONVOY IN BRIG, TOO... IRON DOOR IS LOC--- NO! IS OPEN!

8-20

YOUR CAPTAIN SENT ME TO TAKE EXERCISE WITH MY LOVER CANYON AND HAPPY EASTER!

DOES THE CAPTAIN NOT KNOW OF THE PLOTTING THAT COULD GO ON?... OH, VERY WELL—EXERCISE!

PLEASE TO WHISTLE LOUD SO CONVOY CAN TELL BIG STUFF TO LOVER CANYON!

CAPTAIN HAS SLINKISH EVENING GOWN SHE MADE FOR SELF! I THINK SHE'D GIVE UP NAVY CAREER TO GO TO HOLLYWOODS!

MEANWHILE... NO QUESTION ABOUT IT OUR CAPTAIN IS WEARING PERFUME!—THIS CALLS FOR A REPORT DIRECT TO THE POLITICAL OFFICER OF THE SUBMARINE COMMAND!

8-21

OUR CAPTAIN AND HER PERFUME MOVE TO THE AFTERDECK, WHERE THE YANKEE CANYON EXERCISES

AS THE POLITICAL REPRESENTATIVES IN THE CREW, IT IS OUR DUTY TO OBSERVE THIS ACTION FURTHER

CONVOY! EASTER! GO BELOW!

GUARD, GO TO YOUR QUARTERS--I SHALL TAKE CHARGE OF THE PRISONER!

SO WE'VE FINALLY ARRIVED AT THE REAL POINT, EH, CAPTAIN SHARK?

I DID NOT COME TO HEAR WHAT THE WILD WAVES ARE SAYING, CANYON!—TALK!

Steve Canyon

I'VE BEEN TRYING TO GET A STRAIGHT LINE ON YOU FOR A LONG TIME, BUT IT TOOK CONVOY TO REALLY NAIL YOU DOWN...

YOU WERE A WHIZ AT MATH IN SCHOOL! —YOU GOT INTO SUBMARINE SERVICE BECAUSE A GIRL COULD SHINE THERE! IT WAS TOUGH GOING, BUT YOU THOUGHT AND SLUGGED FAST ENOUGH TO RISE TO A COMMAND OF YOUR OWN!...

...YOU WERE SET TO BE THE FIRST REALLY BIG-SHOT WOMAN IN YOUR COUNTRY'S NAVY—THEN IT HAPPENED!

MAYBE IT WAS SOME NICE GUY FROM THE OUTSIDE WORLD WHO STARTED BELLS RINGING IN THE FEMININE SIDE OF YOUR BRAIN — WHICH YOU HAD KEPT DORMANT UP TO THEN BY SHEER FORCE OF WILL...

...MAYBE IT WAS AN AMERICAN MOVIE YOU SAW ON A TRIP...THE GALS IN THE PICTURE LOOKED GOOD IN THOSE NICE, FROTHY HOLLYWOOD CLOTHES!

— SO YOU MADE A GOWN IN SECRET, AND YOUR MIRROR SAID YOU COULD GIVE THEM CURVES ON EVERY PITCH...YOU COULD DO BETTER IN SILK THAN IN A SUBMARINE...

YOU'D BE A REAL SENSATION IN AMERICA, AND YOU KNOW IT! YOU BROUGHT HAPPY EASTER AND ME ALONG AS YOUR EXCUSE FOR TURNING THIS SCOW OVER TO THE U.S. NAVY AS IF WE HAD CAPTURED IT FROM YOU...

—AND WE'LL BE GLAD TO HELP YOU SWING THE DEAL!.. I EVEN HAVE SOME FRIENDS IN HOLLYWOOD WHO COULD TAKE IT FROM THAT END...

I---

OH — I DIDN'T SEE YOU! BUT SINCE YOU ARE HERE, DRAG CANYON BELOW! AFTER WHAT HE JUST SAID I HAVE NO ALTERNATIVE! HE MUST DIE!

8-22

Steve Canyon

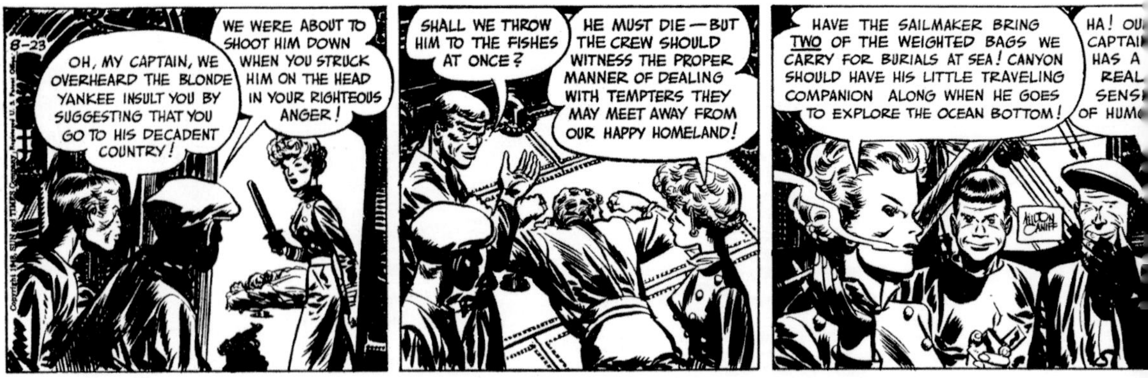
8-23
OH, MY CAPTAIN, WE OVERHEARD THE BLONDE YANKEE INSULT YOU BY SUGGESTING THAT YOU GO TO HIS DECADENT COUNTRY!
WE WERE ABOUT TO SHOOT HIM DOWN WHEN YOU STRUCK HIM ON THE HEAD IN YOUR RIGHTEOUS ANGER!
SHALL WE THROW HIM TO THE FISHES AT ONCE?
HE MUST DIE — BUT THE CREW SHOULD WITNESS THE PROPER MANNER OF DEALING WITH TEMPTERS THEY MAY MEET AWAY FROM OUR HAPPY HOMELAND!
HAVE THE SAILMAKER BRING TWO OF THE WEIGHTED BAGS WE CARRY FOR BURIALS AT SEA! CANYON SHOULD HAVE HIS LITTLE TRAVELING COMPANION ALONG WHEN HE GOES TO EXPLORE THE OCEAN BOTTOM!
HA! OU CAPTAI HAS A REAL SENS OF HUM
MILTON CANIFF

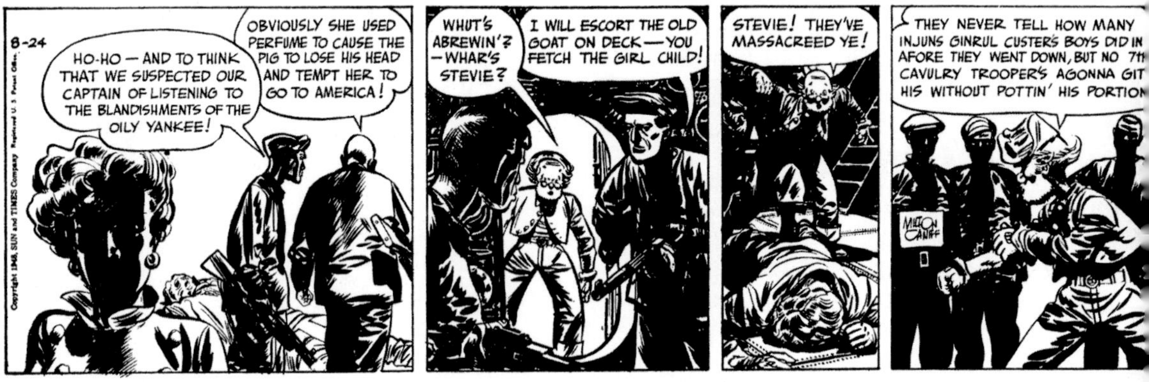
8-24
HO-HO — AND TO THINK THAT WE SUSPECTED OUR CAPTAIN OF LISTENING TO THE BLANDISHMENTS OF THE OILY YANKEE!
OBVIOUSLY SHE USED PERFUME TO CAUSE THE PIG TO LOSE HIS HEAD AND TEMPT HER TO GO TO AMERICA!
WHUT'S ABREWIN'? —WHAR'S STEVIE?
I WILL ESCORT THE OLD GOAT ON DECK — YOU FETCH THE GIRL CHILD!
STEVIE! THEY'VE MASSACREED YE!
THEY NEVER TELL HOW MANY INJUNS GINRUL CUSTER'S BOYS DID IN AFORE THEY WENT DOWN, BUT NO 7TH CAVULRY TROOPER'S AGONNA GIT HIS WITHOUT POTTIN' HIS PORTION
MILTON CANIFF

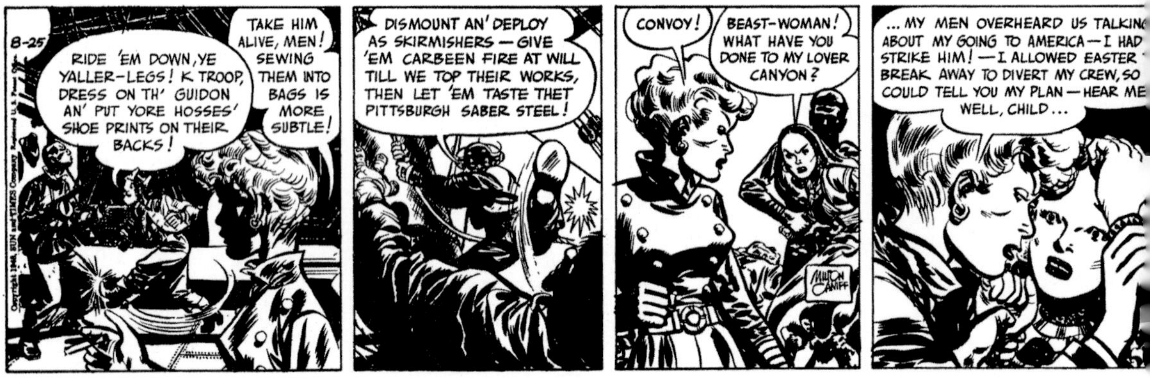
8-25
RIDE 'EM DOWN, YE YALLER-LEGS! K TROOP, DRESS ON TH' GUIDON AN' PUT YORE HOSSES' SHOE PRINTS ON THEIR BACKS!
TAKE HIM ALIVE, MEN! SEWING THEM INTO BAGS IS MORE SUBTLE!
DISMOUNT AN' DEPLOY AS SKIRMISHERS — GIVE 'EM CARBEEN FIRE AT WILL TILL WE TOP THEIR WORKS, THEN LET 'EM TASTE THET PITTSBURGH SABER STEEL!
CONVOY!
BEAST-WOMAN! WHAT HAVE YOU DONE TO MY LOVER CANYON?
MILTON CANIFF
... MY MEN OVERHEARD US TALKIN ABOUT MY GOING TO AMERICA — I HAD STRIKE HIM! — I ALLOWED EASTER BREAK AWAY TO DIVERT MY CREW, SO COULD TELL YOU MY PLAN — HEAR ME WELL, CHILD...

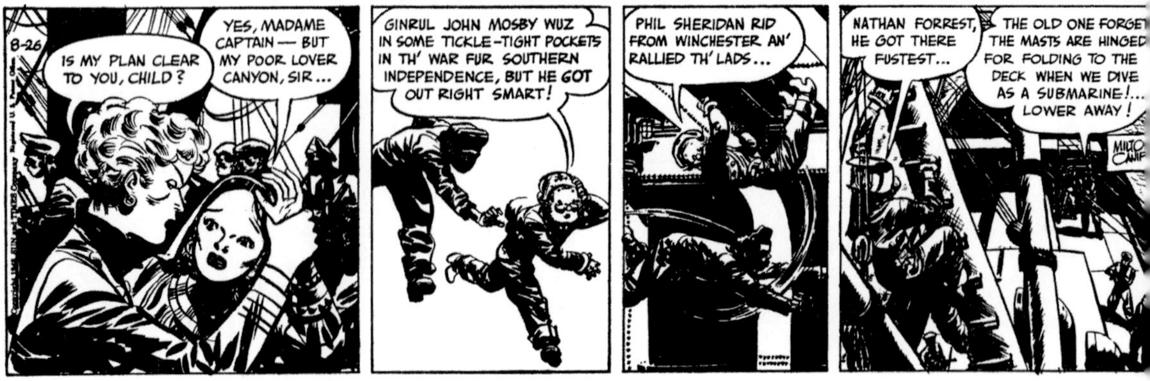
8-26
IS MY PLAN CLEAR TO YOU, CHILD?
YES, MADAME CAPTAIN — BUT MY POOR LOVER CANYON, SIR...
GINRUL JOHN MOSBY WUZ IN SOME TICKLE-TIGHT POCKETS IN TH' WAR FUR SOUTHERN INDEPENDENCE, BUT HE GOT OUT RIGHT SMART!
PHIL SHERIDAN RID FROM WINCHESTER AN' RALLIED TH' LADS...
NATHAN FORREST, HE GOT THERE FUSTEST...
THE OLD ONE FORGE THE MASTS ARE HINGE FOR FOLDING TO THE DECK WHEN WE DIVE AS A SUBMARINE!... LOWER AWAY!
MILTON CANIFF

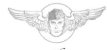

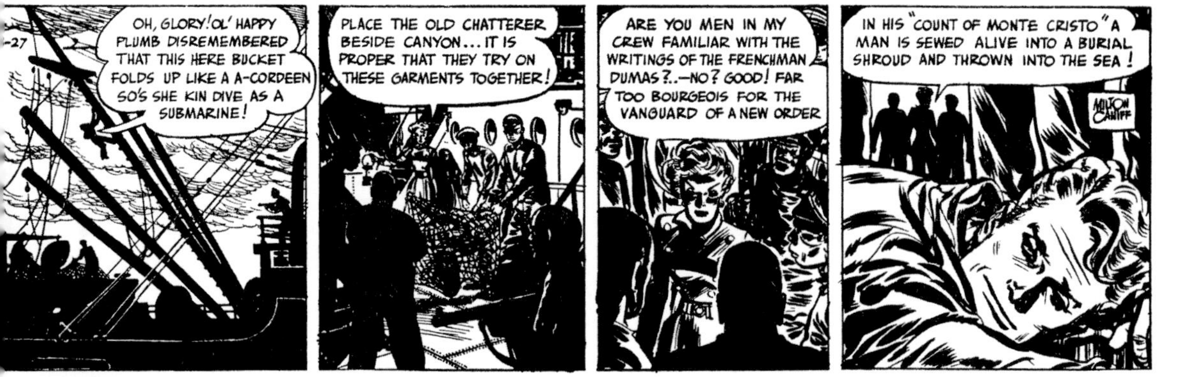
OH, GLORY! OL' HAPPY PLUMB DISREMEMBERED THAT THIS HERE BUCKET FOLDS UP LIKE A A-CORDEEN SO'S SHE KIN DIVE AS A SUBMARINE!
PLACE THE OLD CHATTERER BESIDE CANYON... IT IS PROPER THAT THEY TRY ON THESE GARMENTS TOGETHER!
ARE YOU MEN IN MY CREW FAMILIAR WITH THE WRITINGS OF THE FRENCHMAN DUMAS?..—NO? GOOD! FAR TOO BOURGEOIS FOR THE VANGUARD OF A NEW ORDER
IN HIS "COUNT OF MONTE CRISTO" A MAN IS SEWED ALIVE INTO A BURIAL SHROUD AND THROWN INTO THE SEA!
MILTON CANIFF

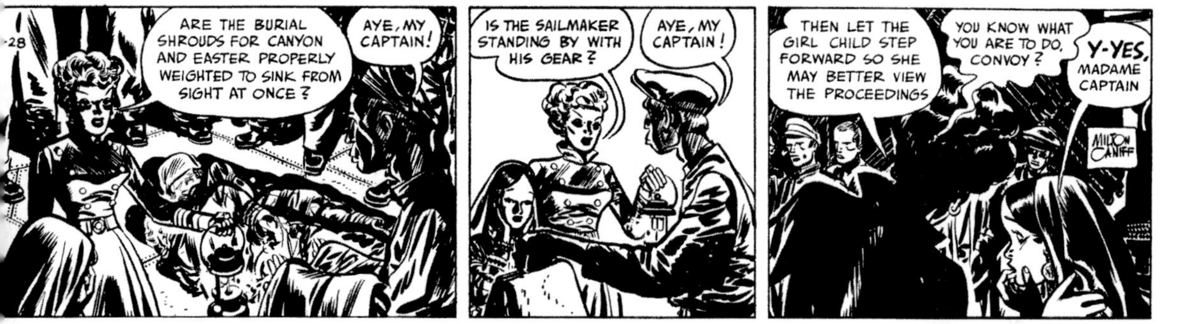
ARE THE BURIAL SHROUDS FOR CANYON AND EASTER PROPERLY WEIGHTED TO SINK FROM SIGHT AT ONCE?
AYE, MY CAPTAIN!
IS THE SAILMAKER STANDING BY WITH HIS GEAR?
AYE, MY CAPTAIN!
THEN LET THE GIRL CHILD STEP FORWARD SO SHE MAY BETTER VIEW THE PROCEEDINGS
YOU KNOW WHAT YOU ARE TO DO, CONVOY?
Y-YES, MADAME CAPTAIN
MILTON CANIFF

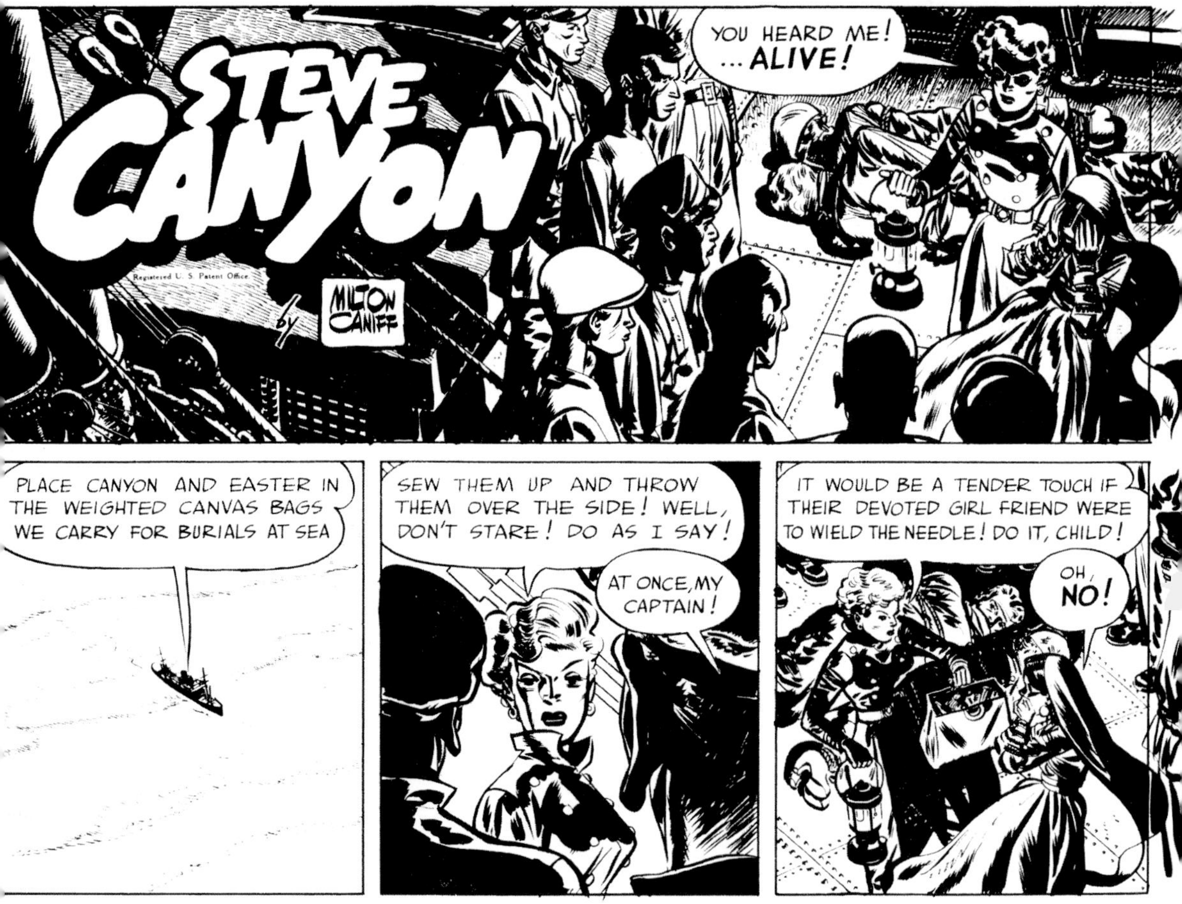
STEVE CANYON
Registered U. S. Patent Office
by MILTON CANIFF
YOU HEARD ME! ...ALIVE!
PLACE CANYON AND EASTER IN THE WEIGHTED CANVAS BAGS WE CARRY FOR BURIALS AT SEA
SEW THEM UP AND THROW THEM OVER THE SIDE! WELL, DON'T STARE! DO AS I SAY!
AT ONCE, MY CAPTAIN!
IT WOULD BE A TENDER TOUCH IF THEIR DEVOTED GIRL FRIEND WERE TO WIELD THE NEEDLE! DO IT, CHILD!
OH, NO!

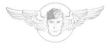

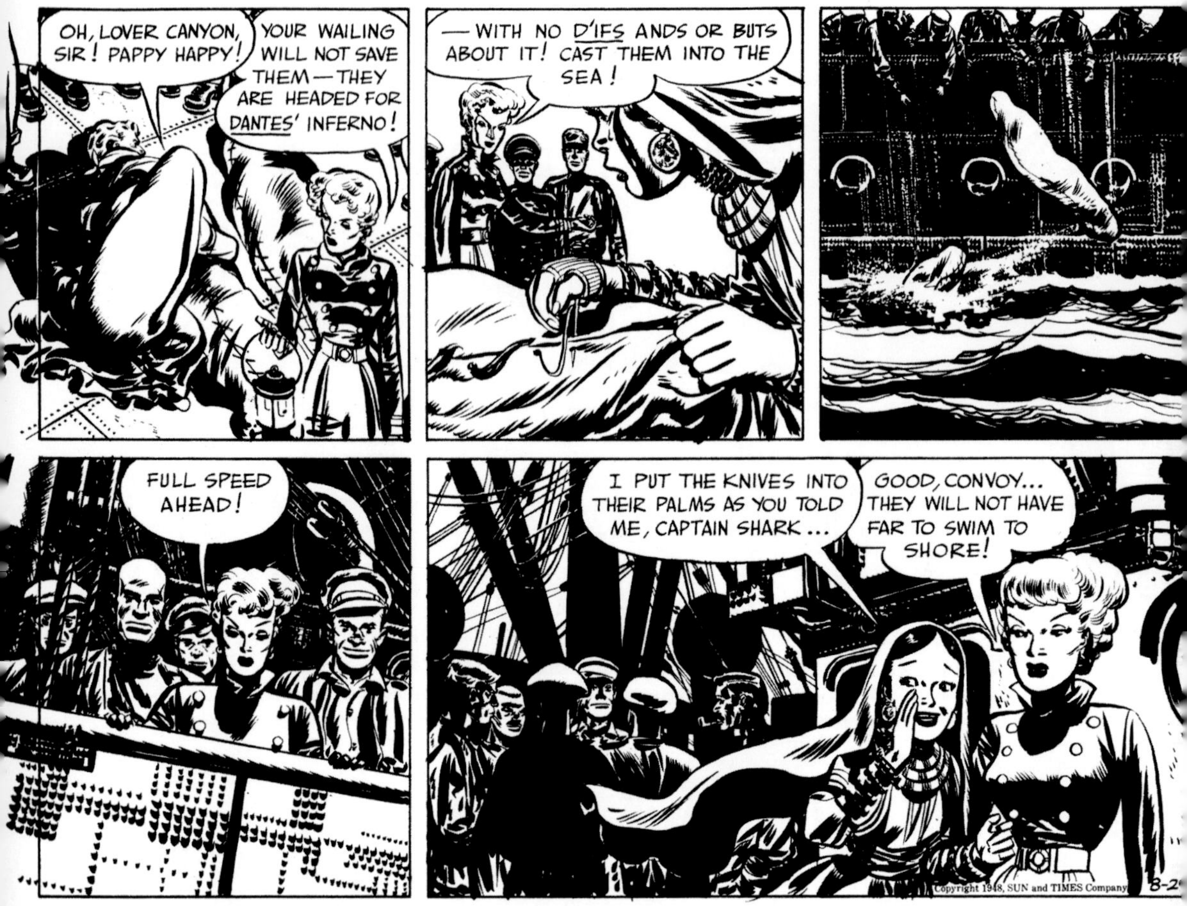
OH, LOVER CANYON, SIR! PAPPY HAPPY!
YOUR WAILING WILL NOT SAVE THEM — THEY ARE HEADED FOR DANTES' INFERNO!
— WITH NO D'IFS ANDS OR BUTS ABOUT IT! CAST THEM INTO THE SEA!
FULL SPEED AHEAD!
I PUT THE KNIVES INTO THEIR PALMS AS YOU TOLD ME, CAPTAIN SHARK...
GOOD, CONVOY... THEY WILL NOT HAVE FAR TO SWIM TO SHORE!
Copyright 1948, SUN and TIMES Company

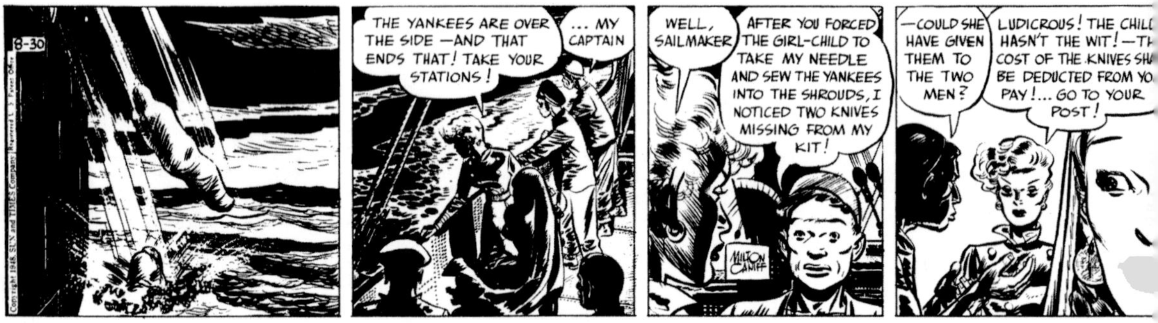
8-30
THE YANKEES ARE OVER THE SIDE — AND THAT ENDS THAT! TAKE YOUR STATIONS!
... MY CAPTAIN
WELL, SAILMAKER
AFTER YOU FORCED THE GIRL-CHILD TO TAKE MY NEEDLE AND SEW THE YANKEES INTO THE SHROUDS, I NOTICED TWO KNIVES MISSING FROM MY KIT!
MILTON CANIFF
— COULD SHE HAVE GIVEN THEM TO THE TWO MEN?
LUDICROUS! THE CHIL HASN'T THE WIT! — TH COST OF THE KNIVES SHA BE DEDUCTED FROM YO PAY!... GO TO YOUR POST!

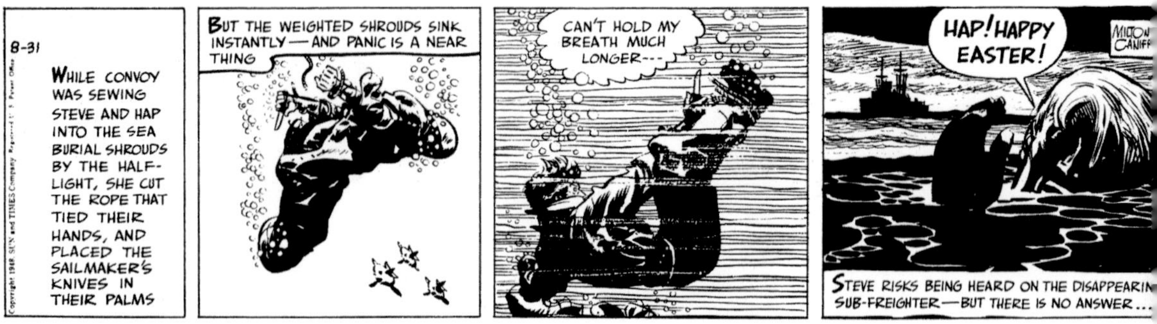
8-31
WHILE CONVOY WAS SEWING STEVE AND HAP INTO THE SEA BURIAL SHROUDS BY THE HALF-LIGHT, SHE CUT THE ROPE THAT TIED THEIR HANDS, AND PLACED THE SAILMAKER'S KNIVES IN THEIR PALMS
BUT THE WEIGHTED SHROUDS SINK INSTANTLY — AND PANIC IS A NEAR THING
CAN'T HOLD MY BREATH MUCH LONGER---
HAP! HAPPY EASTER!
MILTON CANIFF
STEVE RISKS BEING HEARD ON THE DISAPPEARIN SUB-FREIGHTER — BUT THERE IS NO ANSWER...

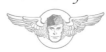

OH, NO! DID HAPPY GET TANGLED UP? DID HE DROP HIS KNIFE?

HAP!... HAPPY EASTER!

MAYBE HE DIDN'T CATCH ON THAT CONVOY WAS CUTTING OUR WRIST BONDS AND PLACING THE KNIFE IN OUR PALMS...

HAP! DON'T YOU HEAR ME?

MAYBE HE WAS SUFFOCATED BEFORE WE WERE TOSSED OVERBOARD...

HAP!

HE COULDN'T HAVE HELD HIS BREATH ANY LONGER THAN I DID—AND HE'D HAVE TO COME UP CLOSE BY—IF HE CAME UP

MILTON CANIFF

THERE SEEMS TO BE A CURRENT OR TIDE RUNNING TOWARD SHORE—THAT'S GOOD

BUT HAP DOESN'T ANSWER MY HAIL—AND THAT'S BAD...

CAN'T SWIM AROUND THIS AREA MUCH LONGER... BEGINNING TO TIRE... HEY! I FELT SOMETHING

IT'S A LOG! ...JUST IN TIME! IT'LL DRIFT IN...

MILTON CANIFF

WHY COULDN'T POOR HAPPY HAVE BEEN SO LUCKY?

OOLP! GOOLP!

?

HAPPY!

YOU MUST HAVE COME UP AND BEEN KNOCKED OUT, SO YOU COULDN'T REMOVE THE GAG! —THEN YOU GOT TANGLED IN THE BRANCHES

GULP! GLUP!

WE'RE NEAR SHORE, HAP! I CAN HEAR SURF...ARE YOU ALL IN ONE PIECE?

MMHMM

THEN JUST REST... I'LL HAVE THE STEWARD CALL YOU WHEN WE DOCK!

MILTON CANIFF

AS STEVE AND HAPPY EASTER LIE EXHAUSTED ON THE BEACH, FROM AROUND A POINT OF LAND COMES A STRANGE SOUND—

STAND UP!... HOOK UP!... CHECK EQUIPMENT!... SOUND OFF EQUIPMENT CHECK!...TEN OKAY! NINE OKAY!EIGHT---

...NOW THE GREEN LIGHT GOES OFF AND THE SERGEANT AND I ARE ALONE IN THIS PLACE THAT WAS SO FULL OF LIFE A FEW MOMENTS AGO...

...I DIDN'T NOTICE THE COLD SO MUCH BEFORE, BUT NOW THE SLIPSTREAM HOWLS THROUGH THE OPEN DOOR... I SETTLE BACK AND REACH FOR A CIGARETTE... THEN I REMEMBER I GAVE MY PACK TO ONE OF THE TROOPERS...

MILTON CANIFF

Steve Canyon

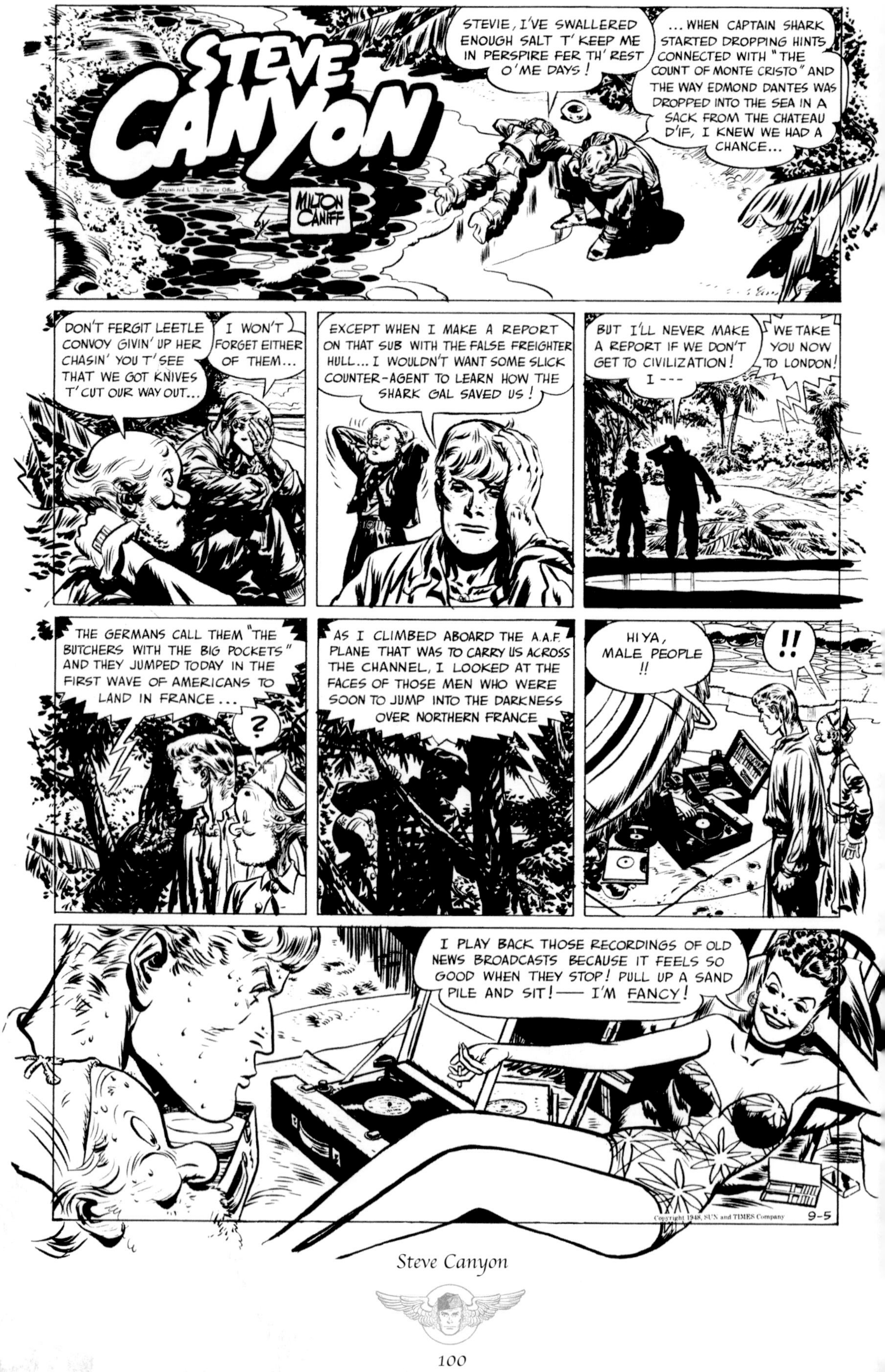
STEVE CANYON
Registered U. S. Patent Office
by MILTON CANIFF
STEVIE, I'VE SWALLERED ENOUGH SALT T' KEEP ME IN PERSPIRE FER TH' REST O'ME DAYS!
...WHEN CAPTAIN SHARK STARTED DROPPING HINTS CONNECTED WITH "THE COUNT OF MONTE CRISTO" AND THE WAY EDMOND DANTES WAS DROPPED INTO THE SEA IN A SACK FROM THE CHATEAU D'IF, I KNEW WE HAD A CHANCE...
DON'T FERGIT LEETLE CONVOY GIVIN' UP HER CHASIN' YOU T' SEE THAT WE GOT KNIVES T' CUT OUR WAY OUT...
I WON'T FORGET EITHER OF THEM...
EXCEPT WHEN I MAKE A REPORT ON THAT SUB WITH THE FALSE FREIGHTER HULL... I WOULDN'T WANT SOME SLICK COUNTER-AGENT TO LEARN HOW THE SHARK GAL SAVED US!
BUT I'LL NEVER MAKE A REPORT IF WE DON'T GET TO CIVILIZATION! I ---
WE TAKE YOU NOW TO LONDON!
THE GERMANS CALL THEM "THE BUTCHERS WITH THE BIG POCKETS" AND THEY JUMPED TODAY IN THE FIRST WAVE OF AMERICANS TO LAND IN FRANCE...
?
AS I CLIMBED ABOARD THE A.A.F. PLANE THAT WAS TO CARRY US ACROSS THE CHANNEL, I LOOKED AT THE FACES OF THOSE MEN WHO WERE SOON TO JUMP INTO THE DARKNESS OVER NORTHERN FRANCE
HIYA, MALE PEOPLE !!
!!
I PLAY BACK THOSE RECORDINGS OF OLD NEWS BROADCASTS BECAUSE IT FEELS SO GOOD WHEN THEY STOP! PULL UP A SAND PILE AND SIT! — I'M FANCY!
Copyright 1948, SUN and TIMES Company
9-5

Steve Canyon

Chapter Four

Plantation Sabotage
September 4 – November 3, 1948

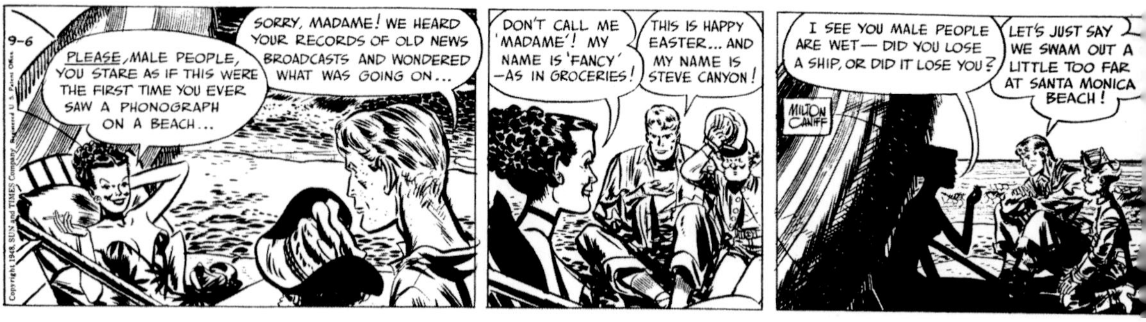
9-6
Copyright 1948, SUN and TIMES Company Registered U.S. Patent Office
PLEASE, MALE PEOPLE, YOU STARE AS IF THIS WERE THE FIRST TIME YOU EVER SAW A PHONOGRAPH ON A BEACH...
SORRY, MADAME! WE HEARD YOUR RECORDS OF OLD NEWS BROADCASTS AND WONDERED WHAT WAS GOING ON...
DON'T CALL ME 'MADAME'! MY NAME IS 'FANCY' —AS IN GROCERIES!
THIS IS HAPPY EASTER... AND MY NAME IS STEVE CANYON!
I SEE YOU MALE PEOPLE ARE WET— DID YOU LOSE A SHIP, OR DID IT LOSE YOU?
LET'S JUST SAY WE SWAM OUT A LITTLE TOO FAR AT SANTA MONICA BEACH!
MILTON CANIFF

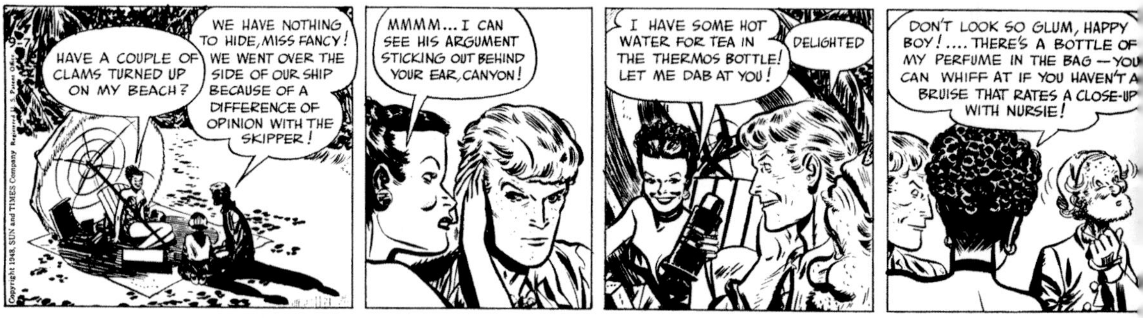
9-7
Copyright 1948, SUN and TIMES Company Registered U.S. Patent Office
HAVE A COUPLE OF CLAMS TURNED UP ON MY BEACH?
WE HAVE NOTHING TO HIDE, MISS FANCY! WE WENT OVER THE SIDE OF OUR SHIP BECAUSE OF A DIFFERENCE OF OPINION WITH THE SKIPPER!
MMMM... I CAN SEE HIS ARGUMENT STICKING OUT BEHIND YOUR EAR, CANYON!
I HAVE SOME HOT WATER FOR TEA IN THE THERMOS BOTTLE! LET ME DAB AT YOU!
DELIGHTED
DON'T LOOK SO GLUM, HAPPY BOY!.... THERE'S A BOTTLE OF MY PERFUME IN THE BAG —YOU CAN WHIFF AT IF YOU HAVEN'T A BRUISE THAT RATES A CLOSE-UP WITH NURSIE!

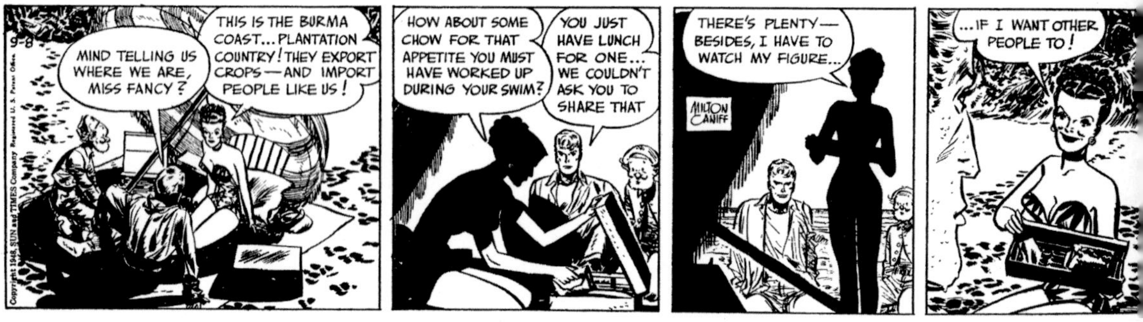
9-8
Copyright 1948, SUN and TIMES Company Registered U.S. Patent Office
MIND TELLING US WHERE WE ARE, MISS FANCY?
THIS IS THE BURMA COAST... PLANTATION COUNTRY! THEY EXPORT CROPS—AND IMPORT PEOPLE LIKE US!
HOW ABOUT SOME CHOW FOR THAT APPETITE YOU MUST HAVE WORKED UP DURING YOUR SWIM?
YOU JUST HAVE LUNCH FOR ONE... WE COULDN'T ASK YOU TO SHARE THAT
THERE'S PLENTY— BESIDES, I HAVE TO WATCH MY FIGURE...
MILTON CANIFF
...IF I WANT OTHER PEOPLE TO!

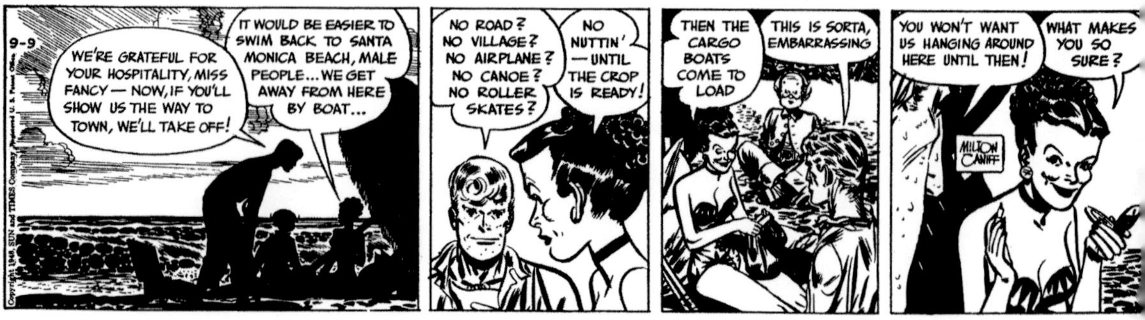
9-9
Copyright 1948, SUN and TIMES Company Registered U.S. Patent Office
WE'RE GRATEFUL FOR YOUR HOSPITALITY, MISS FANCY — NOW, IF YOU'LL SHOW US THE WAY TO TOWN, WE'LL TAKE OFF!
IT WOULD BE EASIER TO SWIM BACK TO SANTA MONICA BEACH, MALE PEOPLE... WE GET AWAY FROM HERE BY BOAT...
NO ROAD? NO VILLAGE? NO AIRPLANE? NO CANOE? NO ROLLER SKATES?
NO NUTTIN' —UNTIL THE CROP IS READY!
THEN THE CARGO BOATS COME TO LOAD
THIS IS SORTA, EMBARRASSING
YOU WON'T WANT US HANGING AROUND HERE UNTIL THEN!
WHAT MAKES YOU SO SURE?
MILTON CANIFF

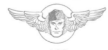

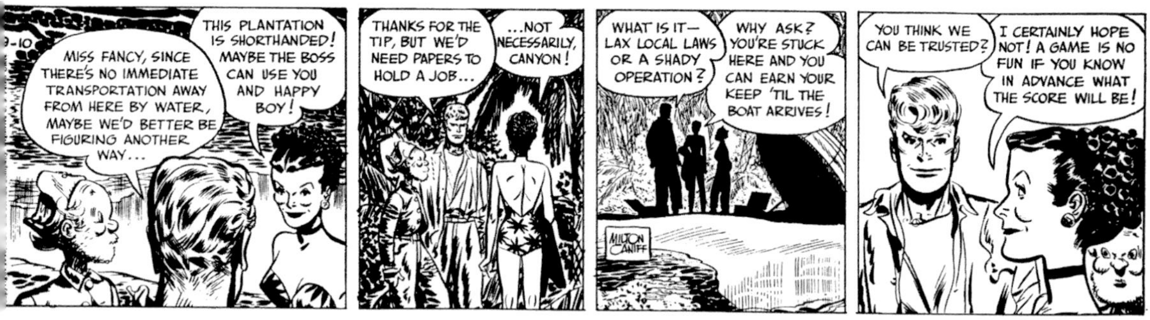
MISS FANCY, SINCE THERE'S NO IMMEDIATE TRANSPORTATION AWAY FROM HERE BY WATER, MAYBE WE'D BETTER BE FIGURING ANOTHER WAY...
THIS PLANTATION IS SHORTHANDED! MAYBE THE BOSS CAN USE YOU AND HAPPY BOY!
THANKS FOR THE TIP, BUT WE'D NEED PAPERS TO HOLD A JOB...
...NOT NECESSARILY, CANYON!
WHAT IS IT— LAX LOCAL LAWS OR A SHADY OPERATION?
WHY ASK? YOU'RE STUCK HERE AND YOU CAN EARN YOUR KEEP 'TIL THE BOAT ARRIVES!
MILTON CANIFF
YOU THINK WE CAN BE TRUSTED?
I CERTAINLY HOPE NOT! A GAME IS NO FUN IF YOU KNOW IN ADVANCE WHAT THE SCORE WILL BE!

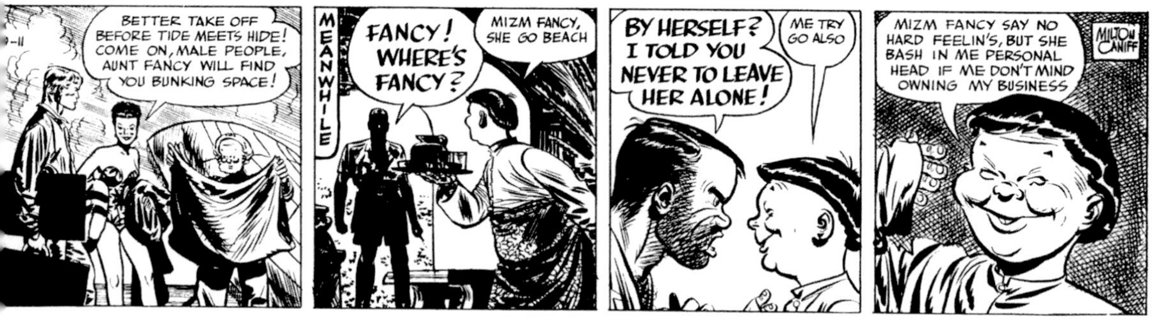
BETTER TAKE OFF BEFORE TIDE MEETS HIDE! COME ON, MALE PEOPLE, AUNT FANCY WILL FIND YOU BUNKING SPACE!
MEANWHILE
FANCY! WHERE'S FANCY?
MIZM FANCY, SHE GO BEACH
BY HERSELF? I TOLD YOU NEVER TO LEAVE HER ALONE!
ME TRY GO ALSO
MIZM FANCY SAY NO HARD FEELIN'S, BUT SHE BASH IN ME PERSONAL HEAD IF ME DON'T MIND OWNING MY BUSINESS
MILTON CANIFF

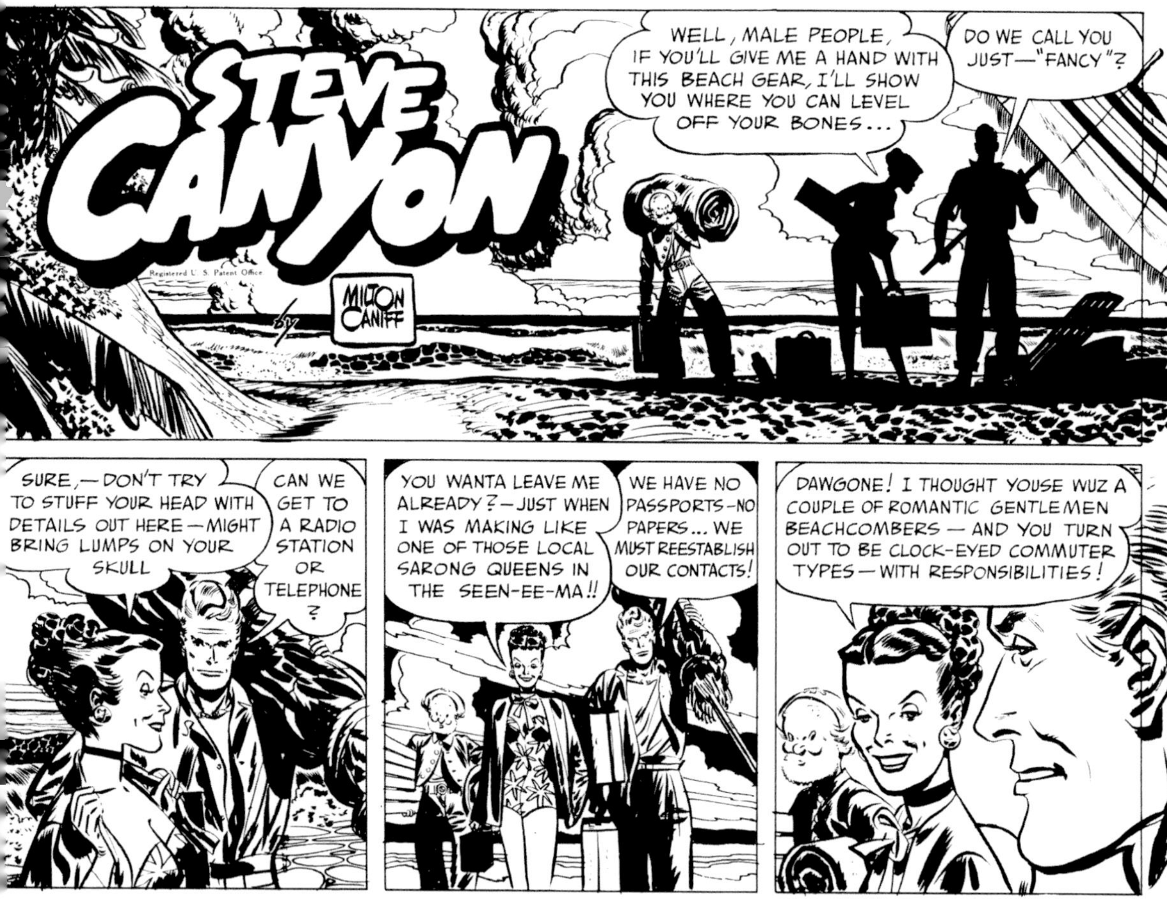
STEVE CANYON
Registered U. S. Patent Office
MILTON CANIFF
WELL, MALE PEOPLE, IF YOU'LL GIVE ME A HAND WITH THIS BEACH GEAR, I'LL SHOW YOU WHERE YOU CAN LEVEL OFF YOUR BONES...
DO WE CALL YOU JUST—"FANCY"?
SURE,—DON'T TRY TO STUFF YOUR HEAD WITH DETAILS OUT HERE—MIGHT BRING LUMPS ON YOUR SKULL
CAN WE GET TO A RADIO STATION OR TELEPHONE?
YOU WANTA LEAVE ME ALREADY?—JUST WHEN I WAS MAKING LIKE ONE OF THOSE LOCAL SARONG QUEENS IN THE SEEN-EE-MA!!
WE HAVE NO PASSPORTS—NO PAPERS... WE MUST REESTABLISH OUR CONTACTS!
DAWGONE! I THOUGHT YOUSE WUZ A COUPLE OF ROMANTIC GENTLEMEN BEACHCOMBERS — AND YOU TURN OUT TO BE CLOCK-EYED COMMUTER TYPES — WITH RESPONSIBILITIES!

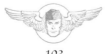

Steve Canyon

BUT WE'RE DEVILS ON OUR NIGHTS OUT... HEY! HEAVY DUTY ROAD BLOCK AHEAD!

FANCY!

WHO ARE THEY?

COUPLE OF STRAYS, RAK—NAMED CANYON AND EASTER...I THOUGHT THEY MIGHT FILL IN ON THE JOB UNTIL---

—UNTIL YOU CAN MAKE THE BIG ONE CRAZY ABOUT YOU!

THE ONLY THING I ASK, STEVIE...WHEN YE BASH HIS FACE IN, LEAVE ME BRING HIM BACK TO CONSCIOUSNESS BY PULLIN' OUT HAIRS — ONE AT A TIME!

Copyright 1948, SUN and TIMES Company   9-12

MISS FANCY'S BOY FRIEND CAN SLUG!

STEVIE! HE SASHAYED UP AN' POKED YE WHILE YORE ARMS WUZ FULL O' TH' GAL'S BEACH TRAPPIN'S — AIN'T YE AGONNA TAKE OUT AFTER HIM?

—AND WALTZ INTO HIS PRIVATE ARMY? — NO, HAP, WE'LL SETTLE WITH THAT RAK WHEN WE KNOW ALL THE DOPE ON THIS GOONEY FARM

HE LOOKED LIKE THET THERE A-DOLPHY HITLER! —D'Y'RECKON...?

I KNEW I'D CATCH YOU SOONER OR LATER, FANCY! YOU'VE BEEN MEETING CANYON ON THE BEACH!

GEE, HOW DID YOU GUESS, RAK? HE AND EASTER HAVE BEEN HIDDEN AT THE BOTTOM OF THE LAGOON IN A PAIR OF WAR SURPLUS DIVING SUITS — LIVING ON K RATIONS...

MILTON CANIFF

SIMMER DOWN, RAK! CANYON AND EASTER EVIDENTLY JUMPED A SHIP — AND TURNED UP ON THIS BEACH...DON'T TRY TO BUILD A PLOT AROUND IT!

WHERE ARE YOU GOING, FANCY?

TO SEND SOYBOY TO PICK UP MY PHONOGRAPH FROM THAT PLACE ON THE PATH WHERE YOU POKED CANYON!

ARE YOU GOING TO PLAY MORE OF THOSE WARTIME NEWS BROADCASTS —? THEY DRIVE ME CRAZY!

A LITTLE TOUCH OF CONSCIENCE —HMMM?

WELL, HAP,'OUR INITIAL BEACHHEAD ASSAULT WAS SUCCESSFUL, BUT WE ENCOUNTERED UNEXPECTED RESISTANCE FURTHER INLAND!.. BETTER FALL BACK AND REGROUP!

HEADS UP, STEVIE! FRUM WHUT'S ACOMIN', WOULD YOU SAY OUR LUCK IS TURNIN' UP, DOWN OR SIDEWISE?

MILTON CANIFF

Steve Canyon

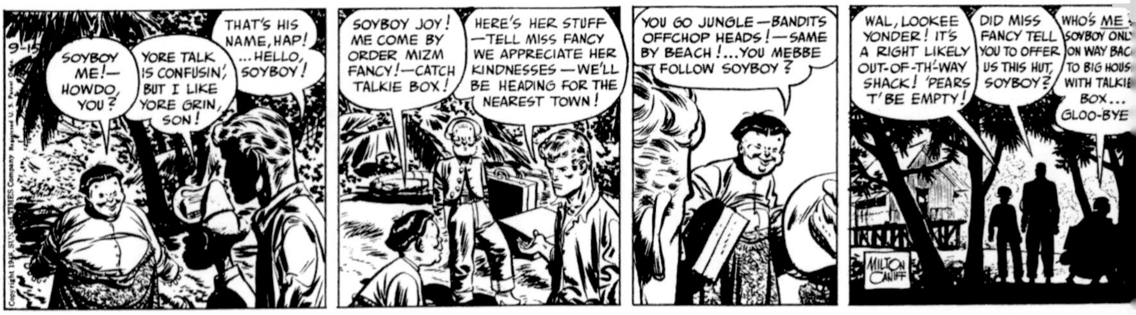
9-15
SOYBOY ME!—HOWDO, YOU?
YORE TALK IS CONFUSIN', BUT I LIKE YORE GRIN, SON!
THAT'S HIS NAME, HAP! ...HELLO, SOYBOY!
SOYBOY JOY! ME COME BY ORDER MIZM FANCY!—CATCH TALKIE BOX!
HERE'S HER STUFF—TELL MISS FANCY WE APPRECIATE HER KINDNESSES—WE'LL BE HEADING FOR THE NEAREST TOWN!
YOU GO JUNGLE—BANDITS OFFCHOP HEADS!—SAME BY BEACH!...YOU MEBBE FOLLOW SOYBOY?
WAL, LOOKEE YONDER! IT'S A RIGHT LIKELY OUT-OF-TH'-WAY SHACK! 'PEARS T'BE EMPTY!
DID MISS FANCY TELL YOU TO OFFER US THIS HUT, SOYBOY?
WHO'S ME SOYBOY ONL ON WAY BAC TO BIG HOUS WITH TALKIE BOX... GLOO-BYE
MILTON CANIFF

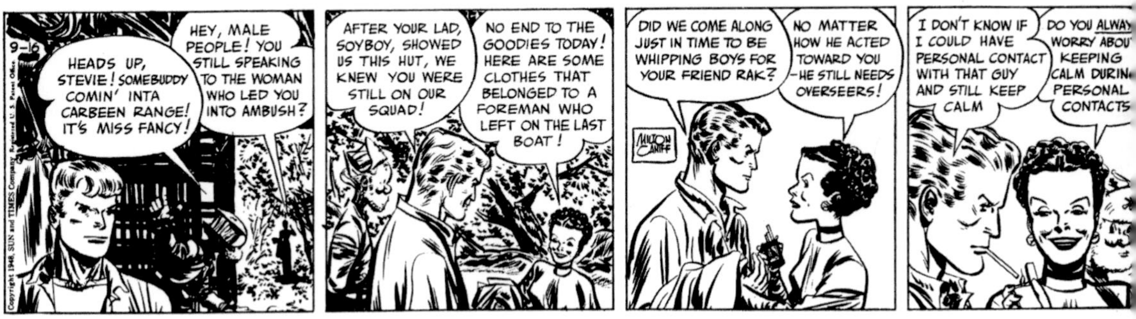
9-16
HEADS UP, STEVIE! SOMEBUDDY COMIN' INTA CARBEEN RANGE! IT'S MISS FANCY!
HEY, MALE PEOPLE! YOU STILL SPEAKING TO THE WOMAN WHO LED YOU INTO AMBUSH?
AFTER YOUR LAD, SOYBOY, SHOWED US THIS HUT, WE KNEW YOU WERE STILL ON OUR SQUAD!
NO END TO THE GOODIES TODAY! HERE ARE SOME CLOTHES THAT BELONGED TO A FOREMAN WHO LEFT ON THE LAST BOAT!
DID WE COME ALONG JUST IN TIME TO BE WHIPPING BOYS FOR YOUR FRIEND RAK?
NO MATTER HOW HE ACTED TOWARD YOU—HE STILL NEEDS OVERSEERS!
MILTON CANIFF
I DON'T KNOW IF I COULD HAVE PERSONAL CONTACT WITH THAT GUY AND STILL KEEP CALM
DO YOU ALWAY WORRY ABOU KEEPING CALM DURIN PERSONAL CONTACTS

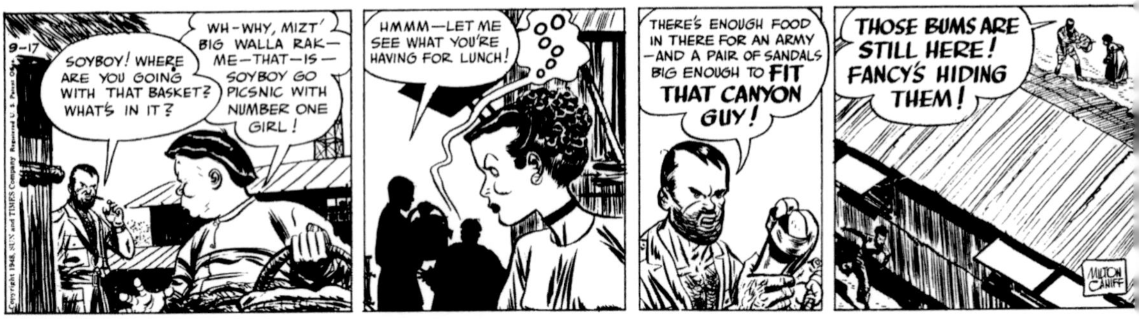
9-17
SOYBOY! WHERE ARE YOU GOING WITH THAT BASKET? WHAT'S IN IT?
WH-WHY, MIZT' BIG WALLA RAK—ME—THAT—IS—SOYBOY GO PICSNIC WITH NUMBER ONE GIRL!
HMMM—LET ME SEE WHAT YOU'RE HAVING FOR LUNCH!
THERE'S ENOUGH FOOD IN THERE FOR AN ARMY—AND A PAIR OF SANDALS BIG ENOUGH TO FIT THAT CANYON GUY!
THOSE BUMS ARE STILL HERE! FANCY'S HIDING THEM!
MILTON CANIFF

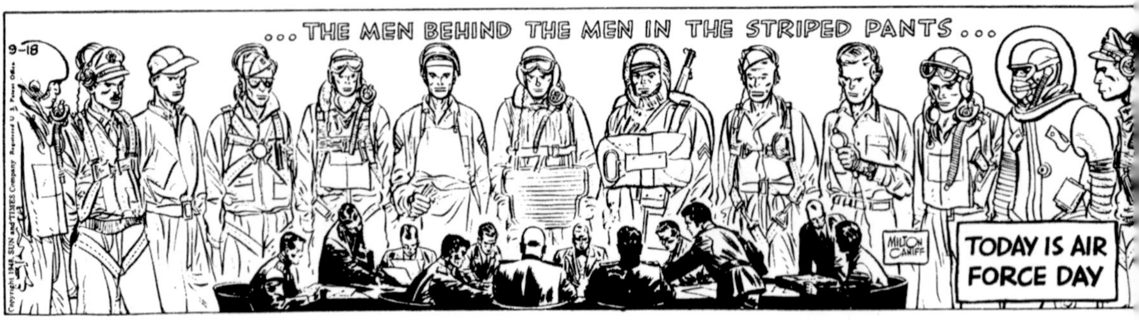
9-18
...THE MEN BEHIND THE MEN IN THE STRIPED PANTS...
MILTON CANIFF
TODAY IS AIR FORCE DAY

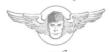

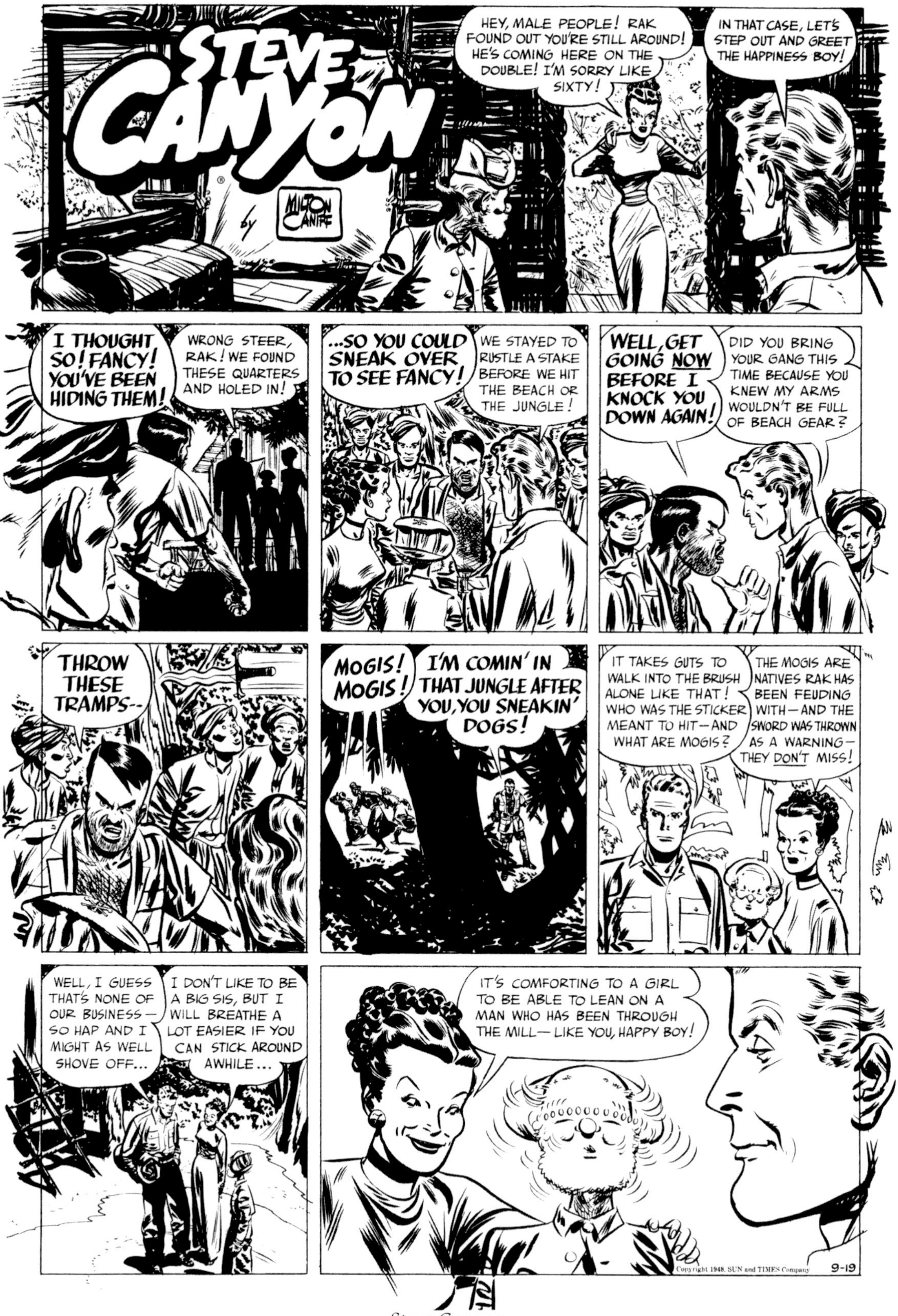
STEVE CANYON
by MILTON CANIFF
HEY, MALE PEOPLE! RAK FOUND OUT YOU'RE STILL AROUND! HE'S COMING HERE ON THE DOUBLE! I'M SORRY LIKE SIXTY!
IN THAT CASE, LET'S STEP OUT AND GREET THE HAPPINESS BOY!
I THOUGHT SO! FANCY! YOU'VE BEEN HIDING THEM!
WRONG STEER, RAK! WE FOUND THESE QUARTERS AND HOLED IN!
...SO YOU COULD SNEAK OVER TO SEE FANCY!
WE STAYED TO RUSTLE A STAKE BEFORE WE HIT THE BEACH OR THE JUNGLE!
WELL, GET GOING NOW BEFORE I KNOCK YOU DOWN AGAIN!
DID YOU BRING YOUR GANG THIS TIME BECAUSE YOU KNEW MY ARMS WOULDN'T BE FULL OF BEACH GEAR?
THROW THESE TRAMPS--
MOGIS! MOGIS!
I'M COMIN' IN THAT JUNGLE AFTER YOU, YOU SNEAKIN' DOGS!
IT TAKES GUTS TO WALK INTO THE BRUSH ALONE LIKE THAT! WHO WAS THE STICKER MEANT TO HIT—AND WHAT ARE MOGIS?
THE MOGIS ARE NATIVES RAK HAS BEEN FEUDING WITH—AND THE SWORD WAS THROWN AS A WARNING—THEY DON'T MISS!
WELL, I GUESS THAT'S NONE OF OUR BUSINESS—SO HAP AND I MIGHT AS WELL SHOVE OFF...
I DON'T LIKE TO BE A BIG SIS, BUT I WILL BREATHE A LOT EASIER IF YOU CAN STICK AROUND AWHILE...
IT'S COMFORTING TO A GIRL TO BE ABLE TO LEAN ON A MAN WHO HAS BEEN THROUGH THE MILL—LIKE YOU, HAPPY BOY!
Copyright 1948, SUN and TIMES Company
9-19

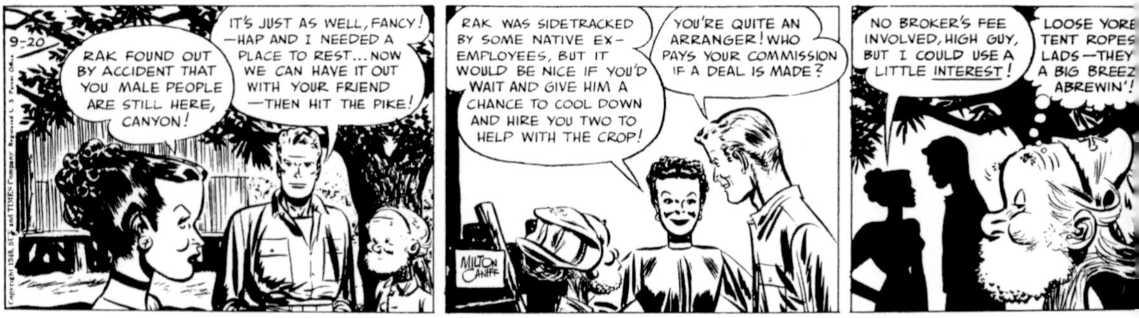
9-20
RAK FOUND OUT BY ACCIDENT THAT YOU MALE PEOPLE ARE STILL HERE, CANYON!
IT'S JUST AS WELL, FANCY! —HAP AND I NEEDED A PLACE TO REST... NOW WE CAN HAVE IT OUT WITH YOUR FRIEND —THEN HIT THE PIKE!
RAK WAS SIDETRACKED BY SOME NATIVE EX-EMPLOYEES, BUT IT WOULD BE NICE IF YOU'D WAIT AND GIVE HIM A CHANCE TO COOL DOWN AND HIRE YOU TWO TO HELP WITH THE CROP!
YOU'RE QUITE AN ARRANGER! WHO PAYS YOUR COMMISSION IF A DEAL IS MADE?
MILTON CANIFF
NO BROKER'S FEE INVOLVED, HIGH GUY, BUT I COULD USE A LITTLE INTEREST!
LOOSE YORE TENT ROPES LADS—THEY A BIG BREEZ ABREWIN'!

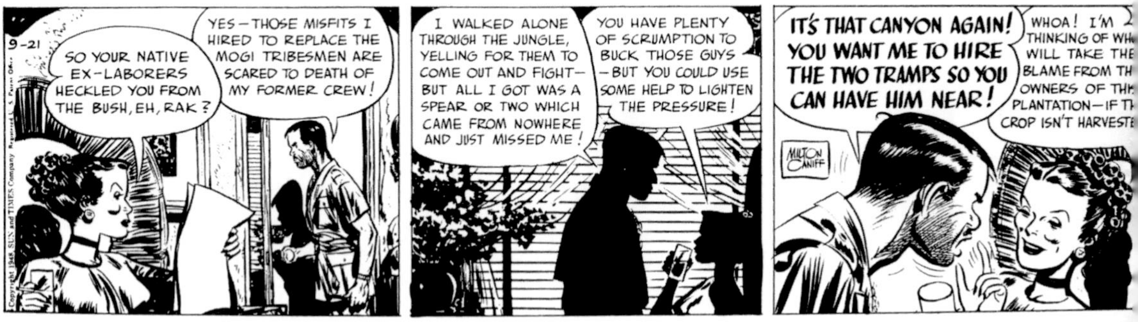
9-21
SO YOUR NATIVE EX-LABORERS HECKLED YOU FROM THE BUSH, EH, RAK?
YES—THOSE MISFITS I HIRED TO REPLACE THE MOGI TRIBESMEN ARE SCARED TO DEATH OF MY FORMER CREW!
I WALKED ALONE THROUGH THE JUNGLE, YELLING FOR THEM TO COME OUT AND FIGHT—BUT ALL I GOT WAS A SPEAR OR TWO WHICH CAME FROM NOWHERE AND JUST MISSED ME!
YOU HAVE PLENTY OF SCRUMPTION TO BUCK THOSE GUYS —BUT YOU COULD USE SOME HELP TO LIGHTEN THE PRESSURE!
IT'S THAT CANYON AGAIN! YOU WANT ME TO HIRE THE TWO TRAMPS SO YOU CAN HAVE HIM NEAR!
WHOA! I'M THINKING OF WH WILL TAKE THE BLAME FROM TH OWNERS OF TH PLANTATION—IF T CROP ISN'T HARVESTE
MILTON CANIFF

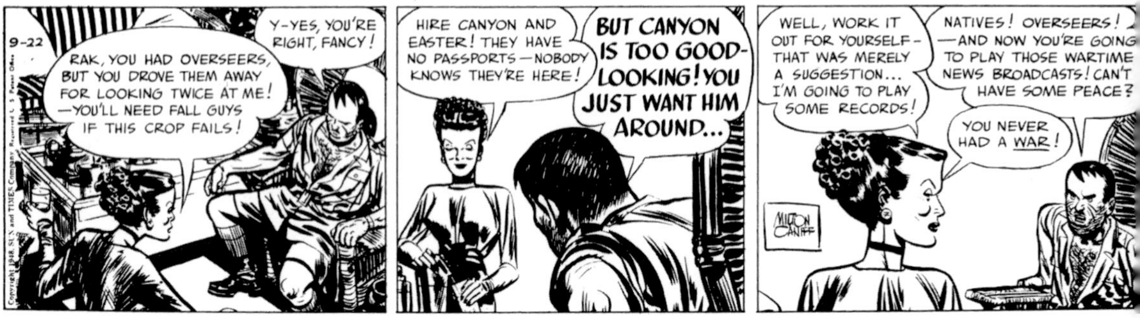
9-22
RAK, YOU HAD OVERSEERS, BUT YOU DROVE THEM AWAY FOR LOOKING TWICE AT ME! —YOU'LL NEED FALL GUYS IF THIS CROP FAILS!
Y-YES, YOU'RE RIGHT, FANCY!
HIRE CANYON AND EASTER! THEY HAVE NO PASSPORTS—NOBODY KNOWS THEY'RE HERE!
BUT CANYON IS TOO GOOD-LOOKING! YOU JUST WANT HIM AROUND...
WELL, WORK IT OUT FOR YOURSELF-THAT WAS MERELY A SUGGESTION... I'M GOING TO PLAY SOME RECORDS!
NATIVES! OVERSEERS! —AND NOW YOU'RE GOING TO PLAY THOSE WARTIME NEWS BROADCASTS! CAN'T HAVE SOME PEACE?
YOU NEVER HAD A WAR!
MILTON CANIFF

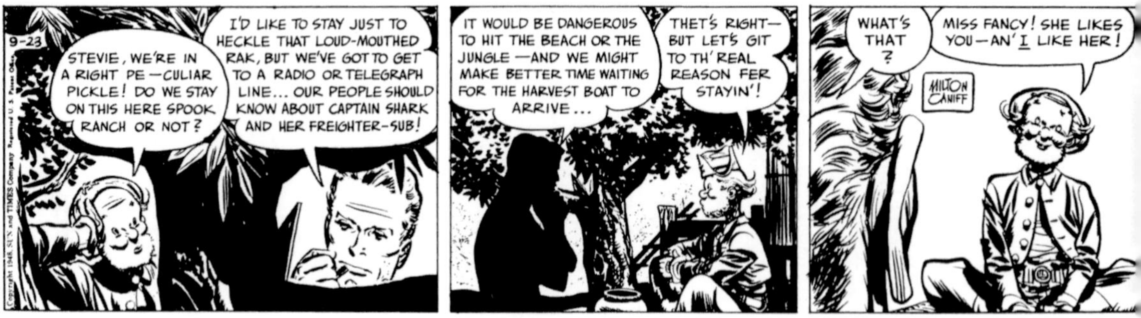
9-23
STEVIE, WE'RE IN A RIGHT PE—CULIAR PICKLE! DO WE STAY ON THIS HERE SPOOK RANCH OR NOT?
I'D LIKE TO STAY JUST TO HECKLE THAT LOUD-MOUTHED RAK, BUT WE'VE GOT TO GET TO A RADIO OR TELEGRAPH LINE... OUR PEOPLE SHOULD KNOW ABOUT CAPTAIN SHARK AND HER FREIGHTER-SUB!
IT WOULD BE DANGEROUS TO HIT THE BEACH OR THE JUNGLE —AND WE MIGHT MAKE BETTER TIME WAITING FOR THE HARVEST BOAT TO ARRIVE...
THET'S RIGHT—BUT LET'S GIT TO TH' REAL REASON FER STAYIN'!
WHAT'S THAT?
MISS FANCY! SHE LIKES YOU—AN' I LIKE HER!
MILTON CANIFF

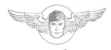

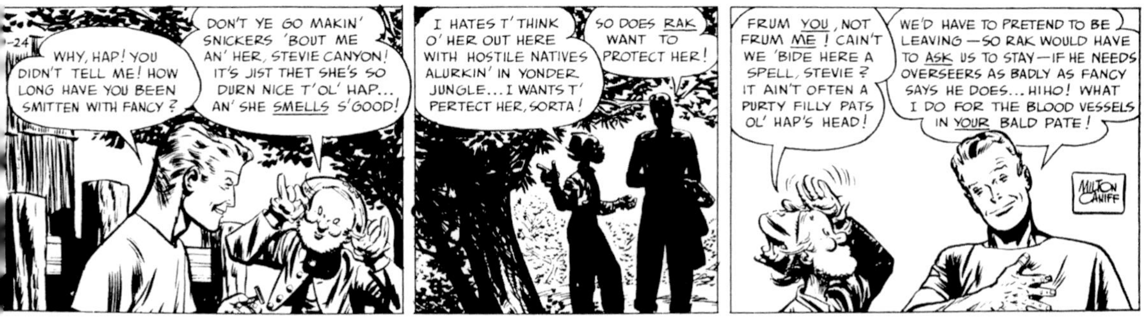
-24
WHY, HAP! YOU DIDN'T TELL ME! HOW LONG HAVE YOU BEEN SMITTEN WITH FANCY?
DON'T YE GO MAKIN' SNICKERS 'BOUT ME AN' HER, STEVIE CANYON! IT'S JIST THET SHE'S SO DURN NICE T' OL' HAP... AN' SHE SMELLS S'GOOD!
I HATES T' THINK O' HER OUT HERE WITH HOSTILE NATIVES ALURKIN' IN YONDER JUNGLE... I WANTS T' PERTECT HER, SORTA!
SO DOES RAK WANT TO PROTECT HER!
FRUM YOU, NOT FRUM ME! CAIN'T WE 'BIDE HERE A SPELL, STEVIE? IT AIN'T OFTEN A PURTY FILLY PATS OL' HAP'S HEAD!
WE'D HAVE TO PRETEND TO BE LEAVING — SO RAK WOULD HAVE TO ASK US TO STAY — IF HE NEEDS OVERSEERS AS BADLY AS FANCY SAYS HE DOES... HIHO! WHAT I DO FOR THE BLOOD VESSELS IN YOUR BALD PATE!
MILTON CANIFF

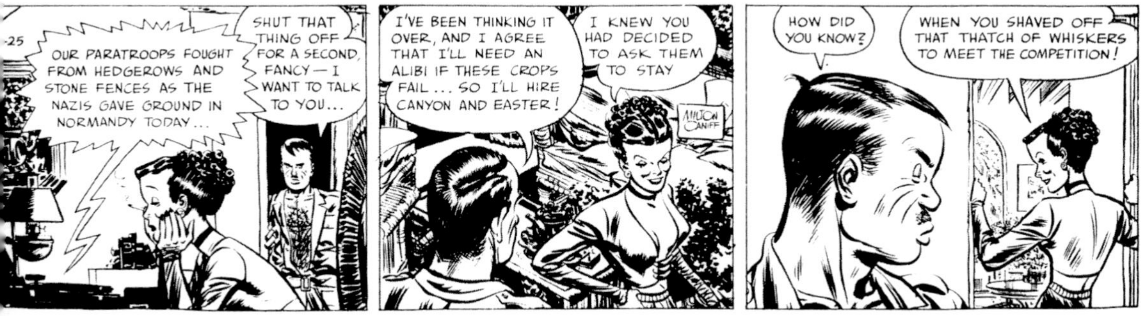
-25
OUR PARATROOPS FOUGHT FROM HEDGEROWS AND STONE FENCES AS THE NAZIS GAVE GROUND IN NORMANDY TODAY...
SHUT THAT THING OFF FOR A SECOND, FANCY — I WANT TO TALK TO YOU...
I'VE BEEN THINKING IT OVER, AND I AGREE THAT I'LL NEED AN ALIBI IF THESE CROPS FAIL... SO I'LL HIRE CANYON AND EASTER!
I KNEW YOU HAD DECIDED TO ASK THEM TO STAY
MILTON CANIFF
HOW DID YOU KNOW?
WHEN YOU SHAVED OFF THAT THATCH OF WHISKERS TO MEET THE COMPETITION!

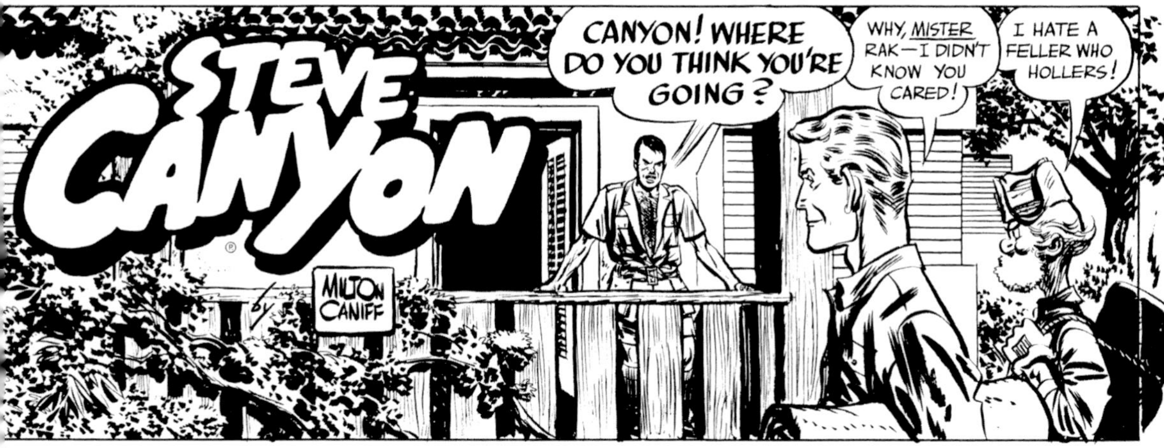
STEVE CANYON
MILTON CANIFF
CANYON! WHERE DO YOU THINK YOU'RE GOING?
WHY, MISTER RAK — I DIDN'T KNOW YOU CARED!
I HATE A FELLER WHO HOLLERS!

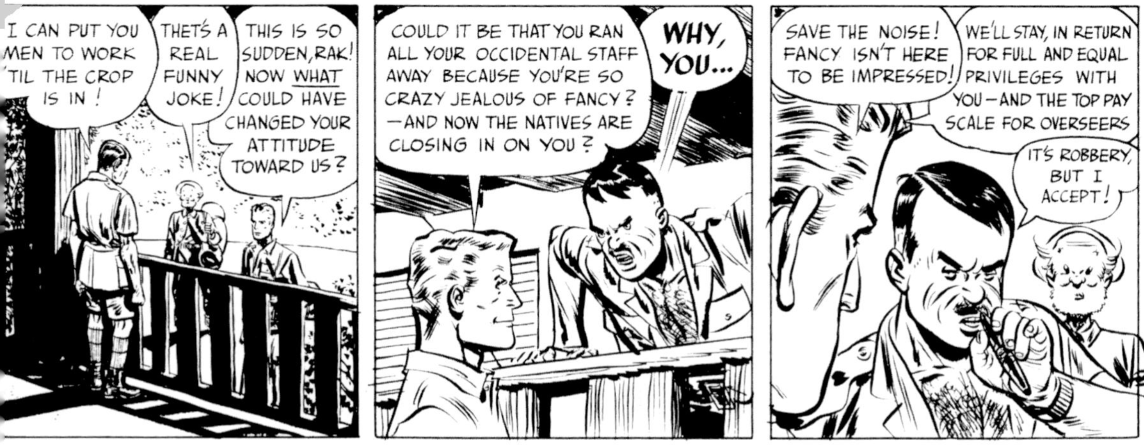
I CAN PUT YOU MEN TO WORK 'TIL THE CROP IS IN!
THET'S A REAL FUNNY JOKE!
THIS IS SO SUDDEN, RAK! NOW WHAT COULD HAVE CHANGED YOUR ATTITUDE TOWARD US?
COULD IT BE THAT YOU RAN ALL YOUR OCCIDENTAL STAFF AWAY BECAUSE YOU'RE SO CRAZY JEALOUS OF FANCY? — AND NOW THE NATIVES ARE CLOSING IN ON YOU?
WHY, YOU...
SAVE THE NOISE! FANCY ISN'T HERE TO BE IMPRESSED!
WE'LL STAY, IN RETURN FOR FULL AND EQUAL PRIVILEGES WITH YOU — AND THE TOP PAY SCALE FOR OVERSEERS
IT'S ROBBERY, BUT I ACCEPT!

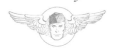

LATER

SO YOU'RE GOING TO BE WITH US FOR A WHILE, BROTHER CANYON...

YEP, FANCY— WE COULDN'T LEAVE YOU HERE WITH THE MOGI TRIBE OF NATIVE EX-EMPLOYEES LURKING OUT THERE IN THE JUNGLE!

I WISH YOU REALLY _WERE_ STAYING TO PROTECT ME!

HUH?

I DON'T KNOW HOW YOU LEARNED THAT RAK FIRED THE MOGIS BECAUSE HE HAD BEEN PAID TO SEE THAT THE CROP THEY WERE TENDING ON THIS PLANTATION DID _NOT_ GET EXPORTED TO AMERICA!

THE MOGIS ARE SMART ENOUGH TO KNOW THAT THE ONLY WAY FOR THEIR COUNTRY TO REGAIN ITS PRE-WAR STATUS IS TO RESUME ITS EXPORT BUSINESS...

...THIS WAY THE UNITED STATES DOESN'T GET A CROP IT NEEDS—AND THE LOCAL COUNTRY DOESN'T GET DOLLARS _IT_ NEEDS...

I DON'T SEE HOW YOU BOYS FIGURED ALL THAT STUFF OUT AND DECIDED TO STAY AND DO SOMETHING ABOUT IT...

9-

9-27

WAL, STEVIE, OL' ADOLPH H. RAK HIRED US T'OVERSEE LET'S START LOOKIN'!

RIGHT, HAP! THE NATIVE STRAWBOSS IS SUPPOSED TO HAVE ALL THE INSTRUCTIONS!

WE'RE HERE TO OVERSEE THE GATHERING OF THE CROP—I--

FUNNY— I LAUGH HA! HA!

MOGI TRIBE ONCE WORK HERE LIKE CRAZY —MIZT RAK HE FIRE ALL SAME—HIRE SCUM OF JUNGLE—

THE SHIPS WILL BE HERE SOON-THAT CROP MUST BE BALED AND READY TO LOAD!

IF _ME_ HAD BEEN GIVE MONEY BY THE POLITICS-TALKERS, ME NOT EVEN BE HERE TO TELL YOU NO CAN DO!

9-28

STEVIE, WHAT KIND OF A RUSTLE BE WE ROPED ONTO HERE?

FANCY TIPPED ME OFF, BUT IT WAS HARD TO BELIEVE, HAPPY! RAK ACCEPTED A BRIBE FOR SABOTAGING HIS OWN CROP!

WHO FRUM? —WHY?

THE LOCAL SUBVERTS WANT TO WRECK THE ECONOMY OF THIS COUNTRY BY STOPPING ITS INCOME FROM FOREIGN TRADE —BY SCUTTLING STUFF AMERICA NEEDS—AND CAN ONLY BUY FROM HERE!

RAK FIRED THE MOGIS WHO WERE GOOD WORKERS— AND HIRED TRAMPS TO STALL ALONG... AND BE BLAMED FOR THE FAILURE

...I'M DOWNRIGHT REMORSEFUL, STEVIE!

WHY?

I THOUGHT MISS FANCY ASKED US T' STAY HERE BECUZ SHE LIKED OUR WINNIN' WAYS!..SHECKS! IT'S US WOT'LL BE BLAMED FUR TH' CROP FAILURE!

Steve Canyon

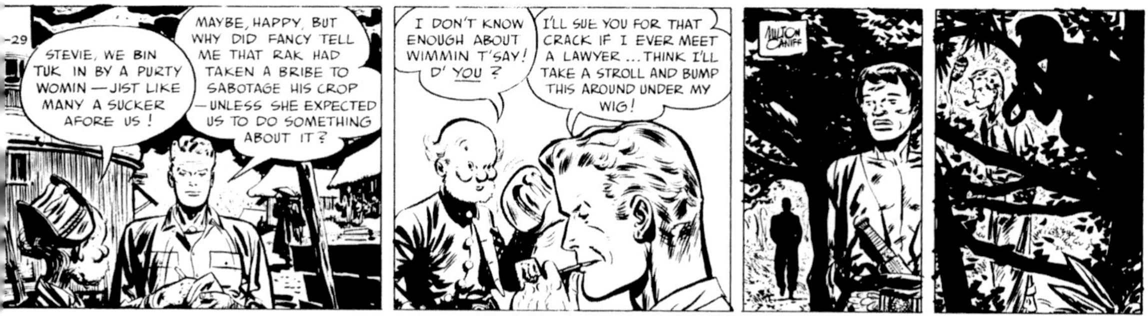
STEVIE, WE BIN TUK IN BY A PURTY WOMIN — JIST LIKE MANY A SUCKER AFORE US!
MAYBE, HAPPY, BUT WHY DID FANCY TELL ME THAT RAK HAD TAKEN A BRIBE TO SABOTAGE HIS CROP — UNLESS SHE EXPECTED US TO DO SOMETHING ABOUT IT?
I DON'T KNOW ENOUGH ABOUT WIMMIN T'SAY! D' YOU?
I'LL SUE YOU FOR THAT CRACK IF I EVER MEET A LAWYER... THINK I'LL TAKE A STROLL AND BUMP THIS AROUND UNDER MY WIG!

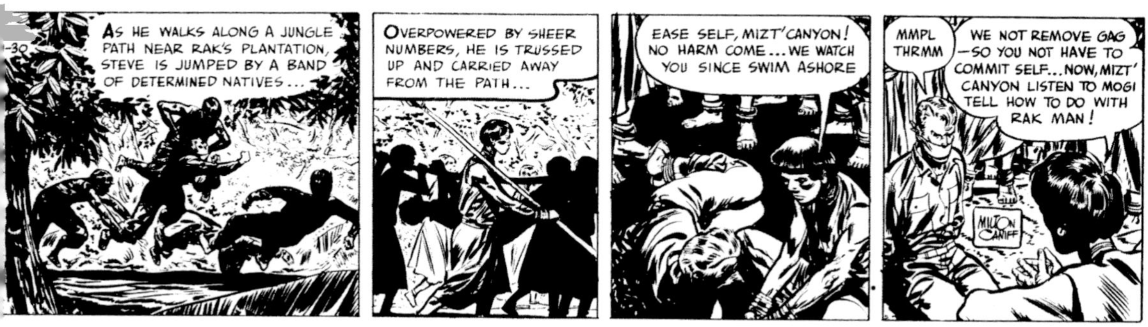
AS HE WALKS ALONG A JUNGLE PATH NEAR RAK'S PLANTATION, STEVE IS JUMPED BY A BAND OF DETERMINED NATIVES...
OVERPOWERED BY SHEER NUMBERS, HE IS TRUSSED UP AND CARRIED AWAY FROM THE PATH...
EASE SELF, MIZT'CANYON! NO HARM COME... WE WATCH YOU SINCE SWIM ASHORE
MMPL THRMM
WE NOT REMOVE GAG — SO YOU NOT HAVE TO COMMIT SELF... NOW, MIZT' CANYON LISTEN TO MOGI TELL HOW TO DO WITH RAK MAN!

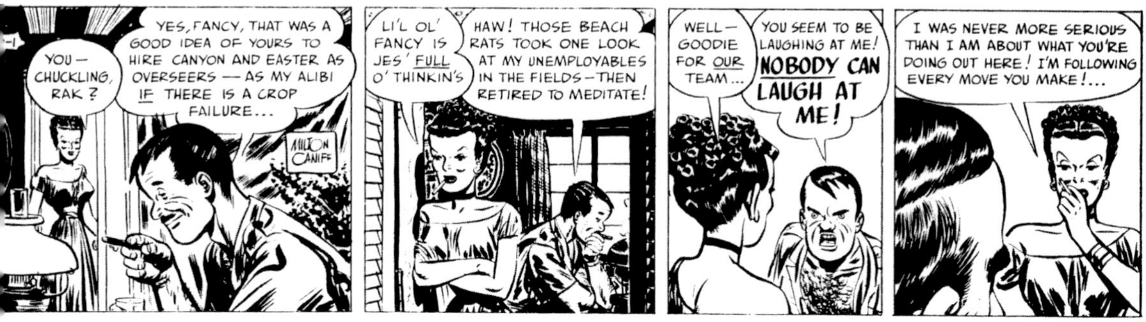
YOU — CHUCKLING, RAK?
YES, FANCY, THAT WAS A GOOD IDEA OF YOURS TO HIRE CANYON AND EASTER AS OVERSEERS — AS MY ALIBI IF THERE IS A CROP FAILURE...
LI'L OL' FANCY IS JES' FULL O' THINKIN'S
HAW! THOSE BEACH RATS TOOK ONE LOOK AT MY UNEMPLOYABLES IN THE FIELDS — THEN RETIRED TO MEDITATE!
WELL — GOODIE FOR OUR TEAM...
YOU SEEM TO BE LAUGHING AT ME! NOBODY CAN LAUGH AT ME!
I WAS NEVER MORE SERIOUS THAN I AM ABOUT WHAT YOU'RE DOING OUT HERE! I'M FOLLOWING EVERY MOVE YOU MAKE!...

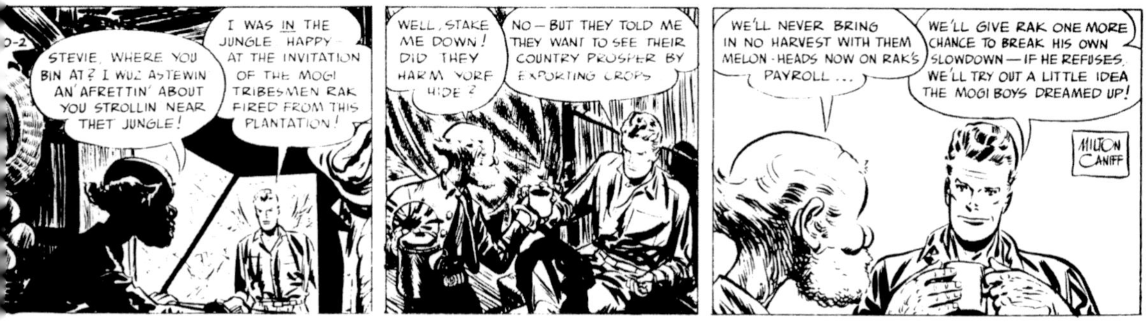
STEVIE, WHERE YOU BIN AT? I WUZ ASTEWIN AN' AFRETTIN' ABOUT YOU STROLLIN NEAR THET JUNGLE!
I WAS IN THE JUNGLE, HAPPY — AT THE INVITATION OF THE MOGI TRIBESMEN RAK FIRED FROM THIS PLANTATION!
WELL, STAKE ME DOWN! DID THEY HARM YORE HIDE?
NO — BUT THEY TOLD ME THEY WANT TO SEE THEIR COUNTRY PROSPER BY EXPORTING CROPS
WE'LL NEVER BRING IN NO HARVEST WITH THEM MELON-HEADS NOW ON RAK'S PAYROLL...
WE'LL GIVE RAK ONE MORE CHANCE TO BREAK HIS OWN SLOWDOWN — IF HE REFUSES, WE'LL TRY OUT A LITTLE IDEA THE MOGI BOYS DREAMED UP!

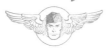

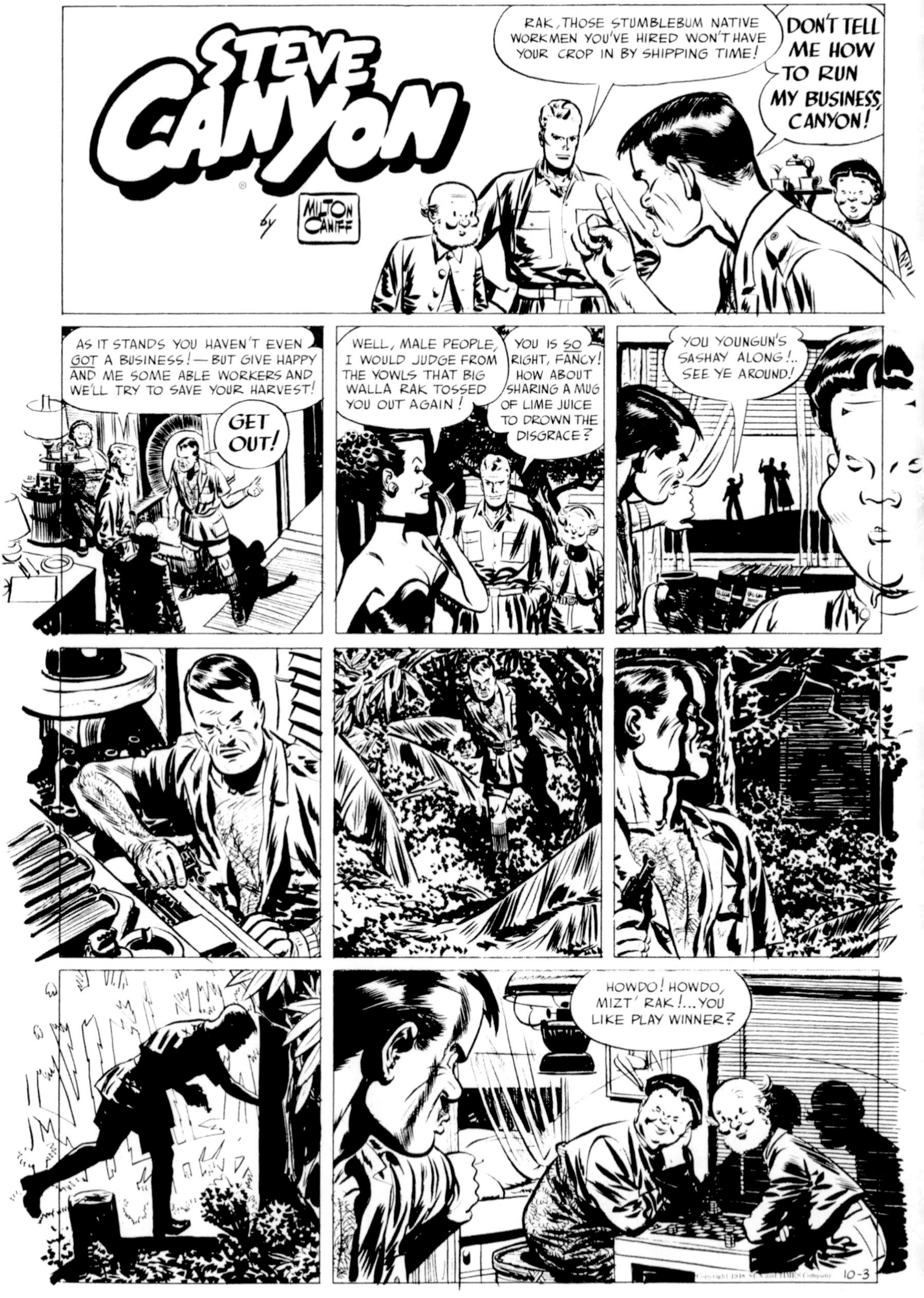
STEVE CANYON
by MILTON CANIFF
RAK, THOSE STUMBLEBUM NATIVE WORKMEN YOU'VE HIRED WON'T HAVE YOUR CROP IN BY SHIPPING TIME!
DON'T TELL ME HOW TO RUN MY BUSINESS, CANYON!
AS IT STANDS YOU HAVEN'T EVEN GOT A BUSINESS! — BUT GIVE HAPPY AND ME SOME ABLE WORKERS AND WE'LL TRY TO SAVE YOUR HARVEST!
GET OUT!
WELL, MALE PEOPLE, I WOULD JUDGE FROM THE YOWLS THAT BIG WALLA RAK TOSSED YOU OUT AGAIN!
YOU IS SO RIGHT, FANCY! HOW ABOUT SHARING A MUG OF LIME JUICE TO DROWN THE DISGRACE?
YOU YOUNGUN'S SASHAY ALONG!.. SEE YE AROUND!
HOWDO! HOWDO, MIZT' RAK!... YOU LIKE PLAY WINNER?
10-3

WELL, HAP, RAK REFUSED TO HIRE COMPETENT NATIVES TO BRING IN HIS CROP, SO WE CAN LET THE MOGIS PUT THEIR PLAN INTO OPERATION!

WHUT D'THEM MOGI LADS ALLOW T'DO, STEVIE?

IT STARTS WITH SOYBOY, RAK'S HOUSEMAN...

SO—THAT EVENING...

HMMM, SOYBOY! MY FAVORITE DISH!

NO THINGS TOO GOODLY FOR MIZT' RAK!

THEN, AFTER DINNER...

SORTA SLEEPY —THINK I'LL TURN IN EARLY...

DO THAT, RAK! YOU'VE GOT A HARD LOAF AHEAD TOMORROW!

SLEEPY ALL OF... SUDDEN, SOYBOY!

IS NIGHT! IS SLEEP TIME! MAKES SENSIBLE, MIZT' RAK!

WELL, FANCY, BIG DAY AHEAD — TRYING TO CONVINCE THOSE GIMPTY COOLIES TO GET TO WORK! GOOD NIGHT!

HEY! WHAT GIVES? DID I SUDDENLY COME UP POISON?

SOYBOY DID HIS JOB OKAY, STEVIE!

YES, HAP, BUT THIS IS JUST THE FIRST NIGHT... HURRY...

AS STEVE AND HAPPY ARRIVE AT ONE OF THE HARVEST FIELDS, A LONG LINE OF WELL-MUSCLED FIGURES FILES OUT OF THE JUNGLE...

NEARLY DAWN! YOU MOGIS MUSTN'T DO TOO MUCH AT ONE TIME!

YOU SAY TRUE, MIZT' CANYON! MOGIS GO!

...THE MOGIS WHO HAVE LABORED EXPERTLY OVER THE CROP DURING THE NIGHT MOVE SILENTLY INTO THE JUNGLE...

...WHILE THEIR WOMEN, WHO HAVE STOOD GUARD OVER THE HUTS OF RAK'S INEPT FIELD HANDS, ROUST OUT THE COOLIES AND HERD THEM TOWARD THE HARVEST AREA....

ONE WORD OF ALL THIS TO ANYONE —AND SKXX-X!

HOW ARE YOU AND EASTER GETTING ALONG WITH MY NATIVE WORKMEN, CANYON?

I TOLD YOU THEY'RE ALL STUMBLEBUMS, RAK — BUT WE'RE DOING WHAT WE CAN!

THEY'LL NEVER MAKE IT IN TIME TO LOAD WHEN THE CARGO BOATS ARRIVE...

DON'T STRAIN YOURSELVES —YOU'LL GET PAID WHETHER THE HARVEST IS ON TIME OR NOT!

SOYBOY— HAVE THE NATIVE STRAW BOSS BRING ME THE FIGURES ON HOW MUCH STUFF IS BALED AND IN THE WAREHOUSE!

RIGHT QUICK SUDDEN, MIZT' RAK— BUT FIRST IS EXTRA FAVORITE DESSERT OF BIG BOSS!

LATER

HMM, SLEEPY! MUSTA EATEN TOO MUCH... GOTTA TURN IN! G' NIGHT!

GOOD NIGHT, RAK!

Steve Canyon

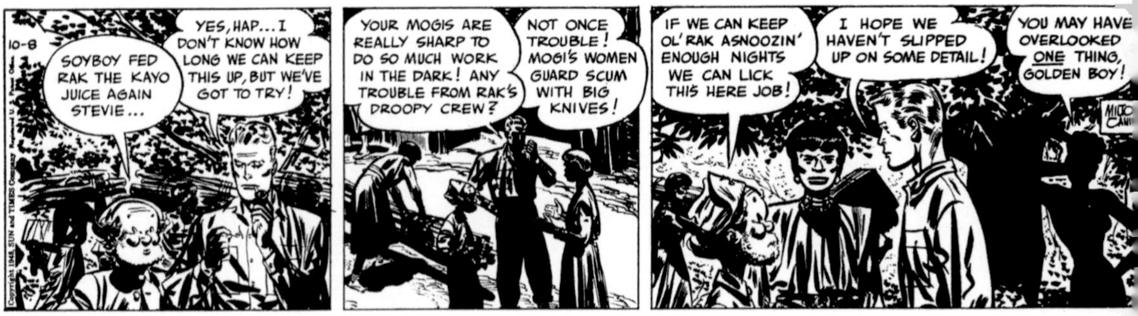
10-8
SOYBOY FED RAK THE KAYO JUICE AGAIN STEVIE...
YES, HAP... I DON'T KNOW HOW LONG WE CAN KEEP THIS UP, BUT WE'VE GOT TO TRY!
YOUR MOGIS ARE REALLY SHARP TO DO SO MUCH WORK IN THE DARK! ANY TROUBLE FROM RAK'S DROOPY CREW?
NOT ONCE TROUBLE! MOGI'S WOMEN GUARD SCUM WITH BIG KNIVES!
IF WE CAN KEEP OL' RAK ASNOOZIN' ENOUGH NIGHTS WE CAN LICK THIS HERE JOB!
I HOPE WE HAVEN'T SLIPPED UP ON SOME DETAIL!
YOU MAY HAVE OVERLOOKED ONE THING, GOLDEN BOY!

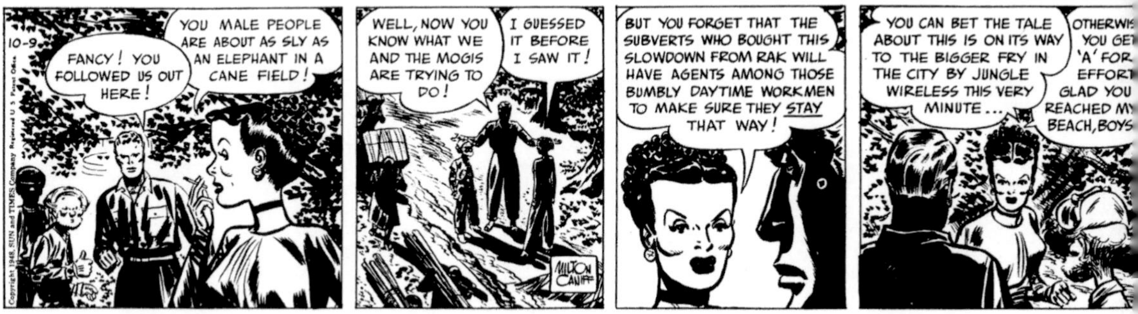
10-9
FANCY! YOU FOLLOWED US OUT HERE!
YOU MALE PEOPLE ARE ABOUT AS SLY AS AN ELEPHANT IN A CANE FIELD!
WELL, NOW YOU KNOW WHAT WE AND THE MOGIS ARE TRYING TO DO!
I GUESSED IT BEFORE I SAW IT!
MILTON CANIFF
BUT YOU FORGET THAT THE SUBVERTS WHO BOUGHT THIS SLOWDOWN FROM RAK WILL HAVE AGENTS AMONG THOSE BUMBLY DAYTIME WORKMEN TO MAKE SURE THEY STAY THAT WAY!
YOU CAN BET THE TALE ABOUT THIS IS ON ITS WAY TO THE BIGGER FRY IN THE CITY BY JUNGLE WIRELESS THIS VERY MINUTE...
OTHERWIS
YOU GET
'A' FOR
EFFORT
GLAD YOU
REACHED MY
BEACH, BOYS

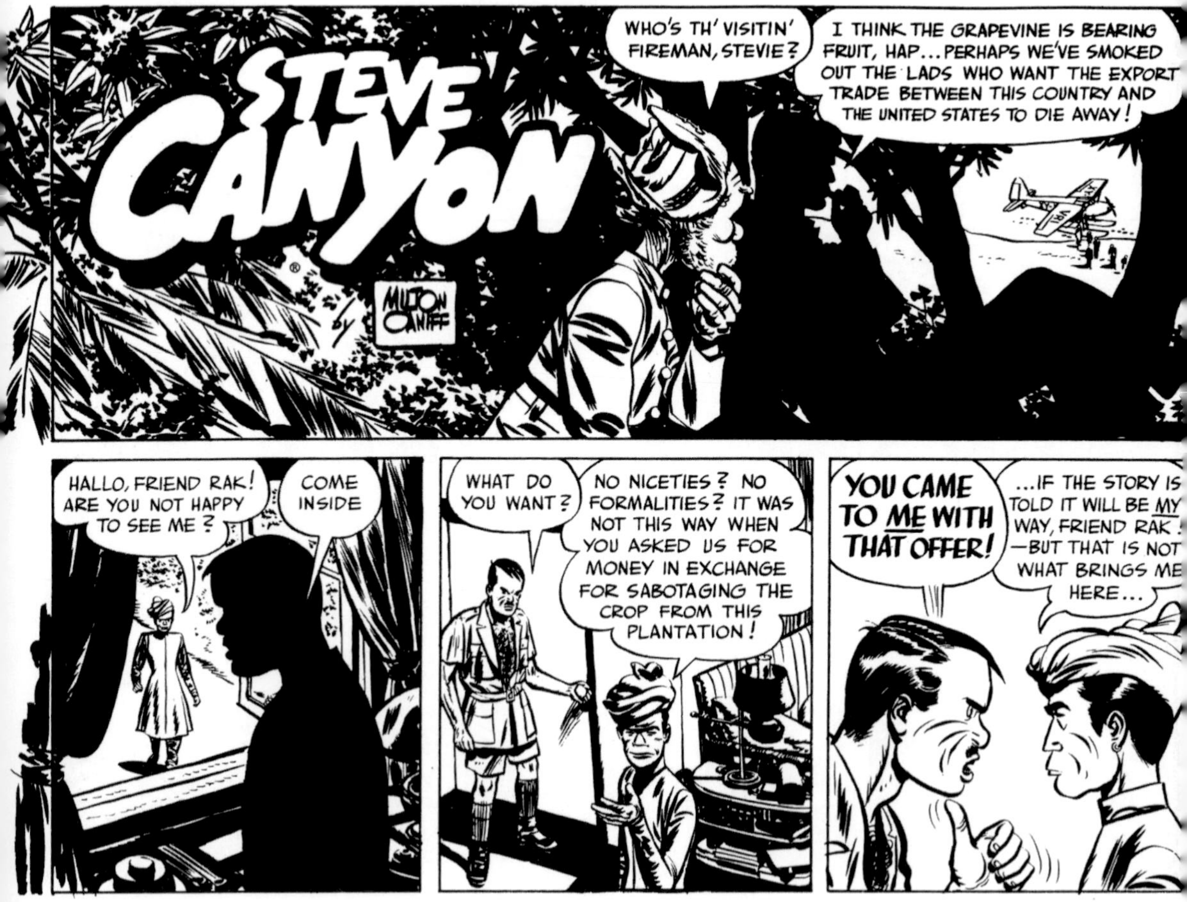
STEVE CANYON
by MILTON CANIFF
WHO'S TH' VISITIN' FIREMAN, STEVIE?
I THINK THE GRAPEVINE IS BEARING FRUIT, HAP... PERHAPS WE'VE SMOKED OUT THE LADS WHO WANT THE EXPORT TRADE BETWEEN THIS COUNTRY AND THE UNITED STATES TO DIE AWAY!
HALLO, FRIEND RAK! ARE YOU NOT HAPPY TO SEE ME?
COME INSIDE
WHAT DO YOU WANT?
NO NICETIES? NO FORMALITIES? IT WAS NOT THIS WAY WHEN YOU ASKED US FOR MONEY IN EXCHANGE FOR SABOTAGING THE CROP FROM THIS PLANTATION!
YOU CAME TO ME WITH THAT OFFER!
...IF THE STORY IS TOLD IT WILL BE MY WAY, FRIEND RAK! —BUT THAT IS NOT WHAT BRINGS ME HERE...

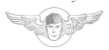

IT IS SAID THAT YOU WILL FAIL TO KEEP OUR BARGAIN! —THAT YOUR CROP WILL BE READY TO SHIP TO AMERICA AFTER ALL...

I HIRED A COUPLE OF TRAMPS — BEACH RATS — AS AN ALIBI FOR THE CROP FAILURE...

...YET SOMEHOW THEY HAVE MADE THE SHIFTLESS NATIVE LABORERS PRODUCE!

BUT HOW SIMPLE! DO AWAY WITH THE MEDDLERS!

AND NOW — PERHAPS THE LADY WHO HAS BEEN LISTENING FROM BEHIND THE CURTAIN WILL JOIN US!

FANCY!

IF YOU YANKEES DO NOT KNOW HOW TO HANDLE YOUR WOMEN, BE ASSURED THAT WE DO...

YOU HIT FANCY! I'LL — I'LL---

...YOU WILL DO NOTHING, MY FRIEND — BECAUSE IF YOU DO, OUR EFFICIENT ORGANIZATION IN AMERICA WILL SEE THAT YOU ARE BRANDED AS A TRAITOR TO YOUR COUNTRY!

10-10

10-11 AT A PLANTATION ON THE BURMA COAST, STEVE CANYON AND HAPPY EASTER ARE HELPING TO BRING IN A HARVEST SCHEDULED TO BE SHIPPED TO THE UNITED STATES...LOCAL SUBVERSIVE INTERESTS ARE DETERMINED TO BLOCK THE PROJECT IN ORDER TO WEAKEN BOTH COUNTRIES...
   AN AGENT FLIES IN FROM THE CITY...

YOU HAVE LITTLE CHOICE, RAK, MY FRIEND! IF YOU DO NOT RUIN YOUR CROP, WE WILL HAVE OUR GROUP IN AMERICA BRAND YOU AS A TRAITOR TO THE UNITED STATES!

YOU COULDN'T DO IT!

DON'T BE NAÏVE! AN ANONYMOUS LETTER OR TWO TO THE PROPER PERSONS, AND YOUR NAME WILL BE ALL OVER THE YANKEE NEWSPAPERS AND WIRELESS!

MY INFORMATION INDICATES THAT THERE ARE TWO NEW YANKEES ON YOUR STAFF...I WILL SPEAK WITH THEM NOW!

YOU WON'T EVEN HAVE TO RAISE YOUR VOICE!

10-12

I WILL SEE THIS YANKEE ALONE!-- BY WHAT NAME IS HE CALLED?

CANYON — AS IN ARIZONA! WHAT'S THE BEEF?

WHO SENT YOU TO THIS PLACE?

I LOST A PRIMARY ELECTION BET—

DIPLOMATIC ATTACHE'S SPY ON US CAN BE ELIMINATED BY RECALL —WE DO NOT HAVE TO BE SO FORMAL WITH UNDERCOVER AGENTS!

YOU WILL WALK INTO THE JUNGLE AHEAD OF ME — AND MAKE NO SIGN TO ANYONE...

Steve Canyon

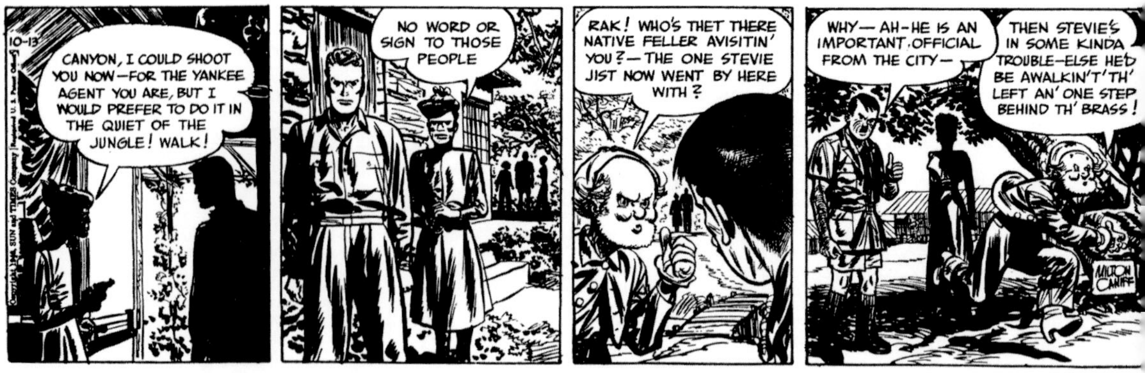
10-13
CANYON, I COULD SHOOT YOU NOW—FOR THE YANKEE AGENT YOU ARE, BUT I WOULD PREFER TO DO IT IN THE QUIET OF THE JUNGLE! WALK!
NO WORD OR SIGN TO THOSE PEOPLE
RAK! WHO'S THET THERE NATIVE FELLER AVISITIN' YOU?—THE ONE STEVIE JIST NOW WENT BY HERE WITH?
WHY—AH—HE IS AN IMPORTANT OFFICIAL FROM THE CITY—
THEN STEVIE'S IN SOME KINDA TROUBLE—ELSE HE'D BE AWALKIN' T' TH' LEFT AN' ONE STEP BEHIND TH' BRASS!
MILTON CANIFF

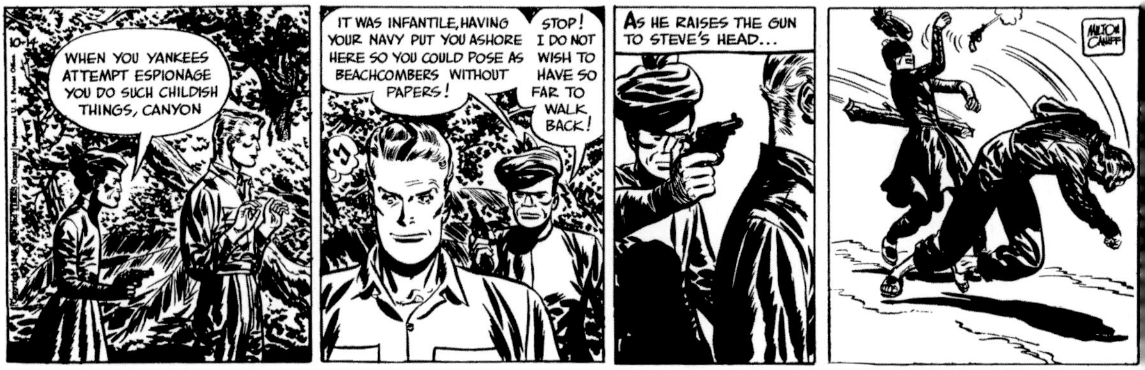
10-14
WHEN YOU YANKEES ATTEMPT ESPIONAGE YOU DO SUCH CHILDISH THINGS, CANYON
IT WAS INFANTILE, HAVING YOUR NAVY PUT YOU ASHORE HERE SO YOU COULD POSE AS BEACHCOMBERS WITHOUT PAPERS!
STOP! I DO NOT WISH TO HAVE SO FAR TO WALK BACK!
AS HE RAISES THE GUN TO STEVE'S HEAD...
MILTON CANIFF

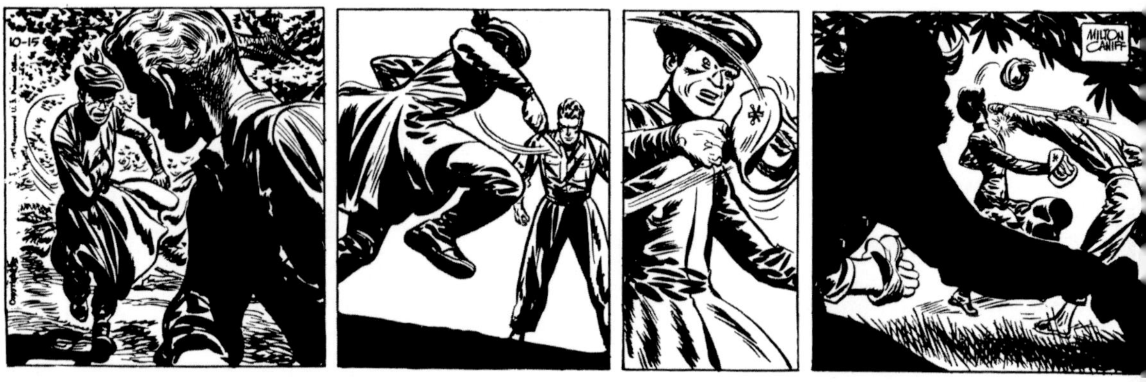
10-15
MILTON CANIFF

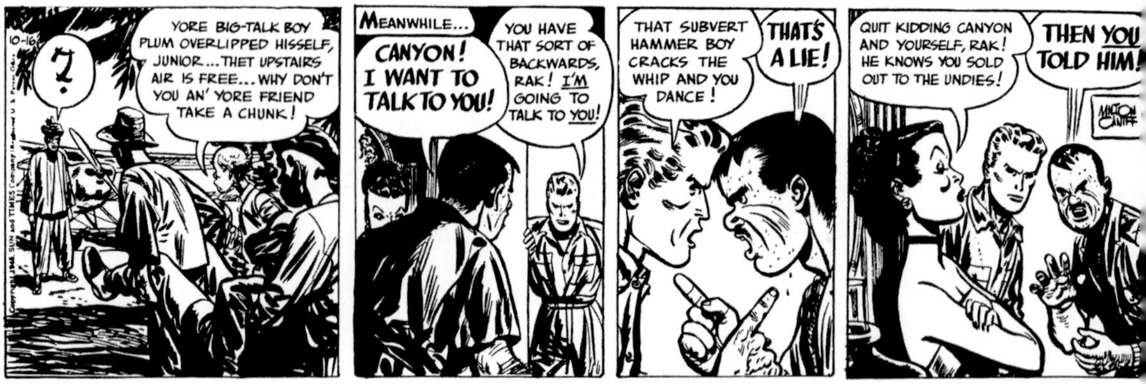
10-16
?
YORE BIG-TALK BOY PLUM OVERLIPPED HISSELF, JUNIOR... THET UPSTAIRS AIR IS FREE... WHY DON'T YOU AN' YORE FRIEND TAKE A CHUNK!
MEANWHILE...
CANYON! I WANT TO TALK TO YOU!
YOU HAVE THAT SORT OF BACKWARDS, RAK! I'M GOING TO TALK TO YOU!
THAT SUBVERT HAMMER BOY CRACKS THE WHIP AND YOU DANCE!
THAT'S A LIE!
QUIT KIDDING CANYON AND YOURSELF, RAK! HE KNOWS YOU SOLD OUT TO THE UNDIES!
THEN YOU TOLD HIM!
MILTON CANIFF

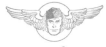

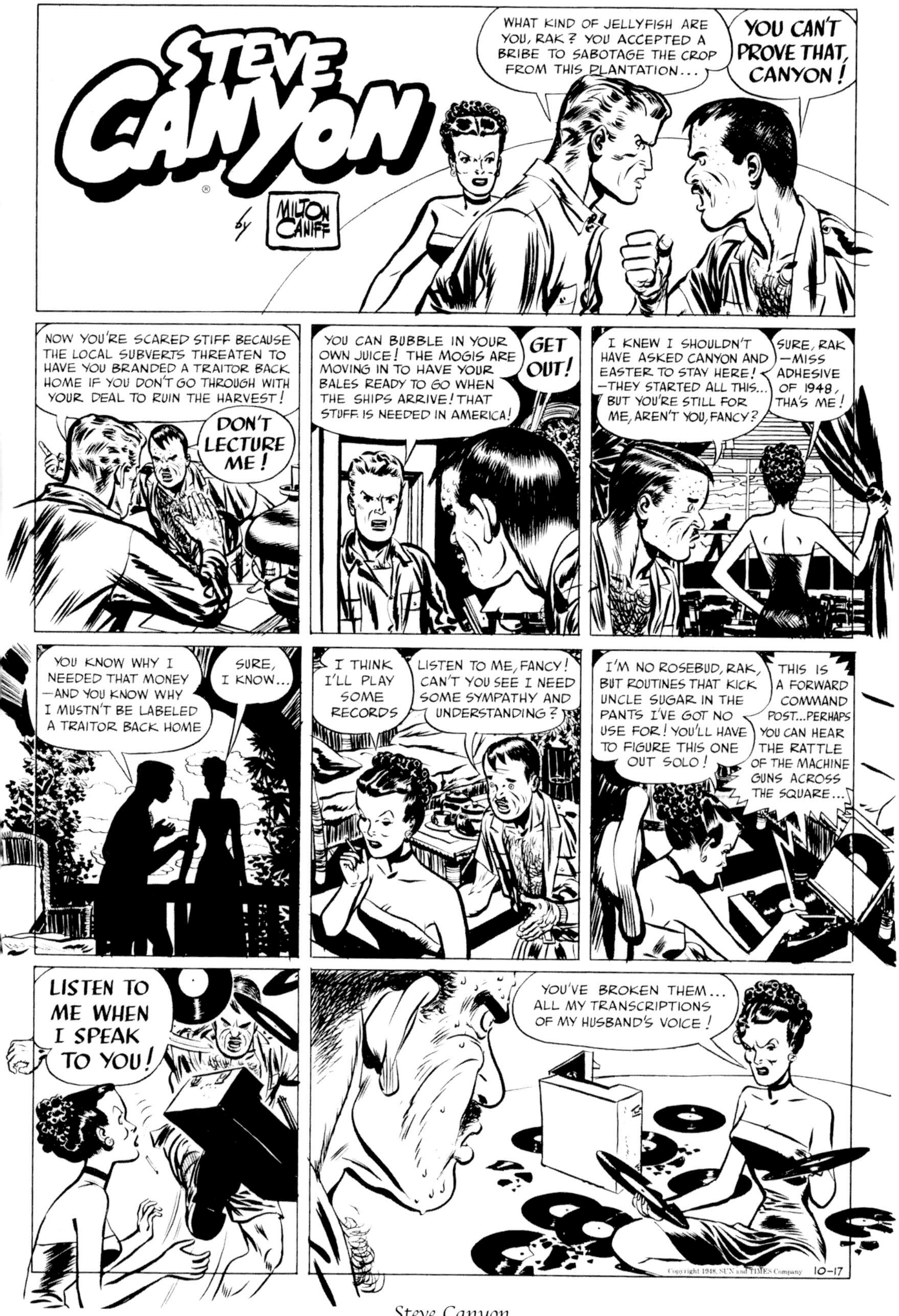
STEVE CANYON
by MILTON CANIFF
WHAT KIND OF JELLYFISH ARE YOU, RAK? YOU ACCEPTED A BRIBE TO SABOTAGE THE CROP FROM THIS PLANTATION...
YOU CAN'T PROVE THAT, CANYON!
NOW YOU'RE SCARED STIFF BECAUSE THE LOCAL SUBVERTS THREATEN TO HAVE YOU BRANDED A TRAITOR BACK HOME IF YOU DON'T GO THROUGH WITH YOUR DEAL TO RUIN THE HARVEST!
DON'T LECTURE ME!
YOU CAN BUBBLE IN YOUR OWN JUICE! THE MOGIS ARE MOVING IN TO HAVE YOUR BALES READY TO GO WHEN THE SHIPS ARRIVE! THAT STUFF IS NEEDED IN AMERICA!
GET OUT!
I KNEW I SHOULDN'T HAVE ASKED CANYON AND EASTER TO STAY HERE! —THEY STARTED ALL THIS... BUT YOU'RE STILL FOR ME, AREN'T YOU, FANCY?
SURE, RAK —MISS ADHESIVE OF 1948, THA'S ME!
YOU KNOW WHY I NEEDED THAT MONEY —AND YOU KNOW WHY I MUSTN'T BE LABELED A TRAITOR BACK HOME
SURE, I KNOW...
I THINK I'LL PLAY SOME RECORDS
LISTEN TO ME, FANCY! CAN'T YOU SEE I NEED SOME SYMPATHY AND UNDERSTANDING?
I'M NO ROSEBUD, RAK, BUT ROUTINES THAT KICK UNCLE SUGAR IN THE PANTS I'VE GOT NO USE FOR! YOU'LL HAVE TO FIGURE THIS ONE OUT SOLO!
THIS IS A FORWARD COMMAND POST...PERHAPS YOU CAN HEAR THE RATTLE OF THE MACHINE GUNS ACROSS THE SQUARE...
LISTEN TO ME WHEN I SPEAK TO YOU!
YOU'VE BROKEN THEM... ALL MY TRANSCRIPTIONS OF MY HUSBAND'S VOICE!
Copyright 1948, SUN and TIMES Company
10-17

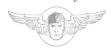

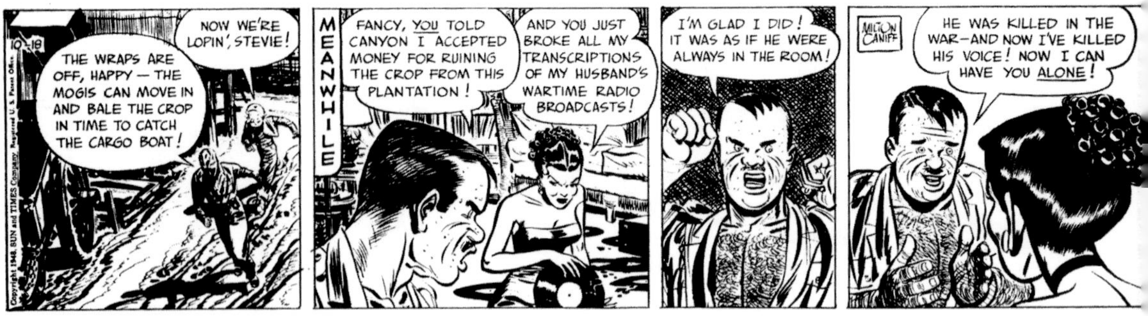
10-18
NOW WE'RE LOPIN', STEVIE!
THE WRAPS ARE OFF, HAPPY — THE MOGIS CAN MOVE IN AND BALE THE CROP IN TIME TO CATCH THE CARGO BOAT!
MEANWHILE
FANCY, YOU TOLD CANYON I ACCEPTED MONEY FOR RUINING THE CROP FROM THIS PLANTATION!
AND YOU JUST BROKE ALL MY TRANSCRIPTIONS OF MY HUSBAND'S WARTIME RADIO BROADCASTS!
I'M GLAD I DID! IT WAS AS IF HE WERE ALWAYS IN THE ROOM!
MILTON CANIFF
HE WAS KILLED IN THE WAR—AND NOW I'VE KILLED HIS VOICE! NOW I CAN HAVE YOU ALONE!

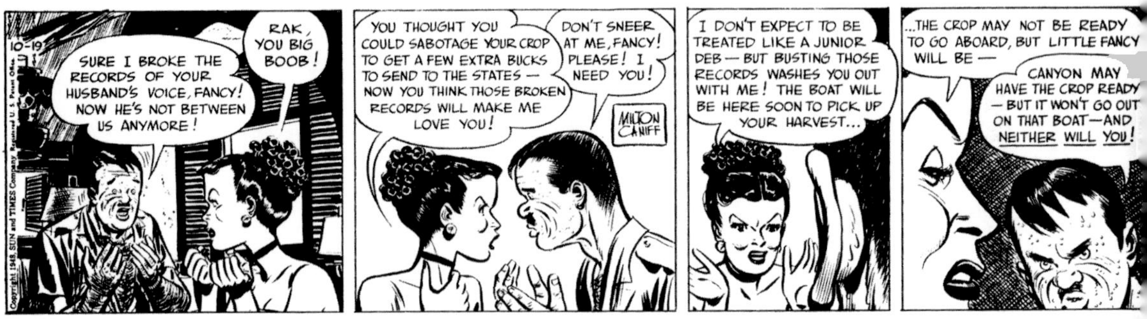
10-19
RAK, YOU BIG BOOB!
SURE I BROKE THE RECORDS OF YOUR HUSBAND'S VOICE, FANCY! NOW HE'S NOT BETWEEN US ANYMORE!
YOU THOUGHT YOU COULD SABOTAGE YOUR CROP TO GET A FEW EXTRA BUCKS TO SEND TO THE STATES — NOW YOU THINK THOSE BROKEN RECORDS WILL MAKE ME LOVE YOU!
DON'T SNEER AT ME, FANCY! PLEASE! I NEED YOU!
MILTON CANIFF
I DON'T EXPECT TO BE TREATED LIKE A JUNIOR DEB — BUT BUSTING THOSE RECORDS WASHES YOU OUT WITH ME! THE BOAT WILL BE HERE SOON TO PICK UP YOUR HARVEST...
...THE CROP MAY NOT BE READY TO GO ABOARD, BUT LITTLE FANCY WILL BE —
CANYON MAY HAVE THE CROP READY — BUT IT WON'T GO OUT ON THAT BOAT—AND NEITHER WILL YOU!

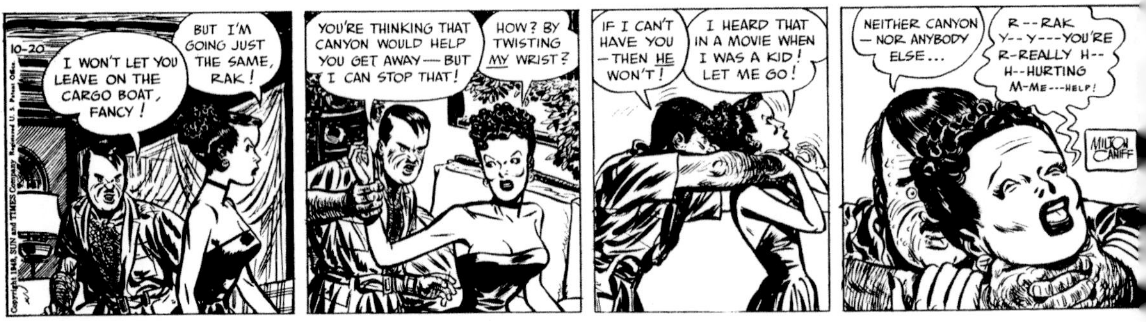
10-20
BUT I'M GOING JUST THE SAME, RAK!
I WON'T LET YOU LEAVE ON THE CARGO BOAT, FANCY!
YOU'RE THINKING THAT CANYON WOULD HELP YOU GET AWAY — BUT I CAN STOP THAT!
HOW? BY TWISTING MY WRIST?
IF I CAN'T HAVE YOU — THEN HE WON'T!
I HEARD THAT IN A MOVIE WHEN I WAS A KID! LET ME GO!
NEITHER CANYON — NOR ANYBODY ELSE...
R--RAK Y--Y---YOU'RE R-REALLY H-- H--HURTING M-ME---HELP!
MILTON CANIFF

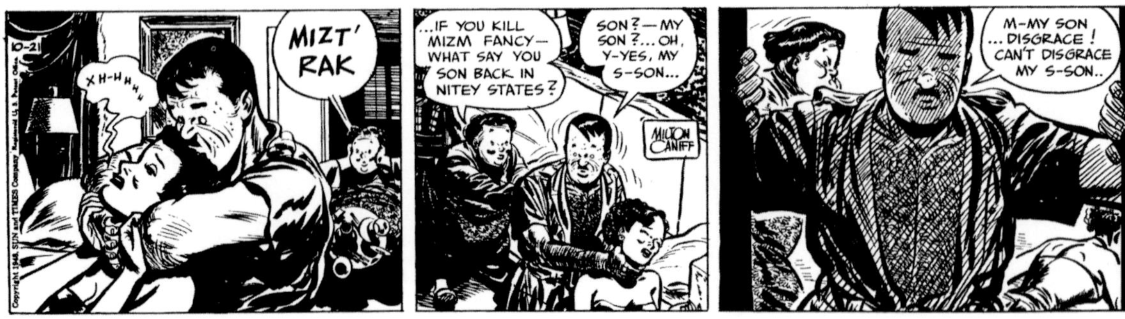
10-21
XH-HHHH
MIZT' RAK
...IF YOU KILL MIZM FANCY— WHAT SAY YOU SON BACK IN NITEY STATES?
SON?—MY SON?...OH, Y-YES, MY S-SON...
MILTON CANIFF
M-MY SON ...DISGRACE! CAN'T DISGRACE MY S-SON..

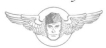

ONE — TWO — ONE — TWO — PLEASE TO WHEEZE, MIZM FANCY!

WHUT TH' DING DANG?

MIZM FANCY CHOKE ON SOMETHING IN THROAT, MIZT' CANYON!

FIND RAK, SOYBOY!

I — I'M... OKAY...

MIZT' RAK HE LOCK HESELF IN HE ROOM — HEAR MOVE AROUND, BUT NO ANSWER TALK!

THE 'SOMETHING IN YOUR THROAT' LEFT FINGER MARKS ON THE OUTSIDE, FANCY! SHALL I BASH IN HIS FACE?

NO, CANYON... HE EXPECTS THAT! THE WORST THING ANYONE CAN DO TO RAK IS TO FORCE HIM TO SIT THERE AND THINK!

STEVIE! TH' NATIVES SAY THERE'S A BOAT BEYOND TH' REEF! MAY BE COMIN' FER OUR CARGO!

THEN THE MOGIS WILL HAVE TO FINISH HARVESTING THE CROP TONIGHT, HAPPY!

WHUT ABOUT RAK — AN' MISS FANCY?

SOYBOY SAYS SHE'S SNAPPING OUT OF IT — RAK CAN SIT IN HIS LOCKED ROOM AND ROT AS FAR AS I'M CONCERNED!

BUT THERE ARE TWO THINGS STEVE DOESN'T KNOW — THAT A PONTOON AIRPLANE IS LANDING IN THE LAGOON — AND THAT RAK IS NOT IN HIS ROOM

STEVE CANYON

by MILTON CANIFF

KEEP YOUR FINGERS CROSSED, HAPPY! RAK'S CROP IS IN THE WAREHOUSES READY FOR THE BOATS TO COME AND LOAD ON SCHEDULE!

NO THANKS T' ANYBUDDY 'CEPTIN' THET MOGI TRIBE WOT PITCHED IN, STEVIE!

IS MISS FANCY FEELIN' FITTIN'?

YES — SINCE I TOLD HER I COULD GET PRESSINGS OF HER DEAD HUSBAND'S WARTIME NEWS BROADCASTS FROM THE MASTER RECORDS BACK HOME...

RAK LOCKED HIMSELF IN HIS ROOM AFTER HE BROKE ALL HER TRANSCRIPTIONS... I FEEL SORTA SORRY FOR THE GUY!

I FELT SORRY FER A HURT COYOTE ONCE'T — THEN HE GOT WELL, BIT ME AN' STOLE MY SUPPER MEAT!

I'M TOO BUSHED FOR PHILOSOPHY ...G'NIGHT!

G'NIGHT, STEVIE...

Steve Canyon

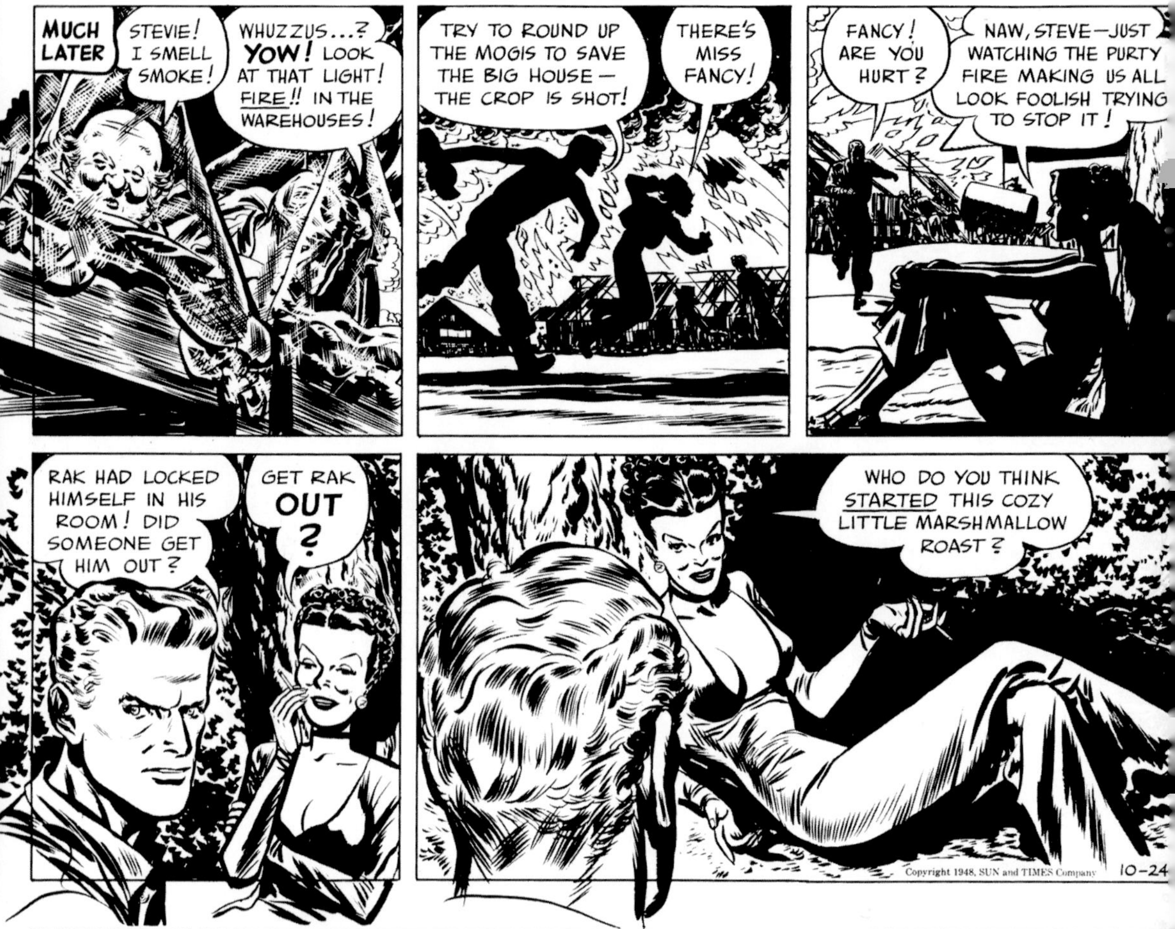

MUCH LATER
STEVIE! I SMELL SMOKE!
WHUZZUS...? YOW! LOOK AT THAT LIGHT! FIRE!! IN THE WAREHOUSES!
TRY TO ROUND UP THE MOGIS TO SAVE THE BIG HOUSE — THE CROP IS SHOT!
THERE'S MISS FANCY!
FANCY! ARE YOU HURT?
NAW, STEVE—JUST WATCHING THE PURTY FIRE MAKING US ALL LOOK FOOLISH TRYING TO STOP IT!
RAK HAD LOCKED HIMSELF IN HIS ROOM! DID SOMEONE GET HIM OUT?
GET RAK OUT?
WHO DO YOU THINK STARTED THIS COZY LITTLE MARSHMALLOW ROAST?
Copyright 1948, SUN and TIMES Company
10-24

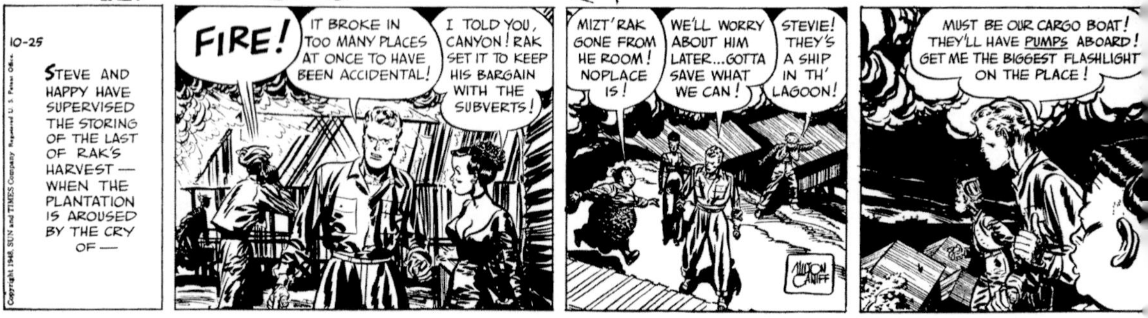

10-25
STEVE AND HAPPY HAVE SUPERVISED THE STORING OF THE LAST OF RAK'S HARVEST — WHEN THE PLANTATION IS AROUSED BY THE CRY OF —
Copyright 1948, SUN and TIMES Company Registered U. S. Patent Office.
FIRE!
IT BROKE IN TOO MANY PLACES AT ONCE TO HAVE BEEN ACCIDENTAL!
I TOLD YOU, CANYON! RAK SET IT TO KEEP HIS BARGAIN WITH THE SUBVERTS!
MIZT'RAK GONE FROM HE ROOM! NOPLACE IS!
WE'LL WORRY ABOUT HIM LATER...GOTTA SAVE WHAT WE CAN!
STEVIE! THEY'S A SHIP IN TH' LAGOON!
MILTON CANIFF
MUST BE OUR CARGO BOAT! THEY'LL HAVE PUMPS ABOARD! GET ME THE BIGGEST FLASHLIGHT ON THE PLACE!

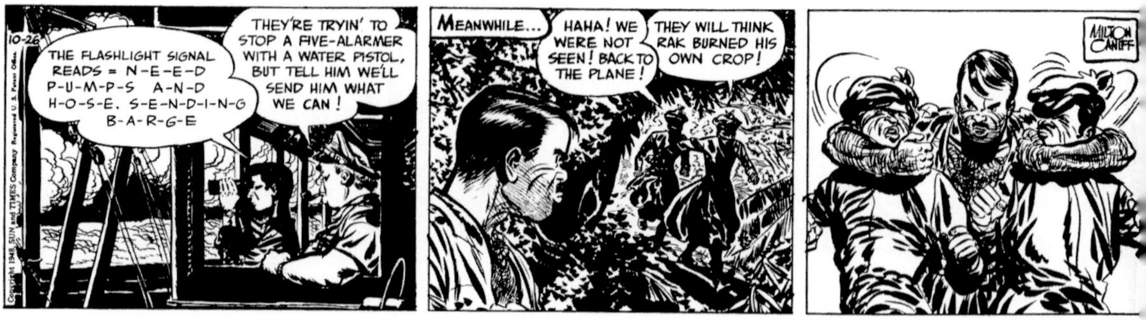

10-26
Copyright 1948, SUN and TIMES Company Registered U. S. Patent Office.
THE FLASHLIGHT SIGNAL READS = N-E-E-D P-U-M-P-S A-N-D H-O-S-E. S-E-N-D-I-N-G B-A-R-G-E
THEY'RE TRYIN' TO STOP A FIVE-ALARMER WITH A WATER PISTOL, BUT TELL HIM WE'LL SEND HIM WHAT WE CAN!
MEANWHILE...
HAHA! WE WERE NOT SEEN! BACK TO THE PLANE!
THEY WILL THINK RAK BURNED HIS OWN CROP!
MILTON CANIFF

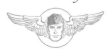

O-27 I WAS IN MY ROOM WHEN I HEARD YOUR AIRPLANE ENGINE... THAT'S WHAT MADE UP MY MIND!

... I TRIED TO CATCH YOU, BUT YOU STARTED THE FIRE BEFORE I COULD GET TO YOU!

SO I CAME TO YOUR USUAL LANDING PLACE TO HEAD YOU OFF...

BUT RAK DOESN'T KNOW THAT A THIRD NATIVE HAD BEEN LEFT BEHIND TO GUARD THE AIRPLANE...

O-28 GOOD WORK! NOW WE WILL FLY THIS RAK FOOL TO THE CITY AND CHARGE HIM WITH ARSON!

THE YANKEE CORRESPONDENTS WILL MAKE A LARGE CLAMOR ABOUT THIS IN THE UNITED STATES!

MEANWHILE... HAP! GET THE SHIP'S HOSE ON THE WORST SPOTS WHILE WE SET UP THE PUMPS!

AYE, STEVIE!

WHILE ON THE CARGO VESSEL... PLEASE, CAPTAIN!

I ADMIT YOU'VE GOT THE BEST REASON IN THE WORLD FOR GOING ASHORE, BOY— BUT I SAY NO!

O-29 I'LL HAVE NO MAN OF MY CREW RISKING HIS HIDE IN A SITUATION NOT OF OUR MAKING! YOU STAY ABOARD THIS SHIP, REED KIMBERLY!

OKAY, THEN—

REED! YOU'VE SIGNED SHIP'S PAPERS! DON'T DISOBEY A DIRECT ORDER!

I SIGNED TO THIS ANCHORAGE —AND I'M HITTING THE BEACH!

O-30 DON'T BE TOO GLOOMY, REED! YOU CAN GO ASHORE AS SOON AS THE SKIPPER THINKS IT'S SAFE!

WE ALL KNOW WHY YOU SHIPPED ON THIS VESSEL, BOY— AND YOU WON'T HAVE LONG TO WAIT!

BUT I CAN'T TELL WHAT'S HAPPENING ON THE PLANTATION! HE MIGHT BE HURT!

NOW, IF THEY'D NEEDED MEDICAL SUPPLIES THEY'D HAVE ASKED!

MEANWHILE... WALK TO THE AIRPLANE, RAK! CANYON WILL BE CERTAIN YOU STARTED THE FIRE!

WHEN YOUR SON IN THE UNITED STATES LEARNS YOU SOLD OUT TO THE UNDERGROUND TO PAY HIS WAY THROUGH SCHOOL, HE WILL BE SO PROUD OF YOU

Steve Canyon

RAK, YOU FAILED TO DESTROY YOUR CROP, AFTER WE PAID YOU TO DO SO... WE WERE COMPELLED TO FLY HERE AND PUT A TORCH TO IT!

YOU DIDN'T FORCE ME TO BURN IT!

SOME DISTANCE AWAY...

NO—BUT WE WILL FLY YOU TO THE CITY AND TURN YOU OVER TO THE GOVERNMENT AS AN ARSONIST! YANKEE NEWS SERVICES WILL RELAY THE STORY TO AMERICA AT ONCE!

YOU SEEM TO FORGET THAT WE ARE KNOWN AS PATRIOTIC CITIZENS!

INTO THE AIRPLANE, RAK!

RAK WAITS UNTIL THE SHIP GAINS CONSIDERABLE ALTITUDE — THEN...

MEANWHILE... ON THE MERCHANT SHIP WHICH HAS COME UP TO TAKE ON THE CROP FROM RAK'S PLANTATION...

WE DID ALL WE COULD, SIR, BUT THERE'LL BE NO CARGO FOR US AFTER THAT HALOCAUST!

PLEASE, CAPTAIN...

PLEASE LET ME GO ASHORE... MAYBE I COULD HELP!

NO, LAD... YOU CAME HERE TO SURPRISE YOUR FATHER — AND I MEAN TO SEE YOU DON'T LEAVE THIS SHIP 'TIL ALL IS CLEAR AND SECURE!

Copyright 1948, SUN and TIMES Company   10-31

Steve Canyon

HAPPY, I THINK WE HAVE THE FIRE UNDER CONTROL, BUT THE HARVEST IS SHOT! THERE'LL BE NO CARGO FOR THE BOAT IN THE LAGOON!

MIZT'CANYON! WHAT A THING ME SEE!

CAME MIZT'RAK PRISONER OF THREE MEN HOLDING GUNS! ALL GO TO IRON BIRD WHICH SITS ON WATER... ME HIDE IN JUNGLE — SCARED TALKLESS! — AS IRON BIRD GO UP!

...ME WATCH IN MOONSHINE! OF SUDDEN, IRON BIRD UP RRR—R—R! INTO SEA-SPOLSH! BOONK! — ALL SILENT! NO TRACE ON WATER TOP!

MEANWHILE — ON THE CARGO VESSEL STANDING BY...

...THE FIRE'S DIED DOWN, REED! YOU CAN GO ASHORE AND SEE YOUR FATHER NOW!

IF SOYBOY SAW THOSE SUBVERTS FROM THE CITY GUNNING RAK INTO THEIR AIRPLANE—THEN SAW IT CRASH INTO THE WATER, IT MIGHT PUT A NEW FACE ON THIS FIRE!

MAYBE THEY FORCED TH' PORE CRITTER T'SET IT— OR DID TH' ARSONING THEMSELVES! HUH, STEVIE!

POWER BOAT PUTTING OUT FROM THE CARGO VESSEL, MIZT'CANYON!

WE MUST HUNT FOR THE WRECKAGE — HEY, SAILOR!

WE'VE HEARD THAT MR. RAK, THE HEAD MAN HERE, HAS CRASHED INTO THE EAST LAGOON IN A FLOAT PLANE! CAN YOU RIDE US OVER TO SEARCH THE AREA?

HE'S TALKING ABOUT MY DAD!

STEVE CANYON

Chapter Five
Puppy Love
November 48 - January 8, 1949

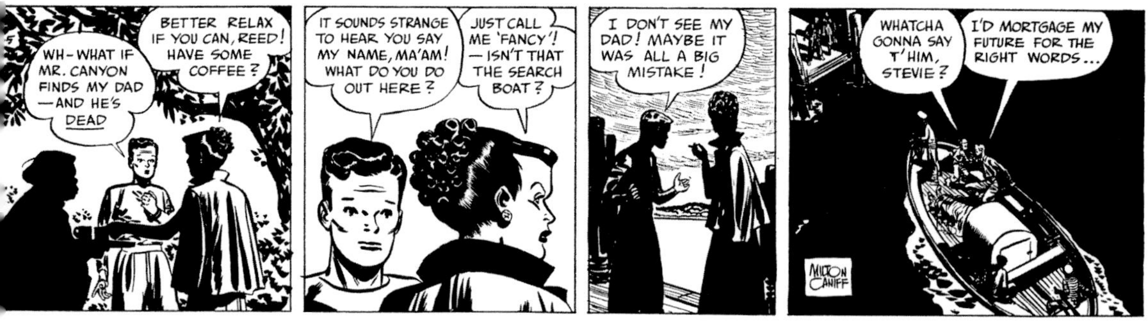
WH-WHAT IF MR. CANYON FINDS MY DAD —AND HE'S DEAD
BETTER RELAX IF YOU CAN, REED! HAVE SOME COFFEE?
IT SOUNDS STRANGE TO HEAR YOU SAY MY NAME, MA'AM! WHAT DO YOU DO OUT HERE?
JUST CALL ME 'FANCY'! —ISN'T THAT THE SEARCH BOAT?
I DON'T SEE MY DAD! MAYBE IT WAS ALL A BIG MISTAKE!
WHATCHA GONNA SAY T'HIM, STEVIE?
I'D MORTGAGE MY FUTURE FOR THE RIGHT WORDS...
MILTON CANIFF

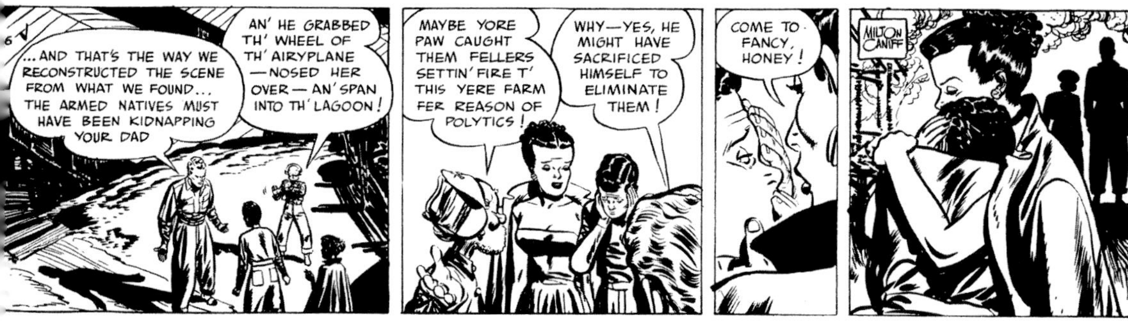
...AND THAT'S THE WAY WE RECONSTRUCTED THE SCENE FROM WHAT WE FOUND... THE ARMED NATIVES MUST HAVE BEEN KIDNAPPING YOUR DAD
AN' HE GRABBED TH' WHEEL OF TH' AIRYPLANE —NOSED HER OVER— AN' SPAN INTO TH' LAGOON!
MAYBE YORE PAW CAUGHT THEM FELLERS SETTIN' FIRE T' THIS YERE FARM FER REASON OF POLYTICS!
WHY—YES, HE MIGHT HAVE SACRIFICED HIMSELF TO ELIMINATE THEM!
COME TO FANCY, HONEY!
MILTON CANIFF

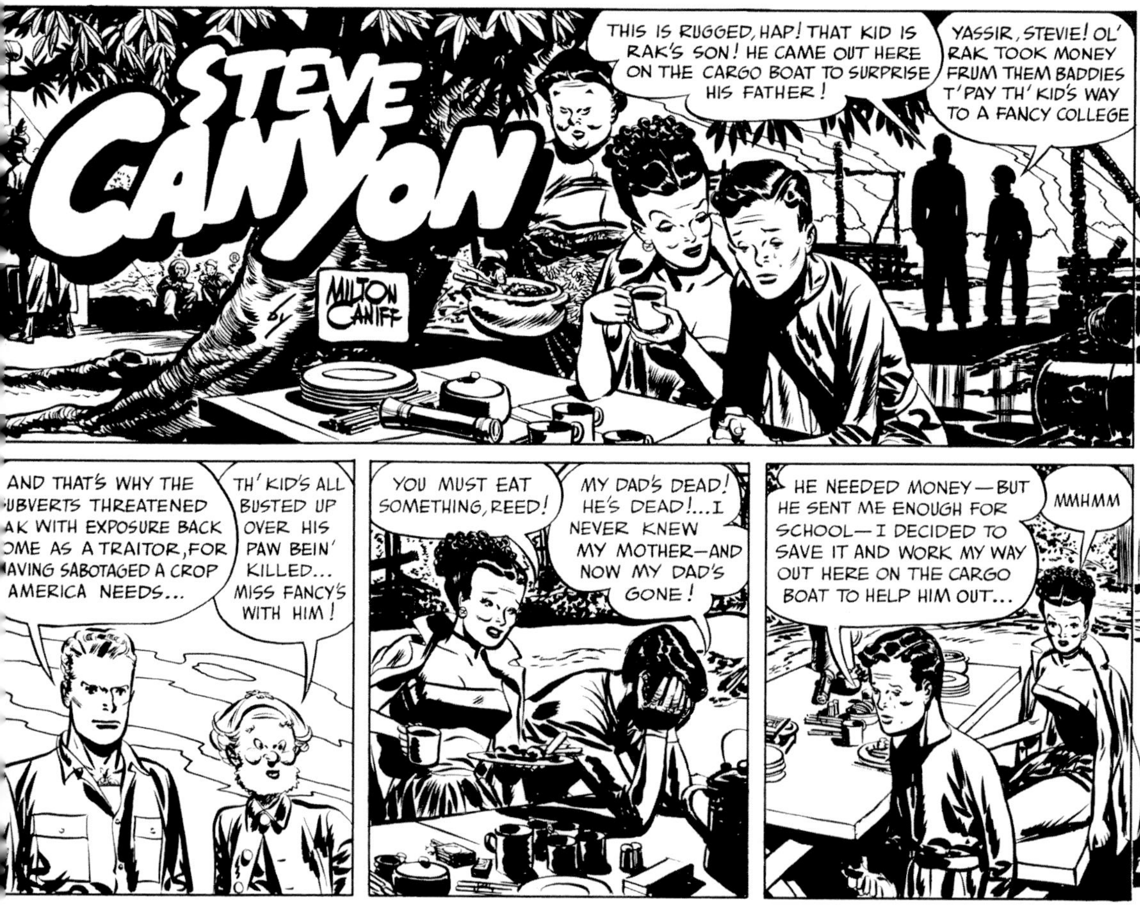
STEVE CANYON
by MILTON CANIFF
THIS IS RUGGED, HAP! THAT KID IS RAK'S SON! HE CAME OUT HERE ON THE CARGO BOAT TO SURPRISE HIS FATHER!
YASSIR, STEVIE! OL' RAK TOOK MONEY FRUM THEM BADDIES T'PAY TH' KID'S WAY TO A FANCY COLLEGE
AND THAT'S WHY THE ubverts THREATENED ak WITH EXPOSURE BACK ome AS A TRAITOR, FOR aving SABOTAGED A CROP AMERICA NEEDS...
TH' KID'S ALL BUSTED UP OVER HIS PAW BEIN' KILLED... MISS FANCY'S WITH HIM!
YOU MUST EAT SOMETHING, REED!
MY DAD'S DEAD! HE'S DEAD!...I NEVER KNEW MY MOTHER—AND NOW MY DAD'S GONE!
HE NEEDED MONEY—BUT HE SENT ME ENOUGH FOR SCHOOL—I DECIDED TO SAVE IT AND WORK MY WAY OUT HERE ON THE CARGO BOAT TO HELP HIM OUT...
MMHMM

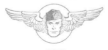

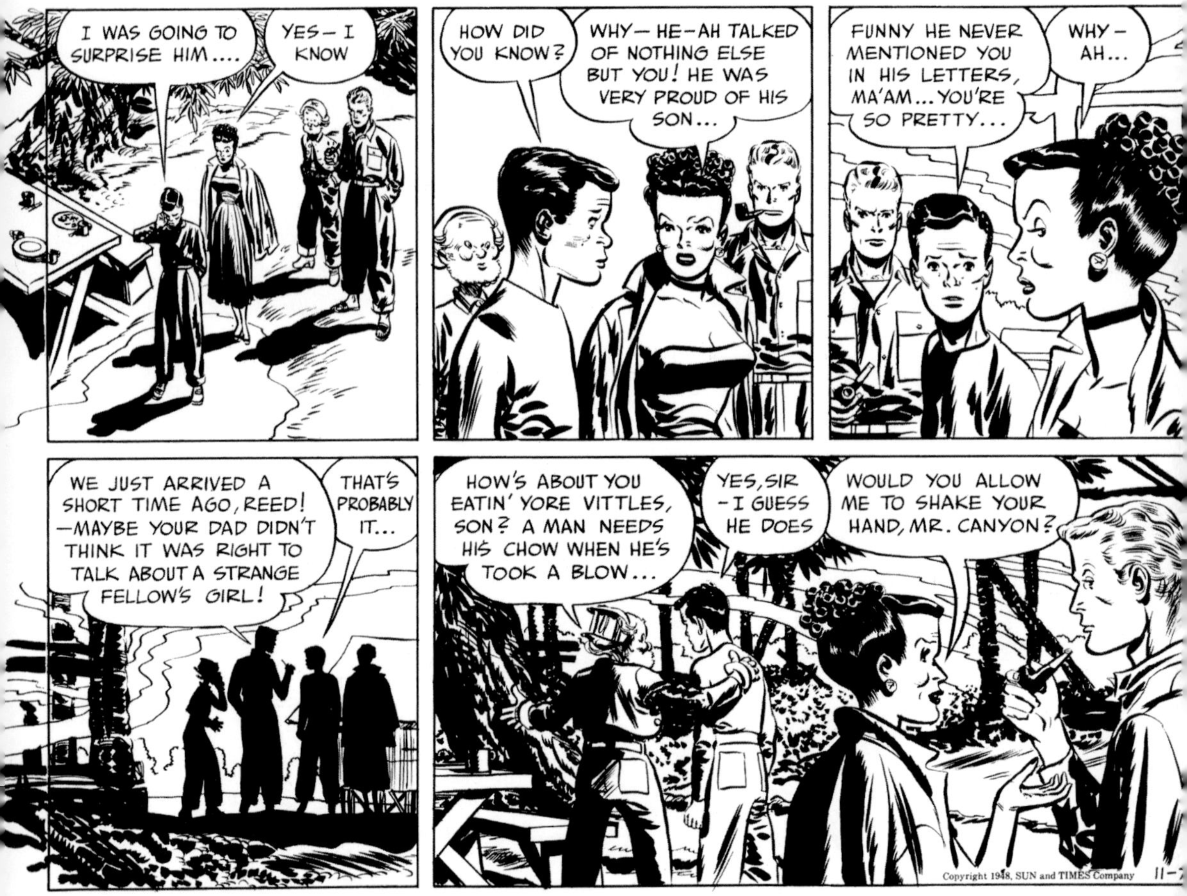
I WAS GOING TO SURPRISE HIM....
YES— I KNOW
HOW DID YOU KNOW?
WHY— HE—AH TALKED OF NOTHING ELSE BUT YOU! HE WAS VERY PROUD OF HIS SON...
FUNNY HE NEVER MENTIONED YOU IN HIS LETTERS, MA'AM... YOU'RE SO PRETTY...
WHY— AH...
WE JUST ARRIVED A SHORT TIME AGO, REED! —MAYBE YOUR DAD DIDN'T THINK IT WAS RIGHT TO TALK ABOUT A STRANGE FELLOW'S GIRL!
THAT'S PROBABLY IT...
HOW'S ABOUT YOU EATIN' YORE VITTLES, SON? A MAN NEEDS HIS CHOW WHEN HE'S TOOK A BLOW...
YES, SIR —I GUESS HE DOES
WOULD YOU ALLOW ME TO SHAKE YOUR HAND, MR. CANYON?
Copyright 1948, SUN and TIMES Company
11-7

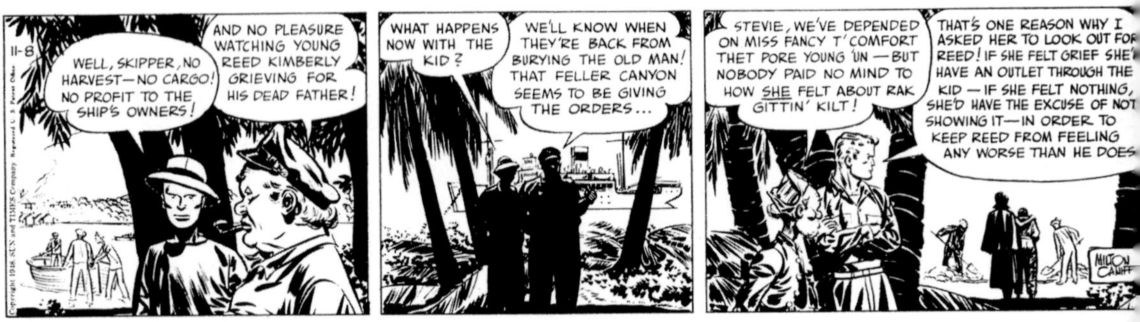
11-8
WELL, SKIPPER, NO HARVEST—NO CARGO! NO PROFIT TO THE SHIP'S OWNERS!
AND NO PLEASURE WATCHING YOUNG REED KIMBERLY GRIEVING FOR HIS DEAD FATHER!
WHAT HAPPENS NOW WITH THE KID?
WE'LL KNOW WHEN THEY'RE BACK FROM BURYING THE OLD MAN! THAT FELLER CANYON SEEMS TO BE GIVING THE ORDERS...
STEVIE, WE'VE DEPENDED ON MISS FANCY T' COMFORT THET PORE YOUNG 'UN —BUT NOBODY PAID NO MIND TO HOW SHE FELT ABOUT RAK GITTIN' KILT!
THAT'S ONE REASON WHY I ASKED HER TO LOOK OUT FOR REED! IF SHE FELT GRIEF SHE' HAVE AN OUTLET THROUGH THE KID — IF SHE FELT NOTHING, SHE'D HAVE THE EXCUSE OF NOT SHOWING IT—IN ORDER TO KEEP REED FROM FEELING ANY WORSE THAN HE DOES
MILTON CANIFF

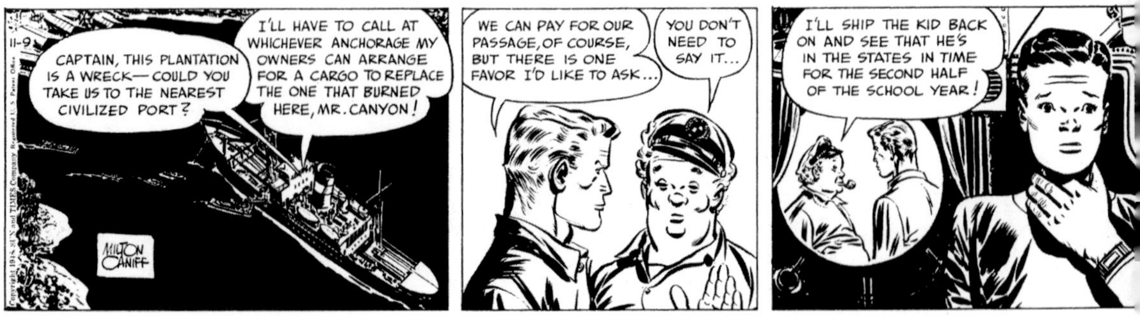
11-9
CAPTAIN, THIS PLANTATION IS A WRECK— COULD YOU TAKE US TO THE NEAREST CIVILIZED PORT?
I'LL HAVE TO CALL AT WHICHEVER ANCHORAGE MY OWNERS CAN ARRANGE FOR A CARGO TO REPLACE THE ONE THAT BURNED HERE, MR. CANYON!
MILTON CANIFF
WE CAN PAY FOR OUR PASSAGE, OF COURSE, BUT THERE IS ONE FAVOR I'D LIKE TO ASK...
YOU DON'T NEED TO SAY IT...
I'LL SHIP THE KID BACK ON AND SEE THAT HE'S IN THE STATES IN TIME FOR THE SECOND HALF OF THE SCHOOL YEAR!

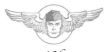

-10 AS THE SUN SINKS IN THE WEST WE TAKE OUR LEAVE OF BEAUTIFUL HEMOGLOBIN!

NOT THAT IT'S ANY OF MY BUSINESS, FANCY, BUT DON'T YOU HAVE ANY —WELL—FEELING ABOUT WHAT HAPPENED TO RAK?

SMART GUYS LIKE YOU CAN BE AWFULLY THICK SOMETIMES—ESPECIALLY ABOUT WOMEN!...I HATED RAK'S GUTS—IN SPADES!

WELL, NOBODY COULD HAVE DONE A BETTER JOB OF STANDING BY THE KID...I WAS PROUD OF YOU...

Y-YOU WERE, STEVE?

YEP!.. WELL, GOTTA CHECK WITH THE SKIPPER ON WHICH PORT HE CAN HAUL US TO!... SEE YOU AT CHOW...

MILTON CANIFF

LIKE T' PLAY SOME CHECKERS ER SOMETHIN', SON?

NO, THANKS, MR. EASTER... I THINK I'LL WALK ON DECK AWHILE...

RECKON I'LL HIT TH' SHUCKS, STEVIE!

...SOME GIN RUMMY, FANCY?

I COULDN'T CONCENTRATE ON CARDS!

MISS FANCY!

WHY, REED! YOU STARTLED ME! WHAT IS IT?

I-I WANT TO ASK YOU A QUESTION...

MILTON CANIFF

12 MAY I ASK YOU A QUESTION, MISS FANCY?

WHY—I SUPPOSE SO, REED...

OH, BROTHER! HERE IT COMES...

IT'S—SORT OF PERSONAL

WELL—I GUESS IT HAD TO COME SOMETIME...

YOU WERE OUT ON THE PLANTATION WITH HIM....

—GET IT OVER WITH!

CANIFF

DO YOU THINK MR. CANYON WOULD ALLOW ME TO TEAM UP WITH HIM?

-3 YOU DIDN'T ANSWER, MISS FANCY!

I'M SORRY, REED—I-I WAS STARTLED FOR THE MOMENT! —I THOUGHT YOU WERE GOING TO ASK SOMETHING —AH—TECHNICAL!

WOULD MR. CANYON MIND IF I WENT ALONG WITH HIM...? I HAVE NO HOME TO GO BACK TO!

I CAN'T SPEAK FOR HIM, REED, BUT HE WOULDN'T RESENT YOUR ASKING...

MR. CANYON IS A REASONABLE SORT OF GUY

THANKS, MA'AM, I'LL TAKE YOUR ADVICE!

MILTON CANIFF

COOL TO HOT NUMBER

YEP—CANYON IS REASONABLE IN HIS APPROACH TO MOST ANYONE WITHOUT A 'FANCY' NAME!

Steve Canyon

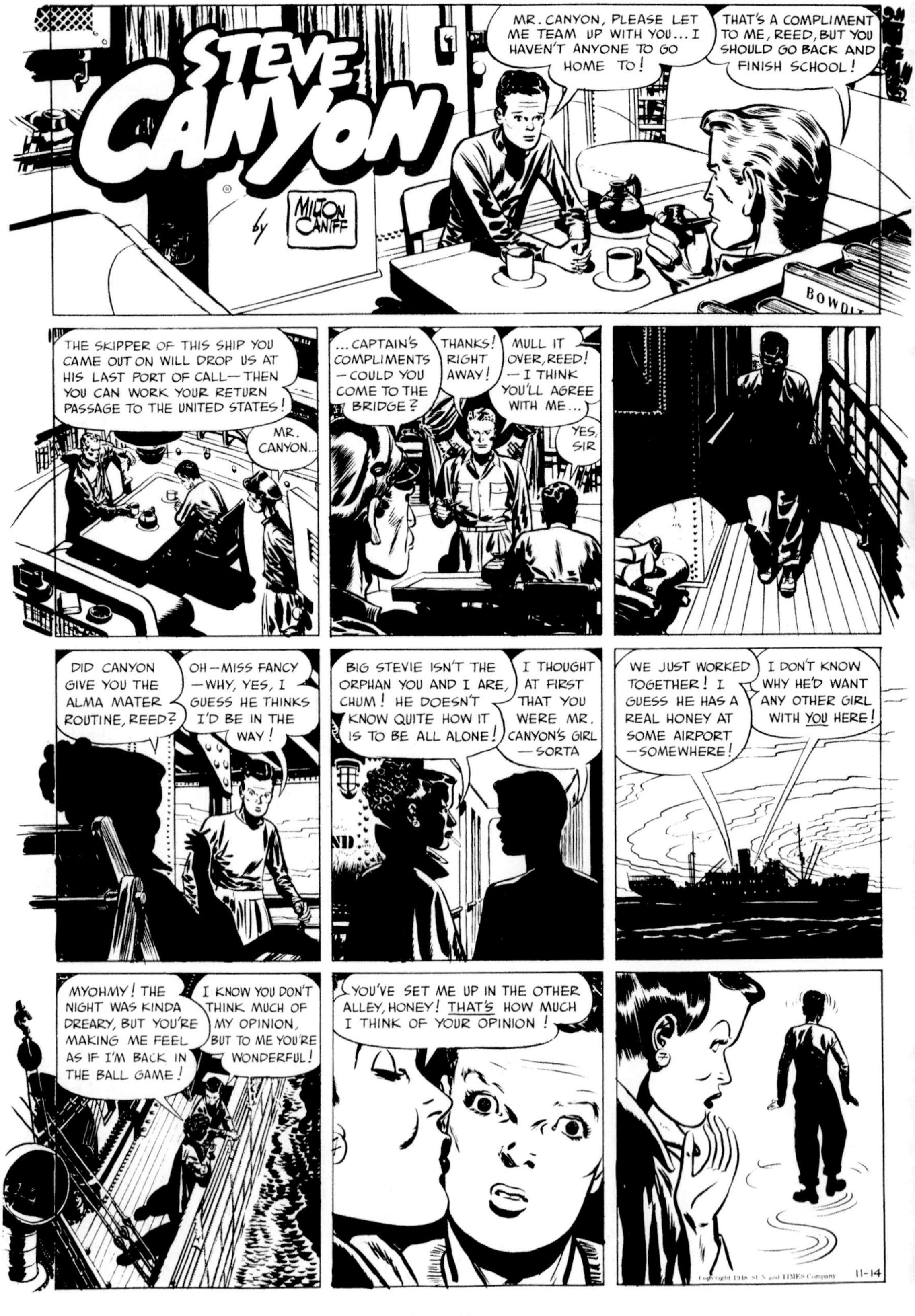
STEVE CANYON
by MILTON CANIFF
MR. CANYON, PLEASE LET ME TEAM UP WITH YOU... I HAVEN'T ANYONE TO GO HOME TO!
THAT'S A COMPLIMENT TO ME, REED, BUT YOU SHOULD GO BACK AND FINISH SCHOOL!
BOWDIT
THE SKIPPER OF THIS SHIP YOU CAME OUT ON WILL DROP US AT HIS LAST PORT OF CALL—THEN YOU CAN WORK YOUR RETURN PASSAGE TO THE UNITED STATES!
MR. CANYON...
...CAPTAIN'S COMPLIMENTS—COULD YOU COME TO THE BRIDGE?
THANKS! RIGHT AWAY!
MULL IT OVER, REED! —I THINK YOU'LL AGREE WITH ME...
YES, SIR
DID CANYON GIVE YOU THE ALMA MATER ROUTINE, REED?
OH—MISS FANCY—WHY, YES, I GUESS HE THINKS I'D BE IN THE WAY!
BIG STEVIE ISN'T THE ORPHAN YOU AND I ARE, CHUM! HE DOESN'T KNOW QUITE HOW IT IS TO BE ALL ALONE!
I THOUGHT AT FIRST THAT YOU WERE MR. CANYON'S GIRL—SORTA
WE JUST WORKED TOGETHER! I GUESS HE HAS A REAL HONEY AT SOME AIRPORT—SOMEWHERE!
I DON'T KNOW WHY HE'D WANT ANY OTHER GIRL WITH YOU HERE!
MYOHMY! THE NIGHT WAS KINDA DREARY, BUT YOU'RE MAKING ME FEEL AS IF I'M BACK IN THE BALL GAME!
I KNOW YOU DON'T THINK MUCH OF MY OPINION, BUT TO ME YOU'RE WONDERFUL!
YOU'VE SET ME UP IN THE OTHER ALLEY, HONEY! THAT'S HOW MUCH I THINK OF YOUR OPINION!
Copyright 1948 SUN and TIMES Company
11-14

CANYON, MY OWNERS HAVE WIRELESSED THAT I CAN PICK UP A CARGO IN TALEEL...

I REMEMBER AN AIR FIELD THERE... WE CAN FLY ON TO RANGOON AND CONTACT THE AMERICAN AUTHORITIES ABOUT NEW PAPERS!

LATER

SO THAT'S THE PICTURE... —I'M A LITTLE SURPRISED THAT YOUNG REED HASN'T SEEMED TOO DOWNHEARTED BECAUSE I TOLD HIM HE COULDN'T GO WITH US!

MAYBE IT'S BECAUSE I KISSED HIS CHEEK AS A SORT OF CONSOLATION

A GAL LIKES TO THINK SHE CAN STILL MAKE THE BELLS RING—EVEN IF THE SUBJECT IS ON THE YOUNG SIDE — BUT THEN I GUESS ALL THAT IS SOMETHING IN WHICH YOU ARE JUST NOT INTERESTED...

YOU SORTA GAVE ME BOTH BARRELS BECAUSE I DIDN'T MAKE A PLAY FOR YOU, DIDN'T YOU, FANCY?...

YEAH, CANYON... I TALK TOO MUCH! WHY SHOULD YOU GIVE ME A NOD?

PLENTY OF REASONS WHY — BUT CATCHING A CHICK LIKE YOU BETWEEN BOY FRIENDS IS LIKE GRABBING AN EMPTY PHONE BOOTH AT RUSH HOUR

I SUPPOSE THE GOLDEN BOY DOESN'T HAVE TO PITCH IN AND COMPETE... PLENTY MORE BABES IN THE NEXT TOWN!

THIS IS ALL SORTA COCKEYED!...YOU'RE IN LOVE WITH YOUR HUSBAND!

I'M NOT A WORSHIPPER OF THE DEAD!

OF COURSE NOT— YOU'RE CONVINCED YOUR GUY IS STILL ALIVE!

CANYON, HOW DID YOU KNOW I THINK MY HUSBAND IS STILL ALIVE?

YOU ASK A PILOT ABOUT THAT, FANCY? MOST OF MY FRIENDS WHO DIDN'T COME HOME JUST SEEM TO BE OVERDUE ON LONG MISSIONS!

MY GUY WAS ON ONE OF THOSE ARMY RECORDING TEAMS...THEY DIDN'T REPORT BACK ONE DAY! MIGHT HAVE BEEN A DIRECT HIT... PRISONERS, MAYBE — NOBODY EVER SAW THEM AGAIN...

...SO YOU THINK EVERY AIRPLANE THAT LANDS MAY HAVE THEM ABOARD! —PICKED UP IN SOME REMOTE PLACE WHERE THEY BAILED OUT...

SORRY I WAS SNEERY AT YOU, CANYON... I'LL KISS YOUR CHEEK FOR BEING SO SIMPÁTICO— THEN PATTER OFF TO MY CABIN...

WHY, REED KIMBERLY! YOU'RE ALWAYS POPPING UP AND STARTLING ME! I THOUGHT YOU WERE IN BED LONG AGO...

I COULDN'T SLEEP BECAUSE MR. CANYON SAID I COULDN'T TEAM UP WITH HIM...AND YOU WERE SO NICE TO ME BEFORE, MISS FANCY...

SO YOU CAME TO THE WELL AGAIN...

IN A WAY— EXCEPT THAT I SAW YOU KISS MR. CANYON ON THE CHEEK JUST NOW — THE SAME WAY YOU KISSED ME!

YOU THINK MAYBE I JUST GO AROUND KISSING EVERY MAN I MEET ON THE CHEEK! —RIGHT?...

WELL— I---

YOU CAN RELAX! I DO NOT GO AROUND KISSING EVERY MAN I MEET — ON THE CHEEK!

OH, GOLLY —THAT'S WHAT I WANTED TO HEAR YOU SAY!

Steve Canyon

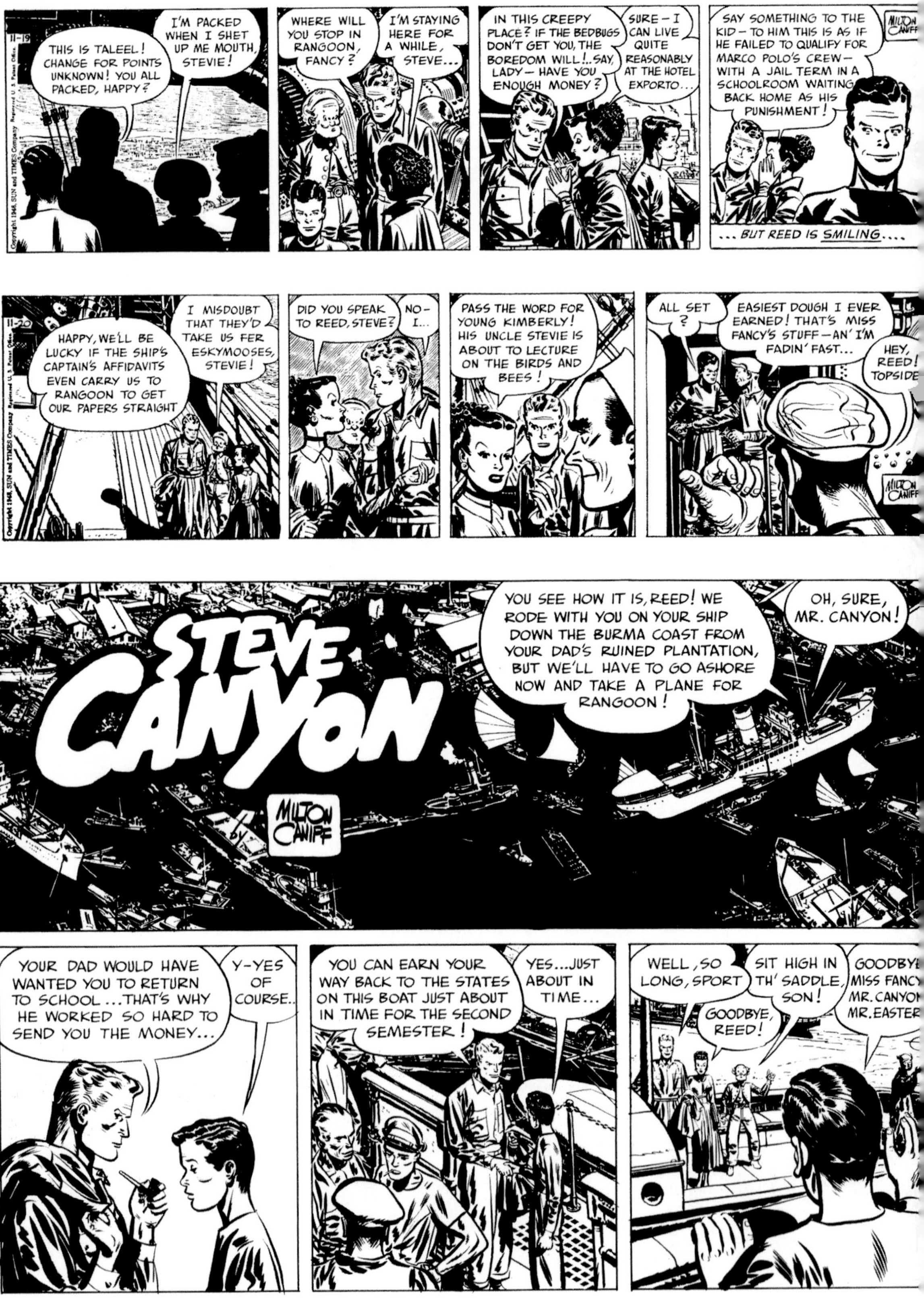
11-19
THIS IS TALEEL! CHANGE FOR POINTS UNKNOWN! YOU ALL PACKED, HAPPY?
I'M PACKED WHEN I SHET UP ME MOUTH, STEVIE!
Copyright 1948, SUN and TIMES Company Registered U. S. Patent Office
WHERE WILL YOU STOP IN RANGOON, FANCY?
I'M STAYING HERE FOR A WHILE, STEVE...
IN THIS CREEPY PLACE? IF THE BEDBUGS DON'T GET YOU, THE BOREDOM WILL!..SAY, LADY—HAVE YOU ENOUGH MONEY?
SURE—I CAN LIVE QUITE REASONABLY AT THE HOTEL EXPORTO...
SAY SOMETHING TO THE KID—TO HIM THIS IS AS IF HE FAILED TO QUALIFY FOR MARCO POLO'S CREW—WITH A JAIL TERM IN A SCHOOLROOM WAITING BACK HOME AS HIS PUNISHMENT!
MILTON CANIFF
...BUT REED IS SMILING....
11-20
HAPPY, WE'LL BE LUCKY IF THE SHIP'S CAPTAIN'S AFFIDAVITS EVEN CARRY US TO RANGOON TO GET OUR PAPERS STRAIGHT
I MISDOUBT THAT THEY'D TAKE US FER ESKYMOOSES, STEVIE!
Copyright 1948, SUN and TIMES Company Registered U. S. Patent Office
DID YOU SPEAK TO REED, STEVE?
NO—I...
PASS THE WORD FOR YOUNG KIMBERLY! HIS UNCLE STEVIE IS ABOUT TO LECTURE ON THE BIRDS AND BEES!
ALL SET?
EASIEST DOUGH I EVER EARNED! THAT'S MISS FANCY'S STUFF—AN' I'M FADIN' FAST...
HEY, REED! TOPSIDE
MILTON CANIFF
STEVE CANYON
by MILTON CANIFF
YOU SEE HOW IT IS, REED! WE RODE WITH YOU ON YOUR SHIP DOWN THE BURMA COAST FROM YOUR DAD'S RUINED PLANTATION, BUT WE'LL HAVE TO GO ASHORE NOW AND TAKE A PLANE FOR RANGOON!
OH, SURE, MR. CANYON!
YOUR DAD WOULD HAVE WANTED YOU TO RETURN TO SCHOOL...THAT'S WHY HE WORKED SO HARD TO SEND YOU THE MONEY...
Y-YES OF COURSE..
YOU CAN EARN YOUR WAY BACK TO THE STATES ON THIS BOAT JUST ABOUT IN TIME FOR THE SECOND SEMESTER!
YES...JUST ABOUT IN TIME...
WELL, SO LONG, SPORT
SIT HIGH IN TH' SADDLE, SON!
GOODBYE, REED!
GOODBYE MISS FANCY MR. CANYON MR. EASTER

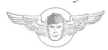

FANCY, ARE YOU SURE YOU WON'T GO TO RANGOON WITH US WHILE I CHECK IN WITH THE AMERICAN AUTHORITIES?

NO, CANYON, I'LL HANG AROUND HERE 'TIL I CATCH MY BREATH, BUT I'LL SEE YOU OFF AT THE AIRPORT!

REED WUZ A RIGHT NICE YOUNG'UN TO HAVE BEEN TH' SON OF THET RAK CRITTER!

I SUPPOSE RAK USED HIS INITIALS AS A NAME IN THE HOPE THAT REED A. KIMBERLY, JUNIOR WOULDN'T BE DISGRACED IF HIS POP'S SCHEMES WENT SOUR!

I KINDA MISS TH' LAD!

SO DO I, HAP, BUT WE COULDN'T HAVE BEEN RESPONSIBLE FOR HIM! THERE GOES REED'S SHIP DOWN THE CHANNEL!

THIS IS MY HOTEL, BOY...

Copyright 1948, SUN and TIMES Company   11-21

STEVIE, IT'S A REAL MERCY YOUNG REED KIMBERLY NEVER DID FIND OUT HIS PAW WUZ SECH A MIXED-UP FELLER!

THE KID'S YOUNG, HAPPY... HE'LL MAKE OUT ALL RIGHT WHEN THE CARGO BOAT GETS HIM BACK TO THE STATES...

I KEEP THINKIN' ABOUT MISS FANCY, ALL BY HER PRETTY SELF THERE IN THET COAST TOWN...

YOU'D BETTER START WORRYING ABOUT WHETHER WE CAN GET NEW PASSPORTS WHEN WE REACH RANGOON!

MEANWHILE, ON THE CARGO BOAT OUTBOUND FROM BURMA...

WHERE'S YOUNG REED KIMBERLY? YOU WERE SEEN TALKING TO HIM BEFORE WE CAST OFF!

HONEST, SKIPPER, YOU TOLD ME OFF TO PUT THE FANCY GAL'S GEAR ASHORE AT HER HOTEL... THE KID PAID ME TO LET HIM DO IT—AN' WHEN HE DIDN'T COME BACK BEFORE WE SAILED, I WAS JUST PLAIN SCARED TO TELL YOU ABOUT IT...

REED KIMBERLY! YOU JUMPED SHIP!

NO, MA'AM, MISS FANCY—I BROUGHT YOUR LUGGAGE FROM THE BOAT, BUT I HADN'T SIGNED ON FOR THE TRIP—SO I DIDN'T GO OVER THE SIDE...

BUT WHY? STEVE CANYON WANTED YOU TO GO BACK TO SCHOOL!

I JUST COULDN'T—AFTER WHAT HAPPENED TO MY DAD...

...STEVE AND HAPPY EASTER HAVE GONE ON TO RANGOON...

...I'M PROBABLY THE ONLY PERSON YOU KNOW IN THIS TOWN!

GEE—THAT'S WON-DERFUL, MISS FANCY!

Steve Canyon

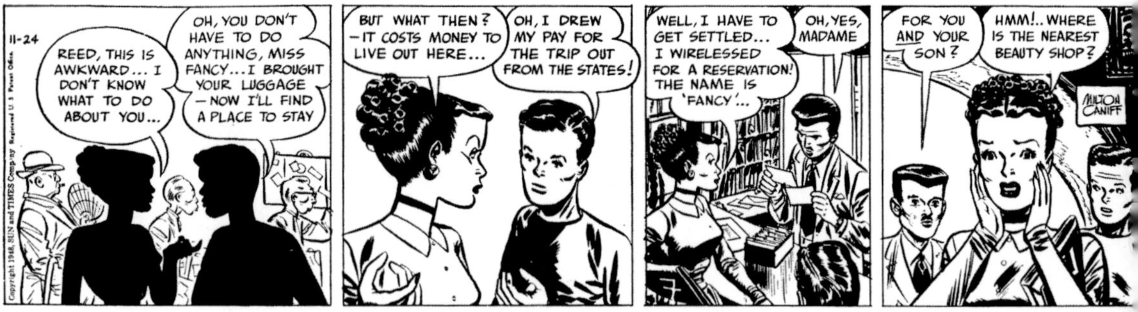
11-24
Copyright 1948, SUN and TIMES Company Registered U.S. Patent Office.
REED, THIS IS AWKWARD... I DON'T KNOW WHAT TO DO ABOUT YOU...
OH, YOU DON'T HAVE TO DO ANYTHING, MISS FANCY... I BROUGHT YOUR LUGGAGE — NOW I'LL FIND A PLACE TO STAY
BUT WHAT THEN? — IT COSTS MONEY TO LIVE OUT HERE...
OH, I DREW MY PAY FOR THE TRIP OUT FROM THE STATES!
WELL, I HAVE TO GET SETTLED... I WIRELESSED FOR A RESERVATION! THE NAME IS 'FANCY'...
OH, YES, MADAME
FOR YOU AND YOUR SON?
HMM!.. WHERE IS THE NEAREST BEAUTY SHOP?
MILTON CANIFF

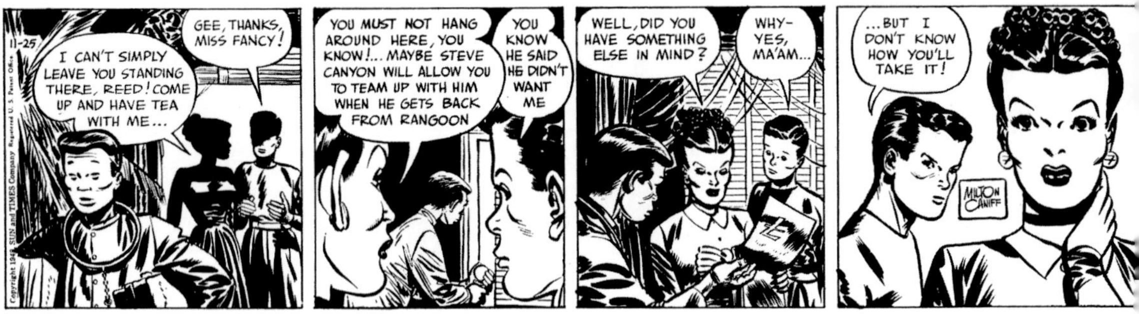
11-25
Copyright 1948, SUN and TIMES Company Registered U.S. Patent Office.
I CAN'T SIMPLY LEAVE YOU STANDING THERE, REED! COME UP AND HAVE TEA WITH ME...
GEE, THANKS, MISS FANCY!
YOU MUST NOT HANG AROUND HERE, YOU KNOW!... MAYBE STEVE CANYON WILL ALLOW YOU TO TEAM UP WITH HIM WHEN HE GETS BACK FROM RANGOON
YOU KNOW HE SAID HE DIDN'T WANT ME
WELL, DID YOU HAVE SOMETHING ELSE IN MIND?
WHY-YES, MA'AM...
...BUT I DON'T KNOW HOW YOU'LL TAKE IT!
MILTON CANIFF

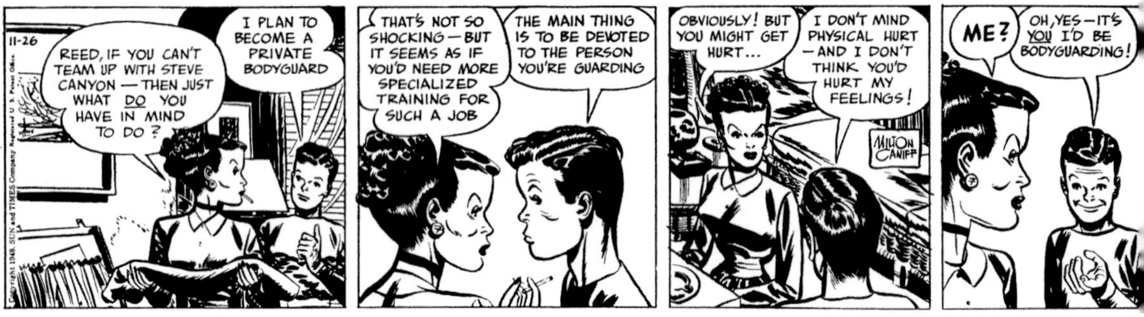
11-26
Copyright 1948, SUN and TIMES Company Registered U.S. Patent Office.
REED, IF YOU CAN'T TEAM UP WITH STEVE CANYON — THEN JUST WHAT DO YOU HAVE IN MIND TO DO?
I PLAN TO BECOME A PRIVATE BODYGUARD
THAT'S NOT SO SHOCKING — BUT IT SEEMS AS IF YOU'D NEED MORE SPECIALIZED TRAINING FOR SUCH A JOB
THE MAIN THING IS TO BE DEVOTED TO THE PERSON YOU'RE GUARDING
OBVIOUSLY! BUT YOU MIGHT GET HURT...
I DON'T MIND PHYSICAL HURT — AND I DON'T THINK YOU'D HURT MY FEELINGS!
MILTON CANIFF
ME?
OH, YES — IT'S YOU I'D BE BODYGUARDING!

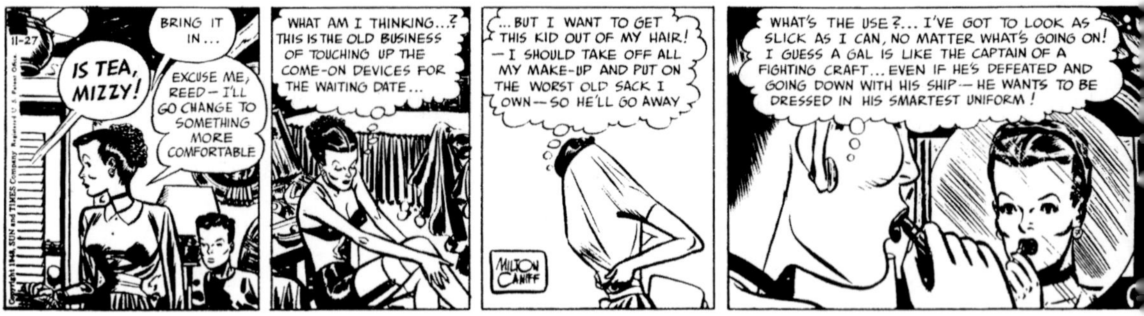
11-27
Copyright 1948, SUN and TIMES Company Registered U.S. Patent Office.
IS TEA, MIZZY!
BRING IT IN...
EXCUSE ME, REED — I'LL GO CHANGE TO SOMETHING MORE COMFORTABLE
WHAT AM I THINKING...? THIS IS THE OLD BUSINESS OF TOUCHING UP THE COME-ON DEVICES FOR THE WAITING DATE...
...BUT I WANT TO GET THIS KID OUT OF MY HAIR! — I SHOULD TAKE OFF ALL MY MAKE-UP AND PUT ON THE WORST OLD SACK I OWN — SO HE'LL GO AWAY
MILTON CANIFF
WHAT'S THE USE?... I'VE GOT TO LOOK AS SLICK AS I CAN, NO MATTER WHAT'S GOING ON! I GUESS A GAL IS LIKE THE CAPTAIN OF A FIGHTING CRAFT... EVEN IF HE'S DEFEATED AND GOING DOWN WITH HIS SHIP — HE WANTS TO BE DRESSED IN HIS SMARTEST UNIFORM!

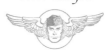

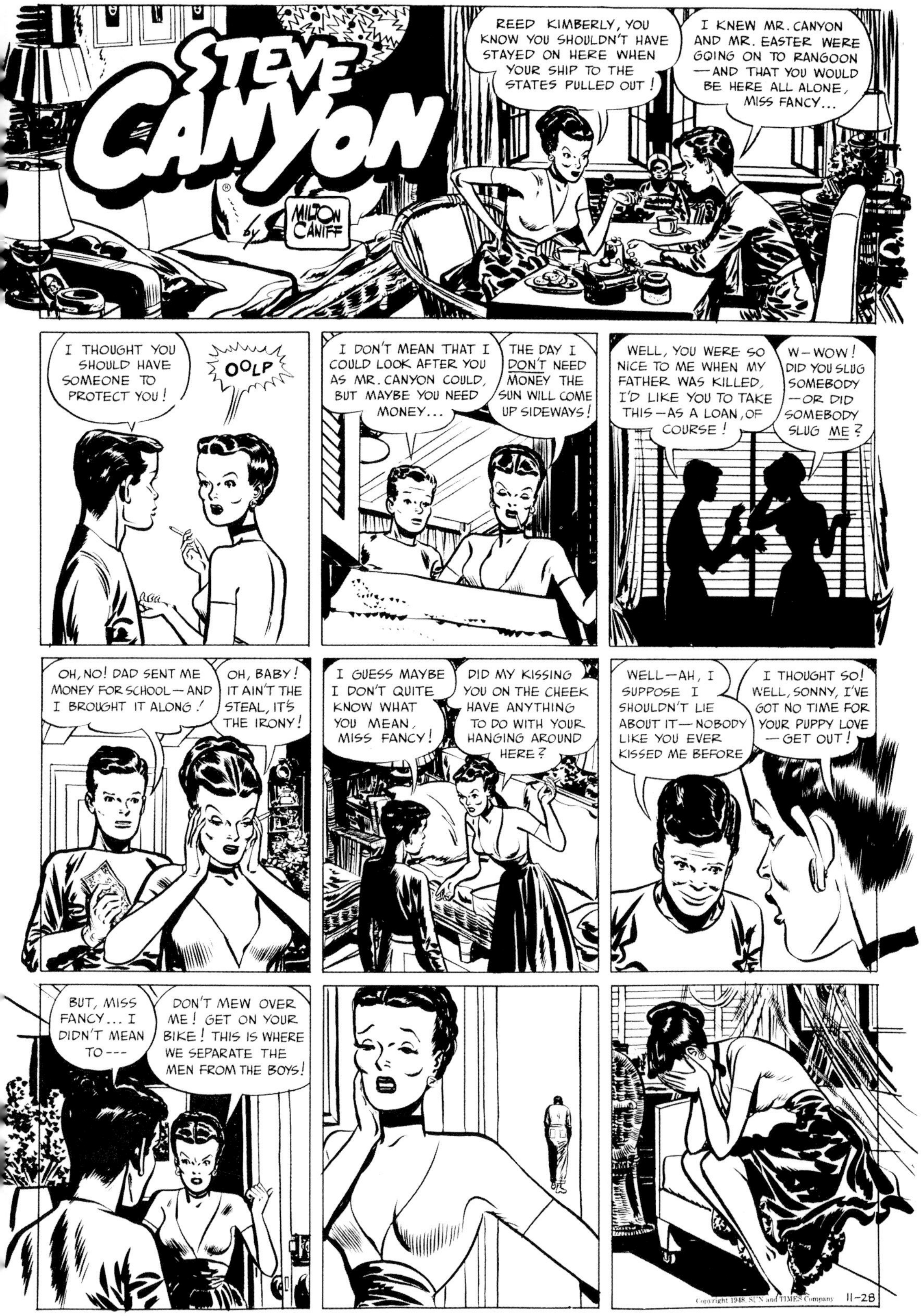
STEVE CANYON
by MILTON CANIFF
REED KIMBERLY, YOU KNOW YOU SHOULDN'T HAVE STAYED ON HERE WHEN YOUR SHIP TO THE STATES PULLED OUT!
I KNEW MR. CANYON AND MR. EASTER WERE GOING ON TO RANGOON —AND THAT YOU WOULD BE HERE ALL ALONE, MISS FANCY...
I THOUGHT YOU SHOULD HAVE SOMEONE TO PROTECT YOU!
OOLP
I DON'T MEAN THAT I COULD LOOK AFTER YOU AS MR. CANYON COULD, BUT MAYBE YOU NEED MONEY...
THE DAY I DON'T NEED MONEY THE SUN WILL COME UP SIDEWAYS!
WELL, YOU WERE SO NICE TO ME WHEN MY FATHER WAS KILLED, I'D LIKE YOU TO TAKE THIS—AS A LOAN, OF COURSE!
W-WOW! DID YOU SLUG SOMEBODY —OR DID SOMEBODY SLUG ME?
OH, NO! DAD SENT ME MONEY FOR SCHOOL—AND I BROUGHT IT ALONG!
OH, BABY! IT AIN'T THE STEAL, IT'S THE IRONY!
I GUESS MAYBE I DON'T QUITE KNOW WHAT YOU MEAN, MISS FANCY!
DID MY KISSING YOU ON THE CHEEK HAVE ANYTHING TO DO WITH YOUR HANGING AROUND HERE?
WELL—AH, I SUPPOSE I SHOULDN'T LIE ABOUT IT—NOBODY LIKE YOU EVER KISSED ME BEFORE
I THOUGHT SO! WELL, SONNY, I'VE GOT NO TIME FOR YOUR PUPPY LOVE —GET OUT!
BUT, MISS FANCY... I DIDN'T MEAN TO---
DON'T MEW OVER ME! GET ON YOUR BIKE! THIS IS WHERE WE SEPARATE THE MEN FROM THE BOYS!
Copyright 1948, SUN and TIMES Company
11-28

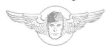

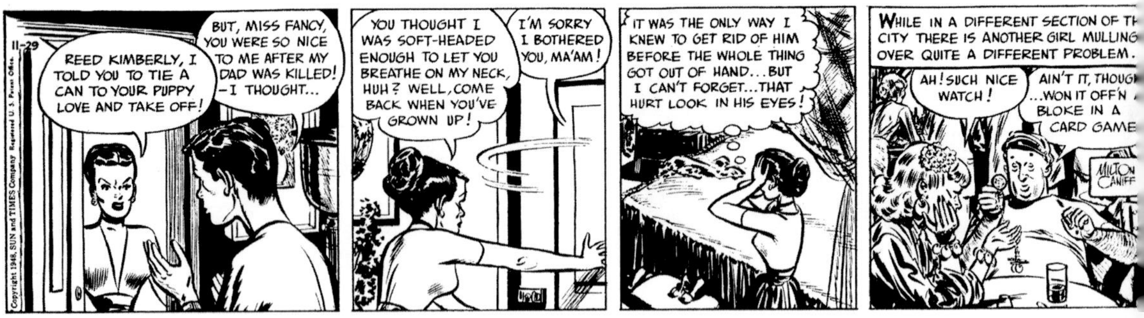
11-29
Copyright 1948, SUN and TIMES Company Registered U.S. Patent Office.
REED KIMBERLY, I TOLD YOU TO TIE A CAN TO YOUR PUPPY LOVE AND TAKE OFF!
BUT, MISS FANCY, YOU WERE SO NICE TO ME AFTER MY DAD WAS KILLED! —I THOUGHT...
YOU THOUGHT I WAS SOFT-HEADED ENOUGH TO LET YOU BREATHE ON MY NECK, HUH? WELL, COME BACK WHEN YOU'VE GROWN UP!
I'M SORRY I BOTHERED YOU, MA'AM!
IT WAS THE ONLY WAY I KNEW TO GET RID OF HIM BEFORE THE WHOLE THING GOT OUT OF HAND... BUT I CAN'T FORGET... THAT HURT LOOK IN HIS EYES!
WHILE IN A DIFFERENT SECTION OF THE CITY THERE IS ANOTHER GIRL MULLING OVER QUITE A DIFFERENT PROBLEM.
AH! SUCH NICE WATCH!
AIN'T IT, THOUGH ...WON IT OFF'N A BLOKE IN A CARD GAME
MILTON CANIFF

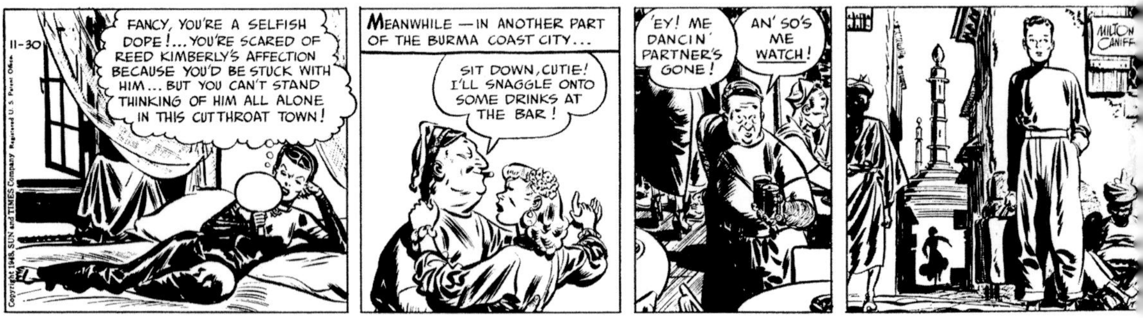
11-30
Copyright 1948, SUN and TIMES Company Registered U.S. Patent Office.
FANCY, YOU'RE A SELFISH DOPE!... YOU'RE SCARED OF REED KIMBERLY'S AFFECTION BECAUSE YOU'D BE STUCK WITH HIM... BUT YOU CAN'T STAND THINKING OF HIM ALL ALONE IN THIS CUTTHROAT TOWN!
MEANWHILE — IN ANOTHER PART OF THE BURMA COAST CITY...
SIT DOWN, CUTIE! I'LL SNAGGLE ONTO SOME DRINKS AT THE BAR!
'EY! ME DANCIN' PARTNER'S GONE!
AN' SO'S ME WATCH!
MILTON CANIFF

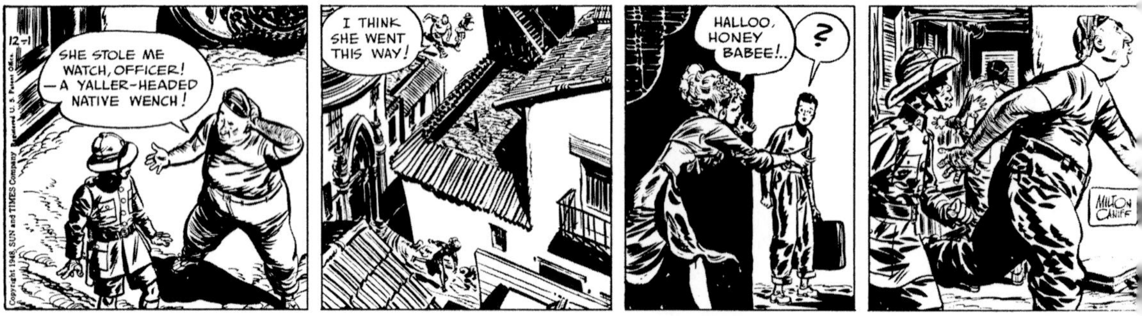
12-1
Copyright 1948, SUN and TIMES Company Registered U.S. Patent Office.
SHE STOLE ME WATCH, OFFICER! —A YALLER-HEADED NATIVE WENCH!
I THINK SHE WENT THIS WAY!
HALLOO, HONEY BABEE!..
?
MILTON CANIFF

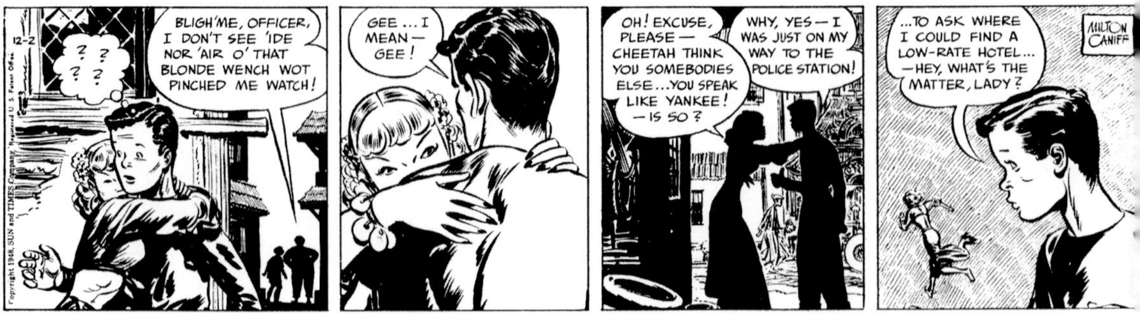
12-2
Copyright 1948, SUN and TIMES Company Registered U.S. Patent Office.
? ? ? ?
BLIGH'ME, OFFICER, I DON'T SEE 'IDE NOR 'AIR O' THAT BLONDE WENCH WOT PINCHED ME WATCH!
GEE ... I MEAN — GEE!
OH! EXCUSE, PLEASE — CHEETAH THINK YOU SOMEBODIES ELSE... YOU SPEAK LIKE YANKEE! —IS SO?
WHY, YES — I WAS JUST ON MY WAY TO THE POLICE STATION!
...TO ASK WHERE I COULD FIND A LOW-RATE HOTEL... —HEY, WHAT'S THE MATTER, LADY?
MILTON CANIFF

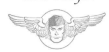

GEE, I CAN'T GET IT OUT OF MY MIND HOW THAT BLONDE NATIVE GIRL THREW HER ARMS AROUND MY NECK — THINKING I WAS SOMEBODY ELSE...

SHE SMELLED SO GOOD... MISS FANCY SMELLS GOOD, TOO, BUT SHE WEARS SOME OTHER KIND OF PERFUME...

I FELT TERRIBLE BECAUSE FANCY KICKED ME OUT—'TIL THAT GIRL RAN UP TO ME...

IF MR. CANYON COULD HAVE SEEN THAT, HE MIGHT NOT THINK I'M SUCH A KID!... HEY! WOULDN'T THE GUYS BACK AT SCHOOL HAVE BEEN IMPRESSED?...

AHUM!... I THINK I'LL GO OUT AND LOOK AROUND! MIGHT RUN INTO SOME WOMEN I'VE MET IN MY TRAVELS!

?

... I DON'T KNOW WHETHER IT WAS SUCH A GOOD IDEA TO COME OUT LOOKING FOR THAT BLONDE NATIVE GIRL....

THESE BABIES LOOK AS IF THEY'D SLIT YOUR NECK FOR YOUR SHOES!... MAYBE MR. CANYON WAS RIGHT — I MIGHT NOT BE READY FOR ADVENTURING — BUT YOU DON'T LEARN IN SCHOOL WHAT I'D LIKE TO KNOW RIGHT NOW!

MEANWHILE

... I'M MISS FANCY...

MANAGER SAY TO GIVE THIS TO MIZZY...

IT'S MY HOTEL BILL!

NO HURRY, OF COURSE, MIZZY! MANAGER MERELY WISH TO BE SURE IT REACH YOU SAFELY...

STEVE CANYON by MILTON CANIFF

FANCY, MY FINE FEATHERED FEMALE, GET ON THE BALL! THE BEST THINGS IN LIFE ARE FREE ONLY TO PEOPLE WITH MONEY!

IF STEVE CANYON AND HAPPY EASTER ARE IN RANGOON—AND YOUNG REED KIMBERLY OFFERS TO LEND ME GOOD YANKEE BUCKS, WHY DO I HESITATE ? A GAL'S GOTTA EAT — NO MATTER HOW YOUNG THE GUY IS WHO PICKS UP THE DINNER CHECK!

I SENT REED AWAY FOR HIS OWN GOOD— NOW I NEED SOMEBODY TO DO SOMETHING FOR MY OWN GOOD!

MEANWHILE—IN ANOTHER SECTION OF THE BURMA COAST CITY....

SHE PINCHED ME POKE...SHE DID! I CAUGHT 'ER 'OT AT IT!

I'VE GOT THE FIX FER THAT CHIPPY! SHE'S A OLD OFFENDER!

Steve Canyon

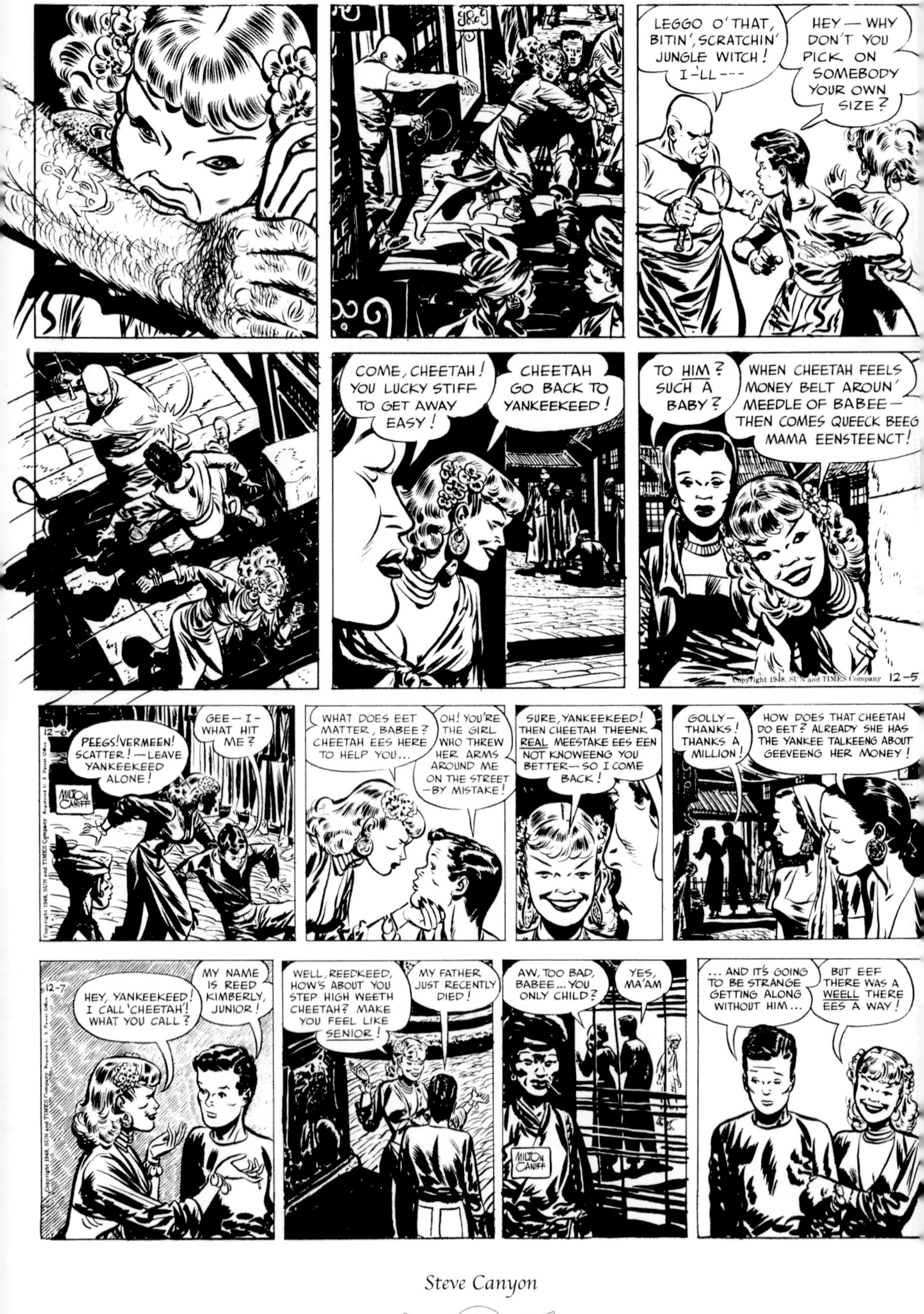

LEGGO O'THAT, BITIN', SCRATCHIN' JUNGLE WITCH! I-'LL---
HEY — WHY DON'T YOU PICK ON SOMEBODY YOUR OWN SIZE?
COME, CHEETAH! YOU LUCKY STIFF TO GET AWAY EASY!
CHEETAH GO BACK TO YANKEEKEED!
TO HIM? SUCH A BABY?
WHEN CHEETAH FEELS MONEY BELT AROUN' MEEDLE OF BABEE — THEN COMES QUEECK BEEG MAMA EENSTEENCT!
Copyright 1948, SUN and TIMES Company 12-5
12-6
PEEGS! VERMEEN! SCATTER! — LEAVE YANKEEKEED ALONE!
GEE — I — WHAT HIT ME?
MILTON CANIFF
Copyright 1948, SUN and TIMES Company
WHAT DOES EET MATTER, BABEE? CHEETAH EES HERE TO HELP YOU...
OH! YOU'RE THE GIRL WHO THREW HER ARMS AROUND ME ON THE STREET — BY MISTAKE!
SURE, YANKEEKEED! THEN CHEETAH THEENK REAL MEESTAKE EES EEN NOT KNOWEENG YOU BETTER — SO I COME BACK!
GOLLY — THANKS! THANKS A MILLION!
HOW DOES THAT CHEETAH DO EET? ALREADY SHE HAS THE YANKEE TALKEENG ABOUT GEEVEENG HER MONEY!
12-7
HEY, YANKEEKEED! I CALL 'CHEETAH'! WHAT YOU CALL?
MY NAME IS REED KIMBERLY, JUNIOR!
Copyright 1948, SUN and TIMES Company
WELL, REEDKEED, HOW'S ABOUT YOU STEP HIGH WEETH CHEETAH? MAKE YOU FEEL LIKE SENIOR!
MY FATHER JUST RECENTLY DIED!
AW, TOO BAD, BABEE... YOU ONLY CHILD?
YES, MA'AM
MILTON CANIFF
... AND IT'S GOING TO BE STRANGE GETTING ALONG WITHOUT HIM...
BUT EEF THERE WAS A WEELL THERE EES A WAY!

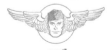

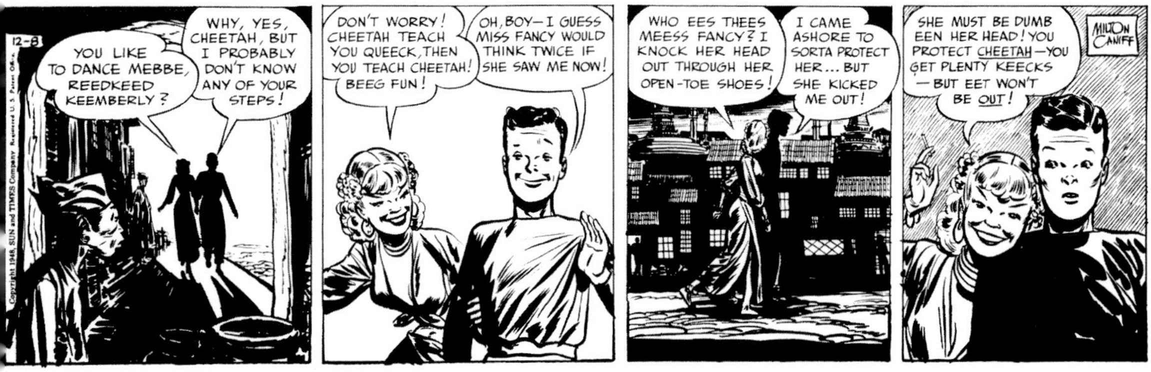
12-8
YOU LIKE TO DANCE MEBBE, REEDKEED KEEMBERLY?
WHY, YES, CHEETAH, BUT I PROBABLY DON'T KNOW ANY OF YOUR STEPS!
DON'T WORRY! CHEETAH TEACH YOU QUEECK, THEN YOU TEACH CHEETAH! BEEG FUN!
OH, BOY—I GUESS MISS FANCY WOULD THINK TWICE IF SHE SAW ME NOW!
WHO EES THEES MEESS FANCY? I KNOCK HER HEAD OUT THROUGH HER OPEN-TOE SHOES!
I CAME ASHORE TO SORTA PROTECT HER... BUT SHE KICKED ME OUT!
SHE MUST BE DUMB EEN HER HEAD! YOU PROTECT CHEETAH—YOU GET PLENTY KEECKS—BUT EET WON'T BE OUT!
MILTON CANIFF

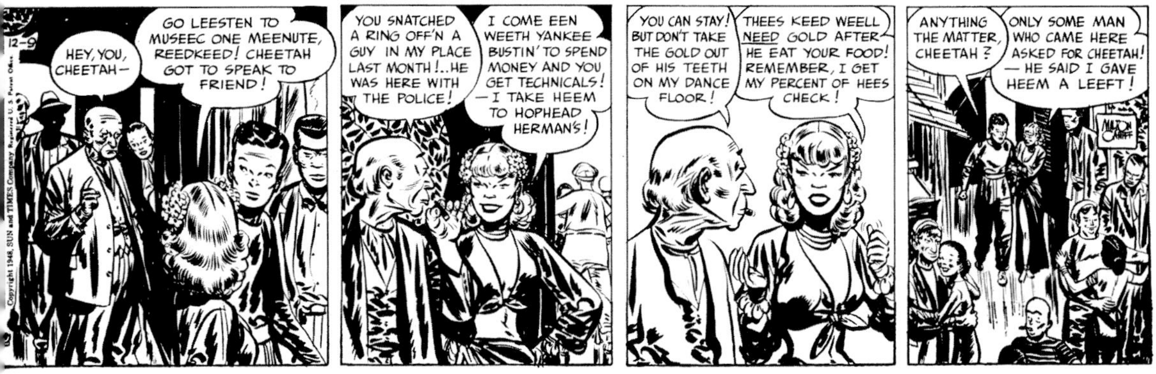
12-9
HEY, YOU, CHEETAH—
GO LEESTEN TO MUSEEC ONE MEENUTE, REEDKEED! CHEETAH GOT TO SPEAK TO FRIEND!
YOU SNATCHED A RING OFF'N A GUY IN MY PLACE LAST MONTH!..HE WAS HERE WITH THE POLICE!
I COME EEN WEETH YANKEE BUSTIN' TO SPEND MONEY AND YOU GET TECHNICALS! —I TAKE HEEM TO HOPHEAD HERMAN'S!
YOU CAN STAY! BUT DON'T TAKE THE GOLD OUT OF HIS TEETH ON MY DANCE FLOOR!
THEES KEED WEELL NEED GOLD AFTER HE EAT YOUR FOOD! REMEMBER, I GET MY PERCENT OF HEES CHECK!
ANYTHING THE MATTER, CHEETAH?
ONLY SOME MAN WHO CAME HERE ASKED FOR CHEETAH! —HE SAID I GAVE HEEM A LEEFT!
MILTON CANIFF

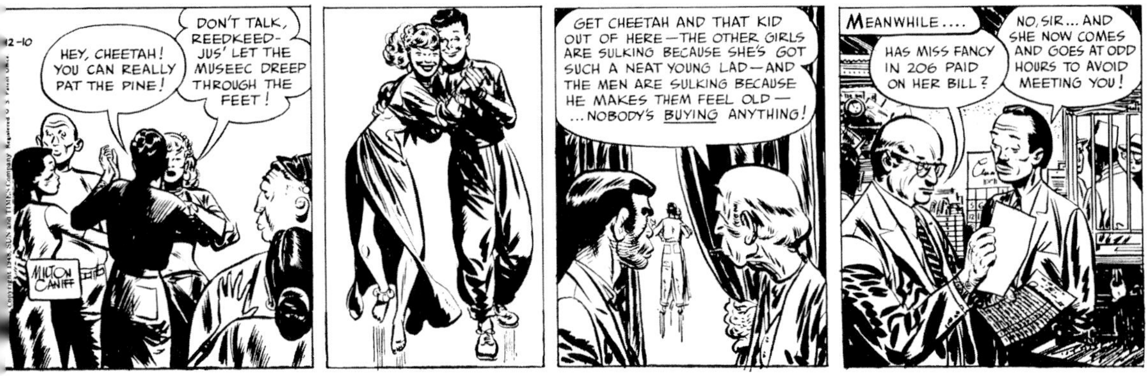
12-10
HEY, CHEETAH! YOU CAN REALLY PAT THE PINE!
DON'T TALK, REEDKEED- JUS' LET THE MUSEEC DREEP THROUGH THE FEET!
MILTON CANIFF
GET CHEETAH AND THAT KID OUT OF HERE—THE OTHER GIRLS ARE SULKING BECAUSE SHE'S GOT SUCH A NEAT YOUNG LAD—AND THE MEN ARE SULKING BECAUSE HE MAKES THEM FEEL OLD— ...NOBODY'S BUYING ANYTHING!
MEANWHILE....
HAS MISS FANCY IN 206 PAID ON HER BILL?
NO, SIR... AND SHE NOW COMES AND GOES AT ODD HOURS TO AVOID MEETING YOU!

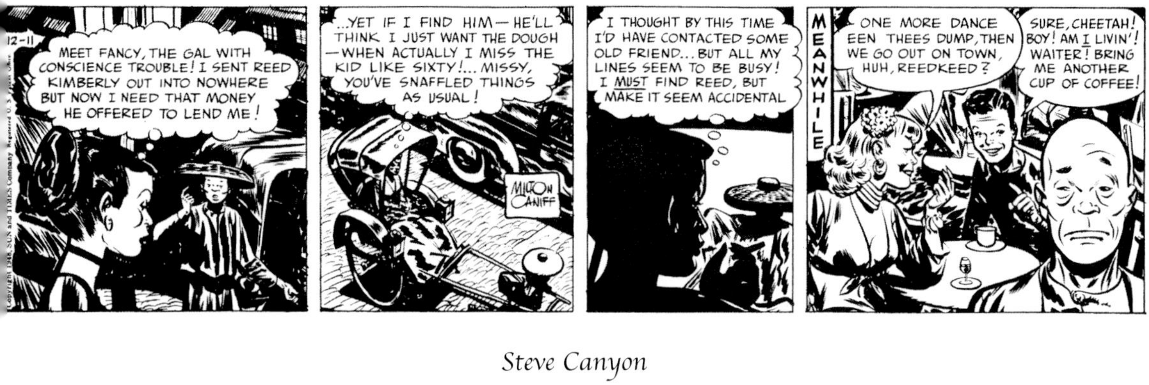
12-11
MEET FANCY, THE GAL WITH CONSCIENCE TROUBLE! I SENT REED KIMBERLY OUT INTO NOWHERE BUT NOW I NEED THAT MONEY HE OFFERED TO LEND ME!
...YET IF I FIND HIM—HE'LL THINK I JUST WANT THE DOUGH—WHEN ACTUALLY I MISS THE KID LIKE SIXTY!... MISSY, YOU'VE SNAFFLED THINGS AS USUAL!
MILTON CANIFF
I THOUGHT BY THIS TIME I'D HAVE CONTACTED SOME OLD FRIEND... BUT ALL MY LINES SEEM TO BE BUSY! I MUST FIND REED, BUT MAKE IT SEEM ACCIDENTAL
MEANWHILE
ONE MORE DANCE EEN THEES DUMP, THEN WE GO OUT ON TOWN, HUH, REEDKEED?
SURE, CHEETAH! BOY! AM I LIVIN'! WAITER! BRING ME ANOTHER CUP OF COFFEE!

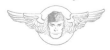

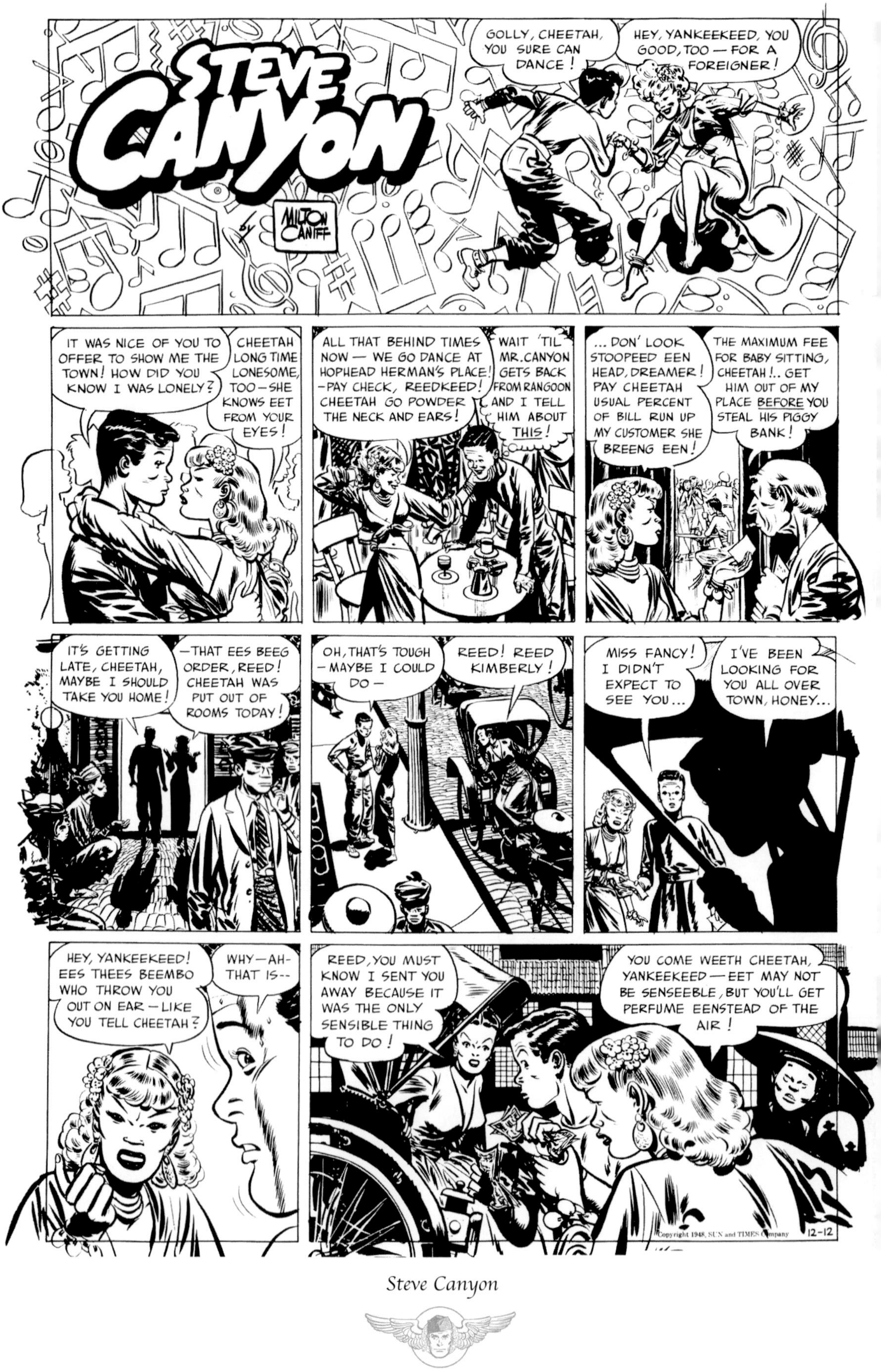
STEVE CANYON
by MILTON CANIFF
GOLLY, CHEETAH, YOU SURE CAN DANCE!
HEY, YANKEEKEED, YOU GOOD, TOO — FOR A FOREIGNER!
IT WAS NICE OF YOU TO OFFER TO SHOW ME THE TOWN! HOW DID YOU KNOW I WAS LONELY?
CHEETAH LONG TIME LONESOME, TOO — SHE KNOWS EET FROM YOUR EYES!
ALL THAT BEHIND TIMES NOW — WE GO DANCE AT HOPHEAD HERMAN'S PLACE! —PAY CHECK, REEDKEED! CHEETAH GO POWDER THE NECK AND EARS!
WAIT 'TIL MR. CANYON GETS BACK FROM RANGOON AND I TELL HIM ABOUT THIS!
... DON' LOOK STOOPEED EEN HEAD, DREAMER! PAY CHEETAH USUAL PERCENT OF BILL RUN UP MY CUSTOMER SHE BREENG EEN!
THE MAXIMUM FEE FOR BABY SITTING, CHEETAH!.. GET HIM OUT OF MY PLACE BEFORE YOU STEAL HIS PIGGY BANK!
IT'S GETTING LATE, CHEETAH, MAYBE I SHOULD TAKE YOU HOME!
—THAT EES BEEG ORDER, REED! CHEETAH WAS PUT OUT OF ROOMS TODAY!
OH, THAT'S TOUGH — MAYBE I COULD DO —
REED! REED KIMBERLY!
MISS FANCY! I DIDN'T EXPECT TO SEE YOU...
I'VE BEEN LOOKING FOR YOU ALL OVER TOWN, HONEY...
HEY, YANKEEKEED! EES THEES BEEMBO WHO THROW YOU OUT ON EAR — LIKE YOU TELL CHEETAH?
WHY — AH — THAT IS --
REED, YOU MUST KNOW I SENT YOU AWAY BECAUSE IT WAS THE ONLY SENSIBLE THING TO DO!
YOU COME WEETH CHEETAH, YANKEEKEED — EET MAY NOT BE SENSEEBLE, BUT YOU'LL GET PERFUME EENSTEAD OF THE AIR!
Copyright 1948, SUN and TIMES Company
12-12

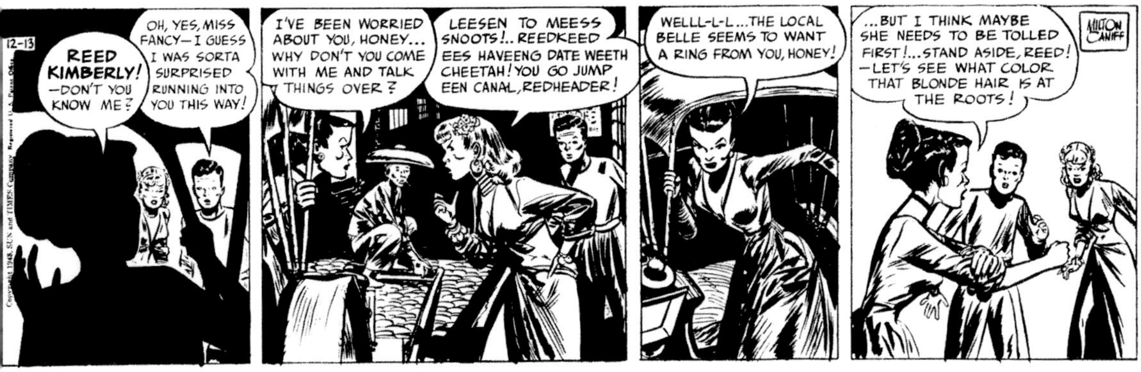
12-13
OH, YES, MISS FANCY—I GUESS I WAS SORTA SURPRISED RUNNING INTO YOU THIS WAY!
REED KIMBERLY! —DON'T YOU KNOW ME?
I'VE BEEN WORRIED ABOUT YOU, HONEY... WHY DON'T YOU COME WITH ME AND TALK THINGS OVER?
LEESEN TO MEESS SNOOTS!.. REEDKEED EES HAVEENG DATE WEETH CHEETAH! YOU GO JUMP EEN CANAL, REDHEADER!
WELLL-L-L...THE LOCAL BELLE SEEMS TO WANT A RING FROM YOU, HONEY!
...BUT I THINK MAYBE SHE NEEDS TO BE TOLLED FIRST!...STAND ASIDE, REED! —LET'S SEE WHAT COLOR THAT BLONDE HAIR IS AT THE ROOTS!
MILTON CANIFF

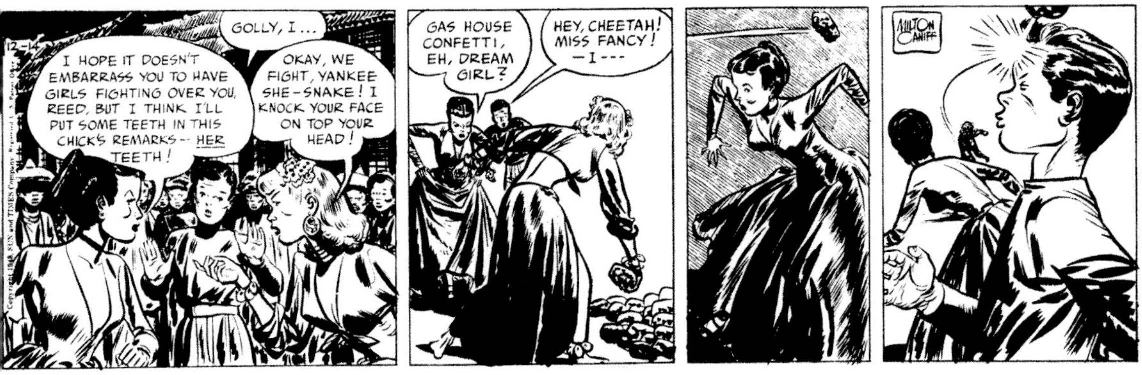
12-14
GOLLY, I...
I HOPE IT DOESN'T EMBARRASS YOU TO HAVE GIRLS FIGHTING OVER YOU, REED, BUT I THINK I'LL PUT SOME TEETH IN THIS CHICK'S REMARKS-- HER TEETH!
OKAY, WE FIGHT, YANKEE SHE-SNAKE! I KNOCK YOUR FACE ON TOP YOUR HEAD!
GAS HOUSE CONFETTI, EH, DREAM GIRL?
HEY, CHEETAH! MISS FANCY! —I---
MILTON CANIFF

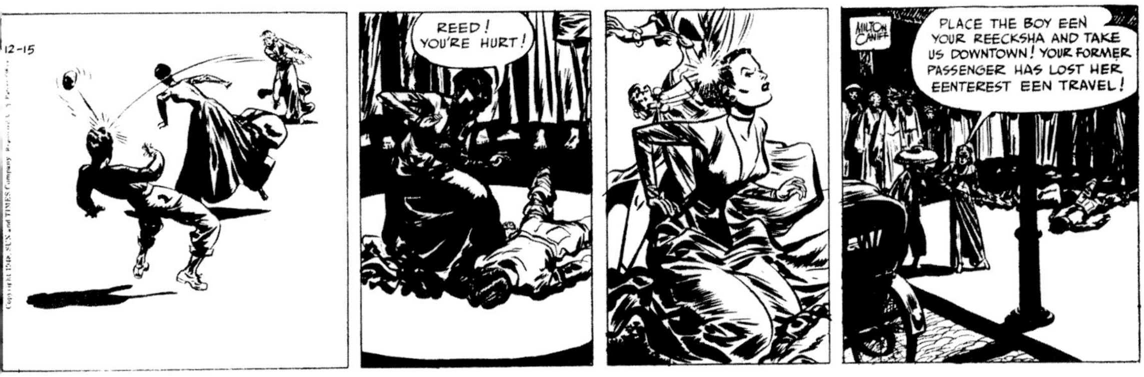
12-15
REED! YOU'RE HURT!
MILTON CANIFF
PLACE THE BOY EEN YOUR REECKSHA AND TAKE US DOWNTOWN! YOUR FORMER PASSENGER HAS LOST HER EENTEREST EEN TRAVEL!

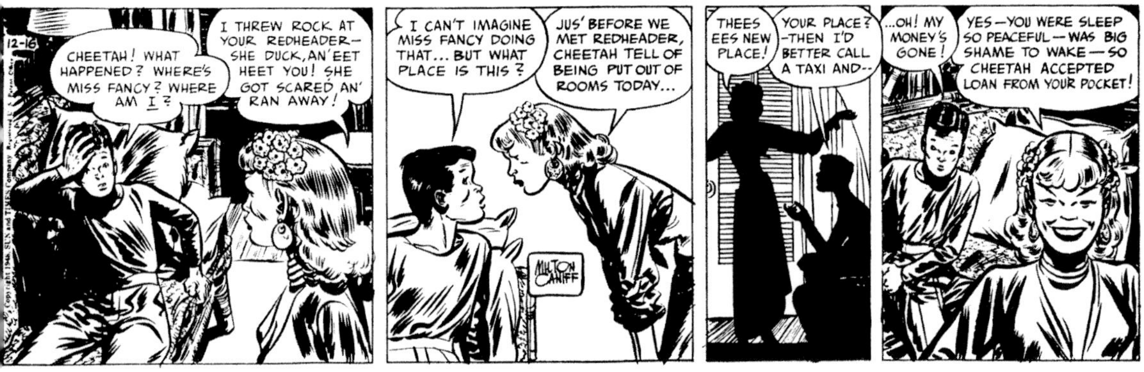
12-16
CHEETAH! WHAT HAPPENED? WHERE'S MISS FANCY? WHERE AM I?
I THREW ROCK AT YOUR REDHEADER— SHE DUCK, AN' EET HEET YOU! SHE GOT SCARED AN' RAN AWAY!
I CAN'T IMAGINE MISS FANCY DOING THAT... BUT WHAT PLACE IS THIS?
JUS' BEFORE WE MET REDHEADER, CHEETAH TELL OF BEING PUT OUT OF ROOMS TODAY...
MILTON CANIFF
THEES EES NEW PLACE!
YOUR PLACE? -THEN I'D BETTER CALL A TAXI AND--
...OH! MY MONEY'S GONE!
YES—YOU WERE SLEEP SO PEACEFUL—WAS BIG SHAME TO WAKE—SO CHEETAH ACCEPTED LOAN FROM YOUR POCKET!

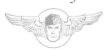

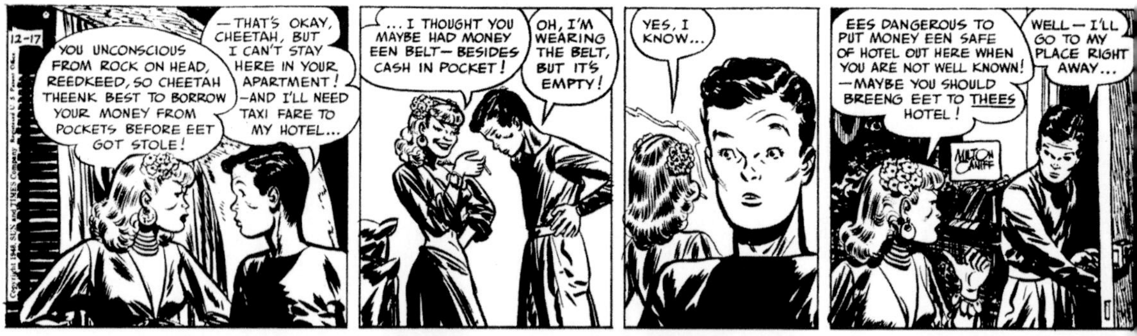
12-17
YOU UNCONSCIOUS FROM ROCK ON HEAD, REEDKEED, SO CHEETAH THEENK BEST TO BORROW YOUR MONEY FROM POCKETS BEFORE EET GOT STOLE!
—THAT'S OKAY, CHEETAH, BUT I CAN'T STAY HERE IN YOUR APARTMENT! —AND I'LL NEED TAXI FARE TO MY HOTEL...
... I THOUGHT YOU MAYBE HAD MONEY EEN BELT— BESIDES CASH IN POCKET!
OH, I'M WEARING THE BELT, BUT IT'S EMPTY!
YES, I KNOW...
EES DANGEROUS TO PUT MONEY EEN SAFE OF HOTEL OUT HERE WHEN YOU ARE NOT WELL KNOWN! —MAYBE YOU SHOULD BREENG EET TO THEES HOTEL!
WELL — I'LL GO TO MY PLACE RIGHT AWAY...
MILTON CANIFF

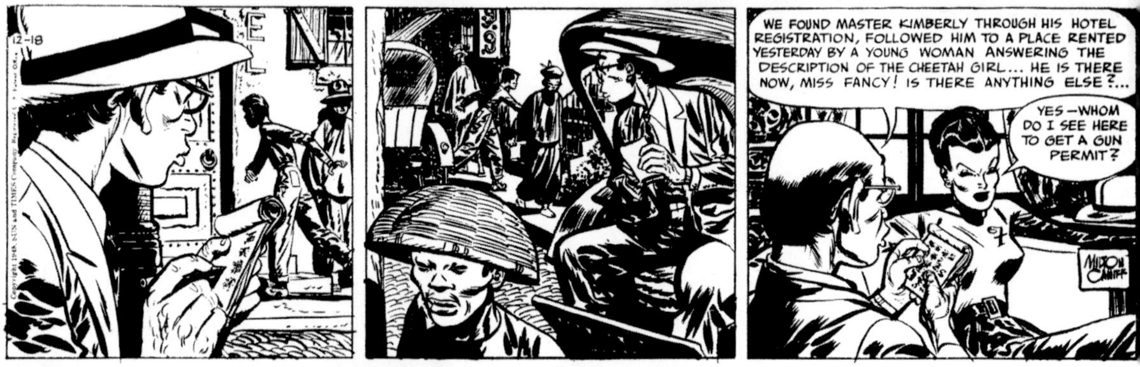
12-18
WE FOUND MASTER KIMBERLY THROUGH HIS HOTEL REGISTRATION, FOLLOWED HIM TO A PLACE RENTED YESTERDAY BY A YOUNG WOMAN ANSWERING THE DESCRIPTION OF THE CHEETAH GIRL... HE IS THERE NOW, MISS FANCY! IS THERE ANYTHING ELSE?...
YES —WHOM DO I SEE HERE TO GET A GUN PERMIT?
MILTON CANIFF

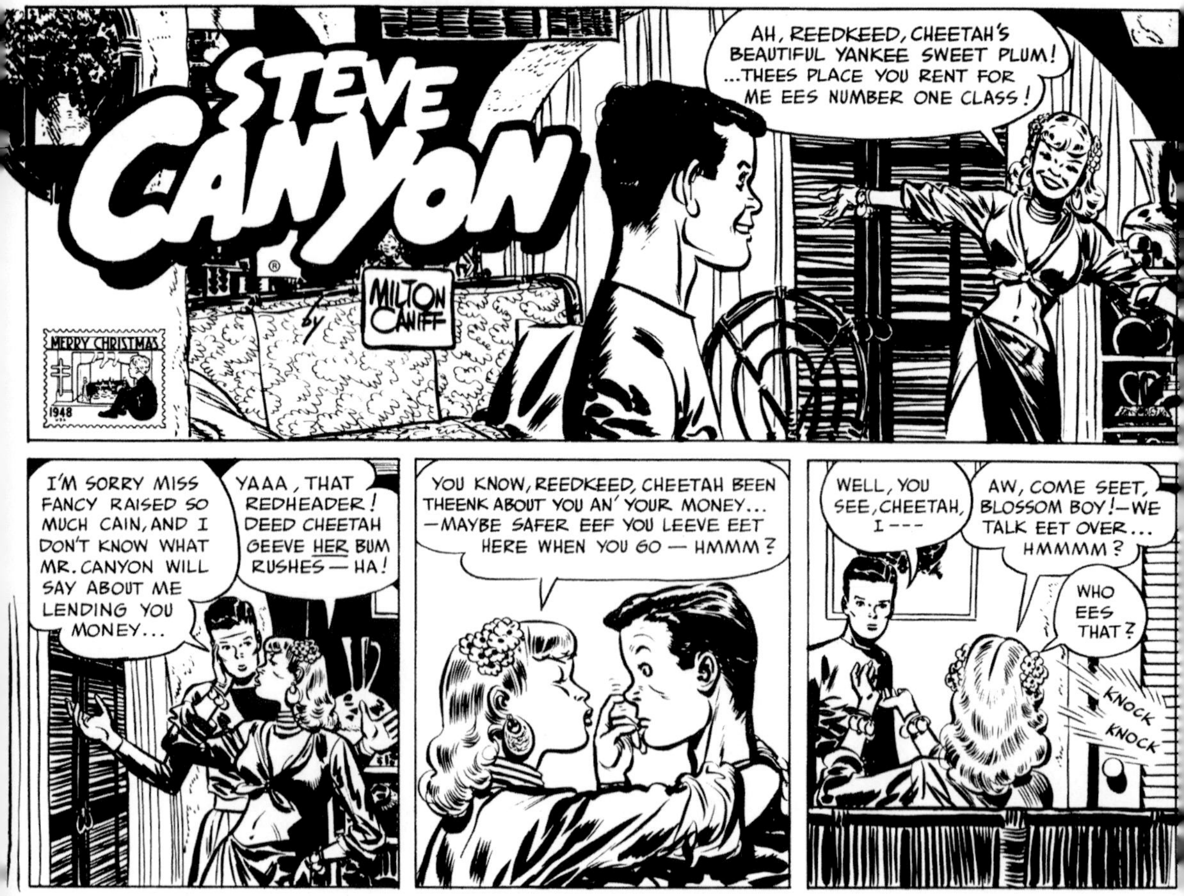
STEVE CANYON
by MILTON CANIFF
MERRY CHRISTMAS
1948
AH, REEDKEED, CHEETAH'S BEAUTIFUL YANKEE SWEET PLUM! ...THEES PLACE YOU RENT FOR ME EES NUMBER ONE CLASS!
I'M SORRY MISS FANCY RAISED SO MUCH CAIN, AND I DON'T KNOW WHAT MR. CANYON WILL SAY ABOUT ME LENDING YOU MONEY...
YAAA, THAT REDHEADER! DEED CHEETAH GEEVE HER BUM RUSHES — HA!
YOU KNOW, REEDKEED, CHEETAH BEEN THEENK ABOUT YOU AN' YOUR MONEY... —MAYBE SAFER EEF YOU LEEVE EET HERE WHEN YOU GO — HMMM?
WELL, YOU SEE, CHEETAH, I---
AW, COME SEET, BLOSSOM BOY!—WE TALK EET OVER... HMMMM?
WHO EES THAT?
KNOCK KNOCK

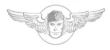

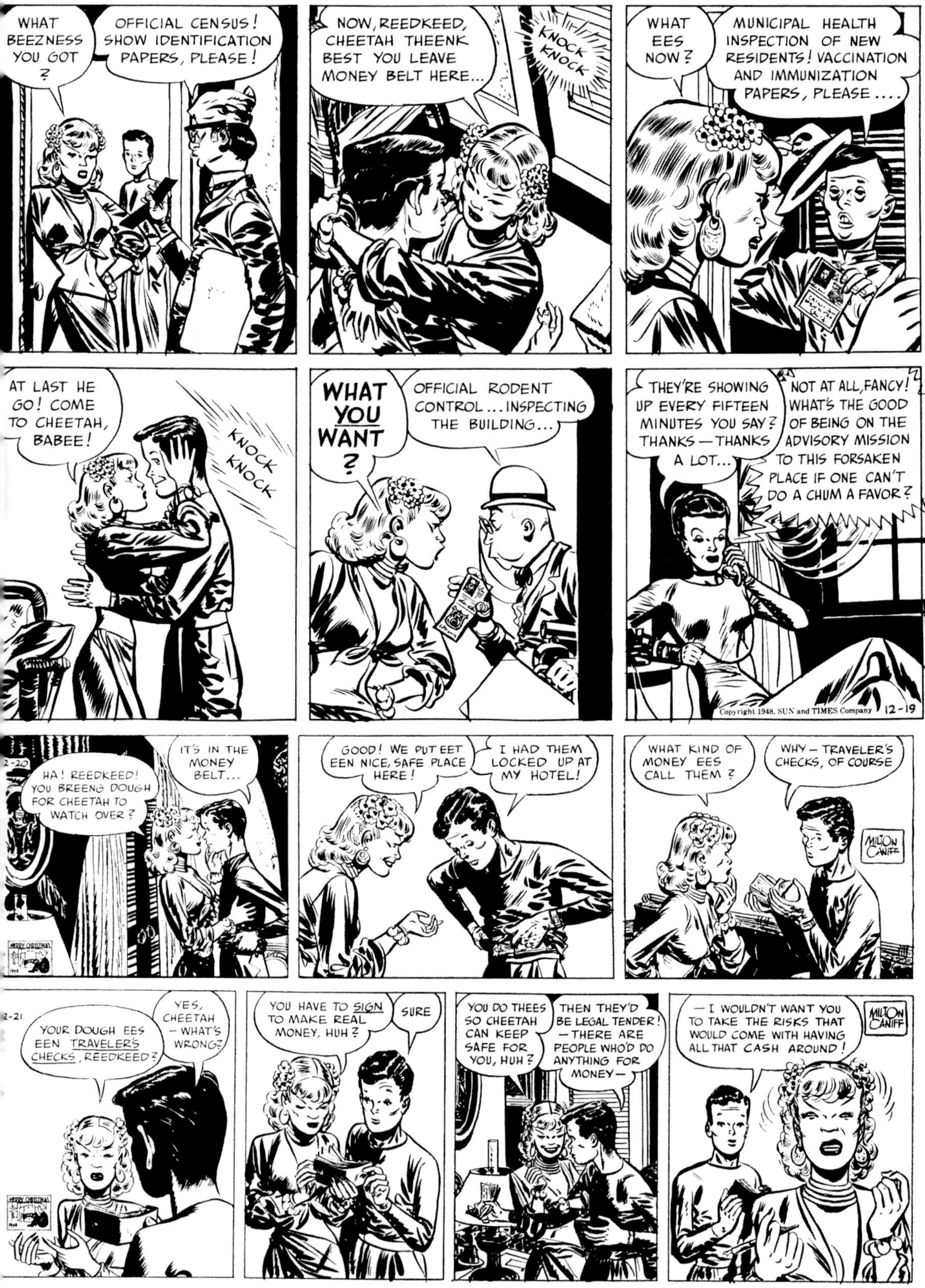
WHAT BEEZNESS YOU GOT ?
OFFICIAL CENSUS! SHOW IDENTIFICATION PAPERS, PLEASE!
NOW, REEDKEED, CHEETAH THEENK BEST YOU LEAVE MONEY BELT HERE...
KNOCK KNOCK
WHAT EES NOW?
MUNICIPAL HEALTH INSPECTION OF NEW RESIDENTS! VACCINATION AND IMMUNIZATION PAPERS, PLEASE....
AT LAST HE GO! COME TO CHEETAH, BABEE!
KNOCK KNOCK
WHAT YOU WANT ?
OFFICIAL RODENT CONTROL... INSPECTING THE BUILDING...
THEY'RE SHOWING UP EVERY FIFTEEN MINUTES YOU SAY? THANKS—THANKS A LOT...
NOT AT ALL, FANCY! WHAT'S THE GOOD OF BEING ON THE ADVISORY MISSION TO THIS FORSAKEN PLACE IF ONE CAN'T DO A CHUM A FAVOR?
Copyright 1948, SUN and TIMES Company
12-19
2-20
HA! REEDKEED! YOU BREENG DOUGH FOR CHEETAH TO WATCH OVER?
IT'S IN THE MONEY BELT...
GOOD! WE PUT EET EEN NICE, SAFE PLACE HERE!
I HAD THEM LOCKED UP AT MY HOTEL!
WHAT KIND OF MONEY EES CALL THEM ?
WHY—TRAVELER'S CHECKS, OF COURSE
MILTON CANIFF
2-21
YOUR DOUGH EES EEN TRAVELER'S CHECKS, REEDKEED?
YES, CHEETAH —WHAT'S WRONG?
YOU HAVE TO SIGN TO MAKE REAL MONEY, HUH?
SURE
YOU DO THEES SO CHEETAH CAN KEEP SAFE FOR YOU, HUH?
THEN THEY'D BE LEGAL TENDER! —THERE ARE PEOPLE WHO'D DO ANYTHING FOR MONEY—
—I WOULDN'T WANT YOU TO TAKE THE RISKS THAT WOULD COME WITH HAVING ALL THAT CASH AROUND!
MILTON CANIFF

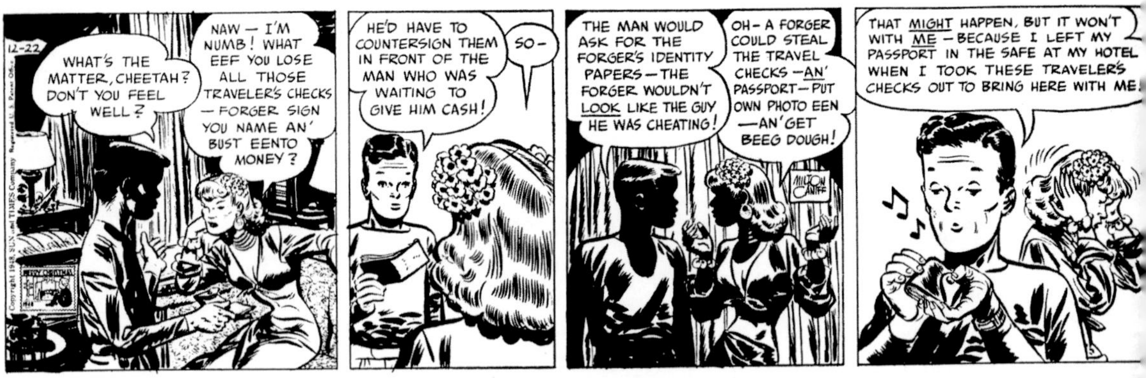
12-22
WHAT'S THE MATTER, CHEETAH? DON'T YOU FEEL WELL?
NAW — I'M NUMB! WHAT EEF YOU LOSE ALL THOSE TRAVELER'S CHECKS — FORGER SIGN YOU NAME AN' BUST EENTO MONEY?
HE'D HAVE TO COUNTERSIGN THEM IN FRONT OF THE MAN WHO WAS WAITING TO GIVE HIM CASH!
SO—
THE MAN WOULD ASK FOR THE FORGER'S IDENTITY PAPERS — THE FORGER WOULDN'T LOOK LIKE THE GUY HE WAS CHEATING!
OH — A FORGER COULD STEAL THE TRAVEL CHECKS — AN' PASSPORT — PUT OWN PHOTO EEN — AN' GET BEEG DOUGH!
MILTON CANIFF
THAT MIGHT HAPPEN, BUT IT WON'T WITH ME — BECAUSE I LEFT MY PASSPORT IN THE SAFE AT MY HOTEL WHEN I TOOK THESE TRAVELER'S CHECKS OUT TO BRING HERE WITH ME.

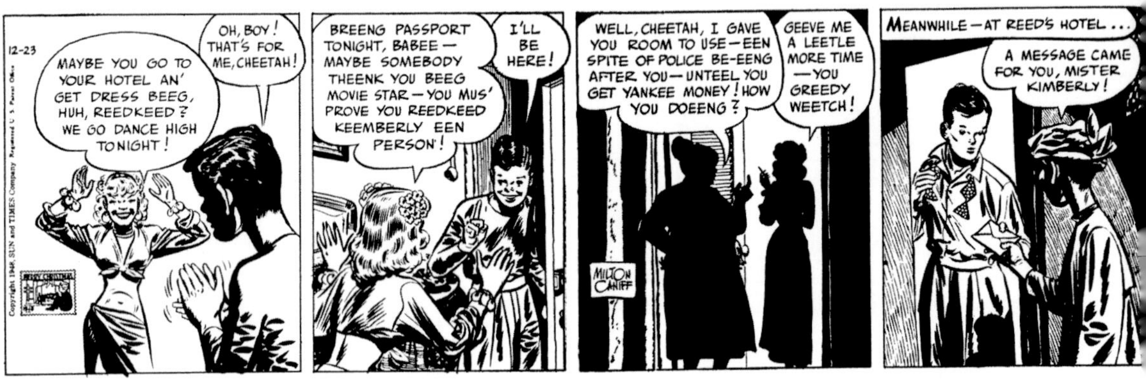
12-23
MAYBE YOU GO TO YOUR HOTEL AN' GET DRESS BEEG, HUH, REEDKEED? WE GO DANCE HIGH TONIGHT!
OH, BOY! THAT'S FOR ME, CHEETAH!
BREENG PASSPORT TONIGHT, BABEE — MAYBE SOMEBODY THEENK YOU BEEG MOVIE STAR — YOU MUS' PROVE YOU REEDKEED KEEMBERLY EEN PERSON!
I'LL BE HERE!
WELL, CHEETAH, I GAVE YOU ROOM TO USE — EEN SPITE OF POLICE BE-EENG AFTER YOU — UNTEEL YOU GET YANKEE MONEY! HOW YOU DOEENG?
GEEVE ME A LEETLE MORE TIME — YOU GREEDY WEETCH!
MILTON CANIFF
MEANWHILE — AT REED'S HOTEL...
A MESSAGE CAME FOR YOU, MISTER KIMBERLY!

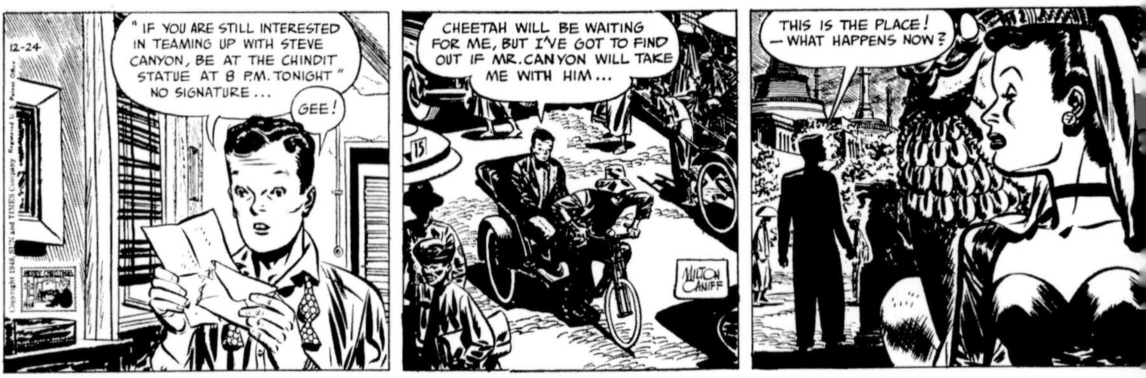
12-24
"IF YOU ARE STILL INTERESTED IN TEAMING UP WITH STEVE CANYON, BE AT THE CHINDIT STATUE AT 8 P.M. TONIGHT" NO SIGNATURE...
GEE!
CHEETAH WILL BE WAITING FOR ME, BUT I'VE GOT TO FIND OUT IF MR. CANYON WILL TAKE ME WITH HIM...
MILTON CANIFF
THIS IS THE PLACE! — WHAT HAPPENS NOW?

" THE SCAR INSIDE THAT WON'T BE WISHED AWAY "

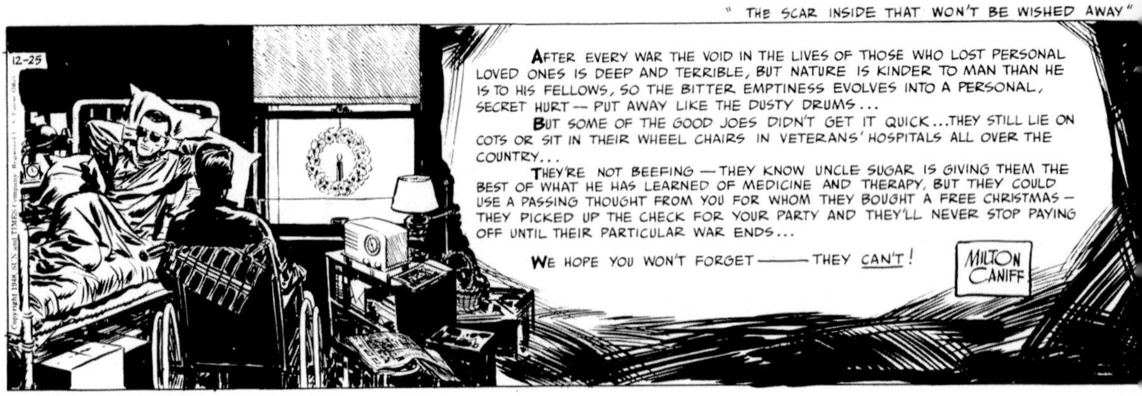
12-25
AFTER EVERY WAR THE VOID IN THE LIVES OF THOSE WHO LOST PERSONAL LOVED ONES IS DEEP AND TERRIBLE, BUT NATURE IS KINDER TO MAN THAN HE IS TO HIS FELLOWS, SO THE BITTER EMPTINESS EVOLVES INTO A PERSONAL, SECRET HURT — PUT AWAY LIKE THE DUSTY DRUMS...
BUT SOME OF THE GOOD JOES DIDN'T GET IT QUICK... THEY STILL LIE ON COTS OR SIT IN THEIR WHEEL CHAIRS IN VETERANS' HOSPITALS ALL OVER THE COUNTRY...
THEY'RE NOT BEEFING — THEY KNOW UNCLE SUGAR IS GIVING THEM THE BEST OF WHAT HE HAS LEARNED OF MEDICINE AND THERAPY, BUT THEY COULD USE A PASSING THOUGHT FROM YOU FOR WHOM THEY BOUGHT A FREE CHRISTMAS — THEY PICKED UP THE CHECK FOR YOUR PARTY AND THEY'LL NEVER STOP PAYING OFF UNTIL THEIR PARTICULAR WAR ENDS...
WE HOPE YOU WON'T FORGET —— THEY CAN'T!
MILTON CANIFF

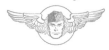

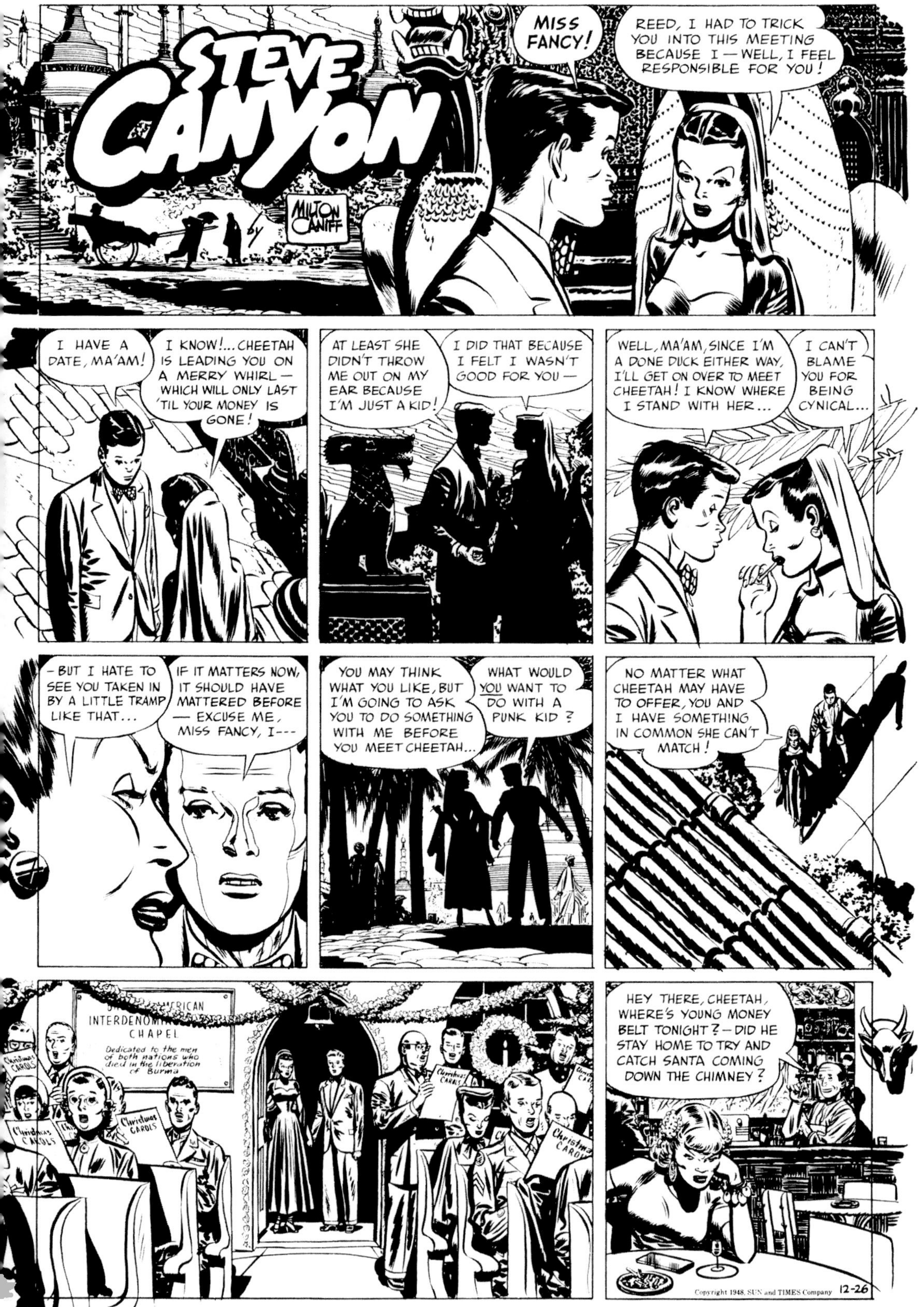
STEVE CANYON
by MILTON CANIFF
MISS FANCY!
REED, I HAD TO TRICK YOU INTO THIS MEETING BECAUSE I — WELL, I FEEL RESPONSIBLE FOR YOU!
I HAVE A DATE, MA'AM!
I KNOW!... CHEETAH IS LEADING YOU ON A MERRY WHIRL — WHICH WILL ONLY LAST 'TIL YOUR MONEY IS GONE!
AT LEAST SHE DIDN'T THROW ME OUT ON MY EAR BECAUSE I'M JUST A KID!
I DID THAT BECAUSE I FELT I WASN'T GOOD FOR YOU —
WELL, MA'AM, SINCE I'M A DONE DUCK EITHER WAY, I'LL GET ON OVER TO MEET CHEETAH! I KNOW WHERE I STAND WITH HER...
I CAN'T BLAME YOU FOR BEING CYNICAL...
– BUT I HATE TO SEE YOU TAKEN IN BY A LITTLE TRAMP LIKE THAT...
IF IT MATTERS NOW, IT SHOULD HAVE MATTERED BEFORE — EXCUSE ME, MISS FANCY, I---
YOU MAY THINK WHAT YOU LIKE, BUT I'M GOING TO ASK YOU TO DO SOMETHING WITH ME BEFORE YOU MEET CHEETAH...
WHAT WOULD YOU WANT TO DO WITH A PUNK KID?
NO MATTER WHAT CHEETAH MAY HAVE TO OFFER, YOU AND I HAVE SOMETHING IN COMMON SHE CAN'T MATCH!
AMERICAN
INTERDENOMIN
CHAPEL
Dedicated to the men of both nations who died in the liberation of Burma
Christmas CAROLS
HEY THERE, CHEETAH, WHERE'S YOUNG MONEY BELT TONIGHT? — DID HE STAY HOME TO TRY AND CATCH SANTA COMING DOWN THE CHIMNEY?
Copyright 1948, SUN and TIMES Company 12-26

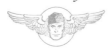

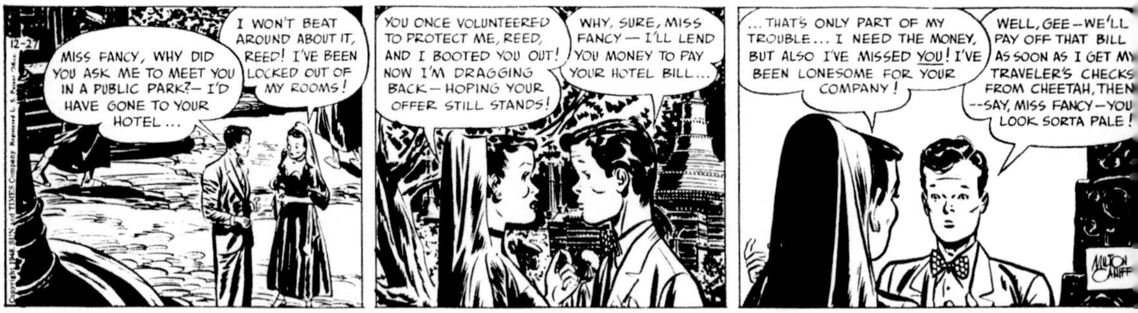
12-27
MISS FANCY, WHY DID YOU ASK ME TO MEET YOU IN A PUBLIC PARK?— I'D HAVE GONE TO YOUR HOTEL...
I WON'T BEAT AROUND ABOUT IT, REED! I'VE BEEN LOCKED OUT OF MY ROOMS!
YOU ONCE VOLUNTEERED TO PROTECT ME, REED, AND I BOOTED YOU OUT! NOW I'M DRAGGING BACK — HOPING YOUR OFFER STILL STANDS!
WHY, SURE, MISS FANCY — I'LL LEND YOU MONEY TO PAY YOUR HOTEL BILL...
...THAT'S ONLY PART OF MY TROUBLE... I NEED THE MONEY, BUT ALSO I'VE MISSED YOU! I'VE BEEN LONESOME FOR YOUR COMPANY!
WELL, GEE — WE'LL PAY OFF THAT BILL AS SOON AS I GET MY TRAVELER'S CHECKS FROM CHEETAH, THEN --SAY, MISS FANCY — YOU LOOK SORTA PALE!
MILTON CANIFF

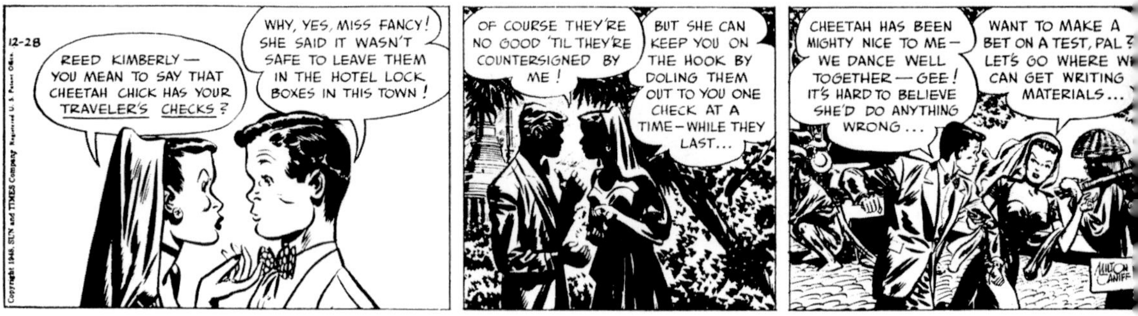
12-28
REED KIMBERLY — YOU MEAN TO SAY THAT CHEETAH CHICK HAS YOUR TRAVELER'S CHECKS?
WHY, YES, MISS FANCY! SHE SAID IT WASN'T SAFE TO LEAVE THEM IN THE HOTEL LOCK BOXES IN THIS TOWN!
OF COURSE THEY'RE NO GOOD 'TIL THEY'RE COUNTERSIGNED BY ME!
BUT SHE CAN KEEP YOU ON THE HOOK BY DOLING THEM OUT TO YOU ONE CHECK AT A TIME — WHILE THEY LAST...
CHEETAH HAS BEEN MIGHTY NICE TO ME — WE DANCE WELL TOGETHER — GEE! IT'S HARD TO BELIEVE SHE'D DO ANYTHING WRONG...
WANT TO MAKE A BET ON A TEST, PAL? LET'S GO WHERE WE CAN GET WRITING MATERIALS...
MILTON CANIFF

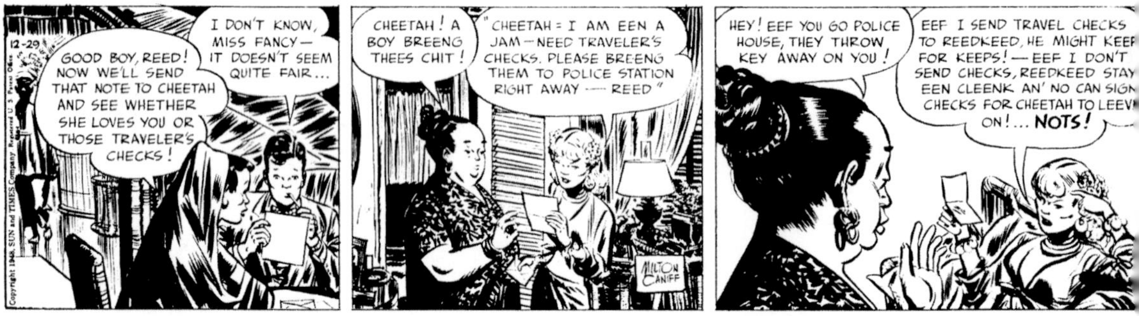
12-29
GOOD BOY, REED! NOW WE'LL SEND THAT NOTE TO CHEETAH AND SEE WHETHER SHE LOVES YOU OR THOSE TRAVELER'S CHECKS!
I DON'T KNOW, MISS FANCY — IT DOESN'T SEEM QUITE FAIR...
CHEETAH! A BOY BREENG THEES CHIT!
"CHEETAH = I AM EEN A JAM — NEED TRAVELER'S CHECKS. PLEASE BREENG THEM TO POLICE STATION RIGHT AWAY — REED"
MILTON CANIFF
HEY! EEF YOU GO POLICE HOUSE, THEY THROW KEY AWAY ON YOU!
EEF I SEND TRAVEL CHECKS TO REEDKEED, HE MIGHT KEEP FOR KEEPS! — EEF I DON'T SEND CHECKS, REEDKEED STAY EEN CLEENK AN' NO CAN SIGN CHECKS FOR CHEETAH TO LEEVE ON!... NOTS!

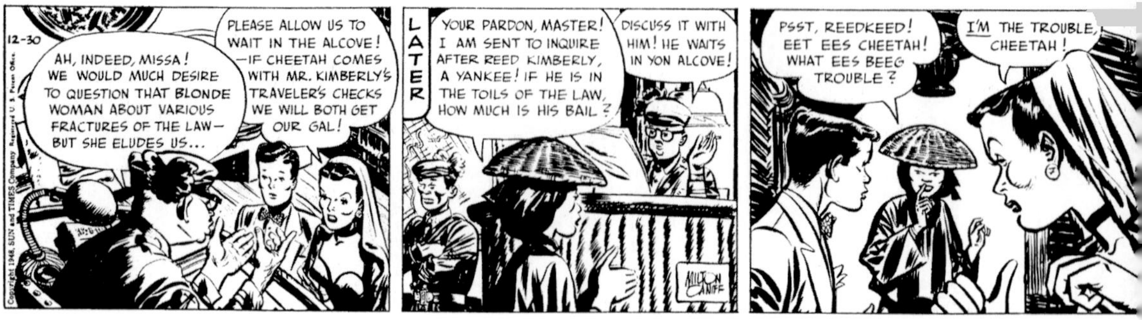
12-30
AH, INDEED, MISSA! WE WOULD MUCH DESIRE TO QUESTION THAT BLONDE WOMAN ABOUT VARIOUS FRACTURES OF THE LAW — BUT SHE ELUDES US...
PLEASE ALLOW US TO WAIT IN THE ALCOVE! — IF CHEETAH COMES WITH MR. KIMBERLY'S TRAVELER'S CHECKS WE WILL BOTH GET OUR GAL!
LATER
YOUR PARDON, MASTER! I AM SENT TO INQUIRE AFTER REED KIMBERLY, A YANKEE! IF HE IS IN THE TOILS OF THE LAW, HOW MUCH IS HIS BAIL?
DISCUSS IT WITH HIM! HE WAITS IN YON ALCOVE!
MILTON CANIFF
PSST, REEDKEED! EET EES CHEETAH! WHAT EES BEEG TROUBLE?
I'M THE TROUBLE, CHEETAH!

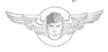

THE YANKEE REDHEADER!

STILL WEARING THE LUMP YOU DEALT ME WITH A ROCK! SHAKE OUT REED KIMBERLY'S TRAVELER'S CHECKS!

YOU GO JUMP EEN DEETCH, WEETCH!

GET THE CHECKS, REED!

I–I CAN'T SEARCH HER, MISS FANCY!

WELL, I CAN!—AND HERE THEY ARE!

WHAT IS THIS SCREECHING IN THE POLICE HOUSE?

HERE'S THE GAL NAMED CHEETAH YOU COPS WANT FOR QUESTIONING!

MISS FANCY, I KNOW I GOT MY TRAVELERS CHECKS BACK, BUT I FEEL BAD ABOUT CHEETAH!

WITH YOUR LOAN I'VE PAID MY HOTEL BILL!—YOU AND I CAN CELEBRATE THE NEW YEAR AND FORGET CHEETAH!

YOU LIKED DANCING WITH CHEETAH—BUT YOU HAVEN'T TRIED DANCING WITH ME! HOW DO YOU LIKE MY NEW YEAR'S EVE GOWN?

OOLP— IT'S BEEN QUITE A YEAR... QUITE A YEAR!

MEANWHILE...IN A NEW YORK RADIO STATION...

CAN WE PUT THE NEW MAN ON THE REMOTE PICKUP FROM THE PETER MINUIT?

WE'LL USE EVERY STAFF ANNOUNCER ON THIS NEW YEAR'S EVE DANCE BAND ROUNDUP—HE MIGHT AS WELL BREAK IN FROM THERE!

CHECK! WELL, GOTTA PUT ON MY MAKEUP AND GO MAKE A TELEVISION STATION BREAK!

GEE, MISS FANCY, I GUESS YOU MUST THINK I'M A FIRST CLASS MEATHEAD!

FORGET ALL THAT, REED! ...NEW YEAR— NEW SHAKE!

STEVE Canyon

by MILTON CANIFF

I THOUGHT CHEETAH SORTA LIKED ME—KINDA FOR MYSELF, NOT THE MONEY I HAD—IF YOU KNOW WHAT I MEAN!

I THINK I CAN PUZZLE IT OUT!

MR. CANYON WILL PROBABLY LAUGH AT ME WHEN HE COMES BACK...

—WE DON'T HAVE TO TELL HIM ABOUT IT, YOU KNOW...

OH, BOY—YOU MEAN YOU'D COVER UP FOR ME SO HE WOULDN'T RUB IT IN?

SURE, REED— CHEETAH'S JUST A NAME OF A JUNGLE ANIMAL FROM NOW ON

Steve Canyon

THE SHORT WAVE NEW YEAR'S DANCE PARADE FROM THE UNITED STATES WILL START SOON, SINCE OUR TIME IS A DAY LATE OUT HERE!

YOU DANCE VERY WELL, REED...

THANKS

WE SWITCH YOU NOW TO TIMES SQUARE IN NEW YORK!..WHEN YOU HEAR THE WHISTLES IT WILL BE TWELVE MIDNIGHT...

THERE THEY GO —SHOULD AULD ACQUAINTANCE

HAPPY NEW YEAR, MA'AM!

HAPPY NEW YEAR, REED!.. WELL, AREN'T YOU GOING TO KISS ME?

THE FIRST STOP ON OUR DANCE BAND ROUNDUP WILL BE THE TWENTY-FOUR CLUB IN HOTEL PETER MINUIT...

GOOD EVENING LADIES AND GENTLEMEN!...WE ARE SPEAKING TO YOU FROM THE FAMOUS TWENTY-FOUR CLUB OF THE PETER MINUIT——

OH!

ARE YOU ILL, MISS FANCY?

THAT ANNOUNCER'S VOICE...IT'S MY HUSBAND!

Copyright 1949, SUN and TIMES Company

1-3

—AS THE SHORT WAVE RADIO BRINGS THE SOUNDS OF THE NEW YEAR CELEBRATION FROM NEW YORK, FANCY AND REED ARE DANCING TO THE MUSIC OF A MANHATTAN BAND—WHEN ALL OF A SUDDEN...

THE HOTEL PETER MINUIT ORCHESTRA REFLECTS THE SPIRIT OF GOOD CHEER WHICH PREVAILS HERE IN THE TWENTY-FOUR CLUB WHEN THEY PLAY "THE HOTFOOT POLKA"

THAT'S MY HUSBAND'S VOICE!

GEE, MISS FANCY—I THOUGHT HE WAS KILLED IN THE WAR!

HE DIDN'T COME BACK FROM HIS LAST MISSION —BUT I WOULD KNOW HIS VOICE ANYWHERE! I'VE GOT TO GET TO HIM —HE MAY BE SICK!

MILTON CANIFF

MEANWHILE...

BEHOLD! CHEETAH, THE JUNGLE WILDCAT, BEGINS THE NEW YEAR IN CAPTIVITY!

NOTS

AFTER A PAUSE FOR STATION IDENTIFICATION WE WILL TAKE YOU TO THE CLUB FRANTIC IN HARLEM!...JACK JAYSON SPEAKING —THIS IS THE UNION BROADCASTING SYSTEM...

THAT'S MY HUSBAND, REED! HIS NAME ISN'T JACK JAYSON, BUT I'M SURE OF THE VOICE!

BUT, MISS FANCY, LOTS OF RADIO ANNOUNCERS SOUND ALIKE OVER THE AIR!

HE MIGHT HAVE BEEN HURT IN THE WAR AND DOESN'T KNOW HIS REAL NAME—BUT I'VE LISTENED TO EVERY RECORDING OF HIS VOICE! I KNOW!!

AT LEAST HE'S SAFE AND HAS A JOB—BUT I'VE GOT TO SEND A RADIOGRAM SO HE'LL KNOW WHERE I AM...

OH, REED, FORGIVE ME, HONEY—WON'T YOU COME WITH ME TO THE TELEGRAPH OFFICE?

NO,—I I—HAV SOME OTHER THINGS TO DO

Steve Canyon

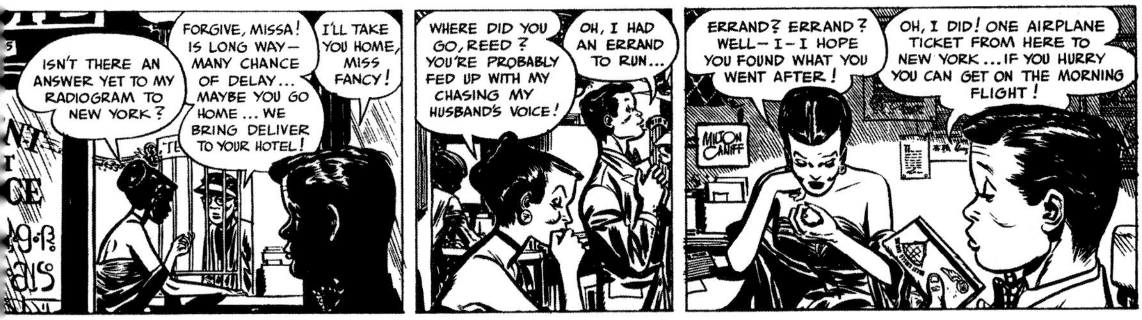
ISN'T THERE AN ANSWER YET TO MY RADIOGRAM TO NEW YORK?
FORGIVE, MISSA! IS LONG WAY— MANY CHANCE OF DELAY... MAYBE YOU GO HOME... WE BRING DELIVER TO YOUR HOTEL!
I'LL TAKE YOU HOME, MISS FANCY!
WHERE DID YOU GO, REED? YOU'RE PROBABLY FED UP WITH MY CHASING MY HUSBAND'S VOICE!
OH, I HAD AN ERRAND TO RUN...
ERRAND? ERRAND? WELL—I—I HOPE YOU FOUND WHAT YOU WENT AFTER!
OH, I DID! ONE AIRPLANE TICKET FROM HERE TO NEW YORK... IF YOU HURRY YOU CAN GET ON THE MORNING FLIGHT!
MILTON CANIFF

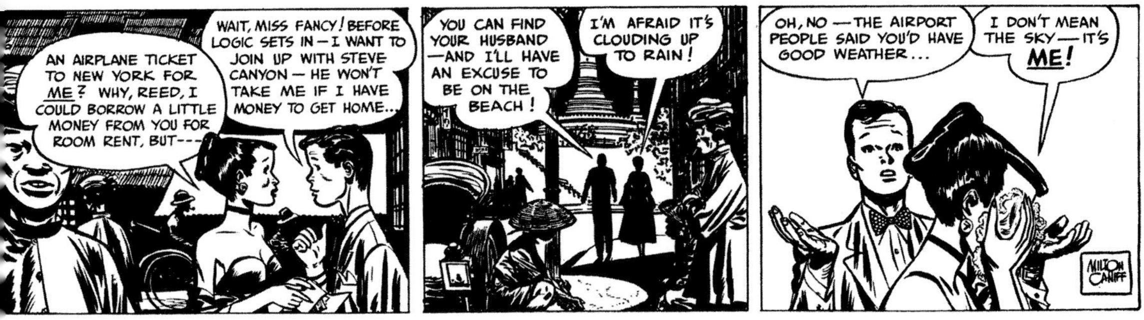
AN AIRPLANE TICKET TO NEW YORK FOR ME? WHY, REED, I COULD BORROW A LITTLE MONEY FROM YOU FOR ROOM RENT, BUT---
WAIT, MISS FANCY! BEFORE LOGIC SETS IN—I WANT TO JOIN UP WITH STEVE CANYON—HE WON'T TAKE ME IF I HAVE MONEY TO GET HOME...
YOU CAN FIND YOUR HUSBAND —AND I'LL HAVE AN EXCUSE TO BE ON THE BEACH!
I'M AFRAID IT'S CLOUDING UP TO RAIN!
OH, NO —THE AIRPORT PEOPLE SAID YOU'D HAVE GOOD WEATHER...
I DON'T MEAN THE SKY—IT'S ME!
MILTON CANIFF

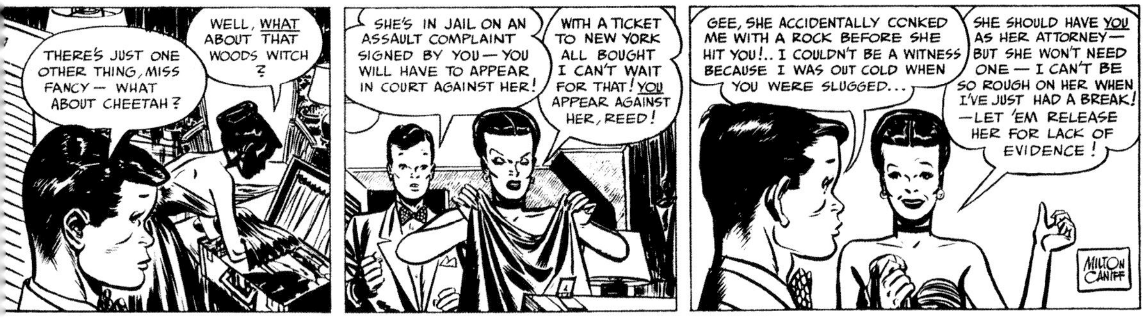
THERE'S JUST ONE OTHER THING, MISS FANCY— WHAT ABOUT CHEETAH?
WELL, WHAT ABOUT THAT WOODS WITCH ?
SHE'S IN JAIL ON AN ASSAULT COMPLAINT SIGNED BY YOU—YOU WILL HAVE TO APPEAR IN COURT AGAINST HER!
WITH A TICKET TO NEW YORK ALL BOUGHT I CAN'T WAIT FOR THAT! YOU APPEAR AGAINST HER, REED!
GEE, SHE ACCIDENTALLY CONKED ME WITH A ROCK BEFORE SHE HIT YOU!.. I COULDN'T BE A WITNESS BECAUSE I WAS OUT COLD WHEN YOU WERE SLUGGED...
SHE SHOULD HAVE YOU AS HER ATTORNEY— BUT SHE WON'T NEED ONE — I CAN'T BE SO ROUGH ON HER WHEN I'VE JUST HAD A BREAK! —LET 'EM RELEASE HER FOR LACK OF EVIDENCE!
MILTON CANIFF

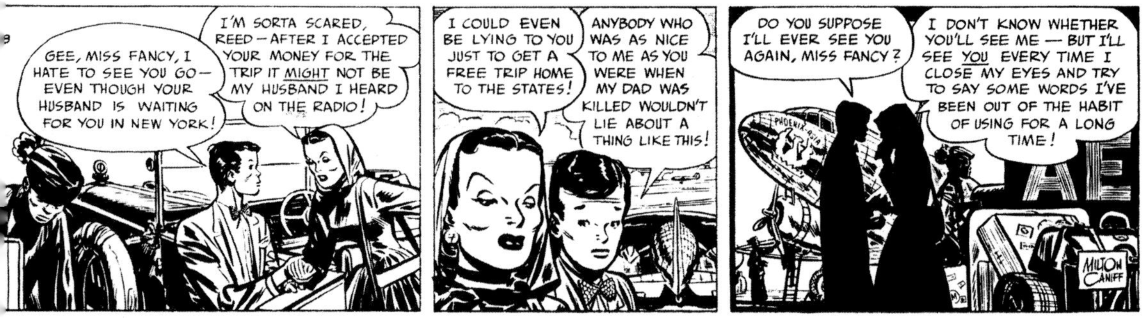
GEE, MISS FANCY, I HATE TO SEE YOU GO— EVEN THOUGH YOUR HUSBAND IS WAITING FOR YOU IN NEW YORK!
I'M SORTA SCARED, REED—AFTER I ACCEPTED YOUR MONEY FOR THE TRIP IT MIGHT NOT BE MY HUSBAND I HEARD ON THE RADIO!
I COULD EVEN BE LYING TO YOU JUST TO GET A FREE TRIP HOME TO THE STATES!
ANYBODY WHO WAS AS NICE TO ME AS YOU WERE WHEN MY DAD WAS KILLED WOULDN'T LIE ABOUT A THING LIKE THIS!
DO YOU SUPPOSE I'LL EVER SEE YOU AGAIN, MISS FANCY?
I DON'T KNOW WHETHER YOU'LL SEE ME — BUT I'LL SEE YOU EVERY TIME I CLOSE MY EYES AND TRY TO SAY SOME WORDS I'VE BEEN OUT OF THE HABIT OF USING FOR A LONG TIME!
MILTON CANIFF

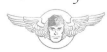

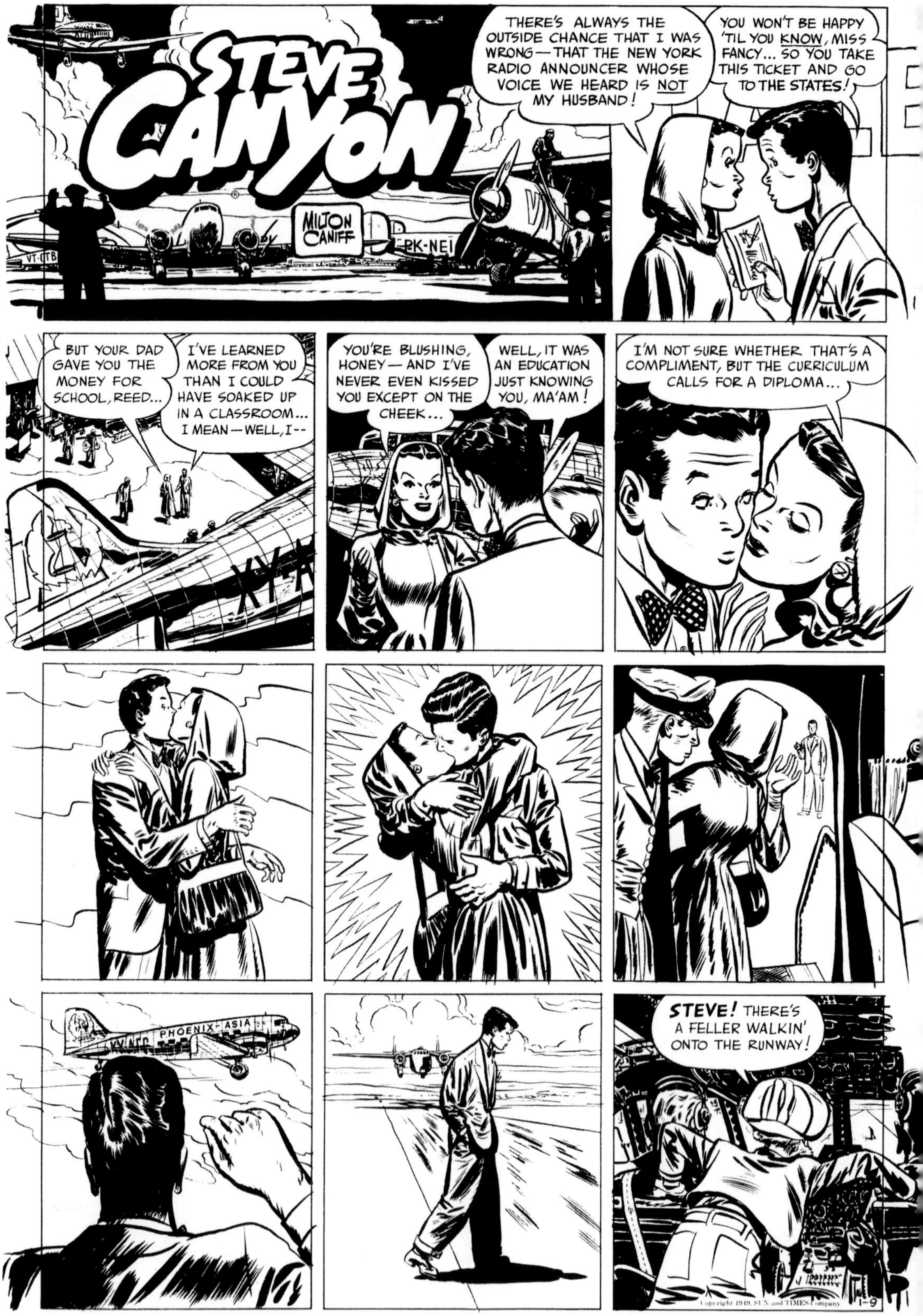
STEVE CANYON
MILTON CANIFF
VT-CTB
PK-NEI
THERE'S ALWAYS THE OUTSIDE CHANCE THAT I WAS WRONG — THAT THE NEW YORK RADIO ANNOUNCER WHOSE VOICE WE HEARD IS NOT MY HUSBAND!
YOU WON'T BE HAPPY 'TIL YOU KNOW, MISS FANCY... SO YOU TAKE THIS TICKET AND GO TO THE STATES!
BUT YOUR DAD GAVE YOU THE MONEY FOR SCHOOL, REED...
I'VE LEARNED MORE FROM YOU THAN I COULD HAVE SOAKED UP IN A CLASSROOM... I MEAN — WELL, I--
YOU'RE BLUSHING, HONEY — AND I'VE NEVER EVEN KISSED YOU EXCEPT ON THE CHEEK...
WELL, IT WAS AN EDUCATION JUST KNOWING YOU, MA'AM!
I'M NOT SURE WHETHER THAT'S A COMPLIMENT, BUT THE CURRICULUM CALLS FOR A DIPLOMA...
PHOENIX-ASIA
STEVE! THERE'S A FELLER WALKIN' ONTO THE RUNWAY!
Copyright 1949, SUN and TIMES Company
1-9

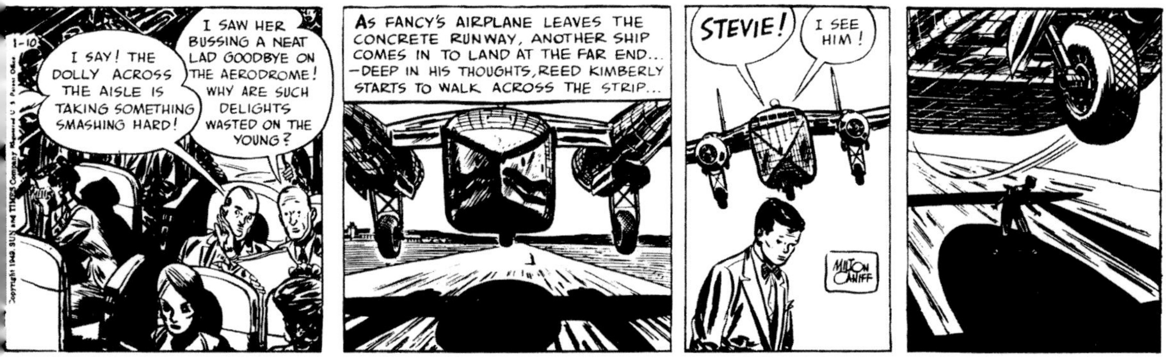
1-10
I SAY! THE DOLLY ACROSS THE AISLE IS TAKING SOMETHING SMASHING HARD!
I SAW HER BUSSING A NEAT LAD GOODBYE ON THE AERODROME! WHY ARE SUCH DELIGHTS WASTED ON THE YOUNG?
AS FANCY'S AIRPLANE LEAVES THE CONCRETE RUNWAY, ANOTHER SHIP COMES IN TO LAND AT THE FAR END... —DEEP IN HIS THOUGHTS, REED KIMBERLY STARTS TO WALK ACROSS THE STRIP...
STEVIE!
I SEE HIM!
MILTON CANIFF

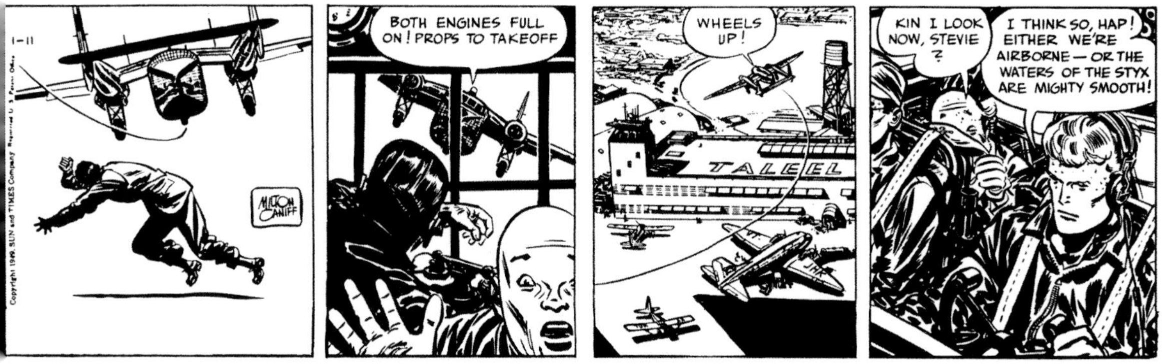
1-11
MILTON CANIFF
BOTH ENGINES FULL ON! PROPS TO TAKEOFF
WHEELS UP!
TALEEL
KIN I LOOK NOW, STEVIE?
I THINK SO, HAP! EITHER WE'RE AIRBORNE — OR THE WATERS OF THE STYX ARE MIGHTY SMOOTH!

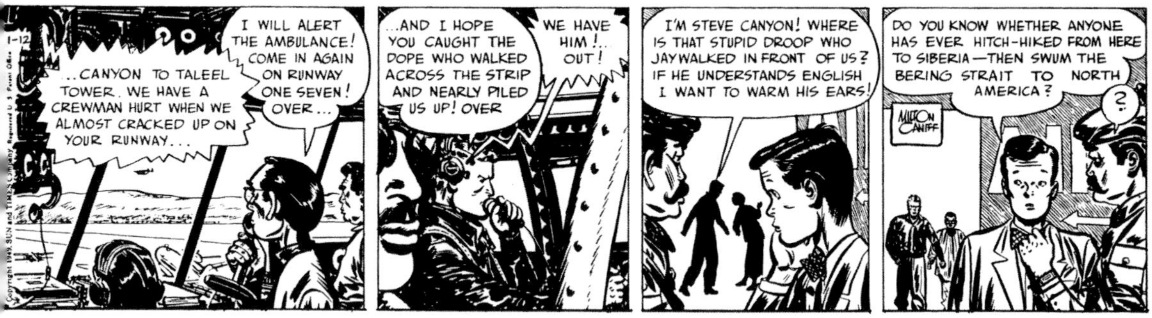
1-12
...CANYON TO TALEEL TOWER. WE HAVE A CREWMAN HURT WHEN WE ALMOST CRACKED UP ON YOUR RUNWAY...
I WILL ALERT THE AMBULANCE! COME IN AGAIN ON RUNWAY ONE SEVEN! OVER...
...AND I HOPE YOU CAUGHT THE DOPE WHO WALKED ACROSS THE STRIP AND NEARLY PILED US UP! OVER
WE HAVE HIM!... OUT!
I'M STEVE CANYON! WHERE IS THAT STUPID DROOP WHO JAYWALKED IN FRONT OF US? IF HE UNDERSTANDS ENGLISH I WANT TO WARM HIS EARS!
DO YOU KNOW WHETHER ANYONE HAS EVER HITCH-HIKED FROM HERE TO SIBERIA—THEN SWUM THE BERING STRAIT TO NORTH AMERICA?
MILTON CANIFF
?

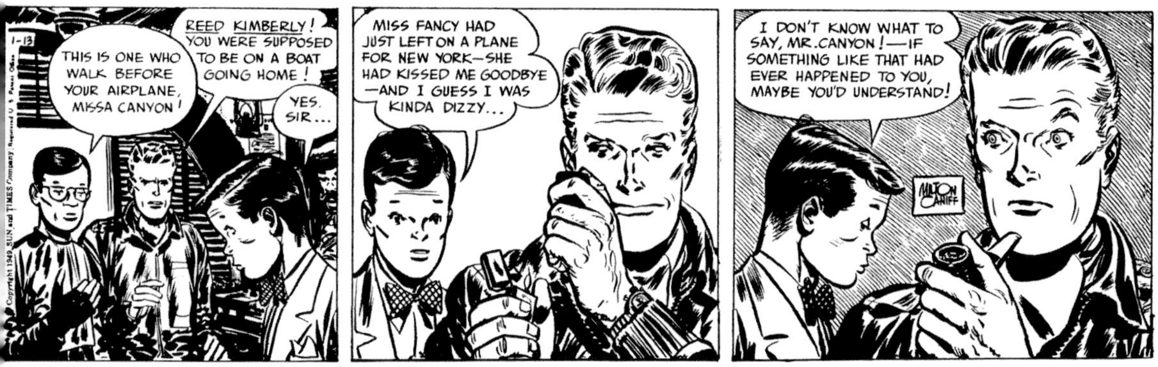
1-13
THIS IS ONE WHO WALK BEFORE YOUR AIRPLANE, MISSA CANYON!
REED KIMBERLY! YOU WERE SUPPOSED TO BE ON A BOAT GOING HOME!
YES. SIR...
MISS FANCY HAD JUST LEFT ON A PLANE FOR NEW YORK—SHE HAD KISSED ME GOODBYE —AND I GUESS I WAS KINDA DIZZY...
I DON'T KNOW WHAT TO SAY, MR. CANYON!—IF SOMETHING LIKE THAT HAD EVER HAPPENED TO YOU, MAYBE YOU'D UNDERSTAND!
MILTON CANIFF

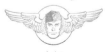

WELL, REED, REGARDLESS OF WHY YOU WERE ON THE RUNWAY, ONE OF MY NATIVE CREWMEN WAS HURT WHEN WE SWERVED TO MISS YOU!

THEN LET ME TAKE HIS PLACE, MR CANYON!

YOU DON'T EVEN KNOW WHERE WE'RE GOING — ANYHOW, I COULDN'T TRUST A KID WHO JAYWALKS ON AIRPORTS!

MEANWHILE...

YANKEE WOMAN DID NOT APPEAR AGAINST CHEETAH — SO SHE GO FREE FOR LACK OF EVIDENCE!

HA! BEEG LAST LAUGH! CHEETAH BEED YOU ALL BAD DREAMS!

YOU SAW THE GIRL — YOU KNOW WHAT TO DO?

EXACTLY...

THERE'S CHEETAH! I THOUGHT SHE WAS IN JAIL!

HER CASE WAS DISMISSED FOR LACK OF EVIDENCE!

SHE'LL BE BROKE, SINCE THAT KID SLIPPED THROUGH HER FINGERS... KEEP YOUR HAND ON YOUR MONEY!

'EY! 'OW ABOUT SOME SERVICE? — THINK I GOT NO BLINKIN' CASH? LOOK 'ERE, BUB!

BUT, MR. CANYON, WON'T YOU EVEN LISTEN TO ME?

I WILL, REED KIMBERLY, AND YOU'D BETTER TALK FAST... I PUT YOU ON A BOAT TO GO BACK TO SCHOOL — AND THE NEXT TIME I SEE YOU YOU JAYWALK IN FRONT OF MY AIRPLANE ON A BURMA LANDING STRIP!

STEVE CANYON

by MILTON CANIFF

I TOLD YOU THE STORY, SIR... I GUESS I WAS DAZZLED BY MISS FANCY KISSING ME GOODBYE!

MY CREWMAN WHO WAS HURT WHEN WE SWERVED TO AVOID HITTING YOU WILL GET COMFORT FROM THAT!

GEE — I FEEL AWFUL ABOUT IT. ISN'T THERE SOMETHING I CAN DO?

WELL, YOU CAN FADE OUT OF HERE WHILE WE TRY TO FIND A MAN WE CAN TRUST TO TAKE HIS PLACE!

YOU SEE, WE'RE FLYING A SORT OF OPERATION VITTLES, JUNIOR GRADE! A SMALL POTATOES AIR LIFT INTO A FRIENDLY STATE IN THE MOUNTAIN COUNTRY, NOW SURROUNDED BY REBEL NATIVE TROOPS...

Steve Canyon

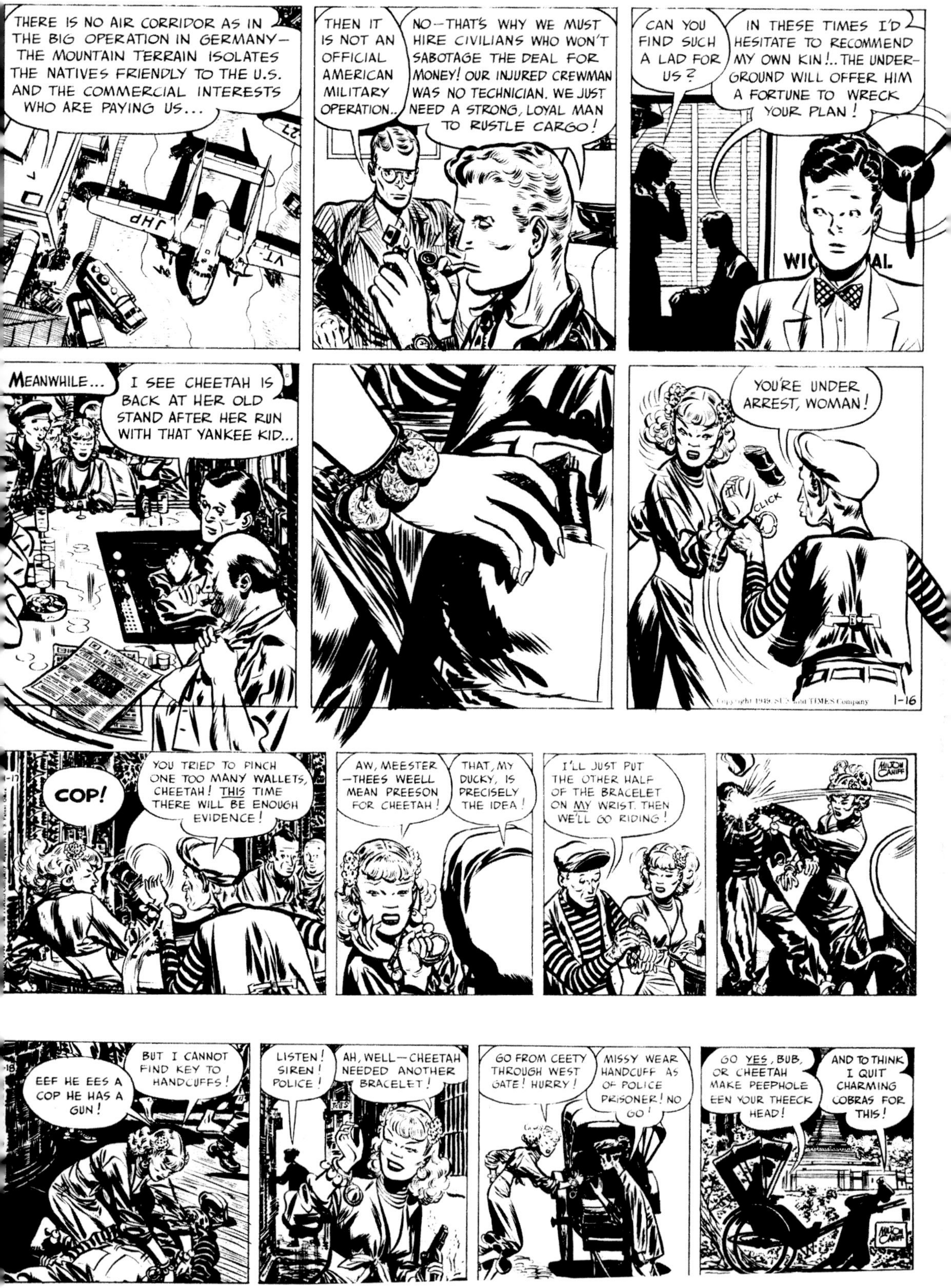
THERE IS NO AIR CORRIDOR AS IN THE BIG OPERATION IN GERMANY—THE MOUNTAIN TERRAIN ISOLATES THE NATIVES FRIENDLY TO THE U.S. AND THE COMMERCIAL INTERESTS WHO ARE PAYING US...
THEN IT IS NOT AN OFFICIAL AMERICAN MILITARY OPERATION..
NO—THAT'S WHY WE MUST HIRE CIVILIANS WHO WON'T SABOTAGE THE DEAL FOR MONEY! OUR INJURED CREWMAN WAS NO TECHNICIAN. WE JUST NEED A STRONG, LOYAL MAN TO RUSTLE CARGO!
CAN YOU FIND SUCH A LAD FOR US?
IN THESE TIMES I'D HESITATE TO RECOMMEND MY OWN KIN!.. THE UNDERGROUND WILL OFFER HIM A FORTUNE TO WRECK YOUR PLAN!
MEANWHILE...
I SEE CHEETAH IS BACK AT HER OLD STAND AFTER HER RUN WITH THAT YANKEE KID...
YOU'RE UNDER ARREST, WOMAN!
CLICK
1-16
COP!
YOU TRIED TO PINCH ONE TOO MANY WALLETS, CHEETAH! THIS TIME THERE WILL BE ENOUGH EVIDENCE!
AW, MEESTER—THEES WEELL MEAN PREESON FOR CHEETAH!
THAT, MY DUCKY, IS PRECISELY THE IDEA!
I'LL JUST PUT THE OTHER HALF OF THE BRACELET ON MY WRIST. THEN WE'LL GO RIDING!
MILTON CANIFF
EEF HE EES A COP HE HAS A GUN!
BUT I CANNOT FIND KEY TO HANDCUFFS!
LISTEN! SIREN! POLICE!
AH, WELL—CHEETAH NEEDED ANOTHER BRACELET!
GO FROM CEETY THROUGH WEST GATE! HURRY!
MISSY WEAR HANDCUFF AS OF POLICE PRISONER! NO GO!
GO YES, BUB, OR CHEETAH MAKE PEEPHOLE EEN YOUR THEECK HEAD!
AND TO THINK I QUIT CHARMING COBRAS FOR THIS!
MILTON CANIFF

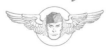

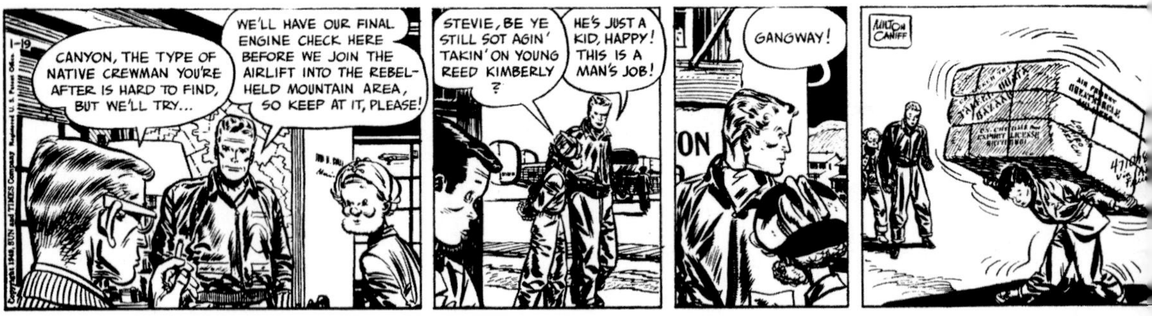
1-19
CANYON, THE TYPE OF NATIVE CREWMAN YOU'RE AFTER IS HARD TO FIND, BUT WE'LL TRY...
WE'LL HAVE OUR FINAL ENGINE CHECK HERE BEFORE WE JOIN THE AIRLIFT INTO THE REBEL-HELD MOUNTAIN AREA, SO KEEP AT IT, PLEASE!
STEVIE, BE YE STILL SOT AGIN' TAKIN' ON YOUNG REED KIMBERLY ?
HE'S JUST A KID, HAPPY! THIS IS A MAN'S JOB!
GANGWAY!
MILTON CANIFF

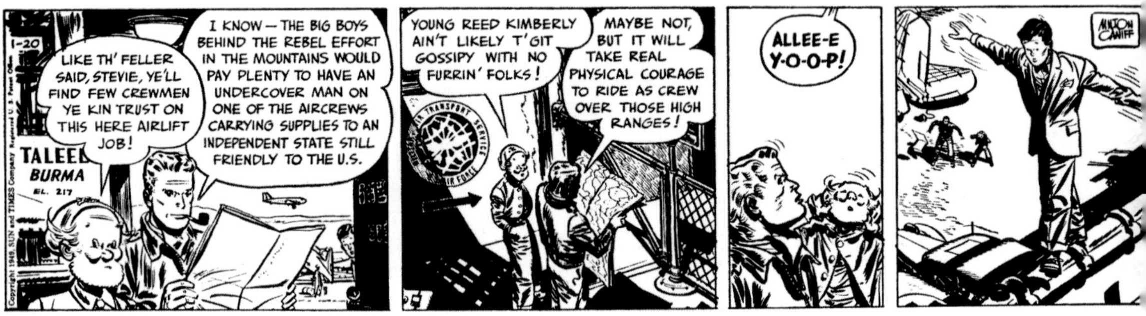
1-20
LIKE TH' FELLER SAID, STEVIE, YE'LL FIND FEW CREWMEN YE KIN TRUST ON THIS HERE AIRLIFT JOB!
I KNOW — THE BIG BOYS BEHIND THE REBEL EFFORT IN THE MOUNTAINS WOULD PAY PLENTY TO HAVE AN UNDERCOVER MAN ON ONE OF THE AIRCREWS CARRYING SUPPLIES TO AN INDEPENDENT STATE STILL FRIENDLY TO THE U.S.
TALEED
BURMA
EL. 217
YOUNG REED KIMBERLY AIN'T LIKELY T'GIT GOSSIPY WITH NO FURRIN' FOLKS!
MAYBE NOT, BUT IT WILL TAKE REAL PHYSICAL COURAGE TO RIDE AS CREW OVER THOSE HIGH RANGES!
ALLEE-E Y-O-O-P!
MILTON CANIFF

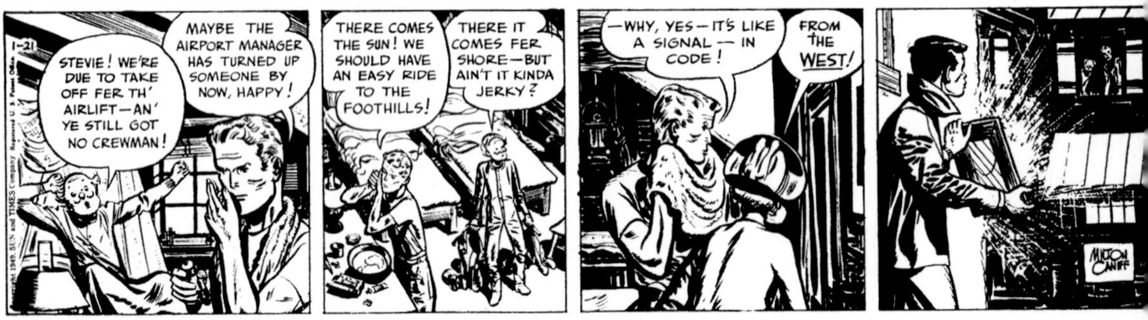
1-21
STEVIE! WE'RE DUE TO TAKE OFF FER TH' AIRLIFT—AN' YE STILL GOT NO CREWMAN!
MAYBE THE AIRPORT MANAGER HAS TURNED UP SOMEONE BY NOW, HAPPY!
THERE COMES THE SUN! WE SHOULD HAVE AN EASY RIDE TO THE FOOTHILLS!
THERE IT COMES FER SHORE—BUT AIN'T IT KINDA JERKY?
—WHY, YES— IT'S LIKE A SIGNAL — IN CODE!
FROM THE WEST!
MILTON CANIFF

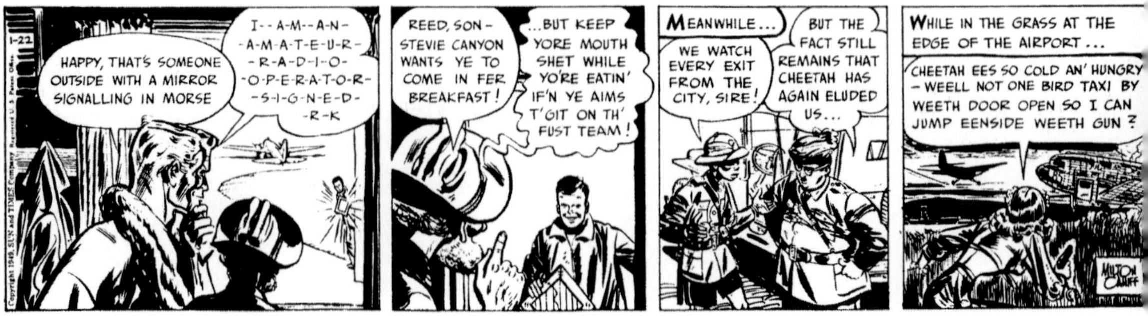
1-22
HAPPY, THAT'S SOMEONE OUTSIDE WITH A MIRROR SIGNALLING IN MORSE
I--A-M--A-N- -A-M-A-T-E-U-R- -R-A-D-I-O- -O-P-E-R-A-T-O-R- -S-I-G-N-E-D- -R-K
REED, SON - STEVIE CANYON WANTS YE TO COME IN FER BREAKFAST!
...BUT KEEP YORE MOUTH SHET WHILE YO'RE EATIN' IF'N YE AIMS T'GIT ON TH' FUST TEAM!
MEANWHILE...
WE WATCH EVERY EXIT FROM THE CITY, SIRE!
BUT THE FACT STILL REMAINS THAT CHEETAH HAS AGAIN ELUDED US...
WHILE IN THE GRASS AT THE EDGE OF THE AIRPORT...
CHEETAH EES SO COLD AN' HUNGRY - WEELL NOT ONE BIRD TAXI BY WEETH DOOR OPEN SO I CAN JUMP EENSIDE WEETH GUN?
MILTON CANIFF

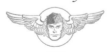

STEVE CANYON
by MILTON CANIFF

I'M SORRY, MR. CANYON!

I SUPPOSE A GUY WHO HAD JUST BEEN KISSED GOOD-BYE BY A GAL LIKE FANCY SHOULD BE EXCUSED FOR JAY-WALKING ACROSS AN AIRPORT RUNWAY—

BUT THAT DOESN'T ALTER THE FACT THAT ONE OF OUR CREWMEN WAS HURT WHEN WE SWERVED TO MISS YOU AS WE LANDED, REED KIMBERLY!

BUT, SIR, I'M PLEADING WITH YOU TO ALLOW ME TO TAKE HIS PLACE!

THAT WOULD BE FINE IF HAPPY AND I HAD SIGNED ON THIS JOB TO DO A MILK RUN, BUT WE'RE GOING TO FLY CARGO INTO THE TOUGHEST KIND OF MOUNTAIN COUNTRY!

THAT HURT CREWMAN WAS NOT A TRAINED MAN—HE WAS STRICTLY A TRUSTWORTHY MUSCLE BOY...

YOU KNOW I'M RELIABLE, MR. CANYON—AND I'VE HAD SOME RADIO TRAINING!

THAT DID IT! WE'LL TRY YOU ON ONE RUN... IF YOU WASH OUT, BACK TO THE TRUANT OFFICER YOU GO... CHECK THE REAR DOORS!

YES, SIR!

...STEVIE CANYON, YE AIMED ALL ALONG T' SIGN THET YOUNGUN' ON THIS HERE CREW!

CAN'T HEAR YOU FOR THE STATIC, HAP!

As STEVE'S AIRPLANE PAUSES AT THE DISTANT END OF THE RUNWAY TO REV UP THE ENGINES

REED KEEMBERLY!

REED KEEMBERLY, TAKE ME WEETH YOU! THE POLICES ARE AFTER ME!

BUT, CHEETAH, I CAN'T! MR. CANYON WOULD NEVER--

LET ME EENSIDE OR I BLAST YOUR YANKEE HEAD OFF!

R-REAR DOORS ARE CLOSED, MR. CANYON!

OKAY, REED!...WELL, HERE WE GO! FOR ONCE NOTHING WENT WRONG!

Copyright 1949, SUN and TIMES Company 1-23

Steve Canyon

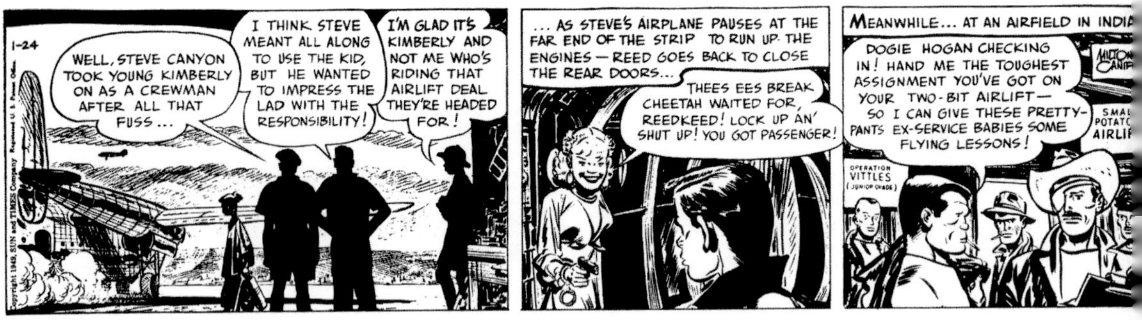
1-24
WELL, STEVE CANYON TOOK YOUNG KIMBERLY ON AS A CREWMAN AFTER ALL THAT FUSS ...
I THINK STEVE MEANT ALL ALONG TO USE THE KID, BUT HE WANTED TO IMPRESS THE LAD WITH THE RESPONSIBILITY!
I'M GLAD IT'S KIMBERLY AND NOT ME WHO'S RIDING THAT AIRLIFT DEAL THEY'RE HEADED FOR!
... AS STEVE'S AIRPLANE PAUSES AT THE FAR END OF THE STRIP TO RUN UP THE ENGINES — REED GOES BACK TO CLOSE THE REAR DOORS...
THEES EES BREAK CHEETAH WAITED FOR, REEDKEED! LOCK UP AN' SHUT UP! YOU GOT PASSENGER!
MEANWHILE... AT AN AIRFIELD IN INDIA
DOGIE HOGAN CHECKING IN! HAND ME THE TOUGHEST ASSIGNMENT YOU'VE GOT ON YOUR TWO-BIT AIRLIFT— SO I CAN GIVE THESE PRETTY-PANTS EX-SERVICE BABIES SOME FLYING LESSONS!
OPERATION VITTLES (JUNIOR GRADE)

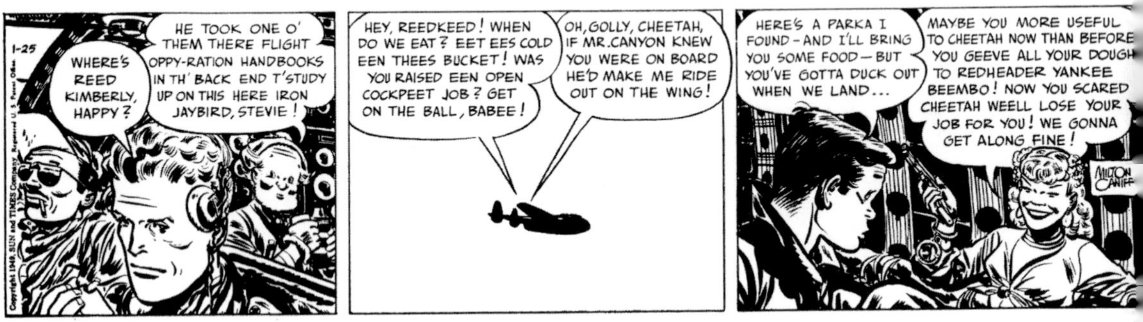
1-25
WHERE'S REED KIMBERLY, HAPPY?
HE TOOK ONE O' THEM THERE FLIGHT OPPY-RATION HANDBOOKS IN TH' BACK END T'STUDY UP ON THIS HERE IRON JAYBIRD, STEVIE!
HEY, REEDKEED! WHEN DO WE EAT? EET EES COLD EEN THEES BUCKET! WAS YOU RAISED EEN OPEN COCKPEET JOB? GET ON THE BALL, BABEE!
OH, GOLLY, CHEETAH, IF MR. CANYON KNEW YOU WERE ON BOARD HE'D MAKE ME RIDE OUT ON THE WING!
HERE'S A PARKA I FOUND — AND I'LL BRING YOU SOME FOOD — BUT YOU'VE GOTTA DUCK OUT WHEN WE LAND...
MAYBE YOU MORE USEFUL TO CHEETAH NOW THAN BEFORE YOU GEEVE ALL YOUR DOUGH TO REDHEADER YANKEE BEEMBO! NOW YOU SCARED CHEETAH WEELL LOSE YOUR JOB FOR YOU! WE GONNA GET ALONG FINE!

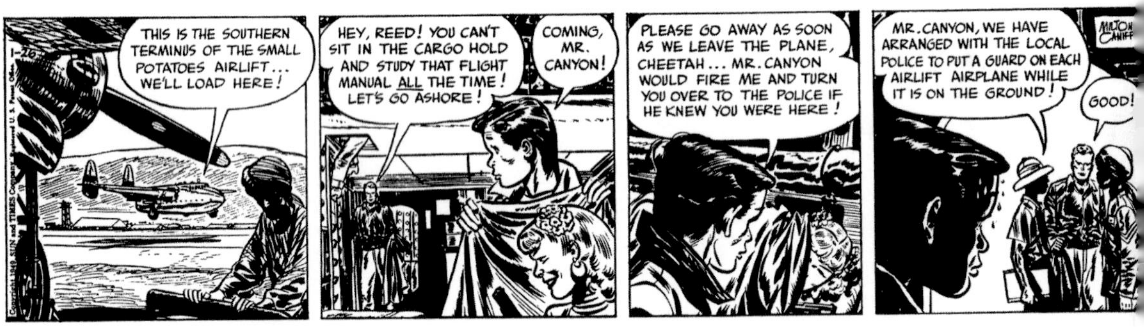
1-26
THIS IS THE SOUTHERN TERMINUS OF THE SMALL POTATOES AIRLIFT... WE'LL LOAD HERE!
HEY, REED! YOU CAN'T SIT IN THE CARGO HOLD AND STUDY THAT FLIGHT MANUAL ALL THE TIME! LET'S GO ASHORE!
COMING, MR. CANYON!
PLEASE GO AWAY AS SOON AS WE LEAVE THE PLANE, CHEETAH ... MR. CANYON WOULD FIRE ME AND TURN YOU OVER TO THE POLICE IF HE KNEW YOU WERE HERE!
MR. CANYON, WE HAVE ARRANGED WITH THE LOCAL POLICE TO PUT A GUARD ON EACH AIRLIFT AIRPLANE WHILE IT IS ON THE GROUND!
GOOD!

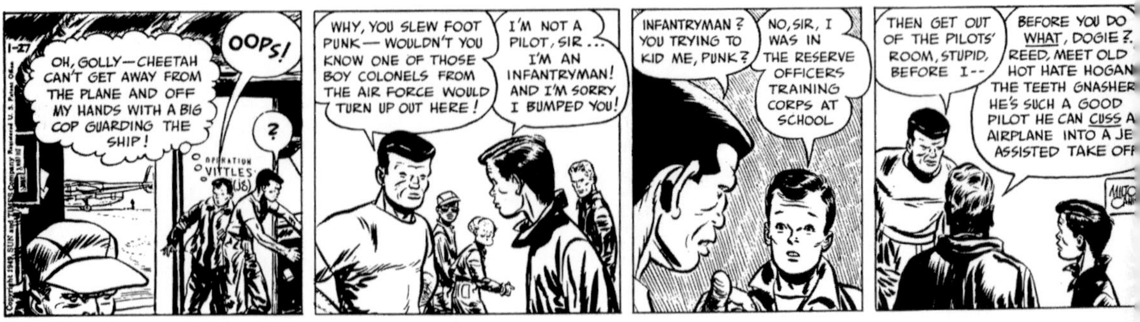
1-27
OH, GOLLY — CHEETAH CAN'T GET AWAY FROM THE PLANE AND OFF MY HANDS WITH A BIG COP GUARDING THE SHIP!
OOPS!
?
OPERATION VITTLES (JG)
WHY, YOU SLEW FOOT PUNK — WOULDN'T YOU KNOW ONE OF THOSE BOY COLONELS FROM THE AIR FORCE WOULD TURN UP OUT HERE!
I'M NOT A PILOT, SIR... I'M AN INFANTRYMAN! AND I'M SORRY I BUMPED YOU!
INFANTRYMAN? YOU TRYING TO KID ME, PUNK?
NO, SIR, I WAS IN THE RESERVE OFFICERS TRAINING CORPS AT SCHOOL
THEN GET OUT OF THE PILOTS' ROOM, STUPID, BEFORE I--
BEFORE YOU DO WHAT, DOGIE? REED, MEET OLD HOT HATE HOGAN THE TEETH GNASHER! HE'S SUCH A GOOD PILOT HE CAN CUSS A AIRPLANE INTO A JE ASSISTED TAKE OF

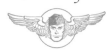

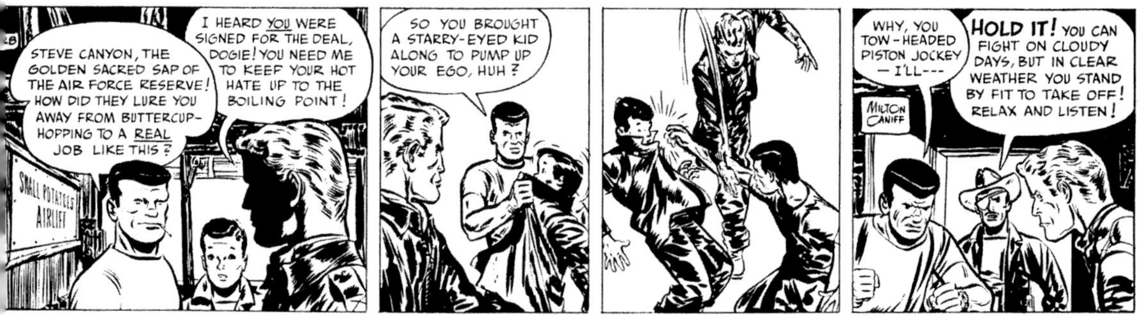
STEVE CANYON, THE GOLDEN SACRED SAP OF THE AIR FORCE RESERVE! HOW DID THEY LURE YOU AWAY FROM BUTTERCUP-HOPPING TO A REAL JOB LIKE THIS?
I HEARD YOU WERE SIGNED FOR THE DEAL, DOGIE! YOU NEED ME TO KEEP YOUR HOT HATE UP TO THE BOILING POINT!
SMALL POTATOES AIRLIFT
SO YOU BROUGHT A STARRY-EYED KID ALONG TO PUMP UP YOUR EGO, HUH?
WHY, YOU TOW-HEADED PISTON JOCKEY — I'LL---
HOLD IT! YOU CAN FIGHT ON CLOUDY DAYS, BUT IN CLEAR WEATHER YOU STAND BY FIT TO TAKE OFF! RELAX AND LISTEN!
MILTON CANIFF

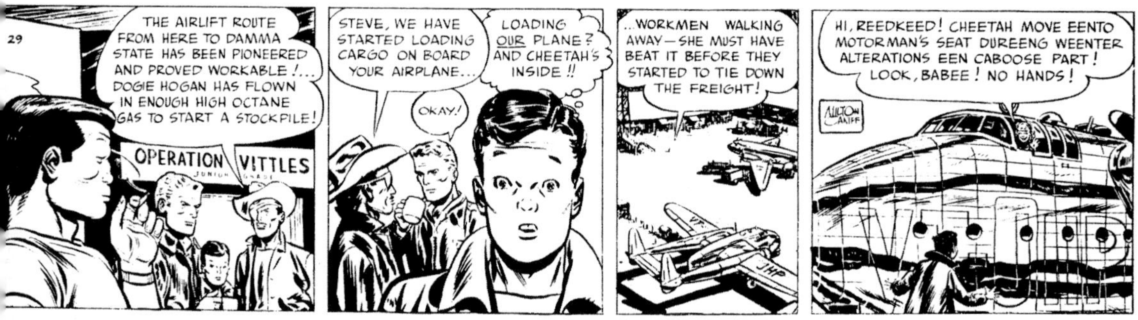
THE AIRLIFT ROUTE FROM HERE TO DAMMA STATE HAS BEEN PIONEERED AND PROVED WORKABLE!... DOGIE HOGAN HAS FLOWN IN ENOUGH HIGH OCTANE GAS TO START A STOCKPILE!
OPERATION VITTLES
STEVE, WE HAVE STARTED LOADING CARGO ON BOARD YOUR AIRPLANE...
LOADING OUR PLANE? AND CHEETAH'S INSIDE!!
OKAY!
...WORKMEN WALKING AWAY—SHE MUST HAVE BEAT IT BEFORE THEY STARTED TO TIE DOWN THE FREIGHT!
HI, REEDKEED! CHEETAH MOVE EENTO MOTORMAN'S SEAT DUREENG WEENTER ALTERATIONS EEN CABOOSE PART! LOOK, BABEE! NO HANDS!
MILTON CANIFF

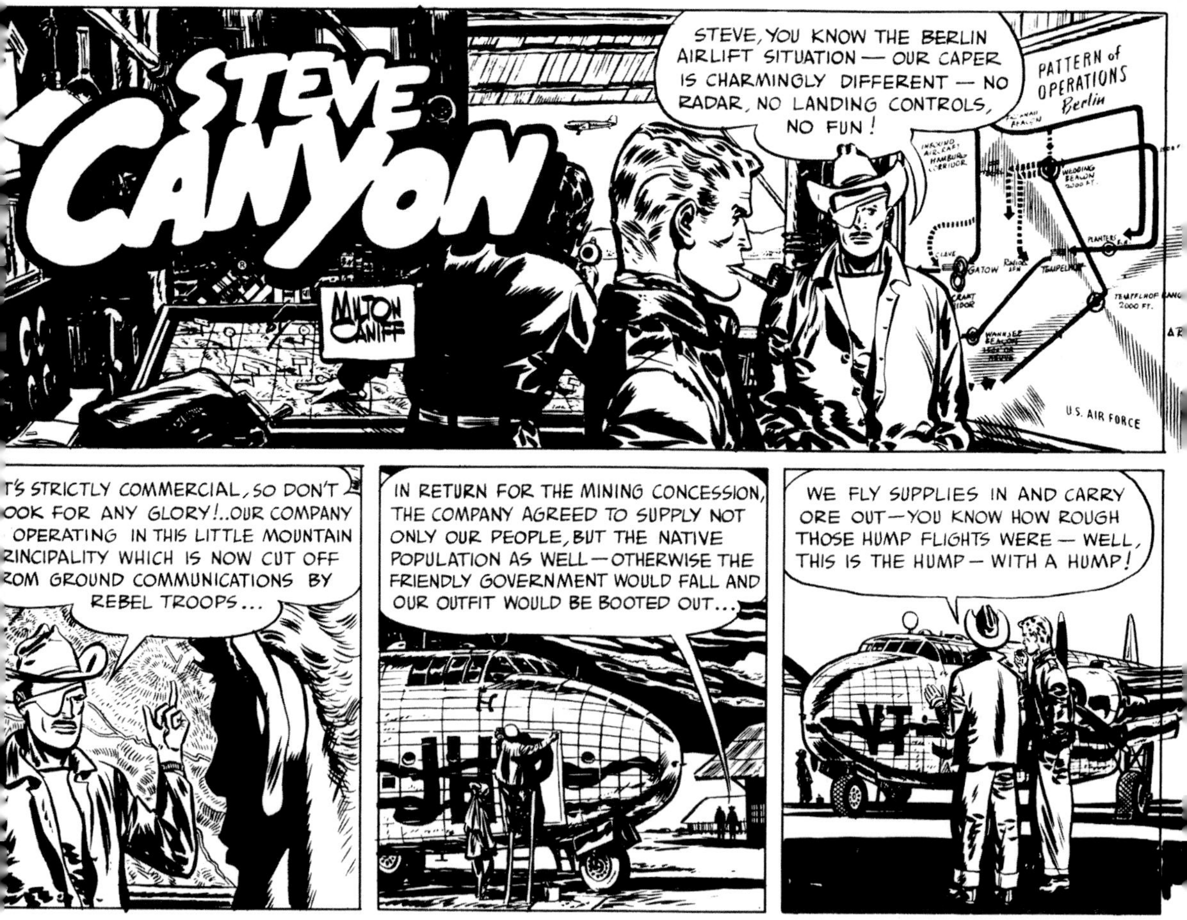
STEVE CANYON
MILTON CANIFF
STEVE, YOU KNOW THE BERLIN AIRLIFT SITUATION — OUR CAPER IS CHARMINGLY DIFFERENT — NO RADAR, NO LANDING CONTROLS, NO FUN!
PATTERN of OPERATIONS Berlin
GATOW
TEMPELHOF
U.S. AIR FORCE
T'S STRICTLY COMMERCIAL, SO DON'T OOK FOR ANY GLORY!..OUR COMPANY OPERATING IN THIS LITTLE MOUNTAIN RINCIPALITY WHICH IS NOW CUT OFF ROM GROUND COMMUNICATIONS BY REBEL TROOPS...
IN RETURN FOR THE MINING CONCESSION, THE COMPANY AGREED TO SUPPLY NOT ONLY OUR PEOPLE, BUT THE NATIVE POPULATION AS WELL—OTHERWISE THE FRIENDLY GOVERNMENT WOULD FALL AND OUR OUTFIT WOULD BE BOOTED OUT...
WE FLY SUPPLIES IN AND CARRY ORE OUT—YOU KNOW HOW ROUGH THOSE HUMP FLIGHTS WERE — WELL, THIS IS THE HUMP — WITH A HUMP!

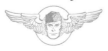

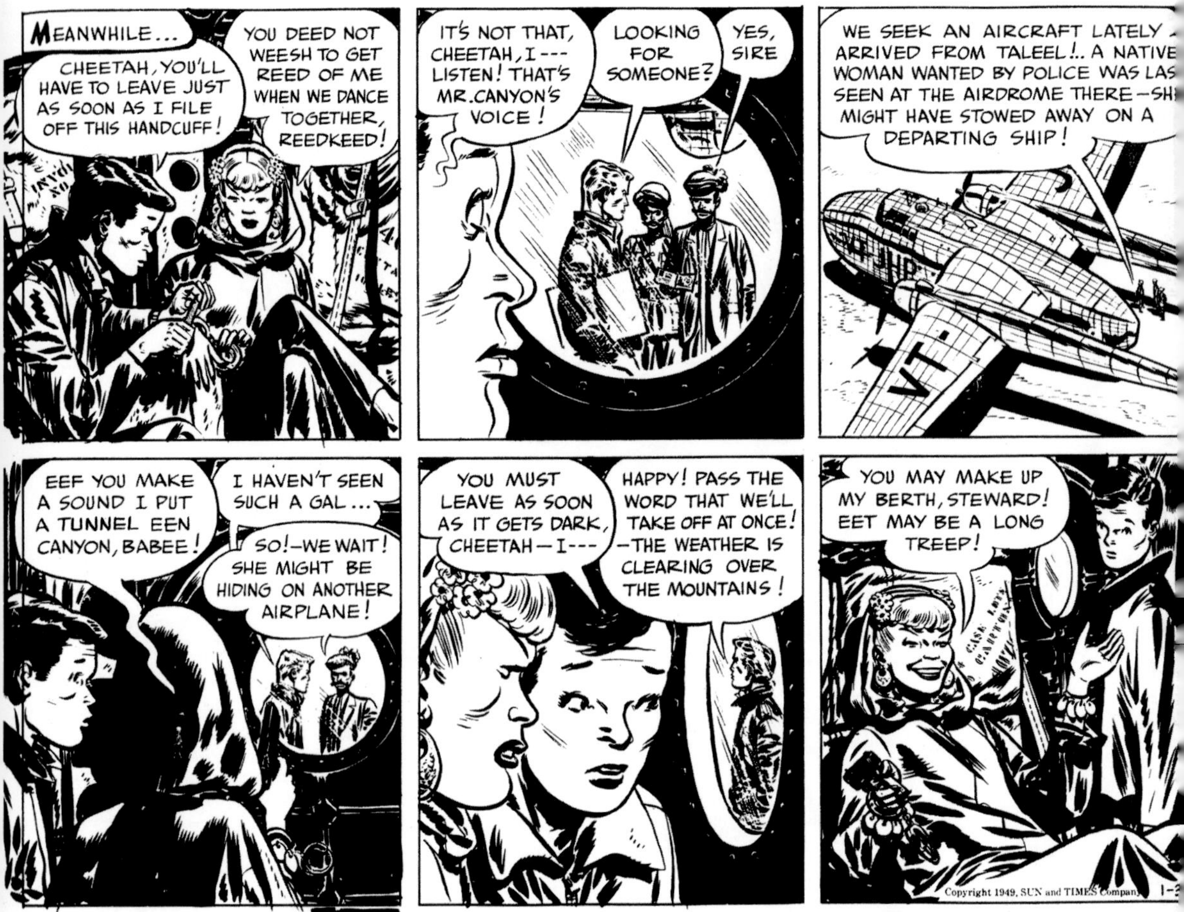
MEANWHILE...
CHEETAH, YOU'LL HAVE TO LEAVE JUST AS SOON AS I FILE OFF THIS HANDCUFF!
YOU DEED NOT WEESH TO GET REED OF ME WHEN WE DANCE TOGETHER, REEDKEED!
IT'S NOT THAT, CHEETAH, I--- LISTEN! THAT'S MR. CANYON'S VOICE!
LOOKING FOR SOMEONE?
YES, SIRE
WE SEEK AN AIRCRAFT LATELY ARRIVED FROM TALEEL!.. A NATIVE WOMAN WANTED BY POLICE WAS LAS SEEN AT THE AIRDROME THERE—SH MIGHT HAVE STOWED AWAY ON A DEPARTING SHIP!
VT-
EEF YOU MAKE A SOUND I PUT A TUNNEL EEN CANYON, BABEE!
I HAVEN'T SEEN SUCH A GAL...
SO!—WE WAIT! SHE MIGHT BE HIDING ON ANOTHER AIRPLANE!
YOU MUST LEAVE AS SOON AS IT GETS DARK, CHEETAH—I---
HAPPY! PASS THE WORD THAT WE'LL TAKE OFF AT ONCE! —THE WEATHER IS CLEARING OVER THE MOUNTAINS!
YOU MAY MAKE UP MY BERTH, STEWARD! EET MAY BE A LONG TREEP!
Copyright 1949, SUN and TIMES Company

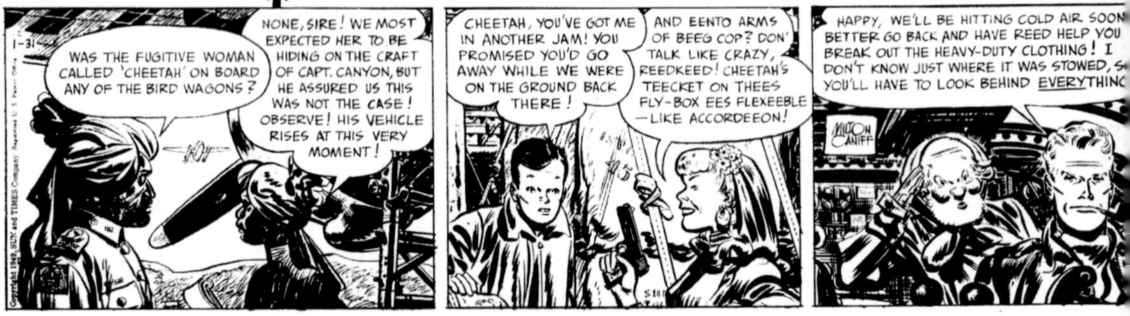
1-31
WAS THE FUGITIVE WOMAN CALLED 'CHEETAH' ON BOARD ANY OF THE BIRD WAGONS?
NONE, SIRE! WE MOST EXPECTED HER TO BE HIDING ON THE CRAFT OF CAPT. CANYON, BUT HE ASSURED US THIS WAS NOT THE CASE! OBSERVE! HIS VEHICLE RISES AT THIS VERY MOMENT!
CHEETAH, YOU'VE GOT ME IN ANOTHER JAM! YOU PROMISED YOU'D GO AWAY WHILE WE WERE ON THE GROUND BACK THERE!
AND EENTO ARMS OF BEEG COP? DON' TALK LIKE CRAZY, REEDKEED! CHEETAH'S TEECKET ON THEES FLY-BOX EES FLEXEEBLE —LIKE ACCORDEEON!
HAPPY, WE'LL BE HITTING COLD AIR SOON BETTER GO BACK AND HAVE REED HELP YOU BREAK OUT THE HEAVY-DUTY CLOTHING! I DON'T KNOW JUST WHERE IT WAS STOWED, S YOU'LL HAVE TO LOOK BEHIND EVERYTHING
MILTON CANIFF
Copyright 1949, SUN and TIMES Company

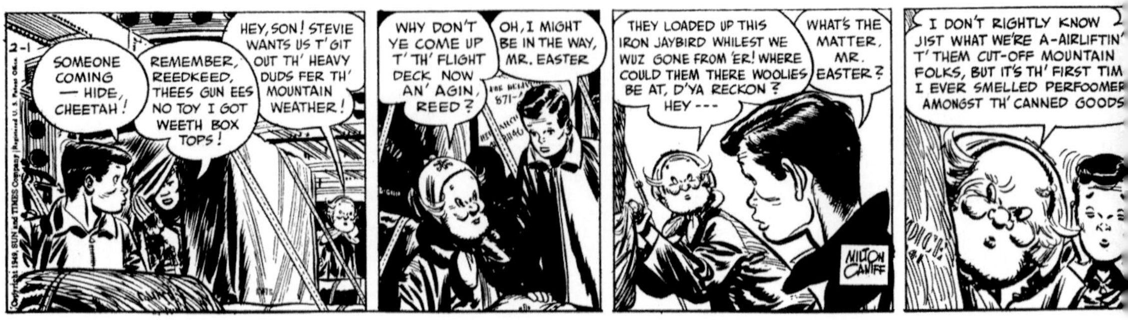
2-1
SOMEONE COMING —HIDE, CHEETAH!
REMEMBER, REEDKEED, THEES GUN EES NO TOY I GOT WEETH BOX TOPS!
HEY, SON! STEVIE WANTS US T' GIT OUT TH' HEAVY DUDS FER TH' MOUNTAIN WEATHER!
WHY DON'T YE COME UP T' TH' FLIGHT DECK NOW AN' AGIN, REED?
OH, I MIGHT BE IN THE WAY, MR. EASTER
THEY LOADED UP THIS IRON JAYBIRD WHILEST WE WUZ GONE FROM 'ER! WHERE COULD THEM THERE WOOLIES BE AT, D'YA RECKON? HEY ---
WHAT'S THE MATTER, MR. EASTER?
I DON'T RIGHTLY KNOW JIST WHAT WE'RE A-AIRLIFTIN' T' THEM CUT-OFF MOUNTAIN FOLKS, BUT IT'S TH' FIRST TIM I EVER SMELLED PERFOOMER AMONGST TH' CANNED GOODS
MILTON CANIFF
Copyright 1949, SUN and TIMES Company

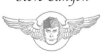

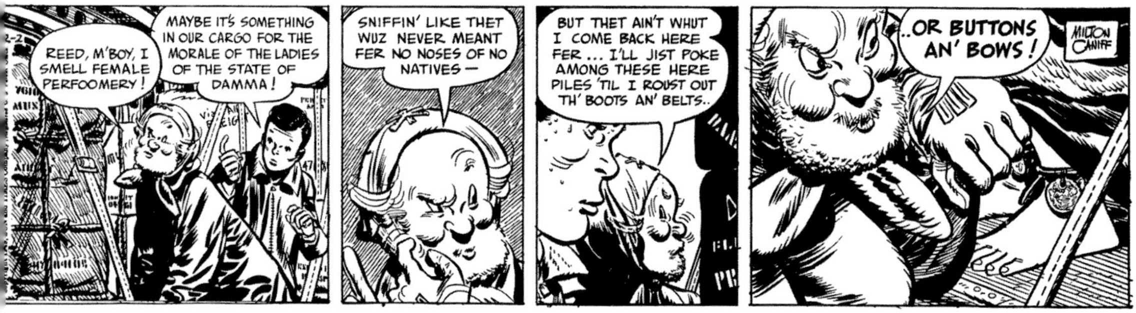
2-2
REED, M'BOY, I SMELL FEMALE PERFOOMERY!
MAYBE IT'S SOMETHING IN OUR CARGO FOR THE MORALE OF THE LADIES OF THE STATE OF DAMMA!
SNIFFIN' LIKE THET WUZ NEVER MEANT FER NO NOSES OF NO NATIVES —
BUT THET AIN'T WHUT I COME BACK HERE FER ... I'LL JIST POKE AMONG THESE HERE PILES 'TIL I ROUST OUT TH' BOOTS AN' BELTS..
..OR BUTTONS AN' BOWS!
MILTON CANIFF

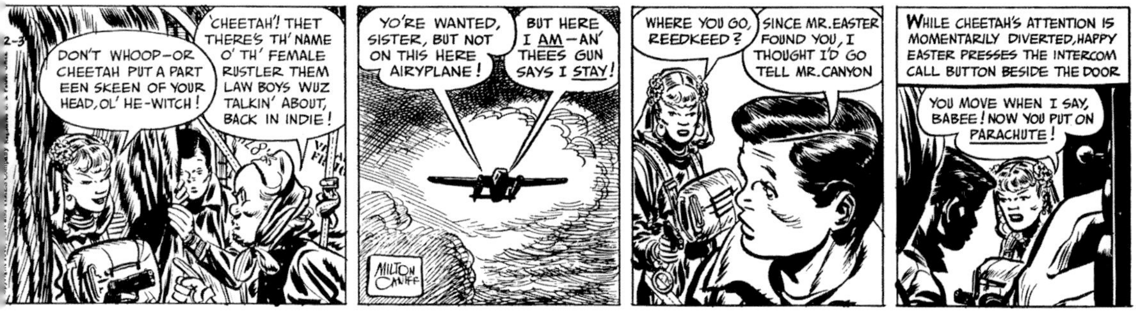
2-3
DON'T WHOOP—OR CHEETAH PUT A PART EEN SKEEN OF YOUR HEAD, OL' HE-WITCH!
'CHEETAH'! THET THERE'S TH' NAME O' TH' FEMALE RUSTLER THEM LAW BOYS WUZ TALKIN' ABOUT, BACK IN INDIE!
YO'RE WANTED, SISTER, BUT NOT ON THIS HERE AIRYPLANE!
BUT HERE I AM—AN' THEES GUN SAYS I STAY!
MILTON CANIFF
WHERE YOU GO, REEDKEED?
SINCE MR. EASTER FOUND YOU, I THOUGHT I'D GO TELL MR. CANYON
WHILE CHEETAH'S ATTENTION IS MOMENTARILY DIVERTED, HAPPY EASTER PRESSES THE INTERCOM CALL BUTTON BESIDE THE DOOR
YOU MOVE WHEN I SAY, BABEE! NOW YOU PUT ON PARACHUTE!

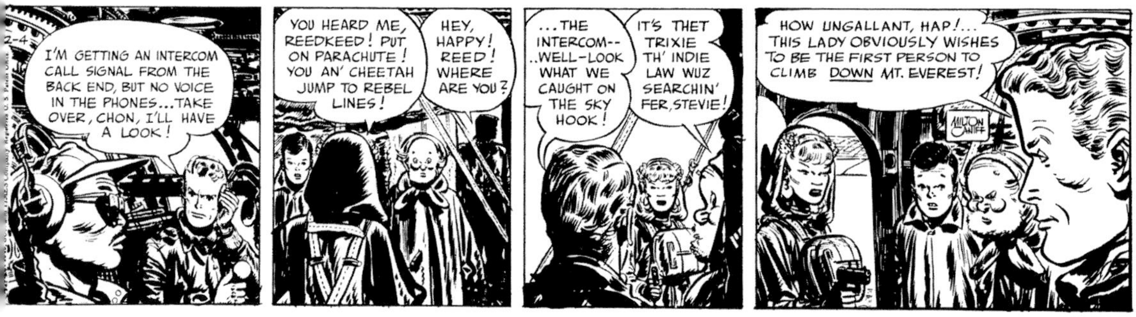
2-4
I'M GETTING AN INTERCOM CALL SIGNAL FROM THE BACK END, BUT NO VOICE IN THE PHONES...TAKE OVER, CHON, I'LL HAVE A LOOK!
YOU HEARD ME, REEDKEED! PUT ON PARACHUTE! YOU AN' CHEETAH JUMP TO REBEL LINES!
HEY, HAPPY! REED! WHERE ARE YOU?
...THE INTERCOM-- ..WELL-LOOK WHAT WE CAUGHT ON THE SKY HOOK!
IT'S THET TRIXIE TH' INDIE LAW WUZ SEARCHIN' FER, STEVIE!
HOW UNGALLANT, HAP!... THIS LADY OBVIOUSLY WISHES TO BE THE FIRST PERSON TO CLIMB DOWN MT. EVEREST!
MILTON CANIFF

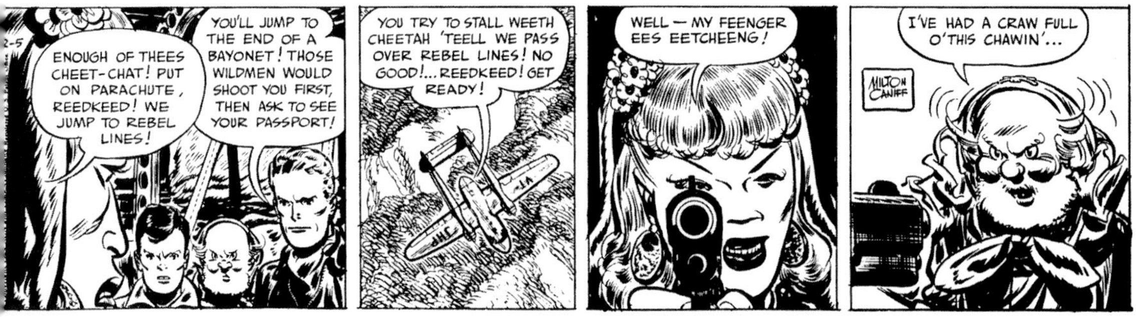
2-5
ENOUGH OF THEES CHEET-CHAT! PUT ON PARACHUTE, REEDKEED! WE JUMP TO REBEL LINES!
YOU'LL JUMP TO THE END OF A BAYONET! THOSE WILDMEN WOULD SHOOT YOU FIRST, THEN ASK TO SEE YOUR PASSPORT!
YOU TRY TO STALL WEETH CHEETAH 'TEELL WE PASS OVER REBEL LINES! NO GOOD!...REEDKEED! GET READY!
WELL — MY FEENGER EES EETCHEENG!
MILTON CANIFF
I'VE HAD A CRAW FULL O'THIS CHAWIN'...

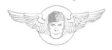

...WE THOUGHT THIS TRIP WAS GOING TO BE DULL AND ROUTINE—THEN UP JUMPED THE FLOOR SHOW!

OKAY, BEEG TOP! YOU MAKE JOKES—CHEETAH MAKE YANKEE SWEESS CHEESE OUT OF YOU EEF YOU GET CUTE!

REEDKEED KIMBERLY IS OUR VICE-PRESIDENT IN CHARGE OF BEING CUTE, BABY!—HE TAKES LITTLE GIRLS RIDING IN OTHER PEOPLE'S AIRPLANES

RELAX! THERE ARE NO BLOCK SIGNALS TO STOP THIS TRAIN IF YOU SHOOT THE ENGINEER!

YOU'RE IN A SQUEEZE—IF WE TURN BACK, THE COPS IN INDIA WILL PICK YOU UP—WHEN WE LAND AT DAMMA I'LL TURN YOU OVER TO THE LOCAL SHERLOCKS! HOW CAN YOU WIN?

THEES CEETY WHEECH YOU CARRY FOOD TO—EET EES SURROUND BY REBEL TROOPS, HEY?

THEY CONTROL ALL THE ROADS AND TRAILS LEADING OUT!

YOU CALL THE CO-PILOT—TELL HEEM TO CIRCLE OVER REBEL LINES!

AND ASK FOR SOME HOMEMADE FLAK?—NOT A CHANCE, DREAMBOAT!

THEN I SHOOT THE OLD MAN!

I-I THINK SHE MEANS IT, MR. CANYON!

YOU SHOULD KNOW HER MOODS, KID! ...CHON, THIS IS STEVE! CIRCLE LEFT WHEN WE'RE OVER THE REBEL LINES!..

NOW, REEDKEED, PUT ON PARACHUTE!

DO EET—OR I SHOOT THE OLD MAN DEAD EEN HEAD!

...HURRY, REEDKEED!—CHEETAH WEELL NEED A HOSTAGE TO GEEVE THE REBELS!

DO EET OR I STEELL SHOOT THE OLD GEEZER!

SO LONG AS A FELLER'S ABOUT T' CASH IN...

...HE MIGHT JIST AS WELL SHET UP A GABBY WOMAN WHILE HE'S AT IT!

Copyright 1949, SUN and TIMES Company 2-6

Steve Canyon

2-7

As CHEETAH LEVELS HER GUN TO FIRE AT HAPPY EASTER — HE THROWS HIMSELF AT HER .. AND THEY BOTH PLUNGE OUT THROUGH ONE OF THE AIRPLANE'S PARATROOP DOORS...

MR. CANYON! THEY HAVE ONLY ONE PARACHUTE!

CHON! CIRCLE LEFT!

LET GO, OLD MAN! I SHOOT!

WHILE YO'RE HOLDIN' THET GUN YE CAIN'T BE PULLIN' TH' UMBERELLY STRING, SISTER!

...THEM ROCKS DON'T LOOK TOO BOUNCY! BETTER MAKE UP YORE MIND T' PULL OR PLUG!!

MILTON CANIFF

2-8

MR. CANYON! THE PARACHUTE OPENED!

THERE THEY GO INTO THE UNDERCAST! HAPPY'S STILL HANGING ON TO THE GIRL!

WH - WHAT CAN WE DO ?

CHON! GET A FIX ON THIS SPOT FROM THE DAMMA STATE RADIO!

SEE IF THEY CAN SEND OUT A FULLY GASSED SEARCH PLANE TO CIRCLE AND WAIT FOR A SIGNAL FROM THE GROUND ... HOLD IT!!

IT WAS MY FAULT THAT CHEETAH WAS HERE! I SHOULD JUMP TO HELP MR. EASTER!

IF YOU JUST DON'T SAY ANYTHING MORE, KID, I DON'T THINK I'LL SOCK YOU!

2-9

CANYON TO DAMMA TOWER — DID YOU SEND OUT THE SEARCH PLANE I REQUESTED ?

DAMMA TOWER TO CANYON...THERE WILL BE FIVE MINUTES OF VISIBILITY BEFORE A STORM HITS HERE FROM THE NORTH!

...CAN'T SEND AN AIRPLANE OUT UNTIL IT CLEARS...YOU JUST MADE IT, YOURSELF! PARK AT THE UNLOADING RAMP ON THE LEFT SIDE OF THE STRIP!

MILTON CANIFF

Steve Canyon

OF PRINTER'S INK AND PATRIOTISM

MILTON CANIFF AND STEVE CANYON

Terry and the Pirates was a contrivance of two seasoned newspaper-men whose motivation was to sell newspapers. The idea for an adventure strip set in the Orient originated with Chicago Tribune chief, General Joseph Medill Patterson, whose bona fides in the successful hawking of newsprint were clearly established. The execution was handed to a young but veteran newspaperman who happened to be a cartoonist – Milton Caniff. Caniff had been haunting newsrooms from the ripe age of 13, chipping in with officed duties, and when needed, his ability to draw. His cartoons sold more papers than his ability to bring lunch to an editor, or rush copy from one office to another, and so his specialty was settled. Newsie first, cartoonist second.

Terry was a smash success under Caniff's control. By the time the U.S. was dragged unceremoniously into the Second World War, he had achieved a level of public adoration (later it might be called superstardom) which will likely never be rivaled again by a cartoonist. As a potential soldier or sailor though, he was unfit due to a childhood insect bite that led to recurring bouts of phlebitis. Three times he was called to serve, three times he failed the military physical. He was 12-F.

But Milton Caniff contributed as much to the Allied effort in World War II as a man deemed unfit to carry a gun or pilot a plane possibly could.

Though he had been the preeminent popular cartoonist prior to hostilities, and would be again following VJ day, his wartime morale-boosting strips saw wider circulation than either Terry and the Pirates or Steve Canyon.

Because of this, and by his own admissions, Caniff earned a reputation as a patriot. "I'm an out-and-out patriot," he told an interviewer in 1945. And for his, "greatest" generation, this was not an unusual thing. World War II was fought and won, not with the superior tech- nology and unrivaled training that our volunteer U.S. armed forces enjoy in this era, but with the unified will of a nation willing to submit to harsh rationing, to invest

every last penny in war bonds, to plant victory gardens, and to donate tin cans and nylons to the war effort.

And because he chose an ex-military hero for his post-War strip, the former Army Air pilot Steve Canyon, he is often viewed today to have been not a patriot, but a militarist. This is not truly the case, though. True, Canyon re-enlisted when the Korean conflict broke out, but only then. To join and support the war effort once the United States had deigned to enter a war in which bullets were flying in the direction of American boys was not something Caniff, and by extension Canyon, even thought twice about. It was a "no brainer" in the current parlance. It was just what one did.

Caniff and Canyon did not champ at the bit and agitate for war in the debate that preceded it, but when it happened, they were there, on the front lines, for the duration.

By the time of Vietnam, of course, much had changed. A new generation, unexposed to the Great Depression, had begun to assert itself, which had very different notions about war. Namely that no war was a "no brainer," even after the lead was flying. Canyon, as he had during Korea, was quick to the frontlines, and there

THIS IS A CATALOG AND PRICE LIST... OF YOUR LINE OF NONEXISTENT MERCHANDISE—

NO DISCOUN[T] FOR EARLY [PAYMENT]

MILTON CANIFF

to win. And though Steve Canyon continued for 20 more years, it was this decision by Caniff that brought about the strip's demise.

Faced with declining syndication as papers dropped the strip for its unabashed pro-military stance during the Vietnam war, Caniff's patriotism was outweighed by his other primary instinct – that of a newspaperman in the business of selling papers. Distancing himself somewhat from the day-to-day scripting, the adventurousness and exoticness that the strip had always offered fell away in favor of the interplay of the Canyon family of characters as they were subjected to detective style plots in an increasingly domestic setting. Though this placated his harshest critics, it never reclaimed many of the papers which had dropped the strip, and was so far from what had originally made the strip what it was, that it couldn't achieve the popularity with readers that would compel papers to pick it up again.

Caniff never expressed much bitterness over this, though it certainly merited it. Steve Canyon died quietly in 1988, with its creator. In the final installment of the 40-year-old strip, Bill Mauldin's Willy, and Caniff's own Steve Canyon planted an inkpen topped with a flight helmet emblazoned "Caniff" upon a grave.

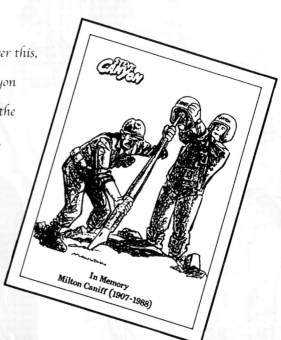

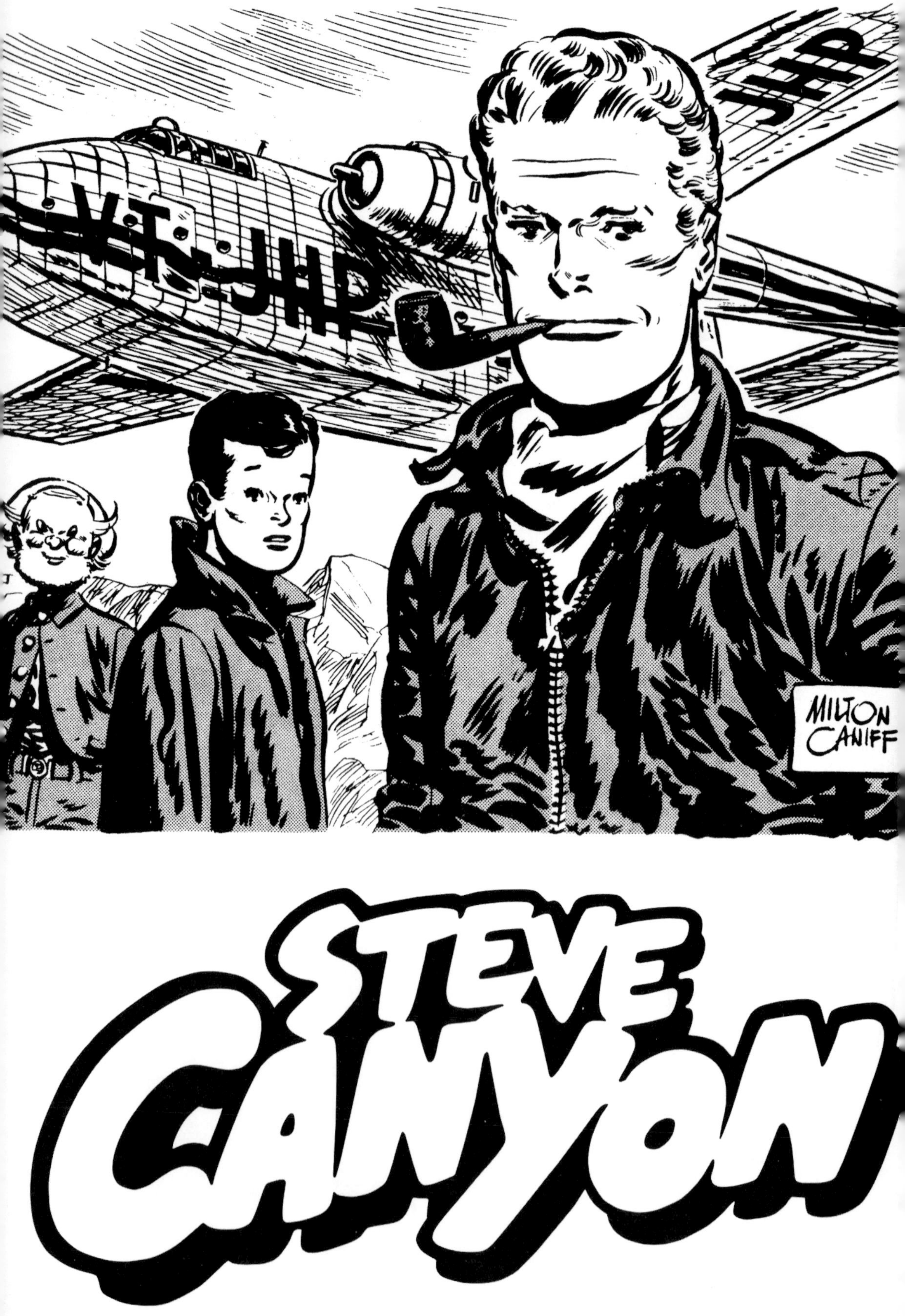
VT-JHP
JHP
MILTON CANIFF

STEVE CANYON

ISBN: 0-9710249-9-5

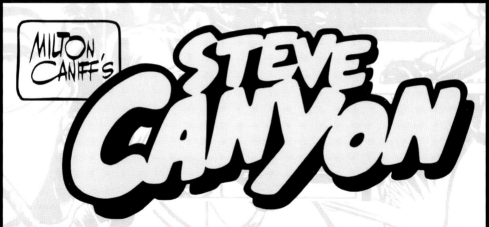

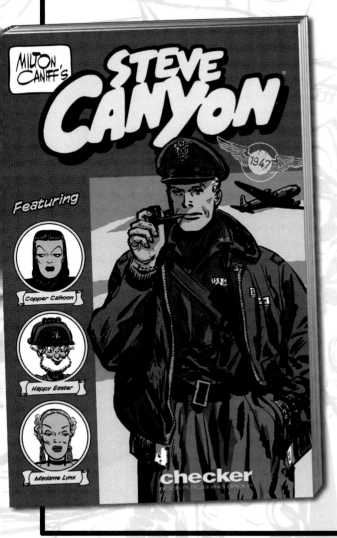

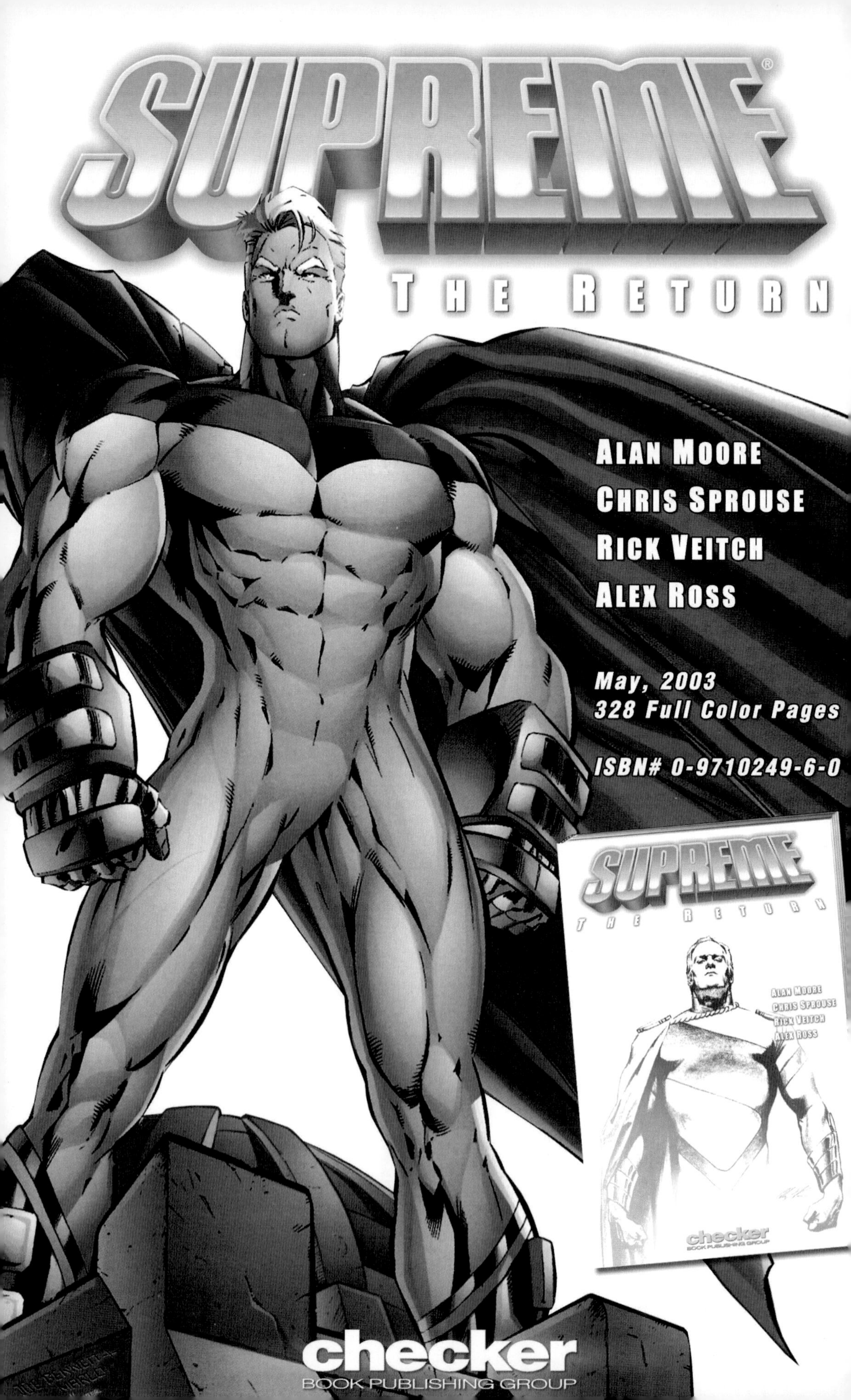
SUPREME®
THE RETURN
ALAN MOORE
CHRIS SPROUSE
RICK VEITCH
ALEX ROSS
May, 2003
328 Full Color Pages
ISBN# 0-9710249-6-0
checker
BOOK PUBLISHING GROUP